Eat What You Kill

The Fall of a Wall Street Lawyer

EAT WHAT YOU KILL

Milton C. Regan Jr.

The University of Michigan Press
Ann Arbor

Copyright © by the University of Michigan 2004
All rights reserved
Published in the United States of America by
The University of Michigan Press
Manufactured in the United States of America
⊗ Printed on acid-free paper

2007 2006 2005 2004   4 3 2 1

A CIP catalog record for this book is available from the British Library.

Library of Congress Cataloging-in-Publication Data

Regan, Milton C.
Eat what you kill : the fall of a Wall Street
lawyer / Milton C. Regan, Jr.
p. cm.
Includes bibliographical references and index.
ISBN 0-472-11437-9 (cloth : alk. paper)
1. Gellene, John—Trials, litigation, etc.   2. Bucyrus-Erie Company—
Trials, litigation, etc.   3. Milbank, Tweed, Hadley & McCloy—Trials,
litigation, etc.   4. Trials (Perjury)—Wisconsin—Milwaukee.
5. Bankruptcy lawyers—United States.   6. Bankruptcy—United States.
7. Legal ethics—United States.   I. Title.

KF224.G45R44   2004
346.7307'8—dc22   2004008335

To Sylvia Leopold &
the memory of Sam Leopold

CONTENTS

ACKNOWLEDGMENTS

This book reflects interviews with several persons who were involved in the events surrounding the bankruptcy of Bucyrus-Erie Corporation and John Gellene's criminal trial; a review of the voluminous documents relating to the Bucyrus leveraged buyout, the major financial transactions in which the company was involved after that buyout until its bankruptcy petition, the Bucyrus bankruptcy trial, the trial regarding professional fees earned in connection with that bankruptcy, and the criminal trial of John Gellene; and extensive discussions with corporate and bankruptcy lawyers, investment bankers, and financial restructuring specialists. I am grateful to Steven Biskupic, John Byrnes, David Goelzer, William Rochelle, Mark Rotert, David Rosenzweig, and Jeff Werbalowsky for the time they spent recounting for me the events relating to Bucyrus-Erie's operations, the company's bankruptcy, and John Gellene's prosecution and criminal trial. Others were willing to speak to me about these matters only on condition of anonymity, which I have honored. None of these latter persons were partners at Milbank Tweed, or worked for or represented Jackson National Life Insurance Company, during the events described in this book, since such parties were subject to obligations that constrained them from speaking with me. Nor did John Gellene agree to talk with me, despite several overtures from me inviting him to do so.

David Epstein, Don Langevoort, Nancy Rapoport, and Nancy Sachs read drafts of the full manuscript and offered insightful suggestions that helped me clarify and think more deeply about a number of issues. I also benefited from exchanges on lawyers, law firms, and legal ethics with Jim Feinerman, Mitu Gulati, Jack Heinz, Abe Krash, David Luban, Steve Lubet, Carrie Menkel-Meadow, Richard Painter, David Wilkins, and Jim Kelley, whose own book *Lawyers Crossing Lines* helped me

ACKNOWLEDGMENTS

sustain the belief that it was possible to write a case study of legal ethics in practice. Steve Case, John Coates, David Epstein, Judge Carolyn Jones, Don Langevoort, Nancy Rapoport, Harvey Miller, and David Skeel all offered valuable instruction on aspects of corporate and bankruptcy law and practice. My special thanks go to Jeff Bauman for our stimulating and enjoyable conversations about lawyers' ethics and corporate practice as we've co-taught a course on that topic over the past few years. I owe much to David Willman, friend and distinguished journalist, who offered valuable guidance on how to approach a project that required extensive interviews and investigation. Finally, my thanks to literary agent Sydelle Kramer, who generously took the time to offer valuable suggestions even though I was not a client of hers.

I had the opportunity to present portions of this book at the Pope and John Lecture at Northwestern Law School at the invitation of Jack Heinz; the Georgetown-Sloan Project on Business Institutions Conference on Field Study Methodology in Legal Research and Teaching about Business organized by Margaret Blair and Don Langevoort; and the Georgetown Law Center Faculty Workshop.

I'm tremendously grateful to many at Georgetown University Law Center in addition to the colleagues whom I've named. Dean Judy Areen made it possible for me to take leave that allowed me to focus for a sustained period on the project; Margaret Blair and Don Langevoort provided a Georgetown–Sloan Project grant that gave me a final semester to finish the book; Dean Areen and Associate Deans Mark Tushnet and Vicki Jackson provided summer stipends and helped with some of the research expenses; and Vivian Campbell, Doug Lind, and Tracey Bridgman of the Edward Bennett Williams Library at the Law Center provided exceptional assistance in locating and obtaining valuable documents. Anna Selden at Georgetown University Law Center shouldered the main burden of preparing the manuscript with care and diligence, and John Showalter of the Law Center also provided valuable assistance.

My greatest debt is to my wife and companion Nancy Sachs, and to my children Rebecca and Benjamin Regan-Sachs. Their presence in my life enriches it far beyond what I could ever describe here.

THE CAST

THE BUCYRUS TEAM

B-E Holdings Co. and Bucyrus-Erie

William Winter, chief executive officer and director

Norbert Verville, chief financial officer and director

David Goelzer, general counsel

Legal Counsel

Larry Lederman, partner, Milbank Tweed
(prebankruptcy planning)

John Gellene, partner, Milbank Tweed
(bankruptcy planning and negotiations)

Cynthia Revesz, associate, Milbank Tweed
(bankruptcy planning and negotiations)

Toni Lichstein, partner, Milbank Tweed
(bankruptcy-related litigation)

David Gelfand, associate, Milbank Tweed
(bankruptcy-related litigation)

Albert Solochek, counsel, B-E Holdings, Inc.

Financial Advisors

Jeff Werbalowsky, Houlihan, Lokey

Eric Siegert, Houlihan, Lokey

THE JACKSON NATIONAL LIFE TEAM

Jackson National Life

John Stark

Melissa D'Arcambal

THE CAST

Legal Advisors
  Andrew Rahl, partner, Anderson, Kill
  Bruce Arnold, partner, Whyte, Hirschboeck
  Anthony Princi, partner, Whyte, Hirschboeck
Financial Advisor
  Joseph Radecki, Jeffries & Co.
South Street Fund
  Mikael Salovaara
  Alfred C. Eckert III

CREDITORS' COMMITTEE COUNSEL
  Brian Rosen, Weil, Gotshal
    (prior to Chapter II petition)
  William Rochelle, Fulbright & Jaworski
    (after Chapter II petition)
  David Rosenzweig, Fulbright & Jaworski
    (after Chapter II petition)

GOLDMAN SACHS

BANKRUPTCY JUDGE
  Hon. Russell A. Eisenberg

U.S. TRUSTEE'S OFFICE
  John R. Byrnes, Assistant U.S. Trustee

U.S. ATTORNEY'S OFFICE, MILWAUKEE
  Steven Biskupic, Assistant U.S. Attorney
  Joseph Wall, Assistant U.S. Attorney

GELLENE DEFENSE COUNSEL
  Mark Rotert, Winston & Strawn

PRESIDING JUDGE, UNITED STATES V. GELLENE
  Hon. J. P. Stadtmueller

[T]here is no private life which has not been
determined by a wider public life . . .

George Eliot
Felix Holt: The Radical

These two cases were far from routine cases. The parties
were not engaged in traditional litigation. The parties
from the first day were engaged in all-out war.

Judge Russell Eisenberg
In re B-E Holdings, Inc. and Bucyrus-Erie Company

PROLOGUE

ON FRIDAY AFTERNOON, December 12, 1997, John Gellene entered the federal courthouse in Milwaukee in the company of Mark Rotert. Rotert was a lawyer from the Chicago law firm of Winston and Strawn. The forty-one-year-old Gellene had been in many courthouses before as a bankruptcy partner at the prestigious Wall Street law firm of Milbank, Tweed, Hadley & McCloy. Milbank traced its roots to the year after the Civil War ended. For more than a century it had provided legal services to the social and economic elite, most notably the Rockefeller family. Gellene was regarded as one of the best bankruptcy lawyers in the country, and had worked on some of the largest corporate reorganizations in the world. The previous year he had earned more than six hundred thousand dollars. He had a residence on the upper East Side of Manhattan, where he lived with his wife and three young daughters.

Gellene had spent most of 1994 in this same courthouse in Milwaukee, guiding local mining tool manufacturer Bucyrus-Erie through a contentious reorganization in bankruptcy. Despite a bitter feud among creditors, Bucyrus had emerged in good shape. Indeed, its business outlook was so bright that it recently had been purchased by a large private investment partnership. The last time Gellene had been in the building was in April 1996 for a hearing to determine the fees that Milbank should receive for its work on the bankruptcy. A month later, U.S. bankruptcy judge Russell Eisenberg approved the firm's receipt of $1.86 million as compensation for the services it provided to Bucyrus. Gellene thus could look back with pride on much of what had happened in this courthouse from February 1994 until May 1996.

Today, however, Gellene was not entering the building as an advocate. Instead, he was a criminal defendant. Rotert was not Gellene's cocounsel; he was his attorney. On the other side of the table were not creditors negotiating how to divide the assets of a financially troubled company. Rather, it was the United States government, acting through Assistant U.S. Attorneys Steven Biskupic and Joseph Wall. Today was the day that Gellene would be arraigned on charges of committing three federal crimes. Today he would enter his plea in the case.

The basis for Gellene's prosecution was something that had happened in this very courthouse. In 1993, Gellene had been asked by powerful Milbank partner Larry Lederman to provide his services to Bucyrus because of Gellene's experience in bankruptcy and financial restructuring. Lederman had advised Bucyrus off and on for five years. He also had provided legal guidance for several years to investment banker Mikael Salovaara. Salovaara had furnished financial advice to Bucyrus over the same five-year period. He was a former Goldman Sachs partner who had recently left the firm with a colleague to establish an investment fund known as South Street. In 1992, South Street had advanced $35 million to Bucyrus in return for a lien on all the company's manufacturing equipment. As the company's major secured creditor, South Street would be first in line to be paid if Bucyrus filed for bankruptcy.

Gellene began working with Bucyrus shortly before the company announced in February 1993 that it would no longer be able to make interest payments on its debt. Bucyrus hoped that it could obtain agreement among its creditors on a reorganization plan under Chapter 11 of the federal Bankruptcy Code. For most of 1993, Gellene helped negotiate the terms of that plan. Ultimately, Bucyrus gained acceptance from all but one large creditor, Jackson National Life Insurance Company (JNL), who strongly opposed it. In February 1994, Gellene filed a Chapter 11 petition on behalf of Bucyrus that laid out the terms of the proposed reorganization plan. JNL immediately contested it. At the same time, Gellene applied to the court for official appointment as Bucyrus's counsel during the Chapter 11 proceedings.

As part of this application for appointment, Gellene was required under Bankruptcy Rule 2014 to list his and Milbank's connections with any party in interest in the bankruptcy. At the time, Milbank also was representing Mikael Salovaara on one matter and South Street on another. Gellene himself was the lead counsel in the South Street matter, although he had done very little work on the case. The work for Salovaara and South Street created a potential conflict of interest for the law firm. As counsel for Bucyrus in its bankruptcy, Milbank would represent a debtor that had a duty to treat fairly all parties with a claim on its assets. As counsel for Salovaara and South Street, Milbank might have an incentive to provide advice to Bucyrus that favored South Street over other creditors.

Gellene didn't disclose these Milbank ties to Salovaara when he submitted the affidavits that accompanied his application. Judge Eisenberg appointed him in March 1994 to represent Bucyrus in the bankruptcy. The judge eventually approved the Bucyrus reorganization plan in December 1994, capping almost two years of intense negotiation and litigation among the parties.

Two years later, JNL discovered Gellene's concealment of Milbank's connections with Salovaara and South Street. By then, JNL controlled Bucyrus. Milbank was forced to return the entire $1.86 million it had been awarded for representing Bucyrus in the Chapter 11 case. Bucyrus also sued it for malpractice, a claim that the firm settled for an amount reported to be between $27 and $50 million.

Finally, in December 1996 federal prosecutors in Milwaukee obtained a grand jury indictment of Gellene. He was charged on two felony counts of making false declarations in the affidavits he had submitted to Judge Eisenberg. He also was charged on one felony count for using a false affidavit under oath to claim that Milbank was eligible to receive payment for its work on the bankruptcy. Each of the first two counts carried a penalty of up to five years in prison and a $250,000 fine. The third count was punishable by up to five years in prison and a $10,000 fine. Any prison sentence over a year would deprive Gellene of his right to vote, his ability to be a teacher, his eligibility to hold public office, and the opportunity to practice law. He was the first lawyer ever charged under federal criminal law for violating Bankruptcy Rule 2014.

WHY DID JOHN GELLENE do it? Why did he risk all he had—his wealth, influence, success, livelihood, and his very freedom, not to mention the security of his wife and children? He had worked brutal hours for years, traveling the country and the world, in pursuit of a partnership granted only to a privileged few at Milbank. Why would he place that in jeopardy by failing to make a simple disclosure?

The answers to these questions are fascinating because they shed light on the tragic fall of a Wall Street lawyer. Gellene's story, however, has broader significance. It offers a window to the dramatic forces that have irrevocably transformed elite law firm practice over the past quarter century. No one who hopes to fathom the ethical landscape that lawyers such as Gellene must navigate can ignore this sea change in what it means to practice in a large law firm. Furthermore, Gellene's experience illustrates the ways in which specialties such as bankruptcy can generate distinct practice cultures with their own norms and understandings of ethical obligations. Appreciating how lawyers identify, frame, and resolve ethical questions thus requires sensitivity to both the types of organizations in which they work and the particular fields in which they practice.

By analyzing John Gellene's story against the backdrop of these forces, this book is a response to the increasing call for work in legal ethics that takes account of the particular contexts in which lawyers practice. In addition, it reflects the view that case studies can be an especially valuable way to deepen our understanding of the complex interaction between context and individual character. As one observer has put it, the narrative focus of case studies can "allow us to visit the psychological and moral realms of legal actors both before and after they make decisions or take actions."

A focus on practice setting illuminates the vast differences in the experiences of lawyers. While it's common to speak of "the" legal profession as if it were a unified body of similar practitioners, the reality is that lawyers work in a variety of practice organizations and are involved in a broad range of activity. The incentives, opportunities, and pressures that confront a lawyer in a large law firm are different from those that lawyers face in a corporate legal department, a government agency, or a small boutique firm. Similarly, lawyers practicing securities law, litigating personal injury cases, providing tax opinions, and bringing criminal prosecutions take account of considerations in their daily work that can be strikingly different. How lawyers respond to the particular forces that shape their practice gives specific content to broad professional ideals and ethical aspirations. For these reasons, it may be more accurate in some respects to speak of "legal professions" rather than "the legal profession."

The large Wall Street firm that is the practice setting for this book is interesting for a couple of reasons. First, it was the rise of such firms in the late nineteenth century that provoked the first sustained efforts to distinguish lawyers as members of a profession with its own unique ethical standards. Anxiety that lawyers were becoming indistinguishable from other commercial occupations led to the formation of the American Bar Association, the creation of a formal canon of ethics for lawyers, and the requirements that persons attend law school and pass a bar examination in order to practice law.

Second, the Wall Street firm was able to influence these reform efforts so as to establish the claim that it represented the pinnacle of professional skill and independence. Reinforced by certain features of the market for corporate legal services, this view prevailed until the last quarter of the twentieth century. Since then, dramatic changes have increased competition among Wall Street firms for both clients and lawyers. On a practical level, these changes have had ripple effects for virtually all lawyers in private practice. On a cultural level, the impact has been at least as profound. Just as the rise of large firms a little over a century ago prompted alarms about lawyers' professional status, so the recent changes that have roiled these firms have rekindled this anxiety. For better or worse, in other words, the large Wall Street firm has served as something of a bellwether of the state of the legal profession for over a hundred years.

UNDERSTANDING THE CASE of John Gellene thus requires placing him into the context of the Wall Street law firm at a particularly unsettling historical moment. It's common to describe that moment as the decline of law practice from a profession to a business. Framed in this way, the ethical implications are straightforward. Individual lawyers and the firms in which they work are motivated more by greed than they were a generation ago. As a result, they are more willing to forsake their ethical obligations than the lawyers who came before them.

The two prevailing explanations for Gellene's behavior reflect this view. The first is that Gellene was a moral rogue, an aberrant partner with a weakness for cutting corners when it suited his purposes. The second is that Gellene was the fall guy, someone pressured by his firm to conceal a conflict of interest so that Milbank could reap a reward of almost $2 million in fees. From this perspective, Gellene was done in by a corrupt organization. The first explanation blames Gellene's fall on flawed character; the second depicts him as the victim of circumstances that he couldn't resist.

Understanding the ethical challenges that large firm lawyers face, however, requires a richer account of how character and circumstance interact in daily practice. We need to move beyond the claim that unethical behavior is attributable mainly to a decline in the personal morality of lawyers or in the integrity of law firms—and that this results from the change in law practice from a profession to a business.

It's true that large law firms now must devote more explicit attention to financial viability than they did a generation ago. Firms unquestionably are subject to greater competition for clients and lawyers than ever before. In recent years they have adopted business principles that their corporate clients embraced far earlier. Law firm leaders speak more openly about profitability and revenues than their predecessors ever did.

Understanding the significance of these changes, however, requires more than broad theories of professional decline. First, we need more detailed accounts of the impact of heightened competition. How precisely do large law firms differ from those a generation ago? What policies and procedures have firms adopted in response to market forces? How does escalating competition shape the career paths of lawyers in large firms? What distinctive opportunities, pressures, and temptations do lawyers face in these firms? What kinds of personal traits are adaptive in this environment?

Focusing on these questions directs attention to three features that are common to practice in modern large law firms. First, a shift to merit-based compensation and away from job security means that partners as well as associates are competitors in a tournament within the firm. Prior scholarship has developed and refined the notion that working life within the large firm is organized as a tournament. That research, however, has focused on competition among associates for partnership. This book suggests that the tournament doesn't end when an associate makes partner. Partners continue to compete for compensation, status, and job stability on an ongoing basis, with their ability to generate revenues serving as the primary scorecard.

The ability to produce revenues in today's large law firm depends primarily on entrepreneurial effort. The firm itself is far less able than before to furnish a permanent base of clients that provide a steady stream of work. The lawyer therefore must seek out his or her own clients. The common way to describe this system in the large firm is that you "eat what you kill." There are two main ways to be an entrepreneur who can compete successfully in a tournament organized around this principle. The first, and preferable, way is to be a "rainmaker": someone who develops contacts with clients that lead to regular business. The second is to cultivate a good relationship with a rainmaker, thereby gaining access to the work that his or her clients generate.

Previous research has suggested that law firms represent an organizational labor market. Associates with large amounts of "human capital" but few client contacts match up with partners whose clients spawn more work than those partners individually can handle.[1] I argue that the same process occurs among partners as well: nonrainmakers with more legal skills than clients compete for relationships with rainmakers who have the clients that can use those skills.

A second feature of large firm practice today is that market forces and greater specialization by lawyers make the particular field in which a lawyer practices an increasingly important source of guidance. Law firms today grow more by acquiring individual lawyers, practice groups, or entire firms than by promoting associates to partner. This means that they tend to house more and more divergent personalities and areas of practice under one roof. This can make it difficult to establish and sustain an overall organizational culture. At the same time, legal work continues to require more refined specialization. As a result, lawyers are likely to draw many of their norms and much of their practice culture from colleagues working in the same specialty, rather than from the firm as a whole. The organizational setting in which lawyers practice thus is not monolithic, but multicultural. The firm establishes the general parameters of competition for reward and punishment. Lawyers' practice specialties, however, may shape how they approach that competition—the obstacles that they perceive, the strategies that they adopt, and the trade-offs that they make.

Finally, lawyers in large firms now work more and more with temporary teams of lawyers and other professionals on discrete projects for intensive periods of time. Teams of persons with varied skills, sometimes from different organizations, are assembled for specific projects, then disassembled and reconstituted for others. Furthermore, competition for clients makes "winning" serve as the central mission for many of these projects. Such teams also can serve as a source of norms for practicing lawyers. The intense interdependence of the experience, combined with close identification with the client, helps create a distinct cognitive and moral universe that can shape how lawyers identify and respond to ethical questions.

This book places the emergence of law firms with these features in historical context, by describing the evolution of Wall Street firms from the late nineteenth century to the dawn of the twenty-first. The experience of Milbank Tweed serves to illustrate this history. I draw on secondary sources, interviews, and internal Milbank Tweed memoranda to tell the story of how the firm evolved from a bastion of the social elite to an aggressive entrepreneurial enterprise. John Gellene

8

began at Milbank just as the old order was crumbling, and was named a partner as the new order was being put in place. His journey from associate to partner thus occurred in a period of economic, political, and cultural transformation at the firm.

APPRECIATING COMMON FEATURES of large firm practice provides a valuable framework for gaining a deeper understanding of the impact of recent changes in the legal profession. We can gain even more insight, however, by applying that framework to examine the experience of individual lawyers in particular instances. Case studies offer the chance to explore how character and circumstance interact in subtle ways, producing distinctive individual stories that nonetheless resonate beyond their specific protagonists. This leads us to the story of John Gellene.

Telling this story requires delving into the details of the Bucyrus bankruptcy in order to get a ground-level view of the circumstances in which Gellene was practicing. What did he understand his assignment to involve? How was that affected by his interaction with others? Whom did he consider his adversaries? What obstacles did he see to achieving a successful result? What alternatives and choices did he perceive himself as having? What pressures did he feel? In other words, how did Gellene see his world? How did the characteristics that he shared with lawyers in other large firms combine with his unique experience to produce a singular perspective that shaped his behavior?

In recounting these details, I draw on transcripts of the Bucyrus bankruptcy case, the record of Gellene's criminal trial and sentencing hearing, documents relevant to the bankruptcy and criminal proceedings, documents prepared in connection with the financial transactions that were the subject of dispute in the bankruptcy, and interviews with participants in and observers of these events, as well as with bankruptcy specialists. These sources help stitch together a narrative that conveys a sense of what it was like for John Gellene to be representing Bucyrus in its bankruptcy in 1993 and 1994. The story includes a discussion of how the pursuit of higher profits led large New

York firms into corporate bankruptcy practice in the early 1980s, and the ways in which this has created tension with bankruptcy conflict of interest rules.

Understanding how Gellene's experience was both similar to and different from other lawyers helps us construct an account of what happened that is more complex than the claim that Gellene was an ethical rogue, or that Milbank was fundamentally corrupt. I use this account to explore the influences and motivations that could have prompted Gellene to act as he did, and the rationalizations that he may have used to justify his behavior. This analysis draws on interdisciplinary insights from behavioral and moral psychology, organizational theory, and business ethics to examine the psychological dynamics of how large firm lawyers may approach ethical issues. Finally, I offer tentative thoughts on how regulation of lawyers' conduct might take account of these dynamics.

My approach to legal ethics thus moves back and forth between a focus on the structural features of large law firm practice, and on how those features intersect with the personal history of individual lawyers. Awareness of structure helps identify potential influences on behavior and possible targets of reform. At the same time, close analysis of behavior can deepen and modify our understanding of the situations that large firm lawyers confront. Ideally, this process will yield a richer ethical portrait of elite law firm practice than either focus alone. Furthermore, it will move us beyond the debate over whether law practice is still a profession or has become a business.

John Gellene's behavior was not as lurid as many of the actors involved in the legal and business scandals of recent years. He didn't loot a company of its assets, or manipulate financial statements to mislead investors. There's no evidence that he withheld information from the bankruptcy court so that he could favor South Street over other creditors. Indeed, Bucyrus's general counsel had high praise for the quality of Gellene's work on behalf of the company. The absence of obvious explanations such as fraud or greed makes Gellene's story an especially good vehicle for analyzing the subtle but powerful forces that shape behavior in today's large law firms. The failure to disclose a conflict of interest in bankruptcy court in Milwaukee may seem light years away from the high-profile combat of Wall Street law practice. This book argues, however, that they are linked in intricate and fundamental ways.

MAGISTRATE AARON GOLDSTEIN presided over John Gellene's arraignment on that cold December day in Milwaukee. He first advised Gellene of his rights: the right to remain silent; the right to a lawyer; and the right to ask that the court appoint a lawyer for him if he were unable to pay for one. Gellene responded that he understood these rights. Assistant U.S. Attorney Biskupic then proceeded to describe the three counts contained in the indictment: two counts of making a false material statement in connection with a bankruptcy case, and one count of using a document while under oath despite knowing that it was materially false. Gellene's attorney Mark Rotert entered a plea on Gellene's behalf of not guilty on all counts.

The final matter at the proceeding was the ability of Gellene to travel while awaiting trial. Before the arraignment, Gellene had been interviewed by the court's pretrial services officer. The officer had recommended to the court that the defendant be released on his own signature on the condition that he surrender his passport and report to the officer as directed. Biskupic indicated that he had no problem with the recommendation. Goldstein ruled that Gellene could travel within New York and New Jersey, to Illinois to visit his counsel, and to the Eastern District of Wisconsin where the trial was to be held. If he wished to travel anywhere else, Gellene would have to notify the Pretrial Services Office in advance.

Goldstein admonished Gellene that if he failed to make any court appearances, he would have his bond revoked and would be charged with the crime of bail jumping. The magistrate also told him that he could be charged with a violation of the Witness Protection Act if he threatened or harmed anyone who was a witness, victim, or informant. If he violated any local, state, or federal law while out on bail, his penalties automatically would be increased.

These warnings seemed more appropriate for a member of organized crime than a bankruptcy lawyer who had spent most of his time helping companies restructure their debt obligations. John Gellene, however, was now within the domain of the criminal law, accused of committing an offense against society. In February 1997, he would be the defendant in a trial that could result in imprisonment, a fine of hundreds of thousands of dollars, and the loss of his ability to practice law. As he left the building, he could not have helped but ask himself a question: How had he fallen so far so fast?

PART I

CONTEXT

CHAPTER ONE

From "Nobody Starves" to "Eat What You Kill"

IN FEBRUARY 1993, Larry Lederman picked up the phone in his fifty-fifth floor office at Milbank, Tweed, Hadley & McCloy in New York. Lederman, a corporate partner, was described as the "800 pound gorilla" at Milbank. He was the highest-paid and most powerful partner at the firm, earning $1.25 million a year. He had an extensive network of contacts with corporations and investment banks, which generated an impressive stream of steady profits. He had been lured to Milbank in late 1991 to shake things up, to transform the firm from an old-line elite institution to an aggressive market-driven enterprise.

Lederman called John Gellene ten floors below, and asked if he "was particularly busy." Gellene was a tall, thin, thirty-six-year-old bankruptcy partner with dark hair who radiated a quiet intellectual intensity behind his glasses. He currently was involved in the international bankruptcy of the company owned by British media tycoon Robert Maxwell. He had recently wrapped up another matter, however, and told Lederman that his work load had "dropped a little bit." Lederman then said, "I have a client named Bucyrus-Erie. They manufacture mining equipment and they are going to need to go through a financial restructuring and I want to get you involved." When Gellene told Lederman that he would take on the job, Lederman promised to send him some material on the company. He also suggested that Gellene call David Goelzer, the company's general counsel, to intro-

15

duce himself. Thus began a series of events that would end with John Gellene in federal prison.

Lederman's presence at Milbank reflected a profound change in the formerly genteel world of the Wall Street lawyer. For one, he was a Jewish partner at a firm that for years had been the epitome of the White Anglo-Saxon Protestant establishment. For another, he had not become a partner by joining the firm as an associate and rising through the ranks. Instead, he had been recruited from another law firm—and one that had been in existence for only a few years. Furthermore, he had a reputation as an aggressive, sometimes abrasive entrepreneurial lawyer who had little interest in social niceties. This reinforced long-held ethnic stereotypes, and was in marked contrast to the long tradition of polite consensus by which the partners at Milbank and other Wall Street firms had run their organizations. Finally, Lederman had been a major player in dismantling the foundations of an implicit arrangement in which corporations never attempted hostile takeovers, and major law firms didn't compete for each other's clients or lawyers.

In short, Larry Lederman represented a changing of the guard—not only for Milbank Tweed, but for the formerly insulated world of the elite law firm. The story of this transformation is the key to understanding the nature of large firm law practice at the dawn of the twenty-first century.

THE WALL STREET LAW FIRM was born in the explosion of industrial activity in the United States during the last third of the nineteenth century. Most law practice before then had been conducted by solo practitioners. The most elaborate practice organization for most of the century was the two-man law office. Lawyers in such an office shared space and overhead costs, but often conducted their own separate practices without sharing clients. In some cases, the two men adopted a division of labor in which one served as courtroom advocate while the other handled nonlitigation matters.

Solo practice and the two-man office both reflected and reinforced the notion that the lawyer was an independent professional whose individual judgment should not be compromised in any way. Practitioners who shared a law office generally had no partnership agreement, nor did they adopt any measures designed to create an organizational entity distinct from their individual practices. The small scale of law practice was suited to an economy in which most clients were individuals or modest economic ventures dominated by a few people at most.

After the Civil War, however, the scale and scope of economic enterprise began to expand in dramatic ways. Railroads, oil exploration and refining, coal mining, and steel production were only a few of the activities whose size and geographic dispersion dwarfed anything that had come before. These and other industries strained the boundaries of existing organizational forms, legal rules, and capital markets. Furthermore, they provoked alarm in some quarters, which led to measures such as the creation of the Interstate Commerce Commission in 1870 and the passage of the Sherman Antitrust Act in 1890.

These developments created an unprecedented need for coordinated, intensive, and ongoing legal services. Lawyers were necessary to revise or invent forms of economic affiliation such as the limited liability corporation, the trust, and the holding company. The economic distress of railroads, for instance, led to the creation of the equity receivership, the forerunner of today's corporate bankruptcy proceeding. This device was designed to solve the problems of creditors with claims on assets, such as stretches of railroad track, that had no value apart from the system of which they were a part. In addition, in many cases lawyers took on the role of liaison to government officials and financial institutions that were assuming increasingly important roles in economic life.

Both the volume and complexity of the corporation's need for these legal services began to strain the capacity of solo practitioners and two-man offices. Lawyers therefore began cautiously to associate in somewhat larger numbers. The move to larger practices was prompted also by an increase in overhead costs, due to the introduction of new technologies such as the typewriter and telephone, and the need for larger reference libraries to contain the increasingly large amount of printed legal material. Adding even one or two lawyers to a two-man practice to share these costs could result in valuable economies of scale.

While lawyers began to practice in larger groups during this period, the increases were gradual, and the organizational forms were far simpler and less integrated than those of corporate clients. Eventual Wall Street powerhouses such as Shearman & Sterling and Davis Polk, for instance, did not have as many as four partners and associates until the 1910s.[1] Lawyers in firms still tended to have parallel practices, and clients typically were regarded as those of the individual attorney rather than the firm. Aspiring young associates, known then as law clerks, learned the law by working without compensation with older practitioners, supporting themselves by serving clients outside the firm.

Why did law firms remain relatively small in the early decades of industrialization? One reason is that, until after World War I, the major economic players were individual entrepreneurs and wealthy investors, such as Andrew Mellon, Cornelius Vanderbilt, and Jay Gould.[2] The attorney-client relationship was based on personal contact between such individuals and prominent members of the bar. Thomas Shearman, for instance, used his relationship with Gould to leave the law firm of the notable David Dudley Field to form his own firm with John Sterling.[3]

Another reason for the limited size and integration of law firm practice was the persistent icon of the lawyer as an independent professional beholden to no one—the virtuous counselor who hung out his shingle and dispensed disinterested legal advice and general wisdom. Many members of the bar warned that lawyers' growing dependence on corporate clients threatened professional independence. They feared that lawyers were becoming mere servants of commercial interests, with little to distinguish them as a singular profession with its own distinct values and traditions. There was some resistance to the notion that a lawyer's freedom of action should be limited in any way by organizational needs and requirements.

The result was that law firm affiliations in the early industrial period were fluid and unstable.[4] Powerful lawyers moved from one firm to another, taking their clients with them. Firms provided no systematic legal training, providing casual apprenticeships for aspiring young lawyers, many of whom were hired because of family connections. To some degree, this was a mirror of the tumultuous economic era, in which many enterprises were extensions of forceful individuals who battled fiercely among themselves for the spoils of industry.

It's striking that lawyers who served corporations were able to preserve their own separate practice organizations, rather than being absorbed as corporate employees. Engineers, for instance, were another occupational group aspiring to professional status in the late nineteenth century that provided services to corporations. In contrast to lawyers, however, the dominant career path for an engineer was to become a corporate employee and rise through the ranks to a management position. Lawyers were resistant to this path because they regarded it as inconsistent with the ideology of the individual practitioner.[5]

Furthermore, corporate enterprises may have been slow to treat legal services as a cost of production. Corporations were subject to relatively little regulation, and may have regarded legal issues as a less regular concern than those relating to financial and operational matters. Furthermore, legal expertise was less amenable to routine organization according to scientific principles.[6] This gave lawyers the opportunity to continue and expand their separate practice organizations. In addition, the existence of separate law firms may have been useful to corporations and their lawyers in arguing that the legal positions that they advanced were the product of neutral and objective analysis of the law, rather than merely self-interested claims.

Finally, notable lawyers of the time not only were able to provide narrow legal advice, but had connections to the world of financiers and government that were extremely useful to economic enterprises.[7] This combination of legal, financial, and political services strengthened their positions and bargaining power vis-à-vis the corporations to which they lent assistance. Knowledgeable and well-connected lawyers, in other words, possessed some degree of market power with respect to their clients.

By the early years of the twentieth century, many industrial enterprises began to move away from the dominance of their founders. They took on a more impersonal and institutional identity as integrated and enduring entities with their own organizational dynamic. Personal connections continued to be valuable, but a class of corporate managers began to arise that emphasized the importance of rational systems and procedures to make operations more stable and predictable.

Some leading Wall Street lawyers believed that law firms likewise

needed to become more integrated organizations. Loose forms of association, haphazard operations, and fierce competition eventually could
prove ruinous for corporate law firms as a group, since it made their
futures and even survival unpredictable. Furthermore, such instability
could weaken lawyers' market power vis-à-vis their corporate clients,
thus undermining the economic foundation of their claim to be independent professionals.

Whatever the reasons, firms began to take more systematic steps to
build enduring organizations in the first two decades of the twentieth
century. The most notable and influential example was the approach
adopted by Paul Cravath for the firm that eventually became known
as Cravath, Swaine & Moore. The Cravath model became the template
for the Wall Street law firm. It provided a structure whose influence
persists to this day.

Cravath joined the firm in 1906 and headed it until his death until
1940. As fellow partner and historian of the firm Robert T. Swaine
noted, "Cravath had a definite philosophy about the organization of
his law firm, its partners, its practice and its relation to its associates."[8] First, Cravath determined that the firm would seek lawyers
almost exclusively from recent law school graduates, rather than from
those in practice elsewhere. He insisted that every incoming lawyer
have a record of accomplishment in both college and law school. The
first choice of the firm was "a Phi Beta Kappa man from a good college
who had become a law review editor at Harvard, Columbia, or Yale."[9]

As these criteria suggest, hiring was limited to members of a narrow
social elite. One observer noted that firms want "lawyers who are
Nordic, have pleasing personalities and 'clean cut' appearances, are
graduates of the 'right schools,' [and] have the 'right' social background
and experience in the affairs of the world."[10] Thirty percent of Wall
Street partners in 1957, for instance, were listed in the *Social Register*.[11]

Second, Cravath broke with tradition by putting every associate on
a salary. Prior to that, the firm had provided no compensation to associates, but simply provided them desk space in return for their assistance. The young lawyers had to support themselves from whatever
business they could develop on their own. Cravath decreed that hence-
forth both partners and salaried associates must devote themselves

exclusively to the practice of law "as a member of the Cravath team."[12] Third, associates would be trained by the firm gradually to take on more responsibility as they gained experience. Ideally, they would not specialize in any particular branch of the law until they had gained exposure to all facets of the firm's practice.

Perhaps the most prominent feature of the Cravath system was the adoption of an "up or out" policy for associates. After a period generally not more than ten years, associates would be considered for promotion to partner. Only a small percentage of men would gain this honor. From 1906 until 1948, for instance, only 44 of 462 associates were made partners.[13] Those passed over were expected to leave the firm, since, according to Swaine, a person with no hope of promotion "tends to sink into a mental rut—to lose ambition; and loss of ambition induces carelessness."[14] The firm took responsibility, however, for finding positions for these lawyers. Many moved to Cravath's corporate clients, while others went to smaller firms to whom the Cravath firm referred work.

The "up or out" policy represented a break from the practice of keeping lawyers on for extended periods as permanent associates. Theoretically, all lawyers at the firm now were either actual or aspiring partners. This ostensibly preserved the ideal of the lawyer as an independent professional rather than an organizational employee.

Marc Galanter and Thomas Palay suggest that such a "promotion to partner tournament" enables law firms to match up partners who have experience and more responsibilities than they alone can handle with young lawyers who have neither.[15] In their terms, partners have excess "human capital," while associates have excess labor. Partners lend their experience and clients to associates, who mix it with their labor to provide legal services. The promise of partnership gives associates an incentive to use partners' capital efficiently and to preserve its value. At the same time, the firm's commitment regularly to make a certain number of partners constrains partners' ability to exploit the work of associates for their own gain. Recent work has questioned whether the tournament is conducted on a level playing field, how many associates actually aspire to be a partner,[16] and the extent to which the tournament is responsible for the rapid growth of large law firms.[17] Nonetheless, the basic point remains that firms conduct competitions for partnership in which only a handful of associates gain promotion.

Despite the up-or-out policy, Cravath and other firms did retain a small group of permanent associates with no hope of promotion to partner. These lawyers typically handled routine legal tasks such as research on state securities law, or worked in specialized fields such as tax and labor law. In addition, firms that had dealings with local New York courts recruited permanent associates from local law schools such as St. John's, Fordham, and Brooklyn. Many graduates of these schools were from the same lower-middle-class background as court administrators and employees, often of Irish or Jewish ancestry.

The animating spirit of Cravath's system was that "all business in the office must be firm business," rather than the business of individual partners or associates. As Swaine put it in his history of the firm:

> Every partner is expected to cooperate with every other in the firm's business, through whichever partner originating, and to contribute to all the work of the firm to the maximum of his ability. The formation of partners of cliques practicing independently of each other, which developed under [a prior partner], would not be allowed today.[18]

Clients, in other words, were those of the firm, not its individual members. All partners were to share in the proceeds from work on behalf of all clients. The hope was that the firm would become an enduring institution, not simply a collection of practitioners.

Put differently, Cravath was attempting to establish a distinctive brand in the legal services marketplace. First, he purported to signal to clients that the firm contained elite lawyers by hiring only top graduates from the supposed best law schools. The requirement that a person graduate from law school and pass a bar examination in order to practice law was still relatively new and not universal. Furthermore, the quality of education offered at the law schools that existed varied considerably. Taking in graduates from only a handful of schools thus served to set the Cravath firm apart from its potential competitors.

Cravath also sought to emphasize that entry into and success within the firm were based on the quality of men's legal skills, not on their political or social connections. "Hence," Swaine declared, "business-getting ability is not a factor in the advancement of a man within the office at any level, except in so far as that ability arise out of competence in doing law work, as contrasted with family or social connections."[19] Swaine undoubtedly overstated the point; his own and other firms tended to look quite favorably on anyone who could bring in clients.[20] Nonetheless, the bulk of the partners distinguished themselves by working for clients whom they inherited from more senior members of the firm.

Furthermore, the Cravath approach was meant to provide clients with assurance of quality control. Lawyers at the firm came fresh from law school and were trained exclusively by the firm in how to provide service to corporate clients. Clients could be confident that all lawyers had received uniform instruction. By contrast, as Swaine noted, those who had practiced elsewhere "might have acquired habits inconsistent with Cravath methods."[21] A corporation therefore need not undertake the expense of developing an elaborate in-house legal department, but could contract out for legal services.

Finally, because the Cravath firm aimed to be a stable and lasting organization, corporate clients could count on continuing access to its legal resources. Those resources consisted not only of technical expertise, but knowledge of the client's particular needs and concerns. The firm ideally would develop an institutional memory as a result of its ongoing and virtually exclusive representation of its clients. Just as corporations were moving from an era of dominance by individual entrepreneurs to one of organizational stability, so Cravath aspired to the same for the corporate law firm.

In time, several other law firms emulated the Cravath system to create a wider type: the Wall Street law firm. Both corporate clients and lawyers came to regard the brand as signifying the pinnacle of law practice. Wall Street firms were involved mainly in "office work" for major corporate clients. They regarded the occasional litigation services that they provided as a "loss leader." The small circle of firms that claimed this brand exerted an influence on legal, political, and economic life far disproportionate to their numbers. These firms also provided the blueprint beyond Wall Street for the emergence of the large law firm as a major institution.

Law practice within this circle was notably insulated from competitive market forces. Indeed, Wall Street firms effectively constituted a cartel whose members would not seek to lure away each other's clients or lawyers. There also was cooperation on costs: salaries for beginning associates were set informally among representatives of the major firms, typically over an annual lunch.

As a result, law firms, partners, and associates had relatively stable and predictable lives. For firms, the relatively powerful market positions of large corporate clients gave those clients minimal interest in aggressively monitoring the cost of legal services. A 1959 Conference Board survey of almost three hundred manufacturing companies, for instance, reported that companies generally indicated that they were happy with their law firm and "have never given any thought to hiring another."[22] As one in-house corporate counsel declared in another setting, legal advice "is probably the only service we buy without some kind of survey of alternate cost."[23] Law firms had little concern that the rare departure of a lawyer would cause the loss of a client. As one observer put it, "U.S. Steel, Standard Oil, and Citibank aren't about to switch law firms at the behest of one man."[24] Banks in particular tended to be especially long-term clients; "once it retains a firm, a bank is stuck with it."[25] Thus, for instance, Milbank Tweed was synonymous with Chase Manhattan Bank, Shearman & Sterling with Citibank, and Davis Polk with J.P. Morgan.

Since corporate clients tended to look to a firm for most of their legal needs, they provided the firm with a steady stream of income. The close connections between a firm and its clients were reinforced by the presence of many firm alumni in the legal departments of those clients, the personal ties between lawyers and corporate executives drawn from the same social class and background, and the accumulation by the firm of detailed knowledge of its clients' operations.

Lawyers were tied to the firm by the implicit promise of other firms not to recruit them, and by the fact that clients generally were unwilling to follow them if they left the firm. Because they had acquired so much experience representing particular clients, the most lucrative professional opportunity for them was to remain with the firm in which they had begun. Furthermore, the firm's training served not only to impart legal skills, but also to socialize lawyers in the culture of the organization. All this comprised what economists call "firm-specific capital." In the law firm context, such capital represents the amount that a lawyer can earn by practicing with a particular firm that exceeds the amount that he could earn by practicing elsewhere.[26] The existence of firm-specific capital resulted in a situation in which, "unlike business executives or college professors, the Brahmins of the Bar don't shop around for better paying positions."[27]

Those who were promoted to partner could look forward to a relatively secure career. In addition to lifetime tenure with the firm, a partner was entitled to a share of the firm's profits, a voice in the firm's governance, and considerable independence from supervision by other lawyers. Competition among partners was muted by reliance on seniority as the primary basis for compensation in most firms. Under the "lockstep" system, those partners promoted to partner in a given year constituted a group that would advance together in the firm and be entitled to the same percentage share of its profits. There were adjustments in some cases for partners who brought in large amounts of business, who were known as "rainmakers." Most partners could be content, however, to rely on the firm's stable of clients for a constant flow of work, and didn't need to seek out clients on their own.

Lockstep compensation served as a form of risk-sharing among lawyers whose individual practices might ebb and flow according to the ups and downs of the business cycle. In addition, advancing years would not automatically diminish a partner's status within the firm. "Courtesy and the recognition that inevitably everyone grows old guarantees that a very old partner, no longer in office, retains his large office, even though he is not currently 'earning' it."[28]

Associates also could look forward to a relatively predictable and linear career path once they entered the firm. "The associate does not have to compete with other lawyers in the market place for clients. He is assured of his salary, his position, or, if he is 'let go,' of one of similar stature someplace else."[29] Those who were promoted to partner, of course, would enjoy all the prerogatives of that status. Those who were not would still be assured of the firm's help in finding well-paying positions in a corporation or another firm, or of receiving referrals from the firm if they started their own practices. Because it was regarded as unprofessional to fire a lawyer, these associates' failures were carefully disguised. As one writer who surveyed the scene described it, the prevailing ethos was "nobody starves."[30]

For the first two-thirds of the twentieth century, Wall Street firms thus were institutions whose freedom from significant competition granted them considerable autonomy in charting their own courses. The firms were quite similar in the backgrounds and social customs of their members, who were drawn from a narrow segment of society. Nonetheless, each firm also had the latitude to establish a distinct culture, based on its history and the personalities of its partners. As one observer has put it:

> How cases were staffed and billed, how partners were selected and paid, and how new partners were admitted to the ranks were issues based on internal considerations rather than market factors. Free to conduct their affairs as they wished, the established practices could all but ignore such boorish concerns as efficiency, productivity, marketing and competition.[31]

The Wall Street law firms that matured in the middle decades of the twentieth century were far more integrated organizations than the firms that had first emerged in the late nineteenth and early twentieth centuries. The reputations and successes of its lawyers were tied more closely to those of the firm than they had ever been before. As John W. Davis of Davis Polk observed, "Now, it is not men, but institutions, that hold the reins of power."[32] Indeed, there was concern in some quarters that lawyers in the Wall Street firm had lost their independence and had become conformist "organization men."

At the same time, however, the large firm was quite loosely organized in comparison to other major business enterprises. It was prohibited by ethical rules from incorporating, on the ground that this would inject too explicit a commercial orientation into the firm. Indeed, members of the Wall Street bar fiercely resisted efforts to permit law firms to incorporate, despite the economic advantages that it would provide.[33]

The Wall Street firm had no extensive managerial hierarchy, differentiating only among partners, associates, and nonlegal staff. It typically had an executive committee of partners, but any major decision was made collegially by all partners. The only formal practice department generally was for tax; otherwise lawyers saw themselves as practicing general corporate law. Firms attempted to formalize assignments to associates, but generally had limited success in doing so. Some firms had no formal partnership agreements, and those that did gave it little attention. As one lawyer put it, "We operate entirely on the basis of trust in each other. We don't want people for partners with whom we need written agreements."[34]

There was a taboo against discussion of financial matters. The firm generally engaged in little formal financial planning, and certainly didn't publicize its profitability or establish revenue goals. Bills usually were not itemized, but were submitted with the notation "For Services Rendered." There was minimal effort to calculate the productivity of lawyers. Data on hours worked were used primarily to construct bills to clients, rather than to evaluate the performance of individual lawyers. The relative insulation of law practice from competition was reinforced by a scarcity of information about matters such as billing rates, firm profits, partnership agreements, partner compensation, associate salaries, and even the identities of the firm's clients.

Indeed, one major study of Wall Street practice noted that absence of the need or inclination to dwell on the business aspects of the firm led some partners to think of themselves as solo practitioners akin to the country lawyer who hung out his shingle. These lawyers thus were able to reconcile the tradition of lawyer independence with practice within a major organization.[35]

The ability of large firms to operate with minimal adoption of business management principles was due to both economic and social factors. Economically, the prosperity of the firm and its long-standing relationships with clients created incentives to cooperate for the welfare of the organization. As one observer noted, the motto was that everyone benefits as long as "no one rocks the boat."[36] Socially, the

27

homogeneity of firm members meant that informal norms could serve in many cases as a substitute for formal rules. All partners knew one another and moved in the same narrow social circles, which made concern for reputation a powerful influence on behavior.

As the Wall Street firm matured over the first two-thirds of the twentieth century, its lawyers were regarded in many quarters as the embodiment of the ethical and public-spirited ideals of the legal profession. Among its ranks, for instance, were John W. Davis, ambassador to Great Britain and Democratic presidential candidate; John McCloy, president of the World Bank, high commissioner of Germany, and secretary of war; and Thomas Dewey, organized crime prosecutor, governor of New York, and Republican presidential candidate. Scores more partners served as officers of the bar and members of law reform commissions.

Studying the Wall Street firm in the late 1950s and early 1960s, Erwin Smigel suggested that only a handful of current lawyers fit Tocqueville's description of lawyers as the American aristocracy. Most prominent among them, he said, was the Wall Street lawyer.[37] "The caliber of men hired and retained . . . by the large firms," he argued, "makes it less likely that many would be willing to risk their reputation by being unethical."[38] Smigel saw such lawyers as positioned to be the conscience of business, because corporations looked to them for independent legal advice.

In another study of lawyers in New York practices of various sizes, Jerome Carlin found that most lawyers were committed to ethical provisions that tracked common moral tenets. Lawyers in the largest firms, however, were more likely to express allegiance to additional, more stringent, provisions distinctive to the profession, such as those relating to conflicts of interest and acceptance of referral fees. Such rules proscribe opportunities for financial gain that are open to most businessmen.

Carlin attributed this heightened ethical sensitivity not to the character of large firm lawyers, but to the conditions under which they practiced. Lawyers in these firms were subject to fewer competitive pressures than other members of the profession, and were exposed to fewer inducements to violate ethical norms. Lower-status lawyers, he suggested, had practices that were less secure and more precarious, with more temptations and pressures to cut corners. Such lawyers were more likely to see the stringent norms that went beyond ordinary moral intuitions as niceties that prevented them from competing effectively in the market for legal services.

Furthermore, concluded Carlin, the restrictive hiring practices of Wall Street firms served to sort lawyers among tiers of the profession according to religion, ethnicity, and social class. The result was that lawyers from elite backgrounds were sorted into practice settings that posed the fewest ethical temptations, while those further down the ladder faced increasing inducements to violate ethical rules. The elite segment of the bar, said Carlin, was able to insulate itself from "ethically contaminating influences."

It's easy, of course, from our perspective to question the supposed high ethical standards of elite members of the bar during the golden age of the Wall Street law firm. The firms themselves openly discriminated on the basis of religion, race, sex, and social background. Their close economic and social connections to clients created the danger that they would subconsciously adopt the outlook of powerful corporate managers rather than stake out strong contrary positions. Certainly, critics of Wall Street firms called the lawyers within them little more than hired extensions of their clients, who had compromised their professional independence.[39]

Nonetheless, a combination of noblesse oblige and protection from competition may have disposed Wall Street lawyers at least to constrain the more aggressive impulses of their corporate clients. It's easy to imagine that lawyers in these firms saw themselves as members of a social elite with some responsibility for the stability and integrity of social institutions. To the extent that a client was tied to its law firm, lawyers may have been able to disagree with managers or offer a long-term perspective without fear that doing so would result in loss of the client. Intimate familiarity with clients' operations also gave lawyers the ability to offer creative alternatives that allowed corporations to achieve their goals with less danger of running afoul of legal rules or creating adverse social consequences.

Milbank Tweed, for instance, was notable for providing conservative advice to Chase Manhattan Bank about activities that might violate restrictions on interstate banking.[40] As one Chase official said of Milbank partner Roy Haberkern, if something was "legally feasible but risky, he would tell his partner that it was a dumb thing to recommend."[41] Similarly, Lord Day & Lord advised the *New York Times* that concern for the public interest should lead the newspaper to accede to the attorney general's request that the *Times* not publish the Pentagon Papers.[42] For better or worse, the notion of aggressively pushing the legal envelope on behalf of corporate clients was not a common philosophy.

It's hard to draw an unqualified conclusion about whether Wall Street lawyers were more likely than others to abide by ethical norms in the golden age of the Wall Street firm. At most, we probably can say that the ethical problems of such lawyers tended to be those of myopia: insensitivity to the inequities of the status quo, and the failure to press their clients toward a more expansive understanding of social responsibility. By contrast, unethical behavior prompted by the prospect of financial gain, especially in any immediate sense, likely was less common.

FOR MORE THAN A CENTURY, Milbank Tweed was the epitome of a traditional Wall Street firm with ties to the corporate and social elite. From its inception in 1866 as Anderson, Adams & Young, it had served as a firm "where clients from the upper class could be served by their peers."[43] Crucial to the ability of the firm to play this role was its tie with the Rockefeller family and its enterprises. George Welwood Murray became a partner in the firm in the late 1880s. As a result of Murray's involvement in religious activities with John D. Rockefeller, Rockefeller began to retain the firm for legal work. Its connection with the family was reinforced by the employment of several Rockefeller in-laws within the law firm. The firm's largest client was the Equitable Trust Company, a bank in which the Rockefellers owned a controlling interest.

In 1931, Rockefeller encouraged the former Anderson firm, known then as Murray, Aldrich & Webb, to merge with Masten & Nichols, another firm that did legal work for the family.[44] Alfred Milbank, the leading partner in the latter firm, had been a college friend of John D. Rockefeller Jr. With its close connection to the various Rockefeller interests, lawyers in the combined firm "just waited for the phone to ring with business."[45]

Much of the legal work for the family for many years was done by Milbank lawyer John Lockwood, who was the main lawyer for the Rockefellers for twenty years after World War II. The close ties between the firm and the family were underscored by the fact that Lockwood's salary was paid roughly half by Milbank and half by the Rockefeller family. Lockwood spent most of his time in the Rockefeller offices, where many Milbank associates did two-year rotations.

Equitable became the Chase National Bank through a merger in 1930, and the Chase Manhattan Bank in another merger in 1955. The flow of banking work to the firm, however, continued unabated. Partner Roy Haberkern was Milbank's primary contact with Chase, and became chair of the firm in the mid-1960s. For twenty years, "The growth of the firm's non-Chase business was put on the back burner; Haberkern ran the firm as though it existed mainly to satisfy the bank's needs."[46] One reflection of this emphasis was that the primary counsel for Chase and for the Rockefellers had permanent positions on the firm's governance committee.

The relationship with Chase provided particular security for Milbank. As one observer of Wall Street firms a generation ago commented, a bank was "the epitome of a locked-in client."[47] Because law firms' banking departments were so large, and their lawyers had such specialized experience with the bank, "it's virtually impossible for a bank—even if it chose—to switch to another firm."[48]

As the 1960s drew to a close, the Wall Street law firm thus "offer[ed] its partners security equivalent to IBM."[49] The comparison to a large corporation was apt, because the stability of both rested on particular economic conditions. During the 1970s, those conditions began to dissolve. By the end of the decade, seismic changes were under way that would irrevocably alter the placid landscape that had existed for more than sixty years. Wall Street law firms—and large law firms in general—would never be the same.

A NUMBER OF DEVELOPMENTS converged in the late 1960s and early 1970s that began to expose large law firm practice on Wall

Street and elsewhere to the forces of market competition. Fittingly enough, one of the first harbingers of change was Cravath, Swaine & Moore. In 1968, the firm breached the gentleman's agreement concerning starting salaries for associates. It unilaterally raised the figure by almost 50 percent, from $10,500 to $15,000. The move provoked howls of protest and criticism by other firms. Nonetheless, most concluded that they had no choice but to match it if they were to compete for the best law school graduates.

Even more significant seeds of change, however, were being sown by new market pressures on corporate clients. Global competition arose, and began to cut into profit margins, creating incentives to reduce labor costs and improve productivity. Companies began to look to mergers and acquisitions as ways to gain economies of scale that would enhance their ability to compete in worldwide markets. In a break with tradition, they even began to launch hostile takeovers of other corporations.

Technological advances also accelerated the forces of competition. They reduced the length of time that existing products could be counted on to generate profits, and created entirely new markets that required wholly new expertise and resources. Changes in investment banking and financial markets also destabilized long-standing operations and relationships. With the deregulation of underwriting fees in 1975, long-term relationships between investment banks and corporations were swept away in a tidal wave of aggressive competition. Banks began to pursue corporate clients by designing ever more novel and complex financial instruments, which they marketed as vehicles for managing risk and improving the bottom line. As capital markets became more globally integrated, these instruments had an increasingly important impact on the economic fortunes of large corporations.

As a result, "the business world of today is more complex than the business world of a generation ago: there are many more players, more products, more intense competition, more fine-grained calculations made about the distribution of risk, and more uncertainty about the rewards of risk."[50]

Several features of this new world have made legal services an increasingly significant cost for large corporations. The breakdown of informal means of resolving disputes in relatively stable markets has resulted in greater use of litigation as a business strategy.[51] Legal regulation has expanded considerably in the past quarter century, affecting matters such as securities issues, taxation, environmental impacts, worker health and safety, pensions, employee relations, workplace discrimination, corporate governance, and many others. Transactions are larger and have bigger stakes, requiring more intricate negotiation and detailed agreements.

Corporations under pressure to control costs began in the 1970s to rethink the way that they obtained legal services. Most notably, they began more directly to rationalize the use of these services by bringing many of them within the corporation. Over the past generation, in-house legal departments have dramatically grown in size, sophistication, and responsibility. Much of the day-to-day work traditionally performed by outside law firms is now done by lawyers who are corporate employees. This development has reduced the steady flow of work on which large law firms used to rely.

This results not only in the loss of a regular source of income. It also attenuates long-term relationships between firms and their clients. Most major corporations now look to outside firms only for discrete large-scale transactions or major litigation that can't be fully staffed in-house. Rather than rely on the same firm for all their outside work, in-house counsel now tend to act as savvy consumers who shop around for representation on each matter. Law firms compete for such work in "beauty contests" in which they present proposals indicating how they plan to provide cost-effective service on particular engagements. Corporations aggressively negotiate alternatives to hourly billing, such as incentive-based fee structures and discounts.

Furthermore, many companies are more concerned with retaining individual lawyers than specific firms. When corporations regularly used outside firms for most of their legal needs, a firm's organizational capacity was an important consideration in assessing the quality of legal services that it could provide to its corporate clients. With clients now tending to shop for representation on discrete, often specialized, high-stakes matters, the emphasis is on obtaining lawyers with the most expertise regardless of what firms they may call home. Indeed, corporations may put together temporary teams for particular projects comprised of the best experts they can find from several different firms. For much of their legal work, corporate clients thus tend to cultivate relationships with particular lawyers rather than particular firms. As a result, partners may move from one firm to another with some confidence that clients will follow them. This has created a phenomenon that was nonexistent a generation ago: an active lateral market for lawyers in which law firms compete with one another for "rainmakers" who can bring along the most business.

Large law firms thus now must face unprecedented fierce competition for both clients and lawyers. One law firm consultant estimates that law firm profit margins in general have fallen from about 33 percent to the range of 10 to 15 percent, with competitive pressures constantly threatening to drive them even lower.[52] Intensifying competition is the widespread availability of information about matters such as profits, compensation, revenues earned from particular projects and cases, billing rates, and the terms of partnership agreements and firm governance.

All this has required firms belatedly to rationalize their operations much more explicitly along business lines. In a significant break with the tradition of collegial peer management, many firms have hired nonlawyer managers to run their practices. Many firms also have incorporated, and others have become limited liability partnerships or companies in order to shield individual partners from personal exposure for the firm's liabilities.

Maintaining and increasing profits per partner has become an especially crucial objective. Keeping this figure high can lure lawyers with profitable clients from other firms, as well as protect the firm from defections by its own lawyers. One way to enhance profits per partner is continued growth through merger with or acquisition of other law firms.[53] As the scale and scope of corporate activity increases, firms must be able to devote greater resources to each matter, and must have the capacity to provide services around the globe. In addition, firms must be able to offer a wide range of diverse specialties to meet the expanding needs of corporate clients. Diversification is important because it allows a firm to capitalize on areas of practice where market demand is high. It also creates opportunities for lawyers working on one matter to "cross-sell" other services that the firm provides.

The quickest way for a firm to develop a specialty that it needs is not to train its associates, but to acquire lawyers, practice groups, or entire law firms with expertise in a particular field.[54] As one partner puts it, "The market is changing quickly, clients' needs are changing quickly. Firms can't develop resources organically fast enough to keep up. They have to go outside to get talent."[55] Most law firms thus see themselves as facing the imperative to continue growing if they are to remain viable competitors. The fastest way to do that is through merging with or acquiring other lawyers. In contrast to a generation ago, an increasingly large percentage of law firm partners are not associates who are promoted from within, but arrivals from other firms.

A second component of maximizing profits per partner is to concentrate on performing "high end" legal work, which involves more customized services for which a firm can charge a premium.[56] This strategy may require jettisoning long-term clients whose business provides more modest profit margins. One law firm consultant, for instance, suggests that law firms fail to appreciate the potential costs of being loyal to clients.[57] Long-term clients may expect the firm to pass on to them the cost savings from the ongoing relationship, and may expect preferential treatment. Furthermore, lawyers may need to spend nonbillable hours nurturing the relationship. "Fickle" clients, which are short-term but provide high profits, "may, in fact, be the most profitable of all."[58] A law firm therefore must ask itself, "Are we actually profiting from client loyalty?"[59]

Firms also try to enhance profits per partner by increasing their leverage, which is the ratio of nonpartner lawyers to partners. Ideally, a partner will generate enough business to keep several other lawyers busy who receive a straight salary rather than a share of the firm's profits. In considering associates for promotion, or partners at other firms for recruitment, the firm tries to determine how much business a lawyer will generate and how much demand there will be for his or her services over the long run. Associates who work in high-demand fields but have little rainmaking potential may be kept on as permanent associates, rather than promoted to partner, in order to keep leverage high. In addition, firms now use contract and temporary lawyers more frequently to cover large projects. Some firms now also differentiate among classes of partners, creating categories such as nonequity partners and partners without voting rights in the firm.[60] This minimizes the number of partners among whom profits must be distributed, and thus maximizes profits per partner.

Firms also attempt to keep profits high by creating incentives for partners to generate revenues. One of the most significant changes in most large law firms from a generation ago is the abandonment of lockstep compensation based on seniority for compensation systems that purport to reflect productivity. As a result, a partner who generates fewer revenues than his or her peers will receive a lower share of profits. Partner compensation thus can be quite volatile from year to year. More drastically, some partners may be demoted to nonequity status, while others may be terminated by the firm if their performance does not improve. In the two years before the large Chicago firm Sidley & Austin merged with New York firm Brown & Wood, for instance, Sidley terminated the partnership of seventy partners.[61]

The result of heightened competition among large law firms is perpetual instability. A prestigious pedigree and impeccable reputation are no guarantees of survival in the new legal services market.[62] Firms must project an image of continued "momentum,"[63] moving into new markets, pursuing new alliances, weeding out unproductive lawyers, and expanding their operations to keep pace with corporate clients. Calculating the revenues for which a partner is given credit in turn reinforces the free agent market, since it provides lawyers with an ostensibly objective basis for marketing their value to other firms.

The large law firm in general, and the Wall Street firm in particular, thus is substantially different from the institution of a generation ago. To some extent, large law firm practice has reverted to the fluid conditions that existed in the late nineteenth century, before Paul Cravath and others sought to create institutions larger than any of the individuals within them. Clients increasingly pursue the services of particular lawyers, rather than specific firms. This creates opportunities for lawyers to take clients with them to other firms that offer more attractive compensation and practice conditions. The demise of lockstep compensation has reduced much of the risk-sharing that law firms provide their members. If partners sniff the beginning of decline in the air, they may well scramble to abandon what they regard as a sinking ship. Few may be willing to take cuts in compensation for the sake of saving the firm.[64]

Ironically, compared to a generation ago, today's large firm has many more formal organizational controls, such as a hierarchical chain of command, more professional managers in positions of authority, distinct practice departments, and detailed financial management and reporting systems. Aside from the need to coordinate the operations of increasingly large organizations, these measures are necessary because firms no longer are able to rely on informal social norms to regulate behavior. The exploding demand for lawyers over the past generation, combined with broader social and political developments, has forced firms to recruit lawyers from a wider and more diverse group of candidates. Furthermore, reliance on the lateral market, rather than solely associate promotion, as a source of new partners makes it difficult to sustain a distinctive and stable culture within the firm. Thus, the irony: large firms a generation ago were loosely organized but tightly integrated, while today's firms are more formally organized but only loosely integrated.

THREE FEATURES of the modern large law firm shape the experience and outlook of lawyers in especially important ways. First, the tournament within the firm is not just for promotion to partner any more. It continues after partnership, as partners must compete for compensation, status, and continued employment. It's not a tournament in the conventional sense, in that there is no single ultimate winner. Indeed, no one is ever assured of winning. Instead, everyone is constantly playing simply to remain in the game. The goal, in other words, is not victory but survival.

The amount of revenues that a partner generates is the main method of keeping score in this tournament. There are two ways that a partner can maximize his score. The first, and preferable, one is to be a rainmaker that brings in clients to the firm. As one observer notes, the "reality of partnership" today is that "business production is paramount."[65] Rainmakers get credit not only for the work they personally do, but also receive some credit for the work that others do for those clients.[66] In other words, rainmakers receive a return on the loan of their human capital to others. The more lawyers a rainmaker can keep busy, the better his standing in the tournament, and the greater his compensation and influence within the firm.

Partners who aren't significant rainmakers must maximize their competitive position by working regularly for partners who are. These lawyers are "service partners"[67] who perform work for other partners' clients. Developing a good relationship with a rainmaker allows a non-rainmaker to generate revenues by regularly billing a large number of hours on lucrative matters. The firm's internal labor market thus serves not only to match the surplus labor of associates with the surplus capital of partners. It also operates among partners to match the surplus labor of nonrainmaker service partners with the surplus capital of rainmakers. A tournament survivor therefore must be a successful entrepreneur and profit center. He must seek out clients in order to acquire excess capital that he can lend to others. In addition, or as an alternative, he must seek out ongoing relationships with rainmakers so that he fully utilizes his own labor.

One function of the tournament is to prevent shirking by partners. The theory is that a partner with fixed compensation and lifetime tenure may be tempted to ease up, thus bringing down revenues and profits per partner. This may make it more difficult for the firm to recruit lawyers from other firms, and leave the firm vulnerable to defections by its own lawyers. It also may hurt a firm's standing with clients by fostering the impression that the firm contains "deadwood." The modern large firm wants lawyers who are "hungry," who can promote the image of constant forward momentum.

At the same time, however, the tournament can penalize those partners whose practice slows down for reasons beyond their control. The demand for particular practice specialties can fluctuate according to larger economic developments. Bankruptcy practice, for instance, tends to be strong during economic downturns but to wane in times of prosperity. Similarly, the burst of the dot-com bubble in 2000 meant a sharp decline in legal work related to high-technology firms. Furthermore, a partner's client may be acquired by another company that prefers to use different lawyers, or may decide to expand its legal department to perform more legal services inside the corporation. These and other developments may reduce the revenues that a partner generates. This leaves him vulnerable to cuts in compensation in the short term and possible termination in the long run. A move from lockstep to compensation ostensibly based on productivity thus sharply lessens the extent to which the law firm serves as an enterprise to share risk among its partners.

A second important feature of the modern large law firm is the influence of practice specialties on lawyers' perspectives. These specialties have taken on greater significance in shaping lawyers' norms as law firms find it increasingly difficult to sustain distinct firmwide cultures. Today's firm contains an increasingly diverse set of lawyers under one roof. Firms now recruit associates from a variety of social backgrounds and law schools, making them far less homogeneous than a generation ago. Furthermore, expanding corporate demand for sophisticated global legal services creates pressure for firms to possess a wide range of practice specialties and office locations. Firms fret constantly about the ability to integrate other lawyers, practice groups, or firms into a seamless organization. In addition, the enhanced ability of lawyers to leave firms with clients in tow makes it hard to enforce firmwide rules and policies. Finally, the sheer size of major law firms makes it difficult to achieve a consensus on values beyond the common denominator of revenues and profits.

Specialists confront issues and problems in their daily work that differ from those faced by other colleagues within the firm. Much of law practice consists of informal understandings about matters such as what arguments are considered within the bounds of good faith, acceptable levels of aggressiveness, the scope of disclosure requirements, how to interact with regulatory agencies, and what constitutes due diligence. These and other issues may be resolved differently by lawyers in specialties such as securities, tax, banking, patents, environmental law, and bankruptcy, to name only a few. Conferences and other professional education activities tend to be organized around specific fields of practice, thereby providing opportunities for lawyers to trade ideas and develop common understandings based on shared experience. In addition, lawyers may be subject to rules of practice particular to their specialty. Practitioners thus may have more in common with lawyers in other firms who practice in the same specialty than with many lawyers in their own firms.

Over time, the shared experiences of practitioners in a particular specialty lead them to develop norms of acceptable behavior. These norms can shape attitudes for at least two reasons. First, lawyers are inclined to regard the norms as legitimate because they are rooted in appreciation of the realities of practice in a particular field. Second, they may influence behavior because those practitioners are "repeat players" who deal with one another on an ongoing basis. This can make concern for reputation an important consideration for a lawyer in deciding how to behave. Lawyers who gain a reputation for cooperation generally will find that other counsel are willing to grant them the courtesies and extend them the trust that can make practice smoother. A lawyer with a reputation for not abiding by the unspoken rules of the game, however, can find himself bogged down in contentious bickering that drains time, energy, and money. Several factors thus combine to make practice specialties an important influence on understandings of what it means to be a lawyer.

Finally, lawyers' experience in the modern large law firm also tends to be shaped by intense involvement on project teams that are assembled to work for the duration of a specific matter. Corporate clients need legal services for increasingly larger and more complex projects.[68] Such projects require the services of several lawyers who devote most of their time and energy to major litigation or a huge transaction, often for extended periods of time. These lawyers then move on to other large cases or deals to work on teams specially created for those matters. Project teams thus represent a version of the "flexible production" approach that has become a more prominent means of providing goods and services in the economy as a whole.[69]

This differs from work in the traditional large law firm in a couple of ways. First, the regular flow of routine business from clients a generation ago included some matters on which individual lawyers could work without the need for extensive coordination with others. While lawyers also worked on teams, that likely constituted a less significant portion of a lawyer's practice than it does today. A project today for a multinational company may require most of a lawyer's time and attention for months and even years on end. During that period, other members of the team can become a significant reference group.

Second, the intensity of the typical corporate project on which outside counsel works has increased from a generation ago. Heightened competition and the faster pace of business have made projects more time-sensitive and have increased their stakes. Furthermore, team members want to achieve a favorable outcome for the client—that is, to "win"—in order to enhance the likelihood that they will receive future business. These factors increase the pressure that teams face when they work on projects for clients.

In addition, it's probably fairly common for lawyers to construct a moral universe that's particular to the matter on which they're working. Both professional training and psychological tendencies incline many lawyers to identify strongly with their clients. This process helps provide the lawyer with a moral orientation in her work. To varying degrees, it permits her to make judgments about the justifiability of other actors' conduct, and to determine what responses are appropriate and defensible. In some cases, it authorizes the lawyer to engage in behavior that otherwise would be subject to moral criticism.

The result of all this is that teams can shape individual perceptions in powerful ways by creating a shared cognitive and moral universe. Members reinforce for one another the idea that their framework for interpreting events is accurate and reasonable. This process can result in "groupthink," a situation in which individuals arrive at a consensus without exploring all options or paying enough attention to information that challenges their framework.[70] Group influence will be especially pronounced when members face stress and ambiguity, and when they perceive an external threat or adversary. It also may be especially potent when a project team is comprised of members from different organizations. The absence of a single entity with overall managerial responsibility in these cases may make it harder to prompt group members to view things from the standpoint of a broader organizational mission.

The large-firm lawyer thus practices under conditions dramatically different from a quarter century ago. Firms are more loosely organized, partners are more akin to individual entrepreneurs, and competition is a relentless fact of life. These changes have been especially vivid at Wall Street firms, because they were the most insulated from competitive pressures for a good part of the twentieth century. All large firms, however, now inhabit a universe whose governing laws are those of the market.

MILBANK TWEED has not been immune to the forces that have rocked large law firms over the past twenty-five years or so. The evolution of its relationships with the Chase Manhattan Bank and the Rockefeller family offer prime examples of how the attenuation of long-term connections with clients can leave a law firm economically vulnerable.

IN THE LATE 1970s, banks began to push the regulatory limits on their ability to engage in interstate banking and investment banking. Milbank lawyers tended to offer conservative advice that discouraged Chase from being very aggressive on these fronts. Meanwhile, however, competitor Citibank was moving ahead in both these areas. Officials at Chase eventually came to regard Milbank's counsel as too risk averse for the rapidly changing landscape of competition. As a result, the firm largely was left out in the cold as Chase began to acquire financial institutions in various parts of the country. Banks such as Chase began significantly to expand their consumer banking activities through the provision of credit cards. Milbank did little of the work on this project as well because of its limited expertise in consumer lending.

Commercial banks during this period began losing corporate business to investment banks, as companies began to turn directly to financial markets for their needs rather than obtain financing from commercial lenders. Investment banks had a competitive edge in this field because of their ability to provide companies with direct access to investors. Milbank had been reluctant over the years to develop connections with investment banks. It feared that representing such clients might create a conflict because the firm regularly represented the New York Stock Exchange, which regulated such banks. As Chase and other commercial banks sought to develop financial products more closely resembling those offered by investment banks, Milbank thus could offer little assistance. The same was true with respect to Chase's development of novel financing techniques such as swaps, which involve the trade between companies of interest rate payments on loans. Other law firms had developed more expertise in these arrangements, and therefore tended to get Chase's business.

The expansion of Chase's inside legal department also cut into Milbank's work for the bank. Even as Chase began to use different lawyers for different projects, as late as 1985 Milbank received 40 percent of its revenues from the bank. Three years later the figure was down to 21 percent. By that point, the firm of necessity had begun to do what in previous years was unthinkable: solicit work from Chase's competitors.

Change also occurred in the firm's provision of legal services to the Rockefeller family. In 1983, at the insistence of the Rockefellers, Milbank partner Donal O'Brien withdrew from the firm and became the head of the family's in-house legal department. Over time, that department assumed more responsibility for the family's legal work. Milbank lawyers began meeting less with family members directly and more with family lawyers, who would pass on the Rockefellers' requests. The firm became less involved in the early stages of various projects, as O'Brien and his lawyers took on a more prominent role as counselors to the family.

In addition, by the mid-1980s the younger generation of Rockefellers had cashed out much of the value of the family's real estate holdings for their own personal use. This meant that there would be fewer entrepreneurial projects that required Milbank's assistance in the future. This fact, along with the insistence of the family's in-house counsel to shop around for law firm assistance, meant that the Rockefeller family no longer would be a steady source of income for Milbank. The special relationship between the family and the firm was gone. In the future, Milbank would have to compete for Rockefeller business like any other law firm.

As Ellen Joan Pollock has recounted, the shifting terrain of law firm practice began to prompt some reaction within Milbank in the late 1970s.[71] There was much resistance, however, to making changes that many partners feared would alter the culture of the firm. Corporate partner Al Lilley headed a study on firm governance in 1978 that altered the composition of the firm committee from life membership to staggered three-year terms. The committee, rather than the partnership, would continue to appoint members to the committee. Its chair, however, could no longer be the partner in charge of the relationship with Chase. The study also recommended abolishing the firm's management committee and bringing in an executive director. In 1980, Milbank hired Ronald Cullis to fill this position. In hiring Cullis, a former vice president and chief accounting officer of Fluor Corporation, the firm was ahead of its time in bringing in a nonlawyer with management experience to administer the firm's operations.

In 1982, Cullis distributed a survey to partners that was designed to elicit their views on the firm and its future. All but four of the firm's sixty-eight partners completed the survey. It revealed that partners were concerned that the firm wasn't generating enough business, that it had an insufficient number of corporate clients, and that it was too dependent on Chase. The survey also pointed up dissatisfaction with inequities in workloads and compensation. This was the first explicit expression of fear from a broad segment of the partnership that the firm might be left behind if it didn't respond to the new dynamics of the legal services market.

The election of a new chair of the firm committee afforded an opportunity for Milbank to begin to explore changes in the firm. Alexander Forger was chosen by the committee as chair in June 1984, and began the delicate task of creating a consensus for measures deemed necessary to assure the firm's viability. Milbank's profits per partner were $370,000 in 1984, compared with $635,000 for Cravath, Swaine & Moore and $795,000 for newcomer Wachtell, Lipton, where Larry Lederman was at the time. The year before, Milbank had seen its first partner leave for practice at another firm. Milbank did little work for investment banks. Furthermore, it had missed the lucrative boom in merger and acquisition practice of the early 1980s, which afforded firms such as Skadden, Arps and Wachtell, Lipton the opportunity to vault into the ranks of the most profitable law firms.

Finally, Milbank's leverage—its ratio of associates to partners—was low compared to its supposed peers. The figure for Milbank in 1980 when Cullis arrived was 1.9:1, compared to Cravath's ratio of 3:1. This figure is crucial in determining profits per partner. The larger the ratio, the more associates the firm can bill at rates above their fixed salaries, and the larger the pool of profits that are available to divide among partners. Milbank had improved to 2.5:1 by 1984. Other firms in competition with Milbank also were focusing on increasing their leverage, however, and Milbank no longer had the predictable stream of work that potentially could be used to keep large numbers of associates busy.

Pressed by younger partners, Milbank adopted a business plan in 1984 that called for the firm to focus on "growth and diversification." Attempts to implement the plan, however, confronted both ambivalence and resistance within the firm. Some members feared that substantial growth of the firm would undermine collegiality. Others didn't like the idea of doing more merger and acquisition work, especially relating to hostile takeovers, because they perceived practice in this field as unduly aggressive. Some chafed at the idea that they needed to take more active steps to cultivate new corporate clients. In addition, some regarded explicit focus on the firm's financial growth as incompatible with an emphasis on putting the client's needs first.

Over time, however, committee members painstakingly addressed partners' concerns and laid out the arguments for change. As law firms began competing more intensively to lure partners from other firms, it soon became apparent that Milbank was vulnerable. Its comparatively low profits per partner provided a selling point for competitors seeking to recruit the firm's top performers. Furthermore, Milbank needed to expand its base of clients, and it didn't have time to develop "rain-makers" from within. Its commitment to lockstep compensation, how-ever, made it difficult to attract high-revenue partners from other firms. As more and more of its Wall Street peers took steps to alter their structures, and as newer firms swooped in to capture important areas of practice, Milbank's partners began to conclude that significant changes were necessary.

At a pivotal March 1986 firm retreat, the partners addressed the crucial issue of compensation. The debate was emotionally charged. The first evening of the retreat, partner Larry Nelson, head of the firm's real estate practice group, gave an impassioned address in defense of lockstep compensation. It allowed partners to focus on serv-ing their clients, he argued, rather than competing with each other. It acknowledged the value of knowledge and skill, rather than simply business generation. It assured that all partners were treated as equals, rather than ranked according to a financial calculus. A firm governed by merit compensation, Nelson asserted, would spawn incessant quar-rels over money and undermine cooperation and teamwork.

Forger's pitch to the partnership was that the committee was proposing that lockstep compensation be modified, rather than drasti-cally revised. It would, he explained, serve only to raise overachievers and lower underachievers. He gained the assent of a large percentage of partners to his argument that some form of alteration was neces-sary. At the same time, most partners wanted lockstep to remain the cornerstone of the compensation system. Eventually the plan passed with no dissent. A compensation committee was charged with imple-menting the new system.

Over the next six months, the committee set about to determine how to carry out the general charge it had been given. Members met with every partner to discuss his or her practice and plans for developing it, as well as the partner's view of the performance of other partners. When the committee issued its report in October, many were surprised at the sweep of its recommendations. Three partners who were high achievers would constitute a class above their lockstep peers, including bankruptcy practice head John Jerome. Three midlevel partners also would receive increases above lockstep. In addition, seven other partners were scheduled to receive such raises beginning January 1, 1987.

More ominously, eight partners received notice that they would not be eligible for lockstep increases, and might in fact suffer a cut in compensation, if they did not increase their productivity. Finally came the most shocking news: two lawyers who had been partners since 1979 would be leaving the firm. The committee insisted that these partners had not been fired. Many members of the firm, however, believed that "evaluations of the two partners had been handled in such a way that the gentlemen had no other logical—or dignified—recourse than to decide to withdraw from the partnership."[72] In all, about twenty partners either gained or lost compared to what they would have received under lockstep compensation. Increases above lockstep averaged about seventy-five thousand dollars, while decreases averaged one hundred thousand dollars.

Many partners were shocked at how aggressively the committee had applied a merit compensation approach. They had assumed that the committee would move slowly and that only a small handful of partners would be subject to deviations from lockstep. Nelson circulated a memo to his peers criticizing the committee for going far beyond the authority that it had been given. He maintained that those partners whose compensation was reduced, and those who in effect were asked to leave, had been denied adequate notice of the complaints against them and an opportunity to defend themselves. Such an explicit expression of disagreement would have been unlikely just a few years earlier, when those who dissented from decisions by the leadership tended to subordinate their objections for the sake of preserving unity within the firm.

Enough other partners expressed reservations about the committee's actions that Forger called a full partnership meeting for January 7, delaying the merit increases that otherwise were scheduled to go into effect on January 1. Critics had the opportunity to air their com-

plaints. Ultimately, however, an overwhelming majority of the partners expressed support for the compensation system as implemented
by the committee. Most lawyers felt that the firm had bestowed considerable discretion upon the committee and that they were not in a
position to second-guess its decisions. Enough of the traditional culture of consensus remained, in other words, that partners were willing
to give the benefit of doubt to committee decisions that could pose a
challenge to that very tradition. Furthermore, those partners who disagreed with the committee's system generally did not have practices
sufficiently portable that they could express their displeasure by going
elsewhere.

In mid-1988, as Milbank approached a decision on whether to name
John Gellene a partner, the firm hired a management consultant to
devise a strategic plan. The consultant's survey research indicated that
Milbank was perceived as not interested in marketing itself or bringing in new clients. The study also revealed that the most important
consideration for potential clients in hiring a firm was not the quality
of the legal work, which companies assumed would be good. Rather,
clients wanted "entrepreneurial lawyers who took initiative and participated fully in their clients' business and made a discernible impact
on transactions."[73] Milbank's leaders concluded that the firm needed
to be more visible in merger and acquisition (M&A) work in order to
be regarded as a contender for major corporate representation.

The strategic plan for the firm approved by the partnership in
March 1990 emphasized how crucial it was for Milbank to develop
expertise in what the plan called "Leading Corporate Transactions."
The number one priority of the firm, said the plan, was to develop a
well-known "General Corporate/M&A" practice. This was necessary
in order to provide the impetus for growth in several other practice
areas, secure "above-average profitability growth levels," and ensure
Milbank's status as an elite firm.

Unfortunately, Milbank currently was regarded as "invisible" in
M&A work. This reflected the "unsatisfactory mix" of its client base,
which was too heavily weighted toward representation of commercial
banks and bankruptcy creditors. By contrast, other firms that had

remained in or moved into the elite ranks had been moved by their investment banking clients to develop a full range of merger and acquisition expertise. In order to compete with such firms, Milbank needed to acquire a group of leading corporate and M&A practitioners "headed by an individual of great reputation and visibility."

The plan directly addressed the issue of the firm's culture. Bringing in a corporate/M&A group, it said, would make the firm "more aggressive, scrappier, more intense, and more highly charged in its desire to accomplish client objectives." To the extent that some within the firm might be disturbed by such a metamorphosis, they "must face up to the trade off that would appear to be necessary if Milbank is to have any chance of holding its own in competing for the business of large publicly-held corporations, investment bankers, merchant bankers, and the like which we now seek."

The planning committee report also noted that work on corporate financial restructuring and bankruptcy was in an upswing, and that Milbank was poised to benefit from this trend by virtue of having the fourth largest bankruptcy department in the nation. One obstacle, however, was the firm's high concentration of creditors in its client base. In order to maximize the benefits of its expertise the firm needed to move more aggressively into the representation of corporate debtors. Developing more extensive connections with investment banks would be important in achieving this objective.

In 1991, Milbank would pursue this strategy by courting the high-powered corporate lawyer Larry Lederman of Wachtell, Lipton, Rosen, & Katz. Because of his ties to major corporations and investment banks, Lederman had the potential to lead Milbank into the promised land of "Leading Corporate Transactions." His contacts also could open the door to more frequent representation of corporate debtors in bankruptcy. Representing such clients could be very beneficial to a young bankruptcy partner like John Gellene. The broad competitive forces that were roiling Milbank and other firms thus would soon touch Gellene's life in dramatic and unforeseen ways. To appreciate more fully how this happened, we need to take a closer look at John Gellene and his career at Milbank Tweed.

CHAPTER TWO

Portrait of a
Young Lawyer

FOR SEVERAL REASONS, Jo]hn Gellene likely was very eager to accept Larry Lederman's request to work on the Bucyrus bankruptcy. The younger partner was keenly aware that he was competing in a tournament with other partners at Milbank for compensation, status, and job security. A good relationship with a powerful rainmaker like Lederman would be a valuable asset in that competition. Furthermore, this asset may have been even more important to Gellene than to his competitors. He was not a rainmaker and was unlikely to become one, because of his personality and the nature of bankruptcy practice. Furthermore, he had an embarrassing blemish on his record at Milbank that had jeopardized his partnership at the firm almost as soon as he had won it. In various ways, these dynamics helped shape the way that John Gellene approached the assignment to help Bucyrus with its reorganization.

JOHN GELLENE was accustomed to competing in, and winning, tournaments. He had grown up in suburban New Jersey about fifteen miles west of New York City. He was the second of six children, four boys and two girls, in a middle-class devoutly Catholic Italian-American family. Gellene's siblings ranged in age from a sister a year older to a brother eleven years younger. His parents' marriage was a traditional one. His father was self-employed as a buyer's representative for chemicals used in textile manufacturing, while his mother was a homemaker.

Gellene's father was a hard-driving man who established extremely high standards of achievement for his children, particularly the boys. As the oldest boy, John was especially shaped by these expectations. He was tightly wound, self-contained, and highly directed. He skipped not one but two grades in school. Despite his youth, fellow students regarded him as a "brainiac," intellectually gifted and driven by an intense desire for academic accomplishment. Gellene participated in student government, chess, and debate at DePaul High School, a Catholic school in Wayne, New Jersey; he was generally well liked by those who knew him, but was not in the most popular social groups. He was a gifted pianist despite no formal training. On rare occasions, he would use music among friends as a release from the strict self-control that he usually imposed on himself.

Gellene acknowledged that recognition for his intellect was a crucial element of his sense of self-worth. "[N]ot just for my adult life but before that," he has said, "I've been recognized as a person with gifts of my intellect and my ability to deal with problems." Larry Lederman described his work as "absolutely brilliant." Another Milbank partner reported a client's view that Gellene was the best bankruptcy lawyer in the United States.

Such expectations, however, also were a burden. They left Gellene afraid to admit that he had made any errors, out of fear that this esteem for him would evaporate. "When I am confronted with a mistake," he said, "it is very difficult for me to stand up and say I did a stupid thing." He was, he admitted, someone "who feels that he had to be perfect because that is where I've gotten my view of myself. That is where I've gotten satisfaction. That's where I've tried for better or worse to have meaning in my life." Adding to the burden was a sense that perhaps Gellene did not deserve the admiration that he seemed to evoke. "For many years," he observed, he had acted as if his supposed gift was "an affliction, something that I had to reject, something that I suppose I wasn't worthy of."

Competing for intellectual achievement offered Gellene a way to validate a sense of self-worth. Success in one tournament led to opportunities to compete in even more demanding ones. He graduated Phi Beta Kappa and summa cum laude from Georgetown with degrees in philosophy and economics. This opened the door to Harvard Law School, from which he graduated cum laude. His performance at Harvard led to a summer position with Milbank Tweed between his second and third years of law school. His work during that summer led to an offer of permanent employment with Milbank. He accepted that offer, but before he began he served as a clerk to Justice Morris Pashman on the New Jersey Supreme Court. He then embarked on the tournament for partnership at Milbank, a prize granted only to a handful of associates each year. With each success, a new challenge arose; with each prize, another appeared on the horizon.

At each step of the way, Gellene had the reputation of being extraordinarily hard-working. Those who knew him in law school recall someone who seemed driven to prove himself, who put in exceptionally long hours even by the standards of students accustomed to punishing schedules. His compulsiveness appeared to be fueled in part by anxiety, prompted perhaps by the fear that he might reveal that he was not as smart as others had been led to believe.

Gellene's work habits continued when he joined Milbank Tweed. He initially worked with a group of litigators who did both commercial litigation and bankruptcy work, and found the environment at the firm "extremely competitive." Eventually, he gravitated to Milbank's bankruptcy practice. In an environment of high achievers who spent most of their waking hours at the firm, he stood out as someone who "works like a dog." Gellene described his typical week as "being in the office ten, twelve, sometimes more hours a day five days a week and then a number of hours in the office on Saturday or Sunday or both." He adopted this schedule, he said, soon after he joined the firm. The desire to make partner in a very competitive environment no doubt intensified any predilection he had for immersing himself in his work.

This pattern of behavior didn't abate, however, after he was named a partner. In 1993, the year leading up to the Bucyrus bankruptcy filing, he billed more than 3,100 hours. In 1994, Gellene's billable hours approached 3,000. Milbank's annual compensation committee reports on Gellene are studded with comments on his hard work from other partners: "works tremendously hard"; "a very hard worker"; "tireless worker"; "overworked"; and "work[s] fiendishly hard."

Colleagues also describe a lawyer who tended to take too much on himself without delegating responsibility to or involving others. In one of its annual reviews, the Milbank compensation committee told Gellene, "There are concerns about practice management as a result of the heavy burdens that you have taken on yourself." The committee expressed the hope that he would "share the burden with your Partners" and use associates more effectively in his projects. Barry Radick, cohead of the firm's bankruptcy practice, put it more vividly: "He is a control freak and a loner. He refuses help; we are concerned that he may get himself into trouble because he is working so hard." Radick observed that Gellene should not be working by himself on a particular major bankruptcy case (not Bucyrus) that the younger partner was heading. The compensation committee's 1995 message to Gellene stated that he could accomplish a lot more if he would "develop better working relationships with others." Gellene himself admitted that he was the sort of person who "if [he] needed help . . . wouldn't necessarily reach out for it."

Gellene's reluctance to share responsibility, his difficulty in seeking help from others, and his insistence on handling several intensive matters at once are consistent with the portrait of perfectionism and anxiety that emerges from his own comments. Perhaps he feared that if others worked closely with him they would come to question his reputation for brilliance. In any event, his approach to his work posed the constant threat of isolation. He ran the risk of cutting himself off from valuable second opinions, and of depriving himself of the sounding board that colleagues can provide.

Gellene's tendency toward intense tunnel vision sometimes led him to ignore the administrative requirements that accompany life in a large law firm. Gellene is "very bright," noted Barry Radick, "but doesn't follow administrative rules." Most glaringly, his chronic failure to submit his "daynotes," or billing records, on time was a source

of frustration. Partner Bob O'Hara repeatedly criticized Gellene's lax-
ity on this score to the compensation committee. Gellene, he said,
tended to submit his records on a monthly basis, sometimes going
longer between reports. "He comes into compliance just enough to get
paid," said O'Hara.

Milbank was sufficiently concerned about daynote delinquencies
that it instituted a penalty for partners who failed to submit them on
time. When the policy was first instituted, Gellene was penalized
$3,125 for his delinquency during the previous quarter. The compen-
sation committee noted that this figure represented one-half the maximum that could be imposed. It withheld only this amount because it
was the first time the committee had applied the new policy. Things
did not improve the next quarter, however. As a result, Gellene was
docked the maximum amount of $6,250 in his next paycheck. Gel-
lene's delinquencies made it especially hard for associates who worked
with him to prepare Milbank's compensation requests to bankruptcy
courts. Associates would frantically try to track him down, only to dis-
cover that he was months behind in compiling his records.

In a similar vein, the head of the firm's summer associate program
reported in 1992 that Gellene had been "[f]ired as partner mentor this
Summer—after 4 weeks had still not made a single contact with his
Summer Associates." In 1994 the compensation committee was told,
"The recruiting staff has determined, based on experience, that Gellene should not be asked to assist the Firm with recruiting or interviewing; he generally refuses or, if he agrees he then cancels." Gellene's intense immersion in his work thus gave rise to a tunnel vision
that obscured anything he saw as not immediately relevant to the task
at hand.

WHEN GELLENE BEGAN his career at Milbank Tweed in 1980,
the old order was beginning to crumble on Wall Street. More of it
remained at Milbank, however, than at many other law firms. A young
associate therefore could assume that the traditional rules of the promotion to partner tournament were still in place. These were that

working long hours and acquiring proficiency in the law provided the best chance for obtaining a partnership. There was little need to worry about where clients would come from. The firm's long-standing relationships with various institutions should provide a steady stream of work.

While it possessed impeccable status as an elite firm, Milbank was somewhat anomalous among such firms for having a fairly substantial bankruptcy practice. Wall Street firms historically tended to look with disdain on this work, particularly since it was associated with Jewish lawyers. Milbank's practice had been developed by a permanent associate named Samuel Ross Ballin, who had obtained his law degree at night from Brooklyn Law School and joined Milbank in 1922. Ballin "taught bankruptcy law to a whole generation of Milbank lawyers, who displayed his primitive-style paintings alongside more expensive art in their offices."[1] Some at the firm believed that he had never been promoted to partner because he was Jewish.[2]

The status of bankruptcy practice changed dramatically, however, in the 1970s. As the economy faltered and revisions to the Bankruptcy Code made Chapter 11 more attractive to corporations, bankruptcy work became highly lucrative. Milbank was well positioned to take advantage of this development. Chase Manhattan was likely to be a creditor in many corporate bankruptcies, which meant regular Chapter 11 assignments. Partner John Jerome eventually became recognized as a leading member of the bankruptcy bar, and headed this practice for many years. A graduate of St. John's Law School, he was described as the "antithesis of the Milbank type" by virtue of his "quick temper and loud voice."[3] Stories abound about his propensity to erupt with anger and throw objects at those who incurred his displeasure. Jerome's preeminence in the field and his lucrative billings, however, gave him an important role within the firm.

Gellene was quite familiar with tournaments. His temperament and habits were well suited to succeed in them. He needed access to a mentor, however, who could enhance his prospects at Milbank by teaching him the intricacies of bankruptcy. He found such a partner in John

Jerome. Gellene began to work "very closely and intensely" with Jerome on various matters. As Gellene put it, John Jerome "taught me how to be a lawyer."

Not long after he began at Milbank, Gellene assumed responsibility in the bankruptcy of Johns Manville, a company facing millions of dollars in potential liability claims against it for exposing workers to asbestos. His work on this and other matters solidified his relationship with Jerome. Jerome's support, along with Gellene's intellect and capacity for hard work, paid off for Gellene at the end of 1988. He was named a partner at Milbank, effective January 1, 1989.

By the time that Gellene achieved his partnership, however, the rules of the Milbank tournament had changed. Long-term relationships with clients were becoming a thing of the past for most Wall Street firms. Lawyers therefore could not afford to assume that their firms would provide them with a regular flow of work. They had to take responsibility for generating work for themselves. Furthermore, the tournament no longer ended with the receipt of a partnership. It continued as long as a partner wanted to stay with his firm. Partnership, in other words, was constantly up for grabs in an ongoing competition.

Willingness to work long hours and mastery of the law thus were no longer a guarantee of job security. If the supply of clients dried up, a partner could be out on the street. Gellene couldn't assume that his relationship with Jerome, or that the fact that he was a skilled bankruptcy lawyer, would shield him from competition. He had to move out from Jerome's shadow and develop his own client base to ensure that he continued to generate profits for the firm.

Gellene's personality, however, didn't easily lend itself to the role of rainmaker. His single-minded, sometimes isolating, concentration was an adaptive trait for winning a prize in the old tournament. It could be a hindrance, however, in the new one, which required cultivating relationships with clients. Many of his colleagues found him a bit abstracted and absorbed. Others regarded him as a little manic, someone spurred by the constant need to perform and to impress others with his intellectual ability.

Even partners who praised Gellene's work sometimes found him difficult to understand. He is "a bit of an enigma," said one. John Jerome, his bankruptcy mentor, observed, "He can get depressed but perhaps this is his nature." Another characterized him as "very smart," but added that "sometimes he gets out on a limb." Still another described him as bright, talented, and ambitious, but suggested, "He should civilize himself more." None of these attributes translated into the kind of easy social skills that are useful in marketing legal services to potential clients.

An equally significant obstacle to Gellene's becoming a rainmaker was the nature of bankruptcy practice, which is both episodic and cyclical. Clients who want to reorganize in response to financial distress need the services of bankruptcy lawyers for a specific purpose for a limited period of time. If everything goes well, the client no longer needs your services. This makes it difficult to build long-term client relationships. By contrast, a corporate lawyer has the potential to tap into a steady stream of work on behalf of clients who may need help with matters such as securities issues, taxation, mergers and acquisitions, the sale of assets, transactional work, regulatory compliance, and litigation, to name only a few. Similarly, lawyers who represent investment banks work on behalf of clients that are constantly involved in corporate deals.

The most natural way for Milbank's bankruptcy practice to build a stable client base was to draw on its work for Chase over the years to sell itself as an expert in creditor representation. That strategy, however, didn't fit in with Milbank's plan to pursue high-end corporate work and become a major player in "Leading Corporate Transactions." Representing debtors was far more lucrative. Corporations in bankruptcy required the services of numerous attorneys to negotiate with creditors, fend off legal challenges, sell assets, and help put together complex reorganization plans that reconciled the interests of shareholders, creditors, employees, customers, suppliers, tort claimants, and government regulators. Debtors' counsel were compensated handsomely for such efforts. Contacts with corporations, not with commercial banks, were critical in landing such work.

In addition to its episodic nature, bankruptcy practice is cyclical. It waxes when the economy is not going well and wanes when times are good. Events such as the failure of many savings and loans in the 1980s, the collapse of many companies in the early 1990s under the burden of debt incurred in leveraged buyouts a few years earlier, and the bursting of the Internet bubble after 2000 create demand for bankruptcy services. When the economy recovers, however, demand can fall off considerably. The flow of work to a bankruptcy lawyer thus is subject to influences over which she has little control.

Internal Milbank Tweed memos indicate that Gellene was acutely aware of the difficulty in developing a stable of clients, and feared that bankruptcy work would dry up. At the end of each year, members of the Milbank compensation committee met with partners to discuss the compensation that they would be receiving under the firm's merit-based system. Reports of this committee indicate that Gellene consistently expressed anxiety about the future of the Milbank bankruptcy practice.

At one point, for instance, he told the compensation committee that he was frustrated by what he perceived as the bankruptcy group's inadequate efforts to develop business. The group had no clients of its own, he fretted, and would remain a practice that simply provided services to others' clients as long as the firm primarily represented financial institutions that periodically had creditor claims in bankruptcy. This was frustrating, Gellene said, since he was at the point in his career when he wanted to develop his own practice. What was necessary, he suggested, was the creation of opportunities to "engage in practice on the debtor side."

On another occasion, Gellene told the committee that there had been a decline in bankruptcy business, as restructuring work flowing from the high corporate debt of the 1980s was slowing down. Bankruptcy work, he said, was in danger of becoming a "commodity," implying fierce competition and declining profit margins. There were "too many lawyers for the available business." In another committee report, Gellene was quoted as lamenting that bankruptcy is "a fee-based practice with only episodic opportunities for premium billing."

He told the committee that "[t]here is less business and more competition," that "[i]t is a little hard to see what is in the pipeline," and that "[t]he business has shrunk so much that our people do not see the upside potential for them." As he was finishing a major bankruptcy case, he fretted that the challenge would be "to find adequate new work."

Gellene complained that the firm in general, and the bankruptcy group in particular, wasn't adequately responding to these challenges. "Both for the Firm as a whole and for the Bankruptcy Department," Gellene argued, "it appears that we can't get a critical mass of partners to make decisions, to implement them and to monitor performance in achieving great results." In addition, Gellene complained, "The crush of daily work makes it difficult to find the time for marketing," and the practice leaders, Jerome in particular, "do not spend enough time on staffing and business development."

The failure to establish a solid business plan for the bankruptcy group led Gellene to express concern about Milbank's relatively new merit-based compensation system. "There is a perception," he said, "that what drove the [compensation] process last year was the pursuance on the part of some partners of their own long-term agendas to build their own practices, and not the interests of the Firm. There is a perception that the best interests of the Firm is not the dominant motivating force." Partners had been led to believe, said Gellene, that a "higher principle would drive the process." In order for the committee's decisions to be credible, he maintained, it must demonstrate that the highest rewards will be given to those who cooperate with others in the firm.

Compensation decisions, said Gellene, "should not be based on unfavorable market developments or the loss of client opportunities but on whether the partner is responding appropriately to these developments." Gellene argued that a "compensation-based" approach to "under-performers" would be unsuccessful. Those who were not pulling their weight, he suggested, should be let go. Compensation sanctions permitted the firm to avoid making such hard choices, and produced ill will among lawyers. "We have a compensation system," he said, "that, in targeting 10–15 percent of the people, creates anxiety in 100 percent." In other words, with Milbank's greater emphasis on an "eat what you kill" system, Gellene had recurring concern about where his next meal was coming from.

WHATEVER ANXIETY Gellene felt about his status at Milbank likely was aggravated by an experience that underscored just how fragile his partnership could be. Only a few months after earning partnership on January 1, 1989, his achievement was in jeopardy. In late May of that year, Milbank was conducting a routine check of the credentials of all its lawyers. It confirmed that he was a member of the New Jersey bar. The firm discovered however, that, contrary to his representation, Gellene was not listed as a member by the New York state bar. This in turn meant that his putative membership in the federal bar in New York City was invalid. In other words, for almost nine years Gellene had practiced law in New York without a license. When confronted with this discrepancy, Gellene did not immediately confirm that Milbank's information was correct. Eventually, however, he admitted that he had never completed the steps necessary to become a member of the New York bar.

The puzzling sequence of events that led to this revelation began when Gellene graduated from law school. Before he began his clerkship with Justice Pashman on the New Jersey Supreme Court, he took both the New Jersey and New York state bar examinations in the summer of 1979. A few months later, he received word that he had passed the New Jersey bar exam and was then sworn in as a member. About the same time, he also learned that he had passed the New York bar exam. In order to become a member of that state's bar, however, Gellene also had to fill out a thirteen-page application, provide affidavits from all his legal employers, and arrange for an interview in Albany with a character and fitness committee of the bar. Only after the state bar association reviewed his documents and received a favorable report from the committee could Gellene be admitted to the bar. The entire process could take up to a year.

After passing the New York bar exam, Gellene simply had not completed this phase of the process. Apparently there was nothing in his background that made him wary about doing so. In all likelihood, his failure was due to a sense that he was too busy at the time with his clerkship duties to fill out the forms and make the trip to Albany—just as he later was too busy at Milbank to submit his billing records on time or help with summer associates. When Gellene joined Milbank, the highly competitive atmosphere of the firm must have reinforced his perception that his schedule didn't provide enough time to finish the process. As the *New York Law Journal* noted, "Faced with the pressure to pile up billable hours, some associates push aside the tedious task of completing the paperwork necessary to gain admission."[4] As a result, according to one partner at a major New York law firm, "There's a long tradition of putting [admission] off in New York."[5]

As time went on, of course, going back and completing the application process would have been, to say the least, awkward for Gellene. It would require him to admit that he had misrepresented his bar status, and could subject him to the charge of engaging in the unauthorized practice of law. Because he had passed the examination itself, someone in his position may well have rationalized his failure as relatively minor. After all, he might reason, the bar's main concern is to prevent people who aren't competent from passing themselves off as knowledgeable about the law. The other paperwork is just a technicality, a formality. Claiming to be a member of the bar under these circumstances, he might tell himself, really is just a "white lie," not a moral transgression.

However Gellene may have rationalized his conduct, Milbank removed him as a partner and granted him a severance payment. There were rumors that he was "exiled" to the firm's outpost in Rockefeller Center. In six months, Gellene had gone from the heights of making partner at a prestigious Wall Street law firm to the depths of being exposed as a fraud. If he were found liable for the misdemeanor of engaging in the unauthorized practice of law, he could face up to one year in jail and a one-thousand-dollar fine. Such prosecutions, however, are extremely rare. At the time that Gellene's case came to light, the division of the court system overseeing his status had permitted around forty attorneys in the recent past who had passed the bar but never finished the application process to take the steps necessary to gain admission.

Gellene was allowed to do the same, then set about to rectify his failure. He completed the forms and submitted them to the appropriate committee. Among the persons who spoke on his behalf at his hearing were John Jerome, Justice Pashman, Chief Judge Burton Lifland of the bankruptcy court of the Southern District of New York, and Gordon Harriss, a partner at the law firm of Davis Polk & Wardwell. Despite his earlier violation, the state accepted his application to be a member of the New York bar. He was sworn in in March 1990, some ten months after the discovery of his misrepresentation.

In May, Milbank designated Gellene as "of counsel" to the firm for the remainder of the year, while Milbank evaluated him and considered what if any further steps to take. Finally, he was reinstated as a partner at the beginning of 1991. The firm did penalize him, however, by putting him in the class with other lawyers who had been named partner at the same time, rather than returning him to his class of 1989. This meant that his compensation would lag behind others who had been named partner along with him two years earlier.

According to a Milbank compensation committee memo at the end of 1991, Gellene may not have been aware of the penalty that the firm imposed until he met with the committee to discuss his salary. The 1991 committee memo indicates that Gellene originally believed that he would be placed in his original partnership class for compensation purposes. When he learned his true status, it "angered him greatly." Gellene apparently was especially concerned that he would be receiving less compensation than fellow bankruptcy practitioner Steven Blauner, who had been named a partner around the same time as Gellene. Subsequent conversation with Gellene "calmed him down somewhat," and emphasized that the firm valued him as highly as it did Blauner. Nonetheless, Gellene may have felt himself under a cloud at the firm and having to prove himself once more.

Because he was a "service partner," not a rainmaker, John Gellene was largely dependent on other partners for work. While he might not be able to compete with other partners by bringing in business, he could do so by billing long hours and being available to others who needed help. He appears to have done this with alacrity. The compensation committee reports on Gellene note the comments of several partners that Gellene was willing to provide help to colleagues on financial restructuring and bankruptcy matters.

The arrival of Lederman at Milbank, however, could open the door to a world that no one else at the firm could offer. Lederman's extensive connections with corporations and investment banks offered the potential for greater access to corporate clients. This would help the firm accomplish its goal of broadening its work to include more debtors as clients. In addition, it could provide a steady stream of work for Gellene, thus easing his concerns about building an ongoing practice. That work would consist of both corporate bankruptcies and financial restructuring of companies outside of bankruptcy.

Bringing in Lederman, however, also could transform Milbank into an even more internally competitive and high-pressure firm. A Brooklyn native born in 1935, Lederman came from a self-described lower middle-class background. He graduated from Brooklyn College in 1957, but did not enter New York University law school until six years later, when he was married and had a child. Upon graduation from law school, Lederman accepted a clerkship with eminent California Supreme Court Justice Roger Traynor. After his clerkship he joined the law firm of Cravath, Swaine & Moore in late 1967.

Cravath, of course, in many ways was the epitome of the Wall Street firm at that time, and still is among the very elite. Only about 10 percent of any group of associates entering the firm ever made partner. The cachet of Cravath in the job market, however, made the experience worthwhile. Lederman came to the firm with the idea of eventually moving to a teaching position in a law school.

His plans eventually changed, however. When Lederman did not make partner at Cravath, he joined the nine-year-old firm of Wachtell,

Lipton, Rosen & Katz. In 1975, the firm had twenty-four lawyers, sixteen of whom were partners. The firm in many ways defined itself as the opposite of Cravath. It was relatively informal and nonbureaucratic, and hired lawyers with the expectation that they would eventually be made partners. The firm had flourished by doing the merger and acquisition work—including involvement in hostile corporate takeovers—that many old-line Wall Street firms had disdained. During the heated takeover activity of the 1980s, Wachtell became enormously profitable because of its expertise in this area.

While the firm represented both acquirers and targets, it became known especially for its work on behalf of takeover targets. In this role, it was often arrayed against Skadden, Arps, Meagher & Flom, the other upstart firm that made the leap to the top tier by specializing in takeover practice.[6] Name partner Martin Lipton and others at Wachtell devised several novel takeover defenses that management could use to fend off undesirable suitors. Wachtell's tendency to represent target companies paralleled Goldman Sachs' policy of not managing hostile takeover efforts. Both the law firm and the investment bank had profited from their decisions, and Wachtell and Lederman worked on a number of transactions with Goldman over the years.

Lederman's practice focused on matters that involved the purchase, sale, and refinancing of corporations. Some of these transactions were necessary because the company was facing financial distress with the prospect of bankruptcy on the horizon. Others resulted from corporate strategy or new financing techniques offered by investment banks. He had worked on LBOs that were launched as takeover defenses as well as those that were vehicles for a buyout group to purchase undervalued companies, streamline corporate operations, and profit from the resale of appreciated stock.

Wachtell's expertise in these matters generally allowed it to abandon hourly billing in favor of the kind of "premium" billing used by investment banks, based on the complexity and outcome of the matter. As Lederman was to remark in a 1992 book on his experiences, investment banking firms tended to be oriented to "doing transactions that brought in fee income and were sensitive to changes in the market."[7] He attributed this to the fact that most partners in such firms earned enough to retire in their early fifties, which meant that younger bankers receptive to change assumed positions of important responsibility.

By contrast, Lederman noted, partners in law firms remained longer. This meant that market developments were filtered through a tier of lawyers who often were older than their banking counterparts and more bound by tradition. In addition, law firms' reliance on hourly billing meant that no particular type of work was more profitable than any other. As a result, Lederman suggested, law firms rarely developed new specialities in response to the market, and lawyers didn't move from firm to firm in search of professional growth as much as did investment bankers.

Because it had come onto the scene much later than many law firms, Wachtell was less constrained by such habits. It was among the first to look to investment banks as organizational models for an increasingly competitive market in legal services. "[T]he opportunities were vast," said Lederman, for a law firm that was "oriented to resolve disputes in favor of doing the deal."[8] This philosophy put Wachtell and Lederman in the thick of many of the major corporate transactions of the day. It also resulted in some bruises, both in corporate America and within Wachtell itself.

A November 4, 1991, memo from the Milbank executive committee recommended that the firm hire Lederman, but also was remarkably candid about the difficulties that he might create. The committee indicated that Lederman was regarded as "one of a handful of the nation's most prominent lawyers in the mergers and acquisitions area." It noted that he consistently generated the second largest amount of business at Wachtell after name partner Martin Lipton.

Lederman's current focus was restructuring the financial obligations of companies that had incurred large debt loads in leveraged buyouts and other transactions in the 1980s. The memo noted his significant connections to Goldman Sachs, and the fact that he had attracted several other clients since leaving Wachtell earlier in the year. It listed eleven matters in which Lederman currently was involved, all of which he would bring with him to Milbank. These were projected to generate $4–5 million in fees in 1992. In addition, the executive committee had identified forty major clients to which Lederman would be introduced if he joined the firm. Discussion with a current Wachtell partner confirmed that Lederman could be expected to generate at least $5 million in new revenues per year, with the potential to be much higher.

At the same time, the executive committee acknowledged that "Larry Lederman arouses intense reactions from his admirers and detractors." Lederman had left Wachtell, Lipton earlier in 1991 because of controversy over his plans to publish a memoir of his corporate practice. The book was entitled *Tombstones: A Lawyer's Tales from the Takeover Decades.* Many Wachtell lawyers felt that Lederman had disclosed confidential information in the book and that it was unduly self-promotional. The memo also described the reactions of nine important lawyers and investment bankers who had worked with Lederman. In addition, the executive committee stated that "there were certain other key conversations which were critical of Larry Lederman and which we felt should not be memorialized in a document circulated as widely as this memorandum." Summaries of these conversations were available in folders in the offices of certain Milbank partners.

The nine individuals whose assessments were described in the memo conceded that Lederman could be difficult to work with. On balance, however, they felt that his creativity and visibility made hiring him a good decision for Milbank. Martin Lipton characterized him as an important presence in merger and acquisition practice, a person of integrity and a skilled lawyer who was very good at generating business. Lipton opined that some of the criticism from Lederman's adversaries was unfair, and was typical of that levied against lawyers in the contentious field of corporate takeovers.

Lipton confirmed that Lederman's decision to publish his book generated considerable criticism from Wachtell partners, although it was Lederman, not the firm, who decided that he should go elsewhere. The memo also cited Lederman's "long-standing personality conflicts" with Lipton as a reason for his departure. Lipton described Lederman as a "very independent person who did not function at Wachtell as a collegial team player." Nonetheless, he generally was allowed "free rein" at the firm.

Wachtell partner Bernard Nussbaum offered a similar assessment. He stated that Lederman had a loyal base of clients that was capable of producing significant business, and that he had trained a large number of the younger Wachtell partners and associates, who regarded him highly. Nussbaum, said the memo, admitted that "Lederman has a difficult personality and made life difficult for some Wachtell partners." He organized his own team of lawyers and "consistently operated outside the sphere of other Wachtell partners and associates." Nonetheless, Nussbaum expressed his belief that Lederman would be a valuable acquisition for Milbank.

Lewis Black, an alumnus of Milbank then practicing corporate law in Delaware, also offered both praise for Lederman and candor about his personality. Black had worked with Lederman on several transactions and found him very imaginative and aggressive in his problem-solving. The memo noted that Black had told Lederman that Milbank "houses a number of very able lawyers who are in addition very nice people who will likely find Larry hard to get along with." Because "Larry can be abrasive and invariably tries to control any situation in which he is involved," Lederman's arrival at Milbank would represent a "clash of cultures." Despite this likely conflict, Black said that it was worth the risk to bring Lederman to Milbank because of his access to areas of practice in which the firm had not been involved.

A memo to the partnership from Milbank partner Al Lilley, attached as an appendix to the committee's memo, set forth his views, based on having worked with Lederman and spoken to others about him. Lilley stated that he strongly favored bringing Lederman to the firm, but that Milbank must appreciate the risks of doing so in order for this step to be successful. The Milbank partner noted that Lederman had especially extensive contacts at Goldman Sachs, which would give the firm an important entree into the investment banking world. In particular, it would give Milbank visibility and prominence in corporate practice by offering the opportunity for its lawyers to participate in the financial restructuring of major corporations.

Lilley noted that Lederman contacts Fred Eckert and Mikael Salovaara would be leaving Goldman to start their own investment fund, but that Goldman had indicated that it would continue regularly to use Lederman. In addition, said Lilly, Eckert and Salovaara "assure us that Lederman and Milbank will be their counsel." Thus, Lederman offered the chance for Milbank to move into "regular representation of investment bankers and their corporate clients (as opposed to creditors) in corporate restructurings." Lilley said that John Jerome and John Gellene of the Milbank bankruptcy practice currently were working with Lederman on a matter that involved a leveraged buyout in which Goldman had been involved (not Bucyrus).

Lilley observed that one of the risks of Lederman's coming to Milbank would be potentially disqualifying conflicts of interest because of Lederman's large roster of clients. While Lilley didn't mention it specifically, Lederman's connections with investment banks would be especially likely to generate such conflicts. Such banks are ubiquitous in corporate transactions, and they themselves must struggle with potential conflicts. Working through the conflicts of interest created by Lederman's presence would take patience and flexibility, said Lilley. This process would be more difficult because "Lederman does not possess great 'statesmanlike' qualities. He has a reputation for being difficult and pressing hard for his position." Lilley also cautioned that some at Milbank might resent Lederman's compensation and stature within the firm, which in turn might undermine the cooperation necessary to make his arrival productive. Ultimately, concluded Lilley, he would not take the risk of having Lederman come to Milbank "without the manifest support and good will" of the partners at the firm.

The executive committee memo admitted that Lederman's joining Milbank "will put added pressure on the cohesiveness of the Milbank partnership." The firm, it said, must be prepared "to accept a number of dislocations" in order to achieve its goal of strengthening its corporate practice and becoming a visible participant in leading corporate transactions. "[T]the costs of this initiative are far outweighed by its likely benefits," the memo stated, benefits that offered a "rare opportunity for the Firm to make significant progress toward remedying its single most critical strategic weakness."

Lederman's compensation for his first full year would be $1.25 million, which reflected an estimate of the portion of the firm's income to which he would be entitled. This would make him the highest paid partner at Milbank. He would join the Corporate and Banking Department's Mergers and Acquisitions and General Corporate Group, serving with Al Lilley as its coleader. In addition, Lederman would be given the honorary title of chairman of the corporate practice. The position would carry with it no significant administrative responsibilities.

The executive committee would authorize Lederman to coordinate with other practice groups the steps necessary to achieve the firm's corporate practice goals, including "identifying and resolving conflict situations." John Jerome would consult with Lederman on conflicts relating to financial restructuring (known as workouts) and bankruptcy matters. The executive committee would "establish a direct, continuing relationship to Lederman" to provide support for his initiatives. A "small, dedicated team of lawyers" would be assigned to work with Lederman, and associates would be rotated to this team in order to broaden the group of lawyers who would receive training from him.

John Jerome planned for Gellene to be a member of Lederman's inner circle. He told the compensation committee in 1991 that he intended "to team Gellene up with Lederman. He will be terrific with the debt/debtor restructuring work." Lederman's comments on Gellene in succeeding years attest to the accuracy of this prediction: "Did a marvelous job on National Gypsum . . . Goldman is crazy about him"; "he is an absolutely brilliant strategist"; "he is wonderful; he has done a great job for us." In turn, Gellene was highly complimentary of Lederman: "His ability to provide guidance and to allow partners in his group to run with significant transactions was terribly impressive." Lederman was "supportive personally and professionally in every way."

By the time that Gellene began to represent Bucyrus, Lederman thus may have begun to replace Jerome as Gellene's main mentor at the firm. As early as Gellene's return to the firm in 1990, one partner suggested that Gellene had grown in his practice because "he is no longer Jerome's boy." In his comments to the compensation committee at the end of 1994, Jerome himself remarked that Gellene was "exiting my orbit, which is very good." Jerome had been the kind of mentor who enabled Gellene to succeed under the old tournament rules; Lederman would be the one who gave Gellene an edge in the new tournament. The Bucyrus bankruptcy was a chance for Gellene to cash in on this opportunity.

CHAPTER THREE

Rust Belt Meets
Wall Street

IN HIS OPENING ADDRESS to the jurors in John Gellene's trial, Gellene's lawyer, Mark Rotert, described his client's first meeting with Bucyrus officials. Gellene didn't know it at the time, said Rotert, but he "was dropped into a war zone. He was dropped into the lawyer's equivalent of the no-man's land between two trenches of warring armies."

It is probably more accurate to say that Gellene arrived in Milwaukee just before the shooting started—and that he himself became an officer in the war. Nonetheless, the seeds of the conflict that permeated the Bucyrus bankruptcy had been sowed five years before Gellene ever became involved with the company. Understanding what happened during that period is crucial in constructing a plausible account of why Gellene acted as he did. These events shaped the pressures that Gellene confronted, the alternatives he believed were available, and the interests that he saw himself as serving. They provide clues to how Gellene viewed the circumstances in which he had to operate and the decisions that he had to make.

The story of the five years from 1988 to 1993 before Gellene agreed to represent Bucyrus reflects the influence of forces both particular to that company and more general to the world of elite law firms and investment banks. They involve a rust belt manufacturing company trying to stave off disaster with the aid of Wall Street lawyers and

bankers; a series of complex financial transactions that would ultimately leave creditors in control of the company; a prominent investment bank's shift from being simply an agent of clients to a direct
investor in capital markets; and the rise of "vulture" investors, who
purchase the debt of financially distressed companies with an eye to
controlling their eventual reorganization.

Those five years also marked the emergence on stage of two men
who would figure significantly in John Gellene's fate: superstar corporate lawyer Larry Lederman and shrewd investment banker Mikael
Salovaara. These men, close personal friends, had worked together for
more than a decade to fashion innovative transactions that had helped
change the face of corporate America. The deals they had arranged for
Bucyrus would become the target of bitter dispute during the bankruptcy, with allegations of fraud and conspiracy filling the air. By the
time that John Gellene walked into his first meeting with Bucyrus in
February 1993, these individuals, organizations, and events had
shaped the terrain he would have to navigate for the next twenty-two
months. For a full understanding of what happened with John Gellene, we therefore must begin our story a few years before he came on
the scene.

IN LATE 1985, Becor Western Corporation in Milwaukee faced a
serious financial crisis. Its shareholders and creditors were clamoring
for a change. The company had been in business for more than a century, manufacturing large mining and construction equipment used
around the world. Company officials were especially proud of the fact
that several of its large shovels had been used to dig the Panama
Canal. The industry in which the company operated was relatively
small, and Becor had been a consistent leader within it. Both domestic
and foreign markets were fiercely competitive, however, with low
prices and profit margins. Furthermore, since some products could
take years to manufacture, cash flow was always a challenge.

During most of the 1970s, Becor had earned healthy profits. By the
late 1970s, however, business had slowed considerably. The growth in
coal mining had fallen well short of industry expectations, and the

Financial Advisor

First Boston

Legal Counsel

Milbank Tweed

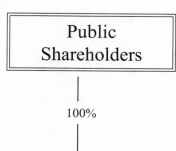

Public Shareholders

|

100%

|

Becor Western Inc.

[Formerly Bucyrus-Erie Company]

$30 Million Notes at 9% due 1999

Total Public Debt: $30 Million

Fig. 1. Before leveraged buyout, December 31, 1987. (Government Exhibit 65, *United States v. Gellene.*)

demand for construction machinery dropped because of a lengthy recession in the construction industry. Beginning in 1981, Becor began winding down its manufacture of construction machinery. The company also undertook a series of plant closings and consolidations to streamline its mining machinery business. Finally, Becor retained First Boston Corporation in October 1985 to advise it on how best to respond to the challenges it faced.

About a year later, Norris Ekstrom, the company's chairman of the board and chief executive officer, reported to the board that management believed that Bucyrus should entertain offers for the sale of the company. This might take the form of a purchase by a competitor. It also could occur through a leveraged buyout (LBO). In an LBO, a small group of investors working with an investment bank would buy up the public shares of the company and convert it to a privately held firm.

One group that was interested in an LBO included about thirty company officials and employees, along with Goldman Sachs and its Broad Street Investment Fund. The core of the management group was William Winter, president and chief operating officer of the company; Ray Olander, a vice president, general counsel, and secretary of Becor Western; Phillip Mork, president of the mining machinery division of Becor Western; and Norbert Verville, recently returned from serving as chief executive of Becor's English subsidiary. These officials would replace Ekstrom and other high-level managers as a result of the buyout. Should the board turn to an LBO, it would mark the union of two quite different sectors of the American economy: an old-line Midwest manufacturing company and Wall Street investment bankers who were devising new transactions to fund changes in the control of major corporations.

The Becor board appointed a special committee of board members to review competing offers for purchase of the company, assisted by First Boston. In February 1987, following the recommendation of the committee, the board voted to accept the offer from the management-Goldman buyout group. When shareholders filed suit alleging that the group had arranged to buy the company for less than full value, the board delayed a decision while considering other offers. Finally, in July 1987 the board recommended to the Becor shareholders that they accept the bid from the management group for a leveraged buyout of the company at a price around $350 million. The transaction was completed on February 4, 1988.

Under the LBO a holding company, B-E Holdings, Inc., was formed to purchase all the stock of the operating company, Becor Western. Thirty current company managers owned one more share of the holding company than did Goldman's Broad Street Investment Fund I. The operating company would be known as Bucyrus-Erie Company. By virtue of its ownership of the holding company that owned Bucyrus-Erie, the buyout group now effectively owned the operating company. The two companies had the same boards of directors. Bucyrus-Erie would continue the manufacture, sales, and service of

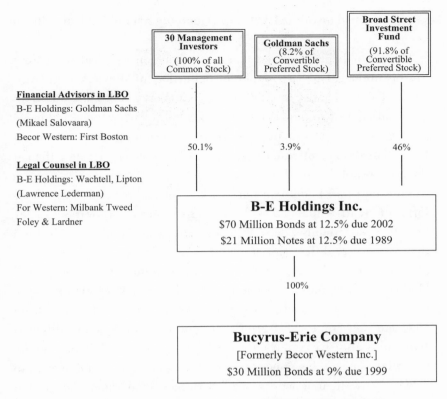

Financial Advisors in LBO

B-E Holdings: Goldman Sachs

(Mikael Salovaara)

Becor Western: First Boston

Legal Counsel in LBO

B-E Holdings: Wachtell, Lipton

(Lawrence Lederman)

For Western: Milbank Tweed

Foley & Lardner

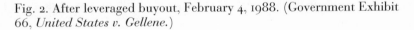

Fig. 2. After leveraged buyout, February 4, 1988. (Government Exhibit 66, *United States v. Gellene.*)

mining machinery. Its profitability would largely determine the value of the holding company that was its sole shareholder.

The managers obtained their stock in B-E Holdings in exchange for contributing cash and operating company shares worth about $1 million. Broad Street contributed $1 million in cash for its shares. Most of the remainder of the purchase price was financed by cash from the operating company and $91 million in B-E Holdings debt. The debt instruments paid 12.5 percent interest semiannually. The holding company would have to repay the full principal on $21 million of them one year from the date of the LBO. The remaining $71 million came due in 2002.

The Becor board received financial advice on the deal from First Boston, and legal advice from Foley & Lardner of Milwaukee and Milbank, Tweed, Hadley & McCloy of New York. Goldman was both financial advisor to, and a member of, the buyout group. Goldman's point man on the transaction was Mikael Salovaara of the Broad Street Fund. The legal counsel to the group was Lawrence Lederman, then at the law firm of Wachtell, Lipton.

Salovaara and Lederman had worked for several years on various forms of creative financial restructurings for large corporations. They had become friends, despite what observers familiar with both describe as very different styles. Salovaara was intense and near-compulsive; as one who dealt with him said, he "knows only one speed." He also had a reputation as a soft-spoken but lethal negotiator, whose approach was, effectively, "We'll burn your village and pour salt on your land so crops can't grow." By contrast, Lederman, although sometimes abrasive, often tended to seek consensus. His philosophy toward those on the opposite side of the bargaining table was to "always leave them a peppercorn." Both men would later play central roles in the tumultuous series of events that began with John Gellene's representation of Bucyrus—and ended with Gellene's confinement in federal prison.

IN THE LATE 1980s, Mikael Salovaara was a newly minted partner in his mid-thirties at Goldman Sachs. The publication *Institutional Investors* had included him on a list of "the next generation's financial leaders."[1] His path to Wall Street was a bit more circuitous than many. The son of a town manager, he graduated from Dartmouth in 1974 with degrees in English and mathematics. He then acquired a master's degree in literature from Cambridge in 1976. Returning to the United States, he entered business and law school at the University of Virginia, graduating in 1980.

Even as a student, Salovaara displayed what the *New York Times* would later describe as a "willingness to play hardball to get what he wanted."[2] During law school, he accused a fellow student of violating the honor code by removing a moot court problem from the Washington office of a student association. A student-run disciplinary committee found the student guilty and expelled him. Salovaara persisted in his accusation through three honor committee trials, two convictions, two appeals, and two further appeals. Only after these proceedings had run their course over a three-year period did Salovaara drop his complaint.

In late 1980, Salovaara joined Goldman Sachs, working primarily on stock and bond underwriting in the corporate finance department. In 1984, he joined a new group at Goldman devoted to the burgeoning LBO market. The group was headed by Alfred C. Eckert III, with whom Salovaara would later become partner in an independent investment fund. The LBO group served as advisors to company managers who sought to take companies private by using debt to acquire underpriced company stock. In 1986, Goldman formed the Broad Street Fund to invest in such buyouts. The most significant feature of this $250 million fund was that Goldman for the first time invested its own capital in the venture, to the tune of $25 million.

The fiercely competitive world of investment banking was a natural milieu for someone like Salovaara, of whom it has been said, "[P]robably no one's elbows are sharper—and no one's tactics so feared and admired."[3] As it turned out, the LBO would be only the beginning of his dealings with Bucyrus. The leverage he would eventually acquire over the company became a flash point for bitter hostility during the Bucyrus bankruptcy. That hostility would make the reorganization a minefield, with John Gellene the most prominent casualty.

THE BUCYRUS LBO was typical of buyouts in the 1980s. The holding company notes were regarded as "junk bonds"—below investment-grade obligations with a high rate of interest to compensate investors for above-average risk. The holding company itself would not generate enough revenues from its operations to cover payments on the bonds. The funds to repay the debt would have to come mostly from dividend payments from Bucyrus-Erie to B-E Holdings. Creditors were betting that managers with a large ownership stake in the operating company would be able to make it more efficient, so that it could afford to pay enough dividends to cover the holding company debt.

The continuous need to make dividend payments, however, could drain the operating company of the funds that it needed for working capital or long-term investment. This could eventually threaten its ability to pay dividends. Furthermore, Bucyrus-Erie had its own debt to repay: $30 million debentures at 9 percent interest, due in full in 1999. If the holding company didn't receive enough dividends from Bucyrus-Erie to cover holding company bond payments, it might have to sell off assets of the operating company.

At the same time, there was cause for optimism. Company officials regarded Bucyrus-Erie's prospects after the LBO as promising because of the company's reputation for producing high-quality equipment for use around the world. The machines that it manufactured lasted for twenty years or more, which meant a predictable market for machine parts for a relatively long period of time. The outlook for the industry as a whole at the time of the buyout generally was seen as good. If business picked up, creditors would receive a handsome return on their investment and members of the buyout group would enjoy substantial appreciation in the value of their shares.

Everyone was aware, however, that the landscape was littered with the wrecks of companies that simply couldn't stay alive with the onerous debt burdens created by an LBO. Indeed, by mid-1987—that is, before the Bucyrus LBO—Salovaara apparently began to anticipate that the market for LBOs was beginning to dry up. The run-up in stock prices had reduced the number of companies that were bargains, and the SEC insider trading investigation of Drexel and others cast a pall on highly leveraged transactions. One observer quotes Salovaara's pessimism in the face of these developments: "I said to myself, 'This market is going to fall apart. These LBOs are going to have to be restructured.'" In other words, many companies would not be able to cover the debt from their LBOs and would have to renegotiate terms with creditors. In preparation for this possibility, the Goldman LBO department expanded to include workouts and junk bond underwriting, activities geared to rearranging companies' capital structures.

In light of all this, how confident was Salovaara that an LBO would help revive Bucyrus's fortunes? When the holding and operating companies filed for bankruptcy five years later, there would be claims that Salovaara was not confident at all. He would be accused of inducing Bucyrus to undergo the LBO because he knew that Goldman would profit from the company's ongoing need to restructure its finances. Furthermore, the buyout group would be charged with fatally weakening Bucyrus-Erie by relying mostly on that company's cash to fund the LBO. This allegedly was part of a conspiracy between managers and Goldman to take over the operating company at virtually no cost to themselves, in order to milk it of its revenues. John Gellene eventually would have to decide whether these claims had merit, and therefore whether the company should sue the buyout group. His response would fuel the fires of a contentious bankruptcy and leave his concealment of Milbank's ties to Salovoara open to sinister interpretation.

THE MARKET FOR Bucyrus-Erie's products did indeed strengthen after the LBO. The company's capital needs grew even more rapidly, however, because mining machines are very expensive to make. In addition, much of Bucyrus's income was being used to service the debt from the LBO. The result was that Bucyrus was a company with the potential for increasing its market share and earning large profits, but it lacked the cash flow necessary to realize that potential. The company tried to improve its financial condition by engaging in three transactions over the next four years. These were an exchange offer, a private sale of notes, and a secured financing. Like the LBO, these transactions would be subject to withering attack by the largest creditor in the bankruptcy.

Management's most immediate concern after the LBO was the $21 million in holding company 12.5 percent notes that were due to be repaid in full on February 4, 1989. The treatment of these notes later would be cited as an example of how Goldman Sachs allegedly continued to prey on Bucyrus-Erie's financial vulnerability. After the LBO,

Goldman had bought some of the notes. Persons on the Goldman trading desk approached Salovaara about Goldman's also purchasing in the secondary market some of the $30 million 9 percent operating company debentures due in 1999. Goldman traders were considering buying the debentures, and then convincing the operating company to offer newly issued debt to replace them. The new debt would carry a higher rate of interest, but would be repaid later in the future.

Since this exchange would enhance the value of the existing 9 percent debentures, Goldman could then resell them at a profit when the exchange offer was announced. Salovaara told the traders that Bucyrus-Erie had good prospects. He later learned that Goldman had already bought the debentures. Indeed, Goldman eventually purchased over 90 percent of the operating company debentures, as well as a third of the holding company notes issued in connection with the LBO.

Salovaara eventually suggested to Bucyrus that it engage in an exchange offer. On January 28, 1989, both the holding and operating companies did so. The operating company issued $75 million in notes due in 1996. The interest rate on these notes was set initially at 10 percent, but would rise to a lucrative 16 percent in 1993. Three groups of existing bondholders could trade in their existing debt for these notes: holders of the $21 million holding company notes due in 1989, the $70 million holding company debentures due in 2002, and the $30 million operating company debentures due in 1999. Most of them did so. Goldman's operating company debentures became more valuable with the announcement of the exchange offer. Their resale netted $10 million in profits for the investment house. The exchange offer also included a $15.5 million dividend payment from Bucyrus-Erie to B-E Holdings.

The exchange offer was especially attractive to investors because it shifted much of the debt repayment obligation from the holding company to the operating company. B-E Holdings reduced its outstanding debt from $70 million to $41 million, while Bucyrus-Erie increased its debt from $30 million to $76 million. The operating company was where the hard assets of the enterprise were located, such as machine

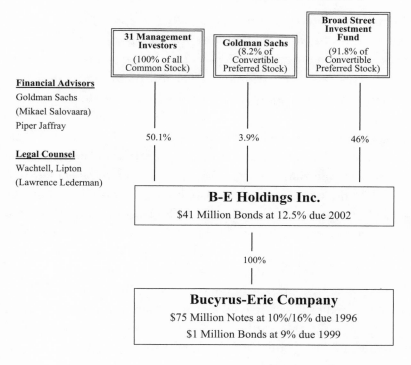

Fig. 3. After exchange offer, January 28, 1989. (Government Exhibit 67, *United States v. Gellene.*)

tools, real estate, inventory, and accounts receivable. If the operating company defaulted on its bonds, creditors could place a lien on these assets. By contrast, the assets of the holding company consisted primarily of stock in the operating company. In the case of default on B-E Holdings bonds, a creditor could seize that stock and become a shareholder of the Bucyrus-Erie. That, however, would only put it in line behind operating company creditors.

From the companies' perspectives, the exchange offer provided an infusion of additional capital and allowed the holding company to avoid having to pay off the $21 million notes due in February 1989. Resetting the interest rate on the new operating company notes to 16 percent in 1993, however, would eventually result in very high interest charges. The ultimate question was whether postponing the company's bond repayment obligations to the more distant future would give Bucyrus enough breathing room to revive the business—or whether it would simply mortgage the future for the sake of the present.

Jackson National Life would later challenge the validity of the exchange offer during the Bucyrus bankruptcy. It would claim that the operating company had been weakened by its assumption of increased debt, while the buyout group and Goldman Sachs profited from the deal. JNL was especially disturbed by Goldman's trading profits on a deal that it had recommended. Whether John Gellene should accede to JNL's demand that Bucyrus sue Goldman for alleged misconduct would be a point of bitter dispute during the bankruptcy.

As 1990 went by, Bucyrus continued to face cash flow problems. The company hoped to raise $80 million. Once again it turned to Goldman and Salovaara for help. Although no one knew it at the time, their solution would bring onto the scene a creditor that would be a fierce antagonist in the bankruptcy proceeding. Salovaara approached Jackson National Life Insurance Company, a Michigan firm owned by Prudential Insurance Company of Great Britain. JNL already had bought $8 million of the new operating company notes issued in connection with the exchange offer. It also had bought from Goldman several issues of junk bonds that had been used to fund leveraged buyouts of other companies.

JNL agreed to purchase $60 million in Bucyrus-Erie notes due in 1996. The operating company was obligated to pay 12.5 percent interest on them, but that rate could increase on January 1, 1993, to as high as 15 percent. The sale went through on June 26, 1990. As with many debt instruments, the agreement with JNL had a covenant restricting the amount that Bucyrus-Erie could borrow after this transaction. The operating company could incur no more than $20 million in additional debt, a provision meant to ensure the company's ability to meet its obligation to JNL on the notes. The deal made JNL the largest creditor of Bucyrus-Erie.

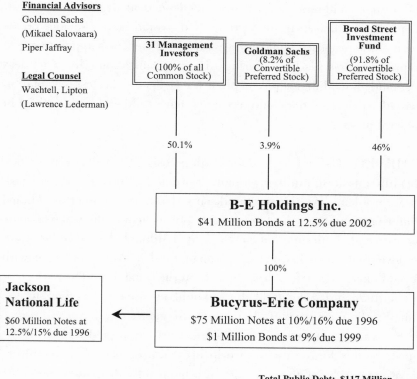

Financial Advisors
Goldman Sachs
(Mikael Salovaara)
Piper Jaffray

Legal Counsel
Wachtell, Lipton
(Lawrence Lederman)

Fig. 4. After sale of notes to JNL, June 26, 1990. (Government Exhibit 68, *United States v. Gellene.*)

The holding company and operating company together now owed a total of $177 million to unsecured creditors. They were obligated to pay semiannual interest on these instruments at rates ranging from 9 percent to eventually as high as 16 percent.

The sale of notes to JNL also would be the subject of accusations during the bankruptcy. JNL claimed that Salovaara sold it the notes knowing that Bucyrus was in trouble and would be unable to meet its obligation. JNL's hostility was further inflamed because it also eventually had to sell at a loss the notes it had bought during the exchange offer that Goldman had recommended—a deal in which Goldman made $10 million in trading profits. JNL would be a tenacious opponent of the proposed bankruptcy plan and of Gellene's appointment to represent Bucyrus-Erie during the reorganization. Its relentless demand that Milbank pay a price for Gellene's disclosure violation would set in motion a chain of events that would end with Gellene in federal prison.

THE LONG-TERM economic prognosis for Bucyrus remained healthy into 1991, but the company continued to have short-term cash flow problems. As the parties discussed different scenarios, Mikael Salovaara and Larry Lederman each left his firm in the wake of some controversy. Lederman, of course, joined Milbank Tweed in late 1991. Salovaara formed his own investment fund in November 1991 with Fred Eckert, who left Goldman Sachs at the same time. The paths that Lederman and Salovaara chose would eventually intersect in the Bucyrus bankruptcy with dramatic consequences.

Salovaara's departure from Goldman was prompted by the investment bank's foray into the world of "vulture" investing. A vulture investor purchases the securities of a financially distressed company. The vulture is betting that the value of the company's assets is higher than the price of these securities would suggest. If the corporation improves its financial condition by restructuring its debt or undergoing a reorganization, the value of its stock and debt increases. The investor then sells its holdings at a handsome profit. Vulture investors often purchase enough interest in a company to take an active role in shaping the terms of its reorganization, doing battle if necessary with both management and other creditors. Indeed, one observer has declared that "the mere presence of flocks of vultures in the market has fundamentally changed the dynamics of bankruptcy from a situation in which management has an overwhelming advantage to one in which these new creditors have great sway."

While such investors have operated at least since the stock market crash of 1929, they began to multiply rapidly in the 1980s. In particular, the collapse of the junk bond market by 1989 created a crisis for many companies that had undergone LBOs earlier in the decade. In 1989, corporations defaulted on $8 billion in debt, four times the amount just two years earlier. By 1990 and 1991, the figure was $18 billion. Investors with experience in LBO funds, such as Salovaara, as well as in junk bonds and financial restructuring, were drawn to the bargains they felt were available from the expanding ranks of distressed companies.

As the pejorative nickname suggests, vultures have provoked criticism. One complaint is that they're too impatient and are interested only in a quick return on their investment, rather than in ensuring that a company is reorganized in a manner that will promote its long-term viability. A vulture may, for instance, resist converting all its debt to equity in order to enhance its priority in any possible future bankruptcy, even though the company attempting to reorganize realistically can't afford the debt load. Or it may promote a reorganization plan that fails to address underlying operational problems but results in a profitable immediate payout to the vulture. The vulture may have enough of an interest in the company to threaten its managers with ouster if they resist its wishes. The result may be that a company emerges from Chapter 11 only to reenter a brief time later.

In addition, vulture investors can elicit fierce resentment from original creditors who paid full price for a company's bonds. Because the vulture bought the debt at a discount, it may be willing to accept a settlement in which the company pays far less than the face value of its outstanding debt securities. The result can be a profit for vulture investors but a substantial loss for other creditors. All this can increase the potential for disharmony in bankruptcy, as the Bucyrus reorganization would graphically illustrate.

For their part, vultures claim that they sustain an active secondary market for a corporation's securities, and free up creditors to make investments in other companies. Indeed, this secondary market may be so robust that by the time bankruptcy occurs all the original creditors have sold their debt to others. This underscores a transformation in corporate bankruptcy to which vulture investors have contributed. The reorganization process no longer reflects the influence of long-term relationships between a corporation and its creditors. As prominent bankruptcy lawyer Harvey Miller put it, in that world gone by a company could say to its banks and bondholders, "You've made a lot of money with me, now help me reorganize." Nowadays, however, a company in Chapter II may confront creditors who are relative strangers, with whom it has no shared history to appeal in trying to gain acceptance of a plan that will ensure a stable future.

In any event, market conditions in 1989—a year after the Bucyrus LBO—convinced Salovaara that Goldman could profit by starting a vulture investment fund. The firm agreed, and committed $100 million of its own money to start the Water Street Corporate Recovery Fund. Goldman began soliciting outside investors in April 1990, with the goal of raising $400 million. By the time the fund accepted its last contribution a few months later, Goldman had raised $683 million. The offering memo explicitly stated that Water Street planned to invest its capital "on a basis that may enable it to influence, directly or indirectly, the recapitalization" of the companies in which it invested. It also declared that the fund's objective was an annual return of 25–35 percent. The plan was to give Water Street four years to see if it could meet its goals.

By early May 1991, the fund had generated returns of over 30 percent. It also, however, had provoked considerable hostility. One concern was that while Salovaara helped run Water Street, he also continued to work in corporate finance at Goldman, advising companies on their capital structure and how to ease their debt burden. Nine of the twenty-one investments that the fund made were in current or former Goldman clients. The fear was that Salovaara's dual roles would allow him to obtain inside information that Water Street could then use to its benefit in making investment decisions. Investment banks had originated so-called Chinese Walls, or firewalls, to prevent information from being passed between their corporate finance and trading operations. Salovaara's activities seemed to ignore the need for this separation. As one observer notes, rival traders joked that Salovaara had "a Chinese Wall in the middle of his brain."

A second source of hostility was that Water Street's profits sometimes came at the expense of Goldman clients. As would any vulture investor, the fund sought advantage in bankruptcies by pushing for reductions in payments to other debtors or by seeking stock in return for the debt that it held. The former tactic of course alienated other creditors, while the latter angered existing shareholders because it reduced the value of their equity. Unfortunately for Water Street, the victims of these tactics often were the large money management funds that regularly bought stocks and bonds from Goldman. Eventually, investors threatened to boycott the Goldman trading desk if the bank continued to operate the fund. This would be devastating to the firm. The profitability of the fund was not worth Goldman's risking being shut out of trading activities. As a result, Goldman began closing down the fund and selling off the investments in it in early May 1991.

After helping to wind down the affairs of Water Street, Salovaara left Goldman at the end of November 1991 to form Greycliff Partners with former Goldman partner Alfred C. Eckert III. Greycliff, owned fifty-fifty by Salovaara and Eckert, would be responsible for the management of South Street Fund. South Street in turn would operate several funds that would engage in the vulture investment activity that had sparked such controversy when conducted by Goldman. The two men sought to raise $150–$200 million for this purpose. Salovaara invested $2.5 million and Eckert $5 million in the enterprise. Salovaara would be in charge of the day-to-day administration of the fund, while Eckert focused on broad oversight. They agreed to split their profits fifty-fifty. Salovaara told Bucyrus-Erie officials that he sought an annual 25 percent return for investors in South Street. It's unlikely that John Gellene even knew at the time that two former Goldman partners had founded an investment fund called South Street. A little more than a year later, however, he would become well aware of this fact.

MEANWHILE, IN MILWAUKEE the discussion of how Bucyrus could address its growing cash flow problem extended into early 1992. The company continued to include both Salovaara and Lederman in these discussions after they moved on to South Street and Milbank, respectively. Bucyrus CEO Bill Winter had had regular Saturday morning discussions with Salovaara about the company in the years since the LBO. Winter had spent his entire working life at Bucyrus, and came to trust and rely on Salovaara to provide Wall Street's perspective on the company's operations.

Salovaara had urged Winter to continue to use Lederman as a legal advisor after he left Wachtell and before he affiliated with Milbank. David Goelzer's notes indicate that Salovaara had been "pushing hard" for this outcome in his conversations with Winter. As a result, Lederman sat in on several discussions about the company's future during middle and late 1991 when he was practicing on his own. Lederman's move to Milbank prompted Bucyrus to switch its legal work from Wachtell, Lipton to Milbank. As it turned out, Salovaara and Lederman would play key roles in arranging the financial transaction that generated the most acrimony during Bucyrus's eventual bankruptcy proceedings.

Richard Hayden had taken Salovaara's place as the Goldman contact with Bucyrus. In late 1991 and early 1992, he told the company that it needed to take some decisive step to address its financial condition. He said that the future of Bucyrus was "not sustainable" under current circumstances, and advised company officials that the company needed a "complete recapitalization." Hayden said that lawyers from Sullivan and Cromwell, a firm used regularly by Goldman, were working on such a plan. The sale of Bucyrus to a third party was another possibility that Goldman discussed with management.

Company officials disagreed with Goldman's dire assessment, and sought the opinions of Salovaara, Lederman, and others on the wisdom of such advice. Should company officials be aggressive in attempting to avoid a sale to outsiders? Or should they be neutral in considering the sale as simply one of several different options? In pursuing a refinancing, should the company make an advance public announcement of its intentions? Or should it approach creditors privately? Questions such as these dominated the discussions among Bucyrus and its advisors as winter turned to spring.

In March, Bucyrus received unwelcome news from its outside auditor, Deloitte & Touche. Deloitte had audited the company's books for decades. Bucyrus was preparing to file its annual Form 10K report with the Securities and Exchange Commission. A day or two before the report was due, Deloitte informed company officials that it would be stating in its portion of the report that it could not express an opinion whether the company would still be in existence a year later. The auditors' decision to include this "going concern" paragraph caught Bucyrus officials by surprise and caused great consternation.

Bucyrus sought and received a fifteen-day extension for its 10K filing. It tried to convince Deloitte to reconsider, but the auditor was unyielding. The 10K was filed on April 15 with Deloitte's statement that it could express no opinion about the viability of the company as a going concern. After the 10K, it became far more difficult for Bucyrus to negotiate with Bank One, its main source of credit. By May and June, "[T]he credit card had been closed," as one company official put it.

As the year progressed, Bucyrus management continued to consult about the company's future with Salovaara, Lederman, and Goldman Sachs. Bucyrus, at Lederman's suggestion, inquired whether Salovaara might be able to fund a refinancing through his new investment fund. Salovaara told Winter that trying to sell the company would be a "waste of time" because it couldn't be sold for more than the outstanding debt. He said that he had $150 million lined up for his new South Street Fund, and that he expected to have the fund operating by early June. In late June, however, Salovaara told Bucyrus that the most that South Street could provide to any one borrower was $35 million. In order to avail itself of this financing, Bucyrus would have to structure any transaction to avoid violating the debt limits it had agreed to when it sold the $60 million in notes to JNL.

The parties began discussing the possibility that Bucyrus would sell its manufacturing assets to South Street, which the company then would lease back from the investment fund. Lederman was the lead attorney for Bucyrus in these discussions, with Salovaara negotiating on behalf of South Street. Under a sale and leaseback arrangement, Bucyrus would receive a much-needed infusion of capital, while South

Street would receive a return on that capital in the form of the lease payments. The payments would not violate any covenants, primarily because they would not constitute debt obligations.

One of the considerations that the company took into account when deciding whether to proceed with the South Street financing was the extent to which Salovaara's and Bucyrus's interests might diverge in the future. In late June, the investor had told company officials that he no longer desired to receive nonpublic information about Bucyrus after the South Street financing. The reason, according to contemporaneous Bucyrus notes, was that "S[outh] S[treet] does not want to be an insider. Wants to be able to trade." In other words, Salovaara wanted to leave open the possibility of acquiring additional Bucyrus securities on the open market. If he did that on the basis of information not available to the market as a whole, he would be in violation of securities laws. For Bucyrus, this signaled a potentially worrisome shift in roles for Salovaara—from advisor to investor. This deprived the company of a trusted long-time financial counselor. It also created the possibility of some tension down the road.

The July 13, 1992, notes of David Goelzer reflect an effort to list the possible implications of entering into a deal with South Street. One concern was that, since South Street was a vulture fund that sought to buy company debt at low prices, Salovaara might have an interest in the continued worsening of Bucyrus's financial condition. Such a decline would make the Bucyrus debt even cheaper on the secondary market. "Recognize that Mikael will profit from a forced restructure scenario," Goelzer wrote. "In fact, that's the scenario that his fund was designed for. He'll buy bonds low and squeeze other debt holders and equity." Indeed, Salovaara might well prefer that the company file for bankruptcy rather than be able to refinance its debt: "NB It appears to be in Mikael's interest that we are *not* able to refinance. The more it looks as though we'll fail, the further down our bond prices will go, and that creates opportunities for him." Furthermore, other vulture funds might become interested, buying up debt from current institutional bond holders. "According to Goldman," Goelzer observed, "this will make a successful restructure more difficult, as the vulture funds will be more cutthroat—take all equity, break up the company, etc."

A second related concern was the amount of influence that Salovaara might gain over the company's future. "Mikael will have a lot of control—from priority position on all necessary assets; ownership of large position in our debt; inside knowledge," say Goelzer's notes. Bucyrus could proceed with South Street, but hire someone else to provide advice on refinancing possibilities. However, Goelzer mused, "[W]ill we be afraid to draw away from Mikael for fear he'll turn on us?" Should these concerns lead the company to "[r]everse course and follow Goldman's advice," or were there provisions that could be added to the South Street financing that might address them? The company had to take account of all these possible scenarios when weighing the costs and benefits of a secured financing arrangement with South Street.

Bucyrus officials eventually decided that a deal with South Street offered the best, and perhaps last, hope to save the company. Bucyrus and South Street agreed on a transaction that involved both conventional debt and the sale and leaseback of certain company equipment. Bucyrus issued to South Street $11.5 million of 10.65 percent notes due July 1, 1995, and $5.25 million of 16.5 percent notes due January 1, 1996. These notes were secured by all the fixed assets of the company except for its manufacturing equipment and real estate.

In addition, the company sold to South Street its manufacturing equipment for $18.25 million. It then leased this equipment back from South Street for a term expiring January 1, 1996. The semiannual lease payments could vary from $2 million to $4 million, depending primarily on whether Bucyrus-Erie elected to defer interest payments. The imputed interest rate on the $18.25 million sale-leaseback portion of the deal was between 25 percent and 27 percent. The so-called blended rate on the total $35 million package was 20.25 percent for 1992 and 20.35 percent for 1993. At the expiration of the lease, Bucyrus-Erie had the right to repurchase the equipment for the original purchase price plus accrued rental payments then due. South Street could require that the company exercise that option.

The closing was held on July 24, 1992, in Milbank Tweed's offices in New York. The transaction was the first investment of Salovaara and Eckert's South Street Fund. It ensured that if Bucyrus ultimately did have to file for bankruptcy, South Street would be first in line among the company's creditors.

This was the deal that would most disturb other creditors in the Bucyrus bankruptcy. Indeed, it would make JNL apoplectic. Holders of debt from the LBO and exchange offer already faced considerable risk that they might not be paid. The South Street deal increased that risk. In the bondholders' view, Salovaara had struck an outrageously lucrative deal with a company in financial trouble, and had protected himself by elbowing other creditors out of the way. From JNL's perspective, the sale-leaseback was a devious way to get around the debt limits that had been designed to ensure payment on the $60 million notes that JNL held. More broadly, JNL claimed that the deal was merely the final stage of Salovaara's ongoing exploitation of Bucyrus-Erie's precarious financial condition. In the bankruptcy that eventually followed, JNL would loudly demand that John Gellene sue Salovaara for allegedly luring Bucyrus into a one-sided deal that effectively gave the investor control over the company.

THE SOUTH STREET transaction bought time for Bucyrus. Both Salovaara and Bucyrus officials knew, however, that increasing the company's obligations by $35 million also posed the risk that Bucyrus would be unable to continue because of its financial obligations. These fears were realized in the last quarter of 1992. The market for machine parts fell off considerably. On January 1, 1993, the interest rate payments on the company's $75 million of 10 percent notes would increase to 16 percent. The rate on the $60 million notes Bucyrus owed to JNL would increase from 12.5 percent to 15 percent. As that date approached, the likelihood that the company would need to declare bankruptcy began to loom large.

Goldman Sachs recommended that Bucyrus officials confer with the financial consulting firm of Houlihan, Lokey, Howard & Zukin about the possibility of reorganizing under Chapter 11 of the federal Bank-

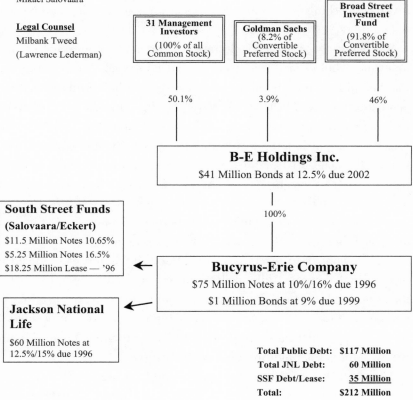

Financial Advisor
Mikael Salovaara

Legal Counsel
Milbank Tweed
(Lawrence Lederman)

31 Management Investors
(100% of all Common Stock)

Goldman Sachs
(8.2% of Convertible Preferred Stock)

Broad Street Investment Fund
(91.8% of Convertible Preferred Stock)

50.1%   3.9%   46%

B-E Holdings Inc.
$41 Million Bonds at 12.5% due 2002

South Street Funds
(Salovaara/Eckert)
$11.5 Million Notes 10.65%
$5.25 Million Notes 16.5%
$18.25 Million Lease — '96

100%

Bucyrus-Erie Company
$75 Million Notes at 10%/16% due 1996
$1 Million Bonds at 9% due 1999

Jackson National Life
$60 Million Notes at 12.5%/15% due 1996

Total Public Debt:	$117 Million
Total JNL Debt:	60 Million
SSF Debt/Lease:	35 Million
Total:	$212 Million

Fig. 5. After South Street Fund financing, July 24, 1992. (Government Exhibit 69, *United States v. Gellene*.)

ruptcy Code. Jeff Werbalowsky of Houlihan's Minneapolis office took the lead on this assignment. Werbalowsky was the thirty-five-year-old head of financial restructuring for the firm. He had practiced law in Los Angeles for five years after graduating from Columbia Law School, working mostly on bankruptcy and financial restructuring issues. He had found, however, that he enjoyed working on the business aspects of problems more than on the legal ones. He thus had joined with a friend to form a business that focused on buying and selling distressed companies. Eventually, he had joined Houlihan, moving to Minneapolis with his wife, a native of the city, and his children. While he was familiar with legal issues, his job primarily involved working on the financial aspects of restructuring and reorganization.

Werbalowsky contacted Goldman to learn more about Bucyrus. The investment house prepared a paper that presented some alternatives for the holding and operating companies, including a merger with or acquisition by another firm. On November 19, 1992, Bucyrus representatives met in Milwaukee with Goldman and Houlihan, Lokey to discuss the company's alternatives and the possibility of retaining Houlihan as financial advisor for a Chapter 11 bankruptcy. Salovaara did not attend this meeting, in light of his earlier request not to be included in internal discussions about the company's affairs. Bucyrus eventually decided in January 1993 to retain Houlihan as financial advisor to both the holding and operating companies.

The November 19 meeting also included discussion of the need to hire a legal advisor. Milbank was chosen for that role. The parties made no final decision about filing for bankruptcy at the meeting. At one point, however, they agreed that if Bucyrus ultimately decided to do so, Larry Lederman would need to designate someone at Milbank who would be the point man for the bankruptcy.

That someone would turn out to be John Gellene.

PART II

THE BANKRUPTCY

CHAPTER FOUR

Rolling the Dice

ON THE MORNING of Saturday February 20, 1993, John Gellene was on a plane to Milwaukee. When he landed at Mitchell Field, he took a taxi to the headquarters of Bucyrus-Erie Corporation in south Milwaukee. There he was ushered into an executive conference room for a meeting of the board of directors. In addition to board members, the meeting included David Goelzer, general counsel of the company; other company managers; Jeff Werbalowsky; and Albert Solochek, a Milwaukee bankruptcy lawyer whom the company had hired the previous month. At this point, Gellene knew little about Bucyrus-Erie. He knew that it had undergone an LBO and that it needed financial restructuring, but he "had no idea really what the problem was or what its size or extent was."

The question before the board was whether the company should suspend interest payments on its outstanding debt. Bucyrus-Erie had a serious cash flow problem. Officials were concerned not only about the ability to make interest payments on the debt. They also feared that when the principal on the bonds came due, the company would be unable to pay it. If the company defaulted on either obligation, it could be thrown into bankruptcy by its creditors, and might have little control over its fate.

Shortly after the meeting began, Goelzer distributed a draft press release stating that Bucyrus would not make the next set of interest payments on its debt that was due in March. The plan was to urge the major creditors to form a committee to negotiate for the exchange of their debt for stock in a new company that would combine the holding

97

and operating companies. Bucyrus would pay the committee's costs for legal and financial advisors. There was a general consensus, including both Gellene and Werbalowsky, that this would be the best way to proceed. It would allow the company to take the initiative in trying to restructure its finances, rather than wait until its creditors started fighting over its assets.

Getting through bankruptcy quickly was important for two reasons. First, the company had over $100 million in net operating losses that it could offset against taxes if it filed for bankruptcy by the end of 1993 or had its reorganization plan approved by the end of 1994. Speed also was important for competitive reasons. Bucyrus sold large and expensive specially engineered machinery that required considerable time to manufacture. Customers, suppliers, and vendors had to have confidence in the long-term viability of the company if they were to enter into transactions with it. Lengthy Chapter 11 proceedings, whose outcome would be uncertain, would undermine that confidence. Customers needing spare parts would begin to look to other firms, and orders for major capital equipment would start to go to Bucyrus's competitors. The company would be able to enjoy the tax benefits it sought only if it was generating income, and its ability to do so would be threatened the longer a reorganization took. A sense of urgency thus pervaded the Bucyrus bankruptcy, which may have played a role in the events that led to John Gellene's undoing.

Participants at the meeting agreed that Bucyrus should suspend interest payments on its outstanding debt. The following Monday, February 22, 1993, Bucyrus issued a press release announcing its decision. The release also stated that the holding company would not be paying dividends on its Series A preferred stock. Bucyrus encouraged its creditors to begin discussing the terms of a bankruptcy plan to ease the company's debt load. All parties with an interest in the company now were on notice that Bucyrus was in financial distress—and that most of them were unlikely to recover the full value of their stake in the company.

WITH THE ISSUANCE of the Bucyrus press release, John Gellene embarked on a journey that would span nearly two years of his life. He would bill over a one thousand hours of his time to the ten months of the Bucyrus bankruptcy proceeding alone, after already working intensively for a year before that on helping form a plan to submit to the court. He would be involved in two acrimonious trials, one related to the bankruptcy plan, the other to Milbank's request for more than $2 million in compensation for its work on behalf of Bucyrus. He would participate in strategy sessions with Bucyrus officials and advisors as they sought to revive a company that was a fixture of the Milwaukee economy. He would formulate advice that combined legal and business judgments, as well as assessments of the motives and tactics of the numerous parties with an interest in the bankruptcy.

Above all, Gellene would negotiate. He and Jeff Werbalowsky would be the point men for Bucyrus in trying to forge an agreement among creditors and shareholders who were battling for the largest possible recovery from a company that was unable to make the interest payments on its debt. As time went by, there would indeed emerge two warring camps, as Mark Rotert told the jury in Gellene's criminal trial. When this became apparent, Gellene would help devise a last-ditch gamble to usher Bucyrus quickly through the bankruptcy process—and would fail. Reeling from his defeat, he would then race the clock in an effort to salvage an agreement that could be accepted by bitterly contending parties. Gellene would do all this while working on other matters as well, flying from city to city and country to country, on the phone from airports and hotel rooms, juggling the relentless demands of high-profile corporate bankruptcies. He would function, in other words, in an environment of constant urgency.

If we're to piece together an account of how John Gellene went wrong, we need a rich understanding of the world that he inhabited at that time. We need a sense of the dynamics of the context in which he acted—and failed to act. What were the contours of his mental map of the Bucyrus bankruptcy? What was his implicit sense of the competing considerations that he had to balance? How might he have justified his decisions not only to others but to himself? Appreciating the ebb and flow of the Bucyrus bankruptcy—the cast of characters, the demands they made, and the battles they fought—is crucial in moving us closer to answers to these questions.

A BANKRUPTCY conducted under Chapter II of the federal Bankruptcy Code would afford Bucyrus an opportunity to continue in business while negotiating with creditors to restructure its existing debt. Once it filed its bankruptcy petition, the company would be protected by an "automatic stay." All debtors would be prohibited from trying to collect on their claims against the company during the reorganization. The process ideally would make Bucyrus more competitive by easing its financial obligations. By agreeing to take reduced payment, or by trading their debt claims for equity in the company, creditors might benefit more from helping the company survive than they would if the company were liquidated and creditors received proceeds from the sale of its assets. Similarly, since existing shareholders would be last to get paid—if they got paid anything—once the company dissolved, a reorganization could be the best way to preserve the value of their investments.

The 1978 Bankruptcy Act revisions had enhanced the attractiveness of bankruptcy as a tool of business planning and restructuring. Prior to that time, the code required that existing managers be removed and a neutral trustee be appointed to run the company and conduct the reorganization. This requirement, championed by William O. Douglas during the New Deal, was a reaction against the perceived abuses that had resulted from allowing existing management to control the reorganization. Company officials, along with their investment bankers and lawyers, were seen as interested primarily in manipulating the bankruptcy process to maintain their influence and line their own pockets.

The 1978 act, however, provided that a trustee need not automatically be appointed when a company filed for bankruptcy. Management would continue to run the corporation, and would be involved in the reorganization process, unless it had engaged in mismanagement or illegal activity. Managers' temptation to pursue their own interest is supposed to be constrained by imposing fiduciary duties upon them.

Filing a Chapter 11 petition creates a bankruptcy "estate," consisting of all the debtor's property, which is held in trust for all parties with claims upon it. Bankruptcy transforms the company into a "debtor-in-possession" (DIP), which must act as a fiduciary to preserve the value of the estate for the benefit of these parties.

The U.S. trustee is charged with overseeing the negotiation process to make sure that all parties have equal access to information that will enable them to make an informed decision about the terms of the plan. The trustee's role is not to take responsibility for ensuring the fairness of the plan that emerges. He or she appoints at least one committee of unsecured creditors. The committee negotiates on behalf of the creditors as a body, and is authorized to conduct an investigation of the company, to monitor its operations during bankruptcy, and to be heard on any issue. Secured creditors, such as South Street, negotiate individually on their own behalf with the debtor.

The parties are given wide leeway in hammering out a plan. The dynamics of their bargaining are shaped to a large degree by the priorities that the Bankruptcy Code establishes among the claimants. Unless the parties agree otherwise, the claims of each group of creditors in the hierarchy must be fully satisfied before the next group can receive any compensation. At the top of the ladder are secured creditors, such as South Street, who have collateral for their loans. A secured creditor is entitled to repayment of both the principal amount of the loan and any interest that accumulates during the bankruptcy proceedings. If the debtor is unable to repay its debt to a secured creditor, the creditor has a right to force a sale of the collateral and to satisfy its claim from the proceeds of that sale. With some exceptions, all unsecured claims are paid on a pro rata basis if there aren't enough funds to repay them in full.

The reorganization plan classifies the claims and interests into categories of substantially similar parties of the same priority, such as general unsecured creditors, preferred stock, and common stock. Each secured claim usually is given a class of its own. The plan must list which classes of claims would be impaired if the plan is adopted—that is, which claims would receive less than the amount to which they otherwise are entitled. Each claim or interest must be treated the same as other members of its class unless the parties agree otherwise.

Creditors and equity security holders whose claims and interests are impaired must vote on whether to accept the plan. The DIP is required to submit to the court a disclosure statement containing information necessary to permit an informed vote. The statement must be approved by the court after a hearing, and then distributed to creditors and equity security holders along with the plan itself. Each class then votes as a unit on the plan, and, in most cases, all classes must approve the plan for it to be effective. Among creditors, a class is deemed to accept the plan if half the number of class members and two-thirds of the amount of the claims vote for it. Among shareholders, a vote of two-thirds of the amount of interests held by members of the class is sufficient to constitute approval of the plan.

Under certain circumstances, a plan may be adopted even if one or more classes have voted against it. The code permits proponents to "cram down" the plan on a dissenting class if the plan is deemed by the court fair to that class and is necessary to the success of the reorganization. The treatment afforded the objecting class must be comparable to that given others with claims or interests of similar priority. A component of this requirement is the "absolute priority" rule. In effect, it requires that if the class that votes against the plan receives only partial compensation under the plan, no junior classes may receive anything.

One option that might have some appeal to Bucyrus was the "prepackaged" bankruptcy. Under this increasingly popular arrangement, bargaining would occur before the company filed for bankruptcy. If negotiations were successful, Bucyrus could provide a disclosure statement to these parties and obtain their votes in favor of the plan. The company then could file the plan simultaneously with its Chapter II petition. If the court ruled that the disclosure statement had afforded adequate information to the voters, the plan would be confirmed in short order. Bucyrus, however, would have to negotiate a prepackaged plan without the protection of an automatic stay. It thus could be vulnerable to enforcement actions by individual creditors during the discussions. Nonetheless, if the parties could reach agreement in advance of a bankruptcy petition, the company might be able to proceed through reorganization fairly quickly.

The holding and operating companies had more than two thousand creditors. Only those whose claims were "impaired"—that is, could not be fully honored on existing terms—would be entitled to vote on a prepackaged plan. This group included most of the large institutional creditors. Bucyrus's two major creditors were JNL, which held an unsecured interest in $60 million worth of bonds, and South Street, with its $35 million secured investment. Since it held an interest in virtually all the company's tangible assets, South Street could thwart any bankruptcy plan that was proposed and effectively shut the company down. Bucyrus's preference was that JNL exchange its bonds for stock in the new company that would emerge from Chapter 11 bankruptcy. The hope was that South Street would either receive immediate payment of a portion of what the company owed it, or could obtain new payment terms for the full amount stretched over a period of time. As it turned out, discussions with both creditors would be time-consuming and, in JNL's case, contentious.

INTENSIVE NEGOTIATIONS between the company and its creditors and shareholders began almost immediately after Bucyrus issued its press release. The unsecured creditors formed an unofficial ad hoc bondholders committee. It consisted of several institutions with holding company and/or operating company bonds. Together, they held somewhat more than half the operating company debt and about 40 percent of the debt of the holding company. The committee's lead attorney as of early May was Brian Rosen of Weil, Gotshal, who represented Franklin Funds, and the committee's financial advisor was Samuel (Skip) Victor of Chanin and Company.

Gellene's official responsibility was for legal matters, while Werbalowsky focused on financial issues. Such lines often were blurred, however, in the workaday world of negotiations. Werbalowsky had a law degree and understood legal issues, while Gellene had familiarity with financial and business concerns by virtue of his extensive bankruptcy experience. Both men played key roles in the effort to broker an agreement among the various parties with an interest in the company. The two men worked smoothly together, but were rather different in personality. Werbalowsky was outgoing and gregarious, while Gellene tended to be more abstracted and intense. Werbalowsky sometimes playfully called Gellene "the professor," because of the Milbank lawyer's occasional tendency to lecture on various aspects of bankruptcy law.

Werbalowsky was more involved on a day-to-day basis than was Gellene. He and Eric Siegert of Houlihan, Lokey took primary responsibility for negotiating with creditors and constructing financial projections. Gellene, however, was in constant contact and periodically broke away from his other cases to fly in and become deeply involved for several days at a time. Gellene's principal daily contact at Bucyrus was general counsel David Goelzer, with whom he spoke virtually every day. The Milbank lawyer also participated at least once a week by conference call with the entire board of directors.

The first meeting between the company and its unsecured creditors was on March 31 in Milwaukee. Parties involved in the Bucyrus bankruptcy negotiations tended to refer to these creditors as the "bondholder," even though a bondholder technically is only one type of unsecured creditor. Senior management, Gellene, Werbalowsky, and representatives of the large bondholder groups, including JNL, all attended. The meeting was tense. John Stark, representing JNL, raised the possibility that all other bondholders should be subordinated to JNL because their bonds had been acquired in fraudulent transactions designed by the buyout group to siphon money from Bucyrus-Erie. Furthermore, many of the bondholders felt resentment toward Salovaara. They believed that he had taken unfair advantage of the operating company in the sale-leaseback. That deal, of course, carried an imputed high interest rate, and also vaulted South Street to the head of the creditor line. As a result, the meeting ended with no clear sense of how to put together a plan that would be agreeable to everyone.

Werbalowsky took the lead in negotiating with South Street. Milbank had done the documents for the sale-leaseback. He therefore relied on the firm at the outset to gain an understanding of the terms of that transaction, which he regarded as one of the most complex he had seen. He was aware that Milbank had a good working relationship with South Street. Regardless of the fact that the South Street Funds were the formal secured creditors of the company, everyone knew that Salovaara controlled them. Salovaara was represented by Matthew Gluck of Fried, Frank, but conducted the bulk of the negotiations himself. His approval would be necessary if there were to be a successful prepackaged plan. The longer the bankruptcy took, the more default interest accumulated on the debt that the company owed him. Obtaining Salovaara's consent to a plan thus was crucial.

Werbalowsky met with Bucyrus's primary lender, Bank One Milwaukee, about providing a financing package that could be used to pay off South Street at a slight discount. Bucyrus was anxious to "cash out" Salovaara because interest on his claims was continuing to run at a high rate while negotiations proceeded. As it turned out, however, the deal never went through, in part because the companies were unable to file for bankruptcy for almost a year.

In early spring, Werbalowsky reported difficulties in reaching an agreement between the bondholders and Salovaara. He expressed concern to Bucyrus officials and Gellene that deep animosity toward Salovaara among the bondholders could threaten the ability to reach an accord. Goelzer was aware at this time that Larry Lederman was providing some information to Gellene about Salovaara's thinking on the bankruptcy negotiations. Goelzer asked Gellene to talk to Salovaara to see if it were possible to get South Street to participate in the restructuring.

Gellene did so, but received no definite answer from Salovaara. He told Goelzer that Salovaara had refused to reveal to Gellene the exact extent of his holdings in Bucyrus. This was not unusual. The investor often didn't buy bonds in his own name, and was well known for becoming involved in bankruptcy cases while attempting to conceal his involvement from others. Bucyrus asked Gellene to call Salovaara on at least one other occasion and inform him in general terms the status of discussions with the other parties. Thus, Gellene had some periodic contact with Salovaara, although Werbalowsky was the companies' main negotiator with the investor.

There was much ongoing discussion about whether Bucyrus-Erie should make the next payment, due June 30, on the debt that the company owed to South Street. Company officials, as well as Gellene and Werbalowsky, were uncertain of the best way to proceed, since Salovaara was a key figure in achieving consensus in favor of a reorganization plan. Eventually, the company decided that it would suspend the upcoming interest payment. Gellene advised, however, that the operating company should meet with Salovaara before doing so.

In June 1993, Winter, Goelzer, and Gellene met with Salovaara at Milbank Tweed's offices in New York. At this meeting, Salovaara apparently wasn't confrontational. He was noncommittal, however, about any concessions that he might be willing to make. He commented in an offhand manner that it might be in his best interest not to negotiate but to force Bucyrus to declare bankruptcy. Bucyrus officials were surprised at how matter-of-fact Salovaara was about this prospect for a company for whom he had served as an advisor for several years. Salovaara made clear, however, that he was weighing what course of action would be best for his investments. As Goelzer would later comment, "Salovaara always seemed to be thinking several moves ahead of the company." "We were probably like a laboratory rat." Goelzer said. "He knew which way we were going to turn even before we did."

Salovaara obviously was in an advantageous negotiating position as the company's only secured creditor. Bucyrus's main source of leverage was the possibility that it might assert that South Street's note on the sale-leaseback was significantly overvalued, because its interest rate was so much higher than the market rate. The company would then subject him to a "cram-up"—that is, give him a note for his claims that was equal to a current market rate instrument but much lower than he would receive under the terms of the original deal. Salovaara undoubtedly would complain to the bankruptcy court that this was unfair. The court, however, might well find his claim unsympathetic in light of what other creditors were receiving.

On July 16, Gellene informed Goelzer that Lederman had talked with Salovaara about possible concessions that South Street might make in connection with a Bucyrus refinancing. He said that Salovaara had expressed some optimism about this prospect. The parties were still sufficiently far apart a week and a half later, however, that on July 28 there was a telephone conversation in which company officials and Gellene discussed the possibility of a "cram-down" of South Street. That is, should the company put together a plan and try to get it confirmed over Salovaara's objections? Bucyrus would have to establish that the plan provided South Street with securities equal to the value of its claim. The problem with that strategy, however, was that Gellene and Werbalowsky had already suggested that JNL was unlikely to agree to a prepack and that a cram-down of it might be necessary. The parties agreed that a court probably would not approve a plan over the objections of the company's two main creditors. As a result, Bucyrus continued to try to reach an agreement with South Street.

JOHN STARK'S CONTENTION that all other creditors should be subordinated to JNL gave Bucyrus even less optimism that it could reach terms that would be agreeable to the company's largest bondholder. In February 1989, JNL had bought some of the notes that Bucyrus had issued as part of its exchange offer. The deal had been brokered through Goldman Sachs. JNL had sold the notes two years later at a loss of $550,000. This naturally didn't create warm feelings at the company toward Goldman.

Concern about this and other investment losses prompted JNL's English parent company, Prudential Corp., PLC (not affiliated with the United States insurance company) to establish PPM America to manage JNL's investment portfolio, and to bring John Stark in to run PPM in November 1990. At that time JNL's portfolio was about $10 billion. Stark went through the portfolio and conducted a "triage" operation, identifying which investments were in trouble. He took charge of managing the resulting "special investments" portfolio, which contained investments that were either in default or at risk of defaulting. These totaled about $250 million.

Stark was a stocky thirty-four-year-old Minnesota native who had received his undergraduate education at Wabash College and his law degree from Vanderbilt. He had worked at a Minnesota money management firm before joining PPM. Stark's competitiveness was reflected in his interest in sailboat racing and skiing. He was beginning to acquire a reputation as a tough, no-holds-barred advocate for his client's interests in financial reorganizations.

Stark's hostility to what he perceived as mistreatment of bondholders was forged in particular by his experience with Marriott Corporation, in which his fund held bonds. In October 1992, Marriott announced a restructuring in which its highly profitable management and services business, which produced more than half of Marriott's operating profit, was to be spun off into a new subsidiary owned by the company's common stockholders. Its much less profitable real estate and concession business was left in the parent company, along with debt and preferred stock. The result was to pump up the price of the company's common stock, but the value of Marriott bonds fell by 30 percent. As one account of the events put it, "[B]ondholders were left howling." Among the loudest was Stark, who led an unsuccessful legal challenge to overturn the restructuring that asked for $30 million in damages.

When Stark joined PPM America, the $60 million Bucyrus notes purchased in 1990 constituted the second largest investment in the JNL private placement portfolio. Stark had visited Bucyrus late in 1990 to discuss the company's condition with company officials, and had been in touch periodically since then.

Stark was traveling when Bucyrus issued its February 20 press release announcing the suspension of its debt payments. His office faxed him a copy. Shortly afterward, Verville called him to inform him of the company's action, and to urge Stark to join the unofficial creditors' committee. Stark was noncommittal, telling Verville only that he would think about it. He may have been miffed that Bucyrus had not pursued a JNL offer of refinancing in March 1992, and had instead struck a deal with South Street. That gave the vulture fund priority over other creditors. Fresh off his experience with Marriott, Stark may have been suspicious that Bucyrus would try to undercut the claim of its largest bondholder.

Stark also had an opportunity to meet John Gellene in March 1993, shortly after the company's press release. He was meeting at Milbank's offices with John Jerome, the head of the firm's bankruptcy practice. Milbank had represented PPM and ten other noteholders since August 1992 in a bankruptcy involving the Phar-Mor drugstore chain. Jerome came by Gellene's office and told him that Stark had said that PPM also held some Bucyrus debt. Stark had asked to meet Gellene, so Jerome indicated that he would bring Stark by Gellene's office. He did so, and Stark and Gellene met for fifteen or twenty minutes. The two men had slight familiarity with each other through their involvement in the National Gypsum bankruptcy, but had not before dealt directly with one another.

Stark told Gellene that Goldman had involved JNL in several deals before he had arrived. He expressed his belief that Goldman had sold a lot of junk debt during the 1980s to fund LBOs, and that many of the companies that had issued that debt were unable to pay their creditors. He told Gellene that JNL's $60 million loan made it the largest creditor of Bucyrus.

Gellene told Stark that he was very new to the Bucyrus case, but knew that the company was trying to get an agreement from creditors to a reorganization as soon as possible. Stark told him that the JNL loan to Bucyrus had been made before he had joined JNL, and that he felt that he needed to conduct what he called "due diligence" on the transaction. He said, however, that he was having trouble getting all the documents he needed that related to the deal. He indicated that as soon as he selected lawyers to represent JNL in the Bucyrus bankruptcy, he would contact Gellene about obtaining the materials he would like to review. Gellene described the meeting as a "cordial" one, in which they didn't get much into matters of substance.

Near the end of March, Gellene received a call from lawyers at Anderson, Kill in New York. They indicated that they were representing JNL in the Bucyrus bankruptcy. The lawyers provided a list of documents they would like to review: offering statements for the reset notes purchased by JNL, information on the financial condition of the company, SEC files, Bucyrus's certificate of incorporation, its bylaws, correspondence between Bucyrus and Goldman, and several years' worth of corporate meeting minutes.

Given Stark's earlier comment about his desire to conduct due diligence, Gellene was surprised at the material the lawyers were seeking. He had expected a request for information dealing with the financial condition of Bucyrus, such as financial statements, budgets, and business plans. Those items were on the list. Anderson, Kill, however, also asked for information more "retrospective" in nature, such as minutes of the board of directors, correspondence between Bucyrus and Goldman, and several documents Gellene "would expect to see in connection with a lawsuit."

Meanwhile, JNL declined to accept Bucyrus's invitation to join the committee of unsecured creditors. Stark didn't believe that the committee included a "critical mass" of creditors, and felt that the membership was too fluid and uncertain. In early April, Stark upped the ante. He informed Bucyrus-Erie that he believed the company should file a lawsuit claiming that the LBO, exchange offer, and South Street sale-leaseback were fraudulent transactions designed primarily to benefit the buyout group rather than the operating company. The result, asserted JNL, was that these deals had left Bucyrus-Erie with insufficient working capital and enough funds to pay its debt.

Defendants in such a suit could include company directors who had approved the transactions, management members of the buyout group, Goldman Sachs, holders of the debt issued in these transactions, and possibly the professionals who had worked on the matters. A successful claim could both generate money for the estate and move JNL ahead of other creditors in the bankruptcy. If Bucyrus-Erie didn't file suit, a creditor such as JNL could do so prior to the bankruptcy petition. Once the petition was filed, any cause of action alleging that Bucyrus had been injured would become the property of the bankruptcy estate.

Gellene reported to Bucyrus management that the threat of such litigation was unlikely to intimidate Salovaara into going along with any plan that he otherwise didn't find acceptable. Gellene called Goelzer shortly after lunch on April 22, 1993, to advise him that Stark had drafted a complaint. Gellene told Goelzer that the lawsuit might name not only various institutions, but also directors Winter, Mork, Verville, and retired general counsel Ray Olander.

About ten o'clock that evening, Gellene received the draft complaint from Stark and began to fax it to Goelzer. Goelzer and Winter stood by the fax machine in stunned amazement as the document rolled in, exclaiming to one another as they took turns taking each page off the machine. Gellene suggested that the Bucyrus board meet with Stark as soon as possible to discuss the advisability of a lawsuit. A meeting was set up for the following day at the company's offices in Milwaukee.

THE BUCYRUS-ERIE RESPONSE to JNL's insistence that the company file a lawsuit was to become a crucial and acrimonious point of contention in the bankruptcy proceedings. JNL was incensed that Gellene recommended not only that the company not file suit, but that it give up any future right to sue any of the parties against whom JNL had made allegations. JNL was especially upset that this let Goldman and South Street off the hook for any potential liability. When Gellene's concealment of Milbank's ties to Salovaara and South Street was discovered, JNL painted that failure in especially dark tones by suggesting that those ties were the real reason for Gellene's recommendation against preserving any right to sue.

It is therefore worth lingering for a moment on JNL's claims and Bucyrus-Erie's decision not to pursue them. JNL alleged that the LBO, exchange offer, and sale-leaseback each constituted "fraudulent conveyances." That term comes from bankruptcy law. In general, it's defined as any transaction undertaken by a debtor before filing a bankruptcy petition that's intended to avoid paying obligations to creditors, or that has the effect of rendering the debtor unable to meet them. JNL maintained that each of these deals was part of a larger effort by the buyout group to gain ownership and control of Bucyrus-

Erie at minimal cost. The group would then "realize all the benefits of operating BE, while BE's unsecured creditors assumed all of the financial risk."[1]

The scheme, JNL contended, had begun with the LBO. The buyout group paid an excessively high price to Becor shareholders to acquire the company. Most of the $350 million purchase price came from Becor cash. Managers paid only a total of $500,000 in cash and contributed thirty-two thousand shares of Becor stock for their share of the company. Goldman's Broad Street Fund put up only $1 million. Managers who also were Becor shareholders received holding company bonds with a 12.5 percent interest rate. They presumably would keep pressure on the operating company to continue paying enough dividends to the holding company to permit the latter to make its bond payments. JNL's implication thus was that these managers would be milking income from the operating company for their own benefit.

Goldman Sachs gained a healthy fee for arranging the LBO. In addition, it knew that the debt that B-E Holdings had undertaken in the LBO would require the company to continue to refinance its obligations. Goldman thus could expect a steady stream of fees for structuring these periodic transactions. Because Bucyrus-Erie had contributed a large amount of cash to the LBO without adequate compensation, alleged JNL, and because it would be under pressure to pay substantial dividends, the operating company was fatally weakened by the LBO. Indeed, JNL claimed, the transaction probably left it insolvent.

Gellene and those in the Bucyrus camp, however, regarded these claims as unpersuasive. First, Gellene believed that the statute of limitations barred any claim relating to the LBO. With respect to the merits, why would the buyout group be interested in gaining control of a company whose health they had ruined? If managers unreasonably manipulated Bucyrus-Erie dividend payments to ensure that they received payment on the holding company bonds they had received for their Becor shares, that would eventually weaken the operating company so much that it no longer could pay such dividends. The best strategy for both ensuring repayment of the bonds and enjoying the benefit of an increase in the value of their holding company shares was to run Bucyrus-Erie as prudently as possible, not to strip it of capital. The Bucyrus camp believed that the best evidence that managers had done just that was the fact that the company had continued to operate for almost five years before it suspended payment on its debt.

To be sure, Bucyrus officials and their representatives conceded that the LBO had been a risky transaction. In their view, however, that risk had been disclosed to participants in the deal. The LBO prospectus had bluntly stated, "As a result of the Merger, Holdings will become very highly leveraged." Projections were that in the five years following the LBO the holding company would incur net losses after taxes and a declining net worth. As a result, said the prospectus, "Holdings will not generate internally amounts of cash that are significant" in relation to its ability to service its debt and pay dividends. If it could not meet its obligations, it might have to sell off assets of the operating company. Investors knew they were buying junk bonds that carried these risks. That was why the bonds had high interest rates.

Finally, any company emerging from an LBO had a substantial debt load. Goldman may have anticipated that the holding and operating companies would need to refinance their debt at some point after the LBO. It was not unusual, however, for this to occur given the risk in taking on so much debt. Even if in hindsight the decision to do the deal was unwise, that was different from saying that it was fraudulent. For these reasons, Bucyrus-Erie felt that it had no viable claim with respect to the LBO.

JNL also believed that Bucyrus-Erie could challenge the exchange offer. That transaction had shifted outstanding debt from the holding to the operating company. The holding company's debt went from $102 million to $57.3 million, while the operating company's rose from $27.5 million to $75.4 million. Bucyrus-Erie incurred these additional liabilities, asserted JNL, with no compensating increase in assets.

JNL was especially critical of Goldman's actions surrounding the exchange offer. After the LBO, JNL declared, Goldman had bought up 93 percent of operating company 9 percent debentures and one-third of holding company 12.5 percent notes. Goldman had done this

EAT WHAT YOU KILL

because it knew that the holding and operating companies would have to refinance their obligations after the LBO. As those companies' faltered because of the large LBO debt load, Goldman would have opportunities to buy the bonds and debentures at a discount. Once Salovaara convinced Bucyrus to conduct an exchange offer, the expected easing of that debt load and the more attractive terms on those bonds and debentures caused their value to rise. The result was that Goldman made a $10 million profit when it resold the debt.

In JNL's view, therefore, Goldman had exploited the trust that Bucyrus had in it by giving advice that was driven mostly by its own financial interest. Even though Goldman wasn't the official financial advisor on the exchange offer, Salovaara's fingerprints were all over the deal.

Gellene believed that the statute of limitations also had run on the exchange offer. He and his client regarded that deal as a transaction that had helped the companies through a tight spot. The holding company avoided the need to repay the principal on $21 million in debt, and the operating company was able to raise capital from the sale of new bonds. Exchange offers were not uncommon for corporations that had undergone LBOs, since the future was especially uncertain for these companies.

It's true that Goldman could be seen as aggressive in exploiting market opportunities connected with the Bucyrus companies. An investment bank two decades earlier might not have done so because it could appear unseemly and disloyal to Bucyrus. In the fiercely competitive banking market of the late twentieth century, however, financial institutions looked for every opportunity to trade profitably. Goldman had effectively hedged its bets, reducing the risk it faced as a shareholder by trading in the companies' debt. Bucyrus had independent financial advice on the deal from Piper Jaffray, however, and thus was not a vulnerable lamb that had been led to the slaughter.

JNL reserved special wrath for the sale-leaseback with South Street. The buyout group had arranged for this transaction with Salovaara without seeking other bids for financing. John Stark had informed Bucyrus officials earlier that JNL was prepared to offer financing assistance. Bucyrus, however, never pursued that alternative. Instead, it entered into an agreement that could involve an interest rate of more than 20 percent—a figure more appropriate for a venture capital deal than a secured financing.

Furthermore, asserted JNL, the transaction was a thinly veiled attempt to avoid the covenants accompanying JNL's notes that limited the amount of debt Bucyrus-Erie could incur. B-E's payments to South Street took the form of equipment lease fees rather than debt service, but South Street could require the company to repurchase its equipment at the end of the period. JNL contended that "this repurchase provision unquestionably makes the Sale-Leaseback a financing arrangement and not a true lease transaction."[2]

Salovaara, claimed JNL, had seen Bucyrus-Erie's precarious condition as an attractive opportunity for his vulture fund. He knew that company officials trusted and relied upon him for advice. He therefore urged them in the first half of 1992 not to file for bankruptcy. That gave him time to use the sale-leaseback as a vehicle for gaining priority in the bankruptcy he knew was inevitable. This harmed the companies because it piled more debt on them even though they had no hope of continuing without a reorganization. It also injured existing creditors, who now became subordinate to Salovaara. Salovaara thus had acted as a wolf in sheep's clothing. He had appeared to continue in his role as trusted advisor while in fact preying on Bucyrus as a classic vulture investor who helped profit from the company's misfortune.

According to Gellene and Werbalowsky, however, no court had ever held that a fraudulent conveyance had occurred when a party had actually advanced funds in return for a claim. South Street had given Bucyrus-Erie $35 million that the company was able to put to use in its operations. The terms of the transaction were steep, but it was unlikely that the company would have been able to negotiate better terms anywhere else. Company officials may have felt comfortable dealing with Salovaara. They could not have been under any illusion, however, that he was providing financing out of the goodness of his heart. Salovaara made clear that South Street was a vulture fund. He had told Bucyrus officials that he aimed for a 25 percent annual return. Among those unsecured creditors who became subordinate to South Street as a result of the deal were managers who held operating company bonds they had received for their Becor shares during the LBO. Salovaara had driven a hard bargain, and perhaps Bucyrus should have declined his offer. The fact that the sale-leaseback may have been a bad deal, however, didn't make it fraudulent.

Bucyrus also rejected JNL's claim that the sale-leaseback violated Bucyrus-Erie debt covenants. In its view, the company had taken appropriate steps to avoid a violation. Corporate lawyers deal in form and structure all the time with an eye to meeting legal requirements or avoiding restrictions. A sale-leaseback was not an uncommon transaction. If all legal requirements necessary to effectuate it had been met, then JNL had no basis for claiming that it was really a debt financing.

JNL and Bucyrus also wrangled over a claim that JNL had the ability to assert on its own behalf even after the bankruptcy petition was filed. The creditor claimed that Goldman had sold it $60 million worth of notes on behalf of Bucyrus-Erie without revealing that the company was in serious financial distress. The company had represented to JNL that it would be using a substantial amount of the proceeds to reduce its long-term debt and increase its working capital, but little of the money actually had been used for these purposes. Already stung by its half-million dollar loss on Bucyrus debentures it had purchased after the exchange offer, JNL believed that it had been misled again.

Gellene and Bucyrus, however, maintained that JNL knew perfectly well that it was acquiring junk bonds. JNL had conducted due diligence on the company's condition. It was in a position to ask for any information that it wanted before committing to the deal. Making a bad investment was not the same thing as being defrauded. Furthermore, even if JNL had been the victim of fraud, the remedy was damages, not giving JNL priority over other creditors in the bankruptcy.

Gellene's reaction to the JNL draft complaint also was informed by awareness that asserting fraudulent conveyance claims was a common bargaining ploy in bankruptcy cases. This was especially the case when the debtor earlier had undergone an LBO. Very few of these claims were ultimately pursued, and even fewer proved successful. Gellene thus likely was skeptical from the start about JNL's accusations. Furthermore, he was quite concerned that JNL had named Bucyrus manager-directors individually in its complaint. Such a step seemed an effort to intimidate management at the outset of negotiations. It signaled that JNL's cooperation in forging a prepackaged plan would be difficult to obtain.

ON THE MORNING of April 23, Gellene, Milbank Tweed associate Revesz, Werbalowsky, and Siegel met in Milwaukee with Goelzer and the four board members named in the JNL complaint: Philip Mork, Norbert Verville, William Winter, and Ray Olander. The directors were extremely upset at being included as defendants. A meeting with JNL was scheduled for that afternoon. Gellene insisted that JNL didn't have a viable claim. Although Gellene took the lead in presenting the legal analysis, Werbalowsky agreed with his conclusion. Nonetheless, the company also had to take account of practical considerations. JNL might file the suit on its own. If it did, it could complicate the bankruptcy by putting creditors even more at odds with one another and the company. It also would create unwelcome publicity just as Bucyrus was attempting to reassure workers, suppliers, and customers that it would emerge from bankruptcy fairly quickly. Having four of the company's directors as defendants in the suit could be especially damaging.

That afternoon, the participants in the morning meeting met with Stark and his lawyers from Anderson, Kill who had prepared the complaint. Gellene argued that the claims had no merit. He encouraged JNL to join the unsecured creditors' committee that was forming in order to arrive at an agreement on how the company should be reorganized. JNL refused. Stark said that the members of the bondholders' group had far less Bucyrus debt than did JNL. The major creditor of the company should not be forced to negotiate through a committee. Furthermore, Stark urged, most of the bondholders' claims should be denied in any event because they were acquired through fraudulent conveyances. When Gellene urged JNL not to file the complaint, Stark replied that the statute of limitations might run if JNL delayed any longer. Bucyrus then proposed a tolling agreement that would stop the statute from running, thus preserving JNL's ability to sue later. JNL agreed in return for not naming the company and its officials in the suit it planned imminently to file.

Stark then said that JNL would negotiate with Bucyrus only on three conditions. First, the company must negotiate exclusively with JNL about restructuring the $60 million that Bucyrus owed JNL. Second, any reorganization must subordinate other creditors' interests to those of JNL. Gellene later described this condition as evolving "into the position that the [other] bondholders' interests must be extinguished." Finally, JNL would not negotiate with any other bondholders. The message was clear: as the largest creditor of Bucyrus, JNL expected to receive individual attention, as well as preference, in the process of working out a financial reorganization of the company.

Not surprisingly, the parties reached no consensus on these conditions at the meeting. Bucyrus representatives viewed JNL's insistence that all other creditors' claims be nullified as completely unreasonable, even by the lenient standards applied to positions typically taken in bankruptcy negotiations. They had difficulty imagining how the parties could reach agreement on a plan as long as JNL stuck to this demand.

After the meeting, Goelzer notified Bucyrus's insurance company of the possibility of a lawsuit by JNL. Bucyrus's bylaws provided that a majority of disinterested directors had to conclude that the defendants had acted in good faith in order for the company to indemnify directors' and officers' legal fees. That was not feasible in this case, since three of the four current directors were potential defendants. One way to deal with this problem was to have an opinion from outside counsel attesting to the good faith of the defendants. Goelzer suggested that Lederman would be a good choice to provide such an opinion, since he was familiar with all of the transactions that were the subject of the complaint. As a result, Gellene took responsibility for drafting a submission to the insurance company, which Lederman approved.

IN RETROSPECT, the use of Gellene both to analyze the merits of JNL's proposed lawsuit and to opine on the good faith of the Bucyrus directors could be subject to challenge on the ground that Gellene and Milbank had a conflict of interest. With the exception of the sale of notes to JNL, assessment of the JNL claims and of the directors' good faith related to transactions in which Milbank had provided legal advice. Thus, although JNL had not named the law firm in its draft complaint, Milbank potentially could be a defendant. One therefore might argue that the company should have hired counsel with no connection to these deals to provide opinions on their legitimacy. The fact that Bucyrus didn't do so sheds some light on the competing practical considerations that can have weight in the context of bankruptcy. It also illustrates the complexities of applying conflict-of-interest rules in this area of practice. For these reasons, the issue warrants a closer look.

Bucyrus could argue that it was the client for whom these analyses were conducted, and that it therefore could waive any concern about a conflict. The company was well aware that Milbank had played a role in these transactions. Hiring outside counsel to conduct investigations would have been expensive for a company in financial distress, and could have delayed the reorganization process. For these reasons, Bucyrus was willing to rely on Milbank's analysis of whether it should bring a lawsuit or seek indemnification of its directors' legal expenses. In doing so, it could take the law firm's prior involvement into account in evaluating the quality of the opinions that Milbank provided. Because Bucyrus had not yet filed a bankruptcy petition, it was not a fiduciary for the estate. It therefore could take into account solely its own interests in deciding whether to waive the conflict.

One response to this argument with respect to the issue of the directors' good faith is that the opinion was provided for Bucyrus's insurance company, rather than Bucyrus itself. Professional rules, however, suggest that the opinion was rendered at the request of Bucyrus—the client—for the benefit of a third-party nonclient. In such a case, the company as client has the authority to waive any conflict. Milbank could be deemed to violate its duty to the insurance company, however, if it didn't exercise due care in investigating the issue of good faith. In these circumstances, such care might require that it at least inform the insurance company of the firm's involvement in the transactions in question. That way, the insurer could take this information into account in deciding whether to tentatively approve indemnification, subject to its reservation of rights.

A more significant challenge to Bucyrus's waiver argument, however, is that certain legal precedent implies that a company nearing insolvency—even before it files a bankruptcy petition—assumes a duty to look after the interests of its creditors.[3] David Goelzer testified that Bucyrus was "clearly insolvent" by 1993.[4] If the legal precedent applied to Bucyrus, the company would have the obligation at this point to ask itself whether creditors would be likely to waive the conflict. Bucyrus could argue that they would, because the creditors also would want to avoid the expense and delay involved in hiring outside counsel.

A problem with this analysis, however, is that all the creditors except JNL had a direct interest in upholding the validity of the transactions at issue. If those deals were deemed fraudulent, and the directors found to have acted in bad faith, these creditors' claims might be extinguished. Indeed, some of the creditors were named as defendants in JNL's New York lawsuit. The non-JNL creditors thus were likely to be perfectly happy for legal opinions to be provided by a law firm that also might have an interest in rejecting any challenge to the validity of the transactions.

JNL thus could argue that Bucyrus and the creditors could not provide a disinterested waiver of Milbank's conflict on behalf of the estate, because they had been participants in the transactions that JNL claimed had gutted the value of its bonds. Of course, JNL had an interest in seeing that the deals were deemed fraudulent. Hiring outside counsel to determine if they were fraudulent would place the responsibility on a party whose motives could not be challenged. JNL therefore could claim that it was the only party in a position to waive the conflict on behalf of the estate, that it refused to do so, and that as a result Bucyrus's waiver was ineffective.

The practical difficulty with that position, however, is that it would give parties such as JNL a significant and perhaps unfair bargaining chip in negotiations. Attorneys who have represented a company in prior transactions often are chosen as counsel for the debtor in financial reorganizations because of their familiarity with the company. Simply by alleging that the company had conspired with other creditors to damage its interests, a creditor could threaten to inflict on the company the cost and delay of hiring outside counsel.

Furthermore, in the Bucyrus case itself, Bucyrus and all its other creditors strongly believed that JNL's fraudulent conveyance claim was wholly without merit. In their eyes, JNL's demand that it be given priority over all other creditors was completely unreasonable. They regarded JNL's allegations as simply a bargaining ploy. In light of the fact that Bucyrus regarded JNL's claims as transparently groundless, the company likely believed that hiring outside counsel would confer on JNL's tactics a respectability they didn't deserve.

Milbank's opinions on the colorability of JNL's allegations and the good faith of the Bucyrus directors thus offer examples of how considerations unique to bankruptcy can shape the application of conflict rules to this area of practice. At the same time, they illustrate that applying these rules in a way that's sensitive to such considerations requires awareness by all parties of potential conflicts. Relationships that might lead to disqualification of lawyers in other settings may be tolerated in bankruptcy when those relationships are disclosed and the parties involved are sophisticated corporations. It is important to remember, however, that Bucyrus's reliance on Gellene to assess JNL's claims can be plausibly justified only because everyone was aware of Milbank's potential conflict. Disclosure, in other words, is essential.

AS THE SPRING of 1993 progressed, JNL continued to refuse to join negotiations as a member of the creditors' committee. Stark turned down Bucyrus's proposal that JNL exchange its debt for equity in a reorganized company. In May, the creditor engaged its own financial advisor, Joseph Radecki of Jeffries and Company.

Later that month, Werbalowsky presented a proposal to JNL under which the creditor would exchange its notes for a new 4 percent bond with a later maturity date. All other current creditors would receive equity in the reorganized company. This would make their interests subordinate to JNL after the bankruptcy. JNL felt the proposed rate was unduly low compared with the rate on the notes it currently held. Those had a rate of 12.5 percent, adjustable to 15 percent. Shortly afterward, JNL made a counterproposal under which it would provide postbankruptcy financing to Bucyrus. In return, JNL would exchange its current unsecured debt for secured obligations. By then, however, Bucyrus was convinced that the best course for the company was to have creditors exchange their debt for equity. Both Bucyrus's representatives and the credit committee regarded JNL's proposal as too unreasonable to serve as a starting point for negotiations.

Discussions with JNL thus reached an impasse by early June. Meetings between the creditor and the creditors' committee broke off for several months. Bucyrus and the committee were surprised that, from their perspective, Stark was so rigid. It was far more common for large creditors to wield influence through their membership on a creditors' committee.

Stark, however, seemed to be on a mission that made him unreceptive to the give-and-take of negotiations. One reason may have been antipathy toward Houlihan. The investment bank had performed some work for Marriott in the spin-off of that company's subsidiary that Stark had so vehemently opposed. In addition, Houlihan had recently succeeded in guiding a prepackaged plan through bankruptcy court in Milwaukee, which Stark had done his best to thwart. More generally, Stark may have believed that Goldman and Salovaara had used their access to Bucyrus over the years to advantage themselves at the expense of other creditors. Whatever the reason, Bucyrus representatives found it extremely difficult to make headway in discussions with JNL.

On June 16, Bucyrus and four of its current and past directors entered into a tolling agreement with JNL. This suspended the statute of limitations on JNL's claims. In return, JNL agreed for the time being not to name the company or the individuals as defendants in its lawsuit. On June 23, JNL filed a complaint in federal district court in Manhattan. It alleged that Goldman and Broad Street had committed fraud in the 1990 sale of notes to JNL. It also maintained that they had engineered fraudulent conveyances in connection with the LBO, the exchange offer, and, in concert with defendant South Street, the sale-leaseback. After filing the lawsuit, JNL proposed its own plan under which its claims in the lawsuit it had filed would be put into a "litigation trust" and adjudicated outside of bankruptcy. Neither Bucyrus nor the creditors' committee agreed to this proposal.

With no agreement with JNL in sight, Bucyrus officials, company advisors, and the committee shifted their efforts to reaching a consensus about how equity in the reorganized company should be allocated among other debtholders. The hope was to reach an agreement between the company and the committee that could be presented to JNL or, if necessary, submitted to a court for approval over JNL's objection. As summer turned into fall, the sense of urgency mounted. The first possible deadline for preserving the $100 million in potential tax benefits was approaching: that Bucyrus file for bankruptcy by the end of the year. If it missed this deadline, the company could obtain the benefits only if it both filed for bankruptcy and got its plan confirmed by the court by the end of 1994.

In September, the company signed an agreement in principle with the creditors' committee concerning the distribution of stock in the company after bankruptcy. Werbalowsky notified JNL of this development in September, and then resumed negotiations with South Street. He tried to convince Salovaara to reduce the fund's claims under a restructuring plan, emphasizing that a successful reorganization was the best way for South Street to get paid. Bucyrus and South Street eventually reached a tentative agreement regarding the treatment of the latter's claims against the company in bankruptcy. The creditors' committee, however, believed that it could obtain more favorable terms from the secured creditor. The committee itself then undertook negotiations with South Street in October and November. On December 8, Bucyrus and South Street reached an agreement that reflected a few additional concessions by the secured creditor.

Under the agreement, Bucyrus was still obligated to make good South Street's claim for principal and interest from the 1992 financing, either through a cash payment or the issuance of debt by the reorganized company. The secured creditor did, however, agree to a reduction in its accumulated interest claims against Bucyrus. The total value of these concessions was between $1 million and $1.8 million (depending on the interest that had accumulated by the effective date of the agreement). In return, Bucyrus released South Street from any claims that the company might have against it. South Street particularly desired that the Chapter 11 reorganization be effected quickly. The agreement contained certain incentives for the company to conclude bankruptcy proceedings as soon as possible.

Other pieces of the puzzle then began to fall into place. In addition to the creditors' committee, JNL, and South Street, the other key claimant in negotiations was Goldman Sachs, a major shareholder in the holding company and a bondholder in the operating company. As did many large New York firms, Milbank represented Goldman in various matters unrelated to the bankruptcy. This was due primarily to Lederman's presence at the firm. Goldman, however, had waived any objection to Milbank's representation of Bucyrus in the bankruptcy.

One of Goldman's principal concerns was that it obtain a release from any potential claims that Bucyrus might bring against it in connection with the financings in which Goldman had participated. In mid-1993, Gellene had calculated that if the statute of limitations had not run, and if the company successfully pursued a claim against Goldman, the recovery would be in the neighborhood of $3–6 million. Goldman, however, was adamant from the outset that it would not accept any prepackaged plan that didn't contain releases. In return for this, it was willing to limit its recovery in bankruptcy to the terms set forth in the company's proposed plan. Gellene knew that there was "bad blood" between Goldman and JNL. He anticipated that releases for Goldman and South Street were likely to be a "sore point" with Stark. That was a risk worth taking, he believed, in order to present a plan to the court before the clock ran out.

As the company began narrowing differences among and reaching tentative agreement with its creditors, Gellene and others started to circulate drafts of a plan among creditors other than JNL. The plan afforded all unsecured creditors a percentage of equity in the reorganized company in exchange for their existing Bucyrus debt. Since the bankruptcy plan involved the issuance of new stock, Bucyrus had to file a Form S-4 with the Securities and Exchange Commission. This was accompanied by a disclosure statement and proxy statement-prospectus soliciting each creditor and shareholder's vote for acceptance of the plan.

The company and the unsecured creditors' committee had no hope that JNL would go along with the terms contained in the draft documents. Indeed, they anticipated that a cram-down of JNL probably would be necessary. Their hope was that they could send the draft documents out, gain informal approval from the creditors, and then formally solicit agreement to the plan when the SEC approved a final version of the material. Their fear, however, was that JNL would get wind of the plan and attempt to block solicitation of its acceptance—and that JNL would push for Bucyrus to file for bankruptcy immediately without any plan in place. The company therefore didn't plan to send the draft documents to Stark.

Events, however, took an unexpected turn. In preparation for sending the documents around, Bucyrus sent draft copies to the printer, R. R. Donnelly, in early September. Upon completion of its work, the printer was then to circulate the documents to the parties on the distribution list. The original list contained the names of various individuals affiliated with or representing JNL. Someone had drawn a vertical black line through these names, intending to indicate that they should be stricken from the list of those to receive the material. Unfortunately for Bucyrus, there was some confusion at the printer about this notation. As a result, the documents were sent to JNL along with all the other parties.

From the perspective of Bucyrus and the other creditors, this was the worst possible outcome. JNL was outraged. On September 10, it gave its forty-five-day notice that it was terminating the tolling agreement with the company and individuals. Stark sent a letter to Mork on

September 21 on behalf of PPM America, JNL's parent corporation. The letter said that PPM was "surprised to receive the draft Form S-4 without prior indication from you that it was forthcoming." It went on to say that Stark had given Bucyrus officials several opportunities to mention the Form S-4 in conversations, and that PPM was "extremely disappointed with your lack of candor." Stark reiterated that the creditor would not consent to the plan, or to any plan that provided equity to JNL on a pro rata basis with creditors who held bonds connected with the LBO. Stark vowed to resist any attempt to cram down the plan over JNL's objection.

On October 16, JNL issued a press release describing its own plan for restructuring the company. The proposal was similar to the one that JNL had suggested earlier. On October 20, JNL instructed the trustee for its 1990 notes to send an acceleration notice to Bucyrus declaring the notes to be immediately due and payable. On October 27, it amended its complaint in federal court in New York to add the company, its board members, and other bondholders as defendants.

Stark also complained to John Jerome and Frank Logan in the bankruptcy practice at Milbank in late September about Gellene's handling of the reorganization. He expressed particular concern about the proposed releases for Goldman and South Street contained in the plan. Stark was not satisfied with Milbank's response. He eventually concluded that JNL and the firm were "at odds," and terminated Milbank as JNL counsel in the Phar-Mor matter.

Once JNL had named them as defendants in the lawsuit, the other bondholders were extremely reluctant to negotiate with it. Werbalowsky made a final attempt to arrange a meeting with them and JNL. The parties were scheduled to meet on November 4 in New York at the law offices of Weil, Gotshal. The parties have conflicting accounts, however, of the circumstances of that meeting.

Melissa D'Arcambal of JNL arrived at the meeting about an hour late. She made clear, however, that she would defer any discussion of JNL's position until John Stark arrived. Stark finally made it up to Weil, Gotshal about two hours after the meeting began. The participants in the meeting had already begun to leave. They passed Stark at the elevator on their way out. Stark was then confronted with what he described as an "angry mob of people" who complained that they had been waiting for him a long time. They told him that they could not accept JNL's proposal and then left. JNL later contended that Bucyrus knew that JNL financial advisor Radecki would be on his honeymoon on that day, and that Stark had a prior commitment to appear in bankruptcy court and could not appear at the meeting until late in the day. Whatever the circumstances, the aborted meeting ended any chance of forging an agreement between JNL and the other parties.

When the company and the creditors' committee rejected its plan, JNL pushed Bucyrus to file for bankruptcy immediately, saying that it would hold the company responsible for losing valuable tax benefits if it failed to do so. JNL filed a state court action against Bucyrus to collect on its reset note. A judgment against the company would have the effect of putting the company immediately into bankruptcy. JNL also sought to pressure the company to file voluntarily for Chapter 11. Stark's December 20 letter to Mork said, "[W]e demand that the Company file a voluntary petition for relief pursuant to Chapter 11 prior to December 31 of this year." If the failure to do so cost the company its potential tax savings, the letter stated, "JNL will hold all appropriate parties responsible, including officers and directors."

Bucyrus, however, was concerned that an uncontrolled, or "free fall," bankruptcy would pose a risk to the company by dragging on too long. Bucyrus would have no priority in proposing the terms of a plan. Any party could put forth its own plan for review by the court. Given the widening gulf between JNL and the other creditors, it was likely that a court would have to contend with at least two competing, and radically different, plans. It was unclear how much credibility a judge might assign to each side if JNL's plan were on the table. The result might be fatal delay, as well as the confirmation of a plan that could doom the company's prospects of survival.

As Gellene and Werbalowsky saw it, Bucyrus now had three options: file for bankruptcy without a plan; accept the JNL proposed plan; or attempt to obtain confirmation of a plan with a "cram-down" of JNL along the lines of what Bucyrus and the creditors' committee had agreed to. A free-fall bankruptcy was too risky, and no other creditor would accept JNL's position that its claims should receive priority. Bucyrus therefore decided to proceed with the proposal set forth in the creditors' committee plan, and to seek confirmation of it over the objection of JNL. As Werbalowsky later put it, the inability of the committee and JNL to reach agreement threatened "a destruction of the business through a piecemeal sale of liquidation." Proceeding with a bankruptcy petition on a cram-down basis seemed to be the only way to avoid this result.

At the same time, this course of action was a high-stakes gamble. Prepackaged bankruptcies receive expedited treatment in court because they typically reflect agreement of all parties on the terms of a plan. That obviously was not the case here. Furthermore, a judge might be especially skeptical of any effort to cram down a plan on the company's largest creditor. Bucyrus would have to convince a court unfamiliar with the parties that JNL was so unreasonable that its objection should be ignored. JNL had already made clear, however, that it was prepared to spare no expense in pursuing its interest.

THE BUCYRUS PLAN created primarily by Werbalowsky actually consisted of two separate plans, one for the holding company and one for the operating company. The plan eliminated operating company shareholder interests. Operating company creditors received stock in exchange for their debt. JNL was placed in one operating company creditor class, while the other bondholders were placed in another. Acceptance of the plan by the non-JNL class of creditors would be sufficient to cram down the operating company plan on JNL, subject to court confirmation. With respect to the holding company, both shareholders and creditors received equity under the holding company plan. The two companies then would merge, with the shareholders of each receiving a pro rata share of newly issued stock in the new combined company, Bucyrus International.

This two-step process made it possible for existing shareholders in the holding company to receive equity in the new company. This was of particular concern because many of these shareholders were

Bucyrus managers and employees. Goldman, however, also was a shareholder that would receive equity in the new company—which surely would be unacceptable to JNL. Under bankruptcy law, the objection of any creditor class not receiving the full value of its claims can prevent existing shareholders of the debtor from receiving anything in a reorganization. If the holding and operating companies were treated as a single entity in the plan, JNL thus would be able to prevent holding company shareholders from obtaining anything.

With a separate plan for the holding and operating companies, however, only the consent of the *holding company* creditors was necessary for shareholders to receive equity. Since JNL was a creditor of the operating company, it had no say in the matter. With holding company creditors' consent, existing B-E Holdings shareholders would first receive equity in that company. When the holding and operating companies were combined in the second step, these shareholders, along with JNL and all other creditors, would receive a pro rata share of equity in the new company. JNL would be powerless at that point to prevent this resolution. Nonetheless, JNL would be the largest single shareholder, with just under 40 percent of the equity in the new company.

The disclosure statement noted that the operating company had a claim against B-E Holdings for a little over $26 million, primarily reflecting funds that the operating company had advanced to the holding company to meet interest payments on the latter's debt. That figure had been discounted by 75 percent in the plan. According to the disclosure statement, "The enforceability of the Intercompany Claim is subject to dispute and/or offset by reason of the less than arms' length relationship between Bucyrus and Holdings." The plan provided for a settlement of the claim and an allocation of its value among operating company creditors. The plan's treatment of the intercompany claim eventually would be one basis for JNL's opposition to Bucyrus in the bankruptcy proceedings.

The operating company's obligations to South Street on its secured notes and under the sale-leaseback arrangement would remain in place. South Street made concessions, however, in the form of reduced interest accumulation and a discount for timely cash repayment. Finally, the claims of all other unsecured interested parties, such as vendors and suppliers, would be paid in full. The disclosure statement indicated that Bucyrus and the creditors' committee had considered JNL's proposed allocation of value among the claimants. It stated that they had rejected it because it disproportionately favored JNL at the expense of other creditors.

The plan provided releases for Goldman, Goldman's Broad Street Fund, South Street, and Salovaara from any claims that Bucyrus might have against them. The claims that JNL was pursuing against these entities, with the exception of those dealing with the $60 million sale of notes to JNL, would become the property of Bucyrus by operation of law once the bankruptcy petition was filed. The company therefore had the authority to surrender them in the plan.

The disclosure statement explained the company's decision to grant releases to the parties named in the JNL complaint. Bucyrus, it stated, did not believe that the transactions at issue "constituted in whole or in part a recoverable fraudulent conveyance under applicable statutes or otherwise gave rise to other substantive claims." Furthermore, it declared, many of the issues that would need to be decided if the claims were litigated involve "novel or unresolved issues of law that could take several years to resolve conclusively." In addition, the facts that would need to be established would be contested by the company and others and "would require extensive, costly, and time-consuming discovery." As a result, pursuit of these claims "would prevent a prompt, efficient, and economic reorganization" of Bucyrus.

This was the only major issue on which Werbalowsky and Gellene disagreed. Werbalowsky had argued that the company should not furnish releases without receiving some consideration from all the potential beneficiaries of a release. He believed that Salovaara was entitled to a release because he had made concessions that reduced the recovery that he would receive in the reorganization. Goldman, however, had made no such concessions. It would be receiving equity in the reorganized company as a result of the two-step plan, and so was unlikely to withhold its agreement to the plan if it received no release. Werbalowsky had no reason to believe that the company had any colorable claim against Goldman. Given the central role of the investment bank in the Bucyrus transactions that JNL was challenging, however, furnishing Goldman a release was likely to be a red flag. It would give Stark more ammunition to use against the company. Thus, in return for the releases, Bucyrus might insist that Goldman waive its right to request Bucyrus indemnify it for the costs of defending itself against any claims based on transactions that Goldman had handled for the company.

Gellene, however, argued in favor of providing the release for three reasons. First, he thought it was important to resolve all parties' claims in the Chapter II proceeding, so that the company and the creditors could start fresh. This was customary in corporate bankruptcies, he said. Second, as his earlier analysis had indicated, he didn't believe that the claims against these parties had any merit. Third, Gellene was more concerned than Werbalowsky about Goldman's reaction to the company's failure to give it a release. Goldman was a major shareholder in the holding company and held a number of debt instruments of Bucyrus-Erie. Gellene didn't want to risk antagonizing Goldman for fear that it might vote against the plan. Werbalowsky ultimately brought his argument to the Bucyrus board of directors. The board, however, backed Gellene's view that the plan should provide a release to Goldman.

The company submitted a draft of its material to the SEC in October. It hoped to receive comments from the agency and incorporate them in a submission that could be approved before the end of the year. The process of receiving comments and revising the material took more than one round, however. Eventually it became apparent that the company was unlikely to meet this schedule. In order to preserve the tax benefits potentially available, Bucyrus therefore would be required to file and receive confirmation of its reorganization plan by the end of 1994.

As the company moved ahead with the process of gaining approval from the SEC, the JNL lawsuit in New York also required attention. Milbank litigation partner Toni Lichstein began representation of Bucyrus in the JNL lawsuit when JNL filed its discovery request. JNL, however, claimed that Milbank could not represent Bucyrus in this case because in another case the firm represented a creditors' committee of which JNL was a member. JNL alleged that this created the possibility that Milbank might gain confidential JNL information that could be used to the disadvantage of the company in the firm's defense of Bucyrus against JNL's claims. As a result, another law firm took over the case. Eventually, the JNL litigation was stayed while the bankruptcy was pending.

In October, Milbank provided Bucyrus with an opinion that the company's directors had acted in good faith in the transactions at issue in the JNL suit. This made the directors eligible for indemnification of their legal fees by Bucyrus. Gellene had prepared the opinion, and Lederman had approved it in accordance with Milbank procedures. The opinion was signed on behalf of the firm as a whole.

AS THESE EVENTS were unfolding, Milbank's compensation committee met with Gellene near the end of 1993 for its annual review. His tardy submission of billing daynotes continued to be a source of frustration. Bob O'Hara indicated that Gellene submitted his records only about once a month. At one point, O'Hara reported, "[H]e was retroactively putting in incomplete daynotes; we caught him on it and he has corrected the problem." Billing figures show that Gellene billed an extraordinary 3,129 hours to clients during 1993, and spent a total of 3,361 hours on matters on behalf of the firm. The latter figure translates into nine hours every day of the year.

Gellene reported to the committee that he had spent much of his time on the Maxwell bankruptcy, which had been occupying him when Lederman asked him to work on the Bucyrus-Erie restructuring, and that the approval of the international bankruptcy plan had received considerable favorable attention. The bankruptcy practice had become more "debtor-oriented." The current challenge for the firm was how this practice focus could be expanded, by, for instance, "down-marketing our skills as we did in Bucyrus-Erie." He still, however, expressed considerable fear of a slowdown in business: "The challenge of the post-Maxwell era beginning in mid-1994 will be to find adequate new work." Keeping a flow of work coming from debtors is difficult, Gellene observed, because bankruptcy affords fewer chances than other kinds of work for the development of ongoing relationships. Furthermore, he noted, bankruptcy practice tends to offer only limited opportunities for premium billing. This makes it crucial to ensure that work is divided to maximize leverage—that is, reliance on associates who do not have a direct claim on the firm's profits.

Compensation decisions, said Gellene, should take into account these difficulties in ensuring an adequate ongoing stream of bankruptcy work. "Decisions should not be based on unfavorable market developments or the loss of client opportunities but on whether the partner is responding appropriately to those developments." He continued to express concern that reactions to the firm's greater reliance on ostensible productivity criteria was creating "internal turmoil" that would retard Milbank in addressing its challenges. This suggests some anxiety about his place in the new revenue-driven Milbank.

The committee reported that Lederman was effusive in his praise for Gellene. The M&A partner described Gellene's work as "marvelous" and "brilliant[ ]." Lederman noted that Gellene "is managing the Bucyrus-Erie matter, which is highly contested—we have billed over $1 million, and they will not do anything without talking to Gellene; he is an absolutely brilliant strategist." Gellene, said Lederman, "works like a dog and needs to be well paid." Other partners complimented his work, describing him as one of the best lawyers in the firm. One partner, although remarking that Gellene did outstanding work, suggested that Gellene "should civilize himself more." The image that emerges at this time is of someone intense and single-minded, with some concern about the long-term future of his practice and compensation, who has little time for either social interaction or compliance with the firm's administrative demands. The forces contributing to this sense of pressure and isolation were only to intensify in Milwaukee.

ON JANUARY 12, 1994, the SEC gave final approval of the registration statement for new stock that Bucyrus planned to issue as part of the reorganization. On January 14, the company sent ballots to all the claimants soliciting their approval of the plan. As the balloting proceeded, Bucyrus and South Street were continuing to negotiate the terms on which South Street would provide financing to Bucyrus during the bankruptcy known as debtor-in-possession (DIP) financing. Such financing could give JNL higher priority in Chapter 11 than it currently enjoyed.[5] JNL had discussed the possibility of providing such financing to the company, and submitted its proposal to do so on February 4 in the hope of forestalling the plan. The terms of the financing, however, preserved possible claims against the parties whom JNL had sued in its lawsuit in New York. They thus were unacceptable to Bucyrus.

By the second week in February, all creditors except JNL had cast their votes in favor of the prepackaged plan. The company originally intended to file the bankruptcy petition about a week after receiving the last ballots. When the company announced the results of the balloting, however, it was inundated with calls from customers, vendors, and other interested parties inquiring what was going to happen to Bucyrus. JNL also was continuing to pressure the company to file its Chapter 11 petition.

As a result, company officials decided to compress the period before filing from a week to three days. Gellene had four or five people working almost around the clock to complete the necessary documents, put them on computer disks, and finish the paperwork at the company. Most of those working on the project were up almost two days straight immediately before the petition was filed. It was, as one participant described it, "a circus," with people running around, papers flying, and a large group of lawyers, legal assistants, and financial advisors turning the Bucyrus board room into command central. The stress on everyone was palpable.

Simultaneously with the bankruptcy, Milbank had to file an application with the court for appointment as Bucyrus's counsel in the proceedings. This application comprised only a minuscule portion of the mountain of papers that would accompany the Bucyrus Chapter II petition. Eventually, however, it would come back to haunt both Milbank and Gellene.

CHAPTER FIVE

A New Battlefield

ON FEBRUARY 18, 1994, Bucyrus-Erie and B-E Holdings filed for Chapter II bankruptcy in federal bankruptcy court in Milwaukee. JNL and Bucyrus each had contacted Assistant U.S. Trustee John Byrnes some four to six weeks before the petition was filed to begin pleading their cases. While not unprecedented, such advance contact was unusual, and underscored the ongoing antagonism between the parties. Byrnes was an outspoken trustee who was not averse to expressing himself forcefully when he deemed it necessary. He had spent much of his childhood in Washington, D.C., where his father served as a congressman from the Milwaukee area. Byrnes had returned to Wisconsin for college and law school. Before assuming his position with the trustee's office, Byrnes had been the United States attorney for the Eastern District of Wisconsin, which included Milwaukee, during the Reagan administration.

JNL expressed to Byrnes its strong disagreement with the proposed plan as it was taking shape, and provided Byrnes a copy of the complaint it had filed in New York attacking the LBO and the financing transactions involving Goldman, South Street, and Bucyrus. JNL also raised its concern about any releases that might be included as part of the plan. For their part, lawyers for Bucyrus cautioned Byrnes about accepting JNL's version of events at face value, and set forth the general outlines of the bankruptcy plan. They informed Byrnes that all creditors except for JNL had agreed to the plan.

On the afternoon that the companies filed for bankruptcy, bankruptcy judge Russell Eisenberg held the customary "first day hearing" in his courtroom at 3:30. The purpose of the hearing was to give the judge an opportunity to become familiar with the parties and the issues in the case. Relying on the information presented at this session, the judge would set a schedule for hearings on the various questions that he would have to resolve. In his midfifties, Judge Eisenberg had practiced bankruptcy law in Milwaukee for several years in a law firm in which Albert Solochek, whom Bucyrus had hired as local bankruptcy counsel, also was a partner.

The holding and operating companies had filed a large stack of documents, which neither the judge nor many of the other parties had had an opportunity to review in detail. John Gellene took the lead for the debtors in their presentation to the court. "You're filing this as a prepack?" Judge Eisenberg asked him, referring to a prepackaged bankruptcy. "Yes, Your Honor," replied Gellene. "And you have the consent of the major players in the case?" the judge asked. "We didn't receive acceptance from one class of creditors," said Gellene. That class contains only one member, he explained: Jackson National Life. Eisenberg inquired how much Bucyrus owed JNL. "Including accrued interest," responded Gellene, "[s]eventy million dollars." This made it the largest single creditor in the proceeding, with more than a third of the companies' combined $194 million debt.

Bruce Arnold then spoke up. Arnold was local counsel for JNL from the law firm of Whyte, Hirschboeck. He notified the judge that earlier in the day JNL had filed a motion to terminate Bucyrus's exclusive right to propose a reorganization plan. JNL wanted the court to suspend consideration of Bucyrus's plan on the ground that it could not be confirmed. JNL also moved for authority to present its own plan. Arnold told Eisenberg that JNL also had filed a motion alleging that the debtors had not prepared an adequate disclosure statement to creditors when it solicited their approval of the plan. This defect, JNL contended, had prevented creditors from making an informed decision whether to accept the plan. "I can tell by the tone of your voice that you're a little excited by this hearing," remarked Judge Eisenberg.

"Not as much about the hearing," said Arnold, "but because of the treatment. We are by far and away the largest creditor of these estates, Your Honor."

Before Gellene's summary of the events leading up to the petition, the judge asked if there were any other major parties in the case who were not present. "Yes, Your Honor," replied Gellene, "the major secured lenders, the South Street Funds." Gellene explained that the funds were three limited investment partnerships. They were represented, he said, by the law firm of Fried, Frank. South Street's claim at the time of the petition, including accrued interest, was about $46 million. Gellene's response indicated that he clearly was aware that South Street was a major player in the bankruptcy proceeding. Indeed, given the strenuous negotiations leading up to the filing, he hardly could have believed otherwise. He therefore knew that any ties that Milbank had with South Street would prompt close scrutiny by the court and other parties in the case.

Eisenberg then asked Gellene for a short description of the background of the case. Gellene recounted how the company had decided to suspend interest payments on its debt, and to encourage creditors to form an informal committee to negotiate the terms of a reorganization. JNL, said Gellene, was invited to join the committee but declined to do so. "The gist of what I'm hearing," interjected Eisenberg, "is that Bucyrus tried to put together a consensual out-of-court restructuring of the company's debt, but JNL was not agreeable to it. You ended up in Chapter II. . . . And what is preventing a clean prepack is Jackson National Life. So the thrust of the case is going to be for you to try to do whatever you can do with Jackson National Life and Jackson National Life to do whatever it can to the debtor."

That's 95 percent of what the case is about, replied Gellene. We have a prepackaged plan that all other creditors have accepted, which satisfies the requirements of the Bankruptcy Code. "But," said Eisenberg, "we have a 70 million dollar creditor here that you can't just blow off. That's a substantial amount of debt." True, replied Gellene. We tried to get JNL involved in negotiations over how that debt would be treated in the reorganization. Unfortunately, JNL wouldn't cooperate. Ultimately, he said, the company decided to treat JNL comparably to other unsecured debt by granting it a proportionate share of equity in the reorganized company.

Eisenberg thanked Gellene for his overview of the case, and then turned to Arnold. "Mr. Arnold," he asked, "what is it that makes your client so hostile as to what's going on?" "In a word," Arnold replied, "it's the conflict of interest." Milbank represents both the holding company and the operating company, he explained, which prevents the development of a plan that treats their respective creditors fairly. But, pressed Eisenberg, "a conflict of interest doesn't make business people angry. There has to be a reason why they are angry. Why are they angry?" "Jackson National Life was defrauded," said Arnold. It was misled by Goldman Sachs into purchasing $60 million in reset notes in 1990. Goldman, he informed the judge, is a defendant in a case filed by JNL that is currently pending in federal court in New York. The reorganization plan, however, "calls for the complete settlement and discharge of all of the claims of fraudulent transfers and violations of corporate trust with absolutely no consideration."

"All right," said Eisenberg. "Both sides share the goal of wanting the company to continue in business. With that in mind, let's turn to the motions dealing with the company's operations that we can address today." From that point until the hearing ended shortly after 7:30 P.M., the parties focused on these administrative matters. Each side, however, had already expressed the mutual animosity that would characterize the proceedings.

AT A HEARING a week later, Judge Eisenberg expressed his concern about the hostility between the parties. Toward the end of the morning's proceedings, the judge bluntly asked the parties:

[A]re the debtor and Jackson National Life so far apart that you think that an accommodation just isn't possible? In other words, what I am saying is it too early for me to orient my thinking to the—as I prepare this case so it's easier to start thinking about a consensual plan? . . . If it's clear that this is going to be a fight to the finish, I want the record as easy to follow as is possible for a District Judge.

Gellene responded that the debtor had acted in the preceding year "as a caretaker for the value of this company for the benefit of all of its creditors." Eisenberg acknowledged this, but advised that "you may not reach an agreement with Jackson National Life, unless the debtor divorces itself from Goldman Sachs and whoever else may be involved in the New York litigation." He suggested that "it would be easier for you to try to protect a limited number of people than a large number of people in the plan." That is, perhaps Bucyrus should rethink the unqualified releases contained in the plan if that was a major obstacle to obtaining JNL's agreement.

Eisenberg continued, "The point is to help me orient my thinking as to where this case is headed. If you think it's hopeless, let me know." Andy Rahl, a partner at Anderson, Kill representing JNL, replied, "Your Honor, we have not had a single substantive discussion with the debtor since I would guess June, July, or August." He continued:

This is the first time we have had any meaningful dialogue with the debtor at all in quite some time. It had been our view for several months it would have been desirable for the debtor to file Chapter 11 a lot sooner than this because it would have permitted dialogue in the context of court proceedings like this. The debtor elected to go along in a different course, and essentially shut us out of the process.

We were completely in the dark as to what the debtor was doing. We weren't even aware of the contents of the registration statement until the day that it was mailed to creditors.

The judge expressed his concern about what might happen to the company if the parties could not come to some agreement. If the plan is not consensual, he said, there likely would be an appeal to the district court and then to the Seventh Circuit Court of Appeals. That process could take three or four years. Such prolonged uncertainty could be fatal to the company. This is the reality that each side must

take into account, he said, which underscores the need for cooperation.

On March 4, Trustee John Byrnes appointed the official committee to
negotiate on behalf of the unsecured creditors. The committee consisted
of three members of the prepetition committee—Franklin Funds,
Cowen & Company, and Eaton Vance Management—along with JNL,
Bucyrus supplier Siemens, and Bell Helicopter, which had been involved
in prepetition litigation against Bucyrus in a products liability suit.

Brian Rosen of Weil, Gotshal had represented the group of unsecured creditors that had taken the lead in the negotiations leading up
to the Chapter 11 petition. JNL, however, had made noises that Weil
should not represent the official committee because it represented parties in other bankruptcies who also were Bucyrus creditors. After
Bucyrus filed its petition, the official committee selected William
Rochelle of Fulbright Jaworski as its lead counsel. Rochelle and David
Rosenzweig of that firm assumed the responsibility of advising the
committee during the bankruptcy proceeding. They were instructed
by a majority vote of the committee on what position to take on the
various issues that came before the court.

The presence of JNL on the committee, of course, made it far less
uniform than it had been prior to the petition. Bucyrus could no longer
count on the support it had received when the company and the other
unsecured creditors had been aligned against JNL. In addition,
Rochelle and Rosenzweig came on board without any familiarity with
the parties. This created an opportunity for JNL to make a fresh pitch
for its position. As the case went forward, Rochelle on occasion irri-
tated Bucyrus by offering advice to the committee on certain issues
that reflected JNL's viewpoint. Eventually, the Fulbright lawyers even
came to doubt that the plan could be confirmed in the form that
Bucyrus had submitted to the court.

As the Chapter 11 case proceeded, the first battle was over Milbank
Tweed's application to represent the debtors in bankruptcy. The second, even fiercer, struggle was over the adequacy of the disclosure
statement that Bucyrus had submitted in soliciting creditors' agreement to the plan. In both instances, JNL took the lead in opposition.

First, JNL contended that Milbank could not represent the debtors because the law firm had a potential conflict of interest. Second, JNL contended that disclosure to the creditors had been insufficient to permit them to make an informed decision about whether to accept the prepackaged plan. Judge Eisenberg recognized that JNL had seized upon these issues as vehicles for derailing the bankruptcy plan to which it so vehemently objected. At the same time, he acknowledged that the creditor's self-interest did not necessarily render its opposition groundless. Indeed, to Bucyrus's dismay, the court ultimately found merit in both JNL claims.

THE REQUIREMENT that the court approve the debtor's choice of counsel for the reorganization proceedings is rooted in the desire to preserve public confidence in the bankruptcy system. Once the bankruptcy petition was filed, Bucyrus was no longer authorized to engage in conduct solely in the interest of the company. It became a debtor-in-possession (DIP), and was required to act as a fiduciary to the estate. There is not complete consensus on the precise contours of this duty, but it definitely requires attention to the interests of creditors, probably shareholders,[1] and possibly other parties in interest such as employees.[2] As a result, DIP counsel must advise its client to take account of all the claimants whose interests will be affected by the reorganization plan.[3] Bucyrus therefore was not the only party with an interest in whom the court would appoint to represent it in the bankruptcy case.

The bankruptcy process affects thousands of parties. Most unsecured creditors are unlikely to recover the full amount that the company owes them, and so fight among each other for the largest possible share of a finite pool of resources. They also may challenge the validity of claims by creditors who purport to be secured. Existing shareholders typically receive no payments unless all creditors are paid in full, and will have the value of their shares diluted if the company decides to use equity to pay all or some of its debts to creditors.

Furthermore, bankruptcy law grants the debtor in possession and its counsel considerable power in mediating among these interests.

This power, combined with the fact that creditors sometimes may be unable to engage in close oversight of the reorganization process, creates opportunities for favoritism and self-interested conduct. Concern about such misconduct is long-standing. As Justice William O. Douglas once observed, "The history of fees in corporate reorganizations contains many sordid chapters."[4] Similarly, a more recent expert has stated that "perception that the bankruptcy system is especially prone to fraud and abuse is not new, nor is it ill-founded."[5]

Misconduct can take many forms. One is declining to investigate possible fraud by company officials. Another is supporting a reorganization plan that permits managers to continue in office but provides smaller payments to creditors. Counsel may favor one set of creditors over another, biased by professional and personal connections within the bankruptcy bar. Or it may milk the estate for large fees that deplete the size of the recovery available for creditors.[6]

The criteria that the court would consider in reviewing Gellene's application are set forth in Section 327 of the Bankruptcy Code.[7] Section 327(a) first provides that an applicant may "not hold or represent an interest adverse to the estate." An adverse interest is one that "would tend to lessen the value of the bankruptcy estate or that would create either an actual or a potential dispute in which the estate is a rival claimant."[8] Second, the applicant must be a "disinterested person." Section 101(14) of the code defines "disinterested" as someone who, among other things, is not a creditor of the DIP and who "does not have an interest materially adverse to the interest of the estate or of any class of creditors or equity security holders."

In order for the court to determine if Gellene met such criteria, Rule 2014 required that he file a declaration with the court describing, among other things, "all of [his and Milbank's] connections with the debtor, creditors, or any other party in interest." Significantly, Rule 2014 does not ask counsel to disclose *conflicts;* it asks for disclosure of all "connections." Not all connections necessarily raise concerns about conflicts. State bar ethical provisions generally provide that a connection constitutes a conflict if the representation of one client is "directly adverse" to that of another, or if the representation of a client "may be materially limited by the lawyer's responsibilities to" another party, including the lawyer herself. If the lawyer determines that such a conflict exists, she must disclose it to the client.

Thus, state ethics rules grant lawyers some discretion to determine when a connection rises to the level of a conflict that must be disclosed. By contrast, Rule 2014 provides the lawyer with no such discretion. She must disclose all connections, regardless of whether she thinks that they represent conflicts of interests. It is up to the judge, not the lawyer, to determine whether a connection raises conflict concerns that must be considered before approving the appointment application.

SECTION 327 and Rule 2014 were of more than academic interest to Milbank at the time that Gellene filed his appointment application. The firm had begun work in December 1993 on matters both for Salovaara and for South Street. The first was a dispute between Salovaara and Alfred Eckert, his partner in Greycliff, the entity that served as the manager for South Street Fund. Salovaara, Eckert, and Lederman had known one another professionally and socially for many years, dating back to Lederman's work for Goldman when the two financiers had been employed there. Indeed, Lederman and Salovaara took a bicycle trip together in March 1993, and the three men had shared Thanksgiving dinner together at Salovaara's house later that year.

Right after Thanksgiving, however, Salovaara and Eckert had a falling out over Eckert's plans to take a job with Primerica, a subsidiary of Travelers Insurance Co. Salovaara was concerned that Primerica would compete with South Street. He maintained that the Greycliff partnership agreement prevented Eckert from taking the job. He consulted Lederman about his claim that Eckert's actions would constitute a breach of the partnership agreement. Lederman in turn asked Milbank litigation partner Toni Lichstein to advise Salovaara on the matter. Salovaara threatened legal action against Eckert, and sent a letter to Travelers indicating that he would sue it as well if the company hired Eckert. There were several meetings in the first part of December involving Salovaara, Eckert, and their lawyers.

On December 10, Milbank prepared a new case memorandum for the representation of Salovaara in his dispute with Eckert. The memo listed Lederman as the client contact and client service partner, and Lichstein as the partner in charge of the case. It indicated that a computerized search for potential conflicts had been conducted. The search was for references to Eckert and to Primerica. It did not, however, examine whether Salovaara was potentially adverse to a Milbank client in any matter, such as the Bucyrus bankruptcy. The search turned up one estate planning matter for Eckert on which Milbank had worked in July 1992. Lichstein mentioned the matter to Lederman. Lederman told her that Eckert's attorney had told him that the prior estate work for Eckert posed no problem for Milbank's ability to represent Salovaara in the partnership dispute.

The second matter, in which the firm represented South Street, also arose in early December. Lederman called Gellene and told him that "Mikael ha[s] a deal for us." He told Gellene that Salovaara wanted to buy debt in Busse Broadcasting that was held by another party. Busse owned several television stations, and itself was owned by George Gillett, an entrepreneur who had filed for bankruptcy in Denver on August 13, 1992. Lederman asked Gellene to whom the work should be assigned: to someone in Lederman's mergers and acquisitions practice or to a bankruptcy lawyer supervised by Gellene? Gellene responded that Milbank could use a relatively junior bankruptcy lawyer because members of that practice group were familiar with this type of transaction. As a result, associate Cynthia Revesz was assigned to work with Gellene on the purchase.

Milbank's conflicts search surveyed whether Gillett or any of his businesses were involved in any matters in which Milbank provided representation. As with the conflicts check for the Salovaara dispute with Eckert, however, it did not examine whether Salovaara was potentially adverse to another Milbank client in any other matter. Despite the deficiencies of the conflicts check in each instance, both Gellene and Lederman were aware that Milbank was representing Bucyrus in a bankruptcy in which South Street was the main secured creditor.

Negotiations in the dispute between Salovaara and Eckert continued through December. On December 22, Lederman called Gellene
and told him that he and Lichstein were discussing "some problems"
that Salovaara was having. He asked if Gellene would come up to his
office and join the discussion. In retrospect, this would prove to be a
significant meeting. When Gellene arrived, Lederman informed him
that Salovaara regarded Eckert's plan to go to Travelers as a breach of
the partnership agreement. During the discussion, a phone call came
into Lederman's office from Salovaara. Lederman put him on the
speaker phone, let him know that Lichstein was also in Lederman's
office, and told him that they had just been discussing Salovaara's dispute with Eckert. For ten or fifteen minutes Lederman, Lichstein, and
Salovaara discussed the possibility of filing a lawsuit in New Jersey to
prevent Eckert from following through with his plans.

Near the end of that conversation, Salovaara told Lederman that he
also wanted to talk with him about the Busse purchase. Gellene had
twice earlier called Salovaara to speak with him about the matter, on
December 9 and 19, billing 0.10 and 0.40 hours respectively for the
conversations. Lederman told Salovaara that Gellene was in his office
and suggested that the two of them discuss Busse. Gellene picked up
the phone, which turned off the speaker phone, and spoke with Salovaara for a little over half an hour. At the conclusion of that conversation, Gellene, Lederman, and Lichstein resumed their discussion of
the dispute between Salovaara and Eckert.

As the meeting was winding down, Lederman asked Gellene what
was going on with the Bucyrus bankruptcy, since Gellene periodically
kept him informed of developments in that matter. Gellene told Lederman that they were still waiting on SEC approval of the solicitation
material. Lichstein then asked whether the firm had any potential
conflict of interest by virtue of the fact that it represented Bucyrus at
the same time that it was representing Salovaara, one of the company's major creditors. Gellene responded that he saw no conflict.
Bucyrus's and Salovaara's interests were aligned, he said, since the
investor had agreed to the terms of the prepackaged bankruptcy plan.
Lederman followed up by saying that the two matters were completely

unrelated. The entire discussion lasted about a minute and a half. The lawyers then resumed discussion of Salovaara's dispute with Eckert for about ten minutes, whereupon Lederman left for a lunch appointment. Gellene billed a total of 1.7 hours to work on the Salovaara-Eckert dispute on that day, which constituted the total amount of time that he billed on the case.

On December 30, Milbank prepared a new case memo stating, "We have been asked to advise Greycliff Partners with respect to investments which they manage in Busse Broadcasting Corporation." Lederman was listed as the client contact, the partner in charge, and the client service partner. The memo indicated that a conflict-of-interest search had been completed. That search was for any matter in which Busse, Gillett, or any of Gillett's holdings under various names were involved. It did not, however, inquire into whether South Greycliff or South Street was potentially adverse to a Milbank client in any matter, such as the Bucyrus bankruptcy.

Work on both the Salovaara-Eckert dispute and the Busse Broadcasting matter continued into 1994. Salovaara sued Eckert in New Jersey state court in early February for breach of their partnership agreement. The New Jersey law firm of Sills, Cummis was the counsel of record in the case. Lichstein, however, was in close contact with the firm as the case progressed. Lichstein also prepared Salovaara for his deposition on February 15, which she attended, and did background work for and attended Eckert's deposition on the following day. Shortly afterward, Lichstein had a conversation with Gellene about Salovaara's demeanor as a witness at his deposition.

Meanwhile, Revesz, with some assistance from Gellene, was preparing documents connected with a purchase agreement with the Fetzer Institute for the Busse note. The agreement was dated January 26. An exhibit to it indicated that Fetzer had filed its proof of claim on the note in the Gillett bankruptcy on October 25, 1993, for $19.9 million. The trustee in the bankruptcy had asserted that the claim might be contingent, which suggested that South Street might have to pursue its claim over the opposition of the trustee.

All this work on behalf of Salovaara and South Street created a potential conflict of interest for Milbank in representing Bucyrus in its bankruptcy. South Street was the major secured creditor of Bucyrus, and Salovaara acted on its behalf. Milbank would be required to give legal advice to the debtor that took into account the interests of all claimants on the estate. At the same time, however, it might have an incentive to encourage Bucyrus to favor South Street. The court surely would want at least to know of this connection in deciding whether to approve Milbank's appointment application. Disclosing it, however, might result in the firm's disqualification.

THE MORNING of the day in February that Gellene flew out to Milwaukee to finish preparation of the Bucyrus bankruptcy papers, he told Lederman that the company had pushed to get the filing done in three days rather than seven, but that "everybody's been staying up all night; we're going to get that done." Gellene also told Lederman that he wanted him to know about disclosure issues that could arise in connection with the firm's application to be appointed counsel for Bucyrus. He told Lederman that Milbank would be disclosing that it currently represented Goldman in unrelated matters. He said that the connection would not be a problem for a bankruptcy court in New York, but he didn't know how a court in Wisconsin would react.

Gellene also told Lederman, "I don't believe that we have to disclose that we represent Salovaara because he's not a creditor." Gellene testified that he had thought of Salovaara when preparing the declaration, but had told himself that "it's not related and he's not even a creditor." The latter conclusion apparently was based on the view that Salovaara individually was not someone to whom Bucyrus owed money. Gellene didn't share his reasoning on this issue with anyone else at the time, because "we were in the middle of this fire drill to get everything done, and everybody was off doing something else. There was so much work to be done that everybody had to work on one thing and not really look at what somebody else was doing."

At the time that Gellene filed Bucyrus's Chapter II petition and his own application for appointment as the company's bankruptcy counsel, Milbank had billed Salovaara for just under 28 hours for work on the acquisition of the Busse Broadcasting note (27.65). Those hours were logged primarily by Revesz. It also had billed Salovaara for just under 500 hours for work on his dispute with Eckert (498.4), mostly by Lichstein. Both these lawyers continued to remain active on these matters after the bankruptcy petition was filed. They continued as well to assist Gellene on the Bucyrus reorganization.

Milbank drafted, and Gellene and Goelzer signed, Bucyrus's request that Milbank be appointed to represent the holding and operating companies in bankruptcy. The request stated that the debtors had selected Milbank for two reasons. One was its extensive experience with large corporate reorganization and financial transactions. The other was that the firm had become familiar with the companies' affairs as a result of representing them in general corporate matters and in preparing the reorganization plan. The application went on to say that to the best of the companies' knowledge, "the members and associates of Milbank do not have any connection with the Debtors, their creditors, or any other party in interest," except as set forth in a declaration, or affidavit, signed by Gellene that accompanied the request.

Gellene's affidavit indicated that Milbank formerly and currently represented "certain equity security holders and institutional creditors of the debtors" in unrelated matters, and that it might do so in the future. "Equity security holders" is a term of art in the Bankruptcy Code. Milbank had used the term *institutional creditors* over the years when applying for retention as counsel to financial institutions in bankruptcy matters. One can imagine that this standard phrase was adopted in light of the firm's historically close relationship with Chase Manhattan Bank.

The affidavit stated that one former and current Milbank client was Goldman Sachs, "a holder of debt securities of Bucyrus [-Erie] and of equity securities of [B-E] Holdings." Aside from Milbank's prior work for JNL, Gellene declared that neither he nor anyone at Milbank was aware of any other connection with the Bucyrus companies, their creditors, "or any other party in interest." In sum, he said, there was nothing that compromised Milbank's status as a "disinterested person" under the Bankruptcy Code. The affidavit said nothing of Milbank's ongoing work for Salovaara in his dispute with Eckert, nor of Gellene's current status as lead counsel for South Street in the Busse matter.

Goelzer acknowledged that "in a perfect world" he would prefer that Milbank didn't represent Goldman in any matters. Given the size and scope of the investment house's activities, however, he regarded it as "almost impossible" to find a firm of Milbank's expertise and status that had not at some point represented Goldman or other large financial institutions. Furthermore, Goelzer assumed that a firm as sophisticated as Milbank would have a firewall in place. That arrangement would preclude individuals from working simultaneously on matters for the Bucyrus companies and Goldman, as well as prevent information relating to one client from reaching those working for the other. Given this, as well as the unrelated nature of the respective representations, he wasn't worried that Goldman would induce Milbank to favor it over Bucyrus in the bankruptcy.

Finally, Goelzer noted after the bankruptcy that removing Milbank from the case at that late date, given its familiarity with Bucyrus and the prepackaged plan, would have been "cataclysmic." Bringing another law firm up to speed on the bankruptcy would prolong uncertainty about the companies' future, and jeopardize the tax benefits available if the reorganization were completed by the end of 1994.

Four days after Milbank's request to represent the two Bucyrus companies, JNL filed an objection to the application. It contended first that Milbank represented interests adverse to one another because it sought to represent both the holding and operating companies. The operating company, asserted JNL, was effectively a creditor of the holding company. It had advanced the holding company several million dollars in order to fund the latter's interest and dividend payments. Furthermore, JNL maintained that the transactions that it alleged were fraudulent conveyances gave the operating company a cause of action against B-E Holdings. Finally, the prepackaged plan proposed to allocate $13 million to holding company creditors and shareholders, a figure that JNL alleged was far in excess of that company's value.

By representing the holding company, claimed JNL, Milbank thus would be seeking to pursue the interests of an entity with interests directly adverse to the Bucyrus estate. JNL made the same argument in contending that Houlihan, Lokey should not be appointed financial advisor to both the operating and holding companies.

JNL's second contention was that Milbank was not a "disinterested person" because the plan contained releases for all parties involved in the LBO, the exchange offer, and the South Street financing. JNL, of course, had challenged these transactions in its suit in federal court in New York. Milbank could not be expected to offer neutral advice about whether Bucyrus should sue Goldman in connection with these deals, since the firm represented Goldman in other matters. Furthermore, Milbank had worked on the LBO and on the sale-leaseback, and Milbank partner Larry Lederman had worked on the exchange offer while at Wachtell, Lipton. As a result, JNL argued, Milbank could not be disinterested in investigating and evaluating claims in connection with these deals. The benefits that Milbank would directly and indirectly receive under the releases in the plan created a conflict of interest that precluded it from serving as counsel for the debtors.

To some degree, JNL faced an uphill battle in arguing that Milbank should be disqualified because of its role in prior Bucyrus transactions. It has become more common in recent years for counsel who apply to represent the debtor in bankruptcy to have represented the company in matters before the debtor files for Chapter 11 protection. The familiarity that the lawyers bring to the case can expedite the proceeding, and courts therefore often are disposed to grant the appointment application. If any issues arise during the reorganization about any previous transaction in which counsel was involved, the creditors' committee generally can scrutinize and, if appropriate, challenge the deal.

This safeguard arguably was less likely to function in the Bucyrus case, however. JNL's contentions that the LBO and exchange offer were fraudulent called into question the validity of the claims held by most committee members. Those members therefore were unlikely to press for a searching examination of those transactions. Only with respect to the sale-leaseback might the committee be relatively impartial—although its members obviously would benefit if the court ruled that Bucyrus had no obligations arising out of that agreement.

On February 24, Judge Eisenberg held a hearing at which he considered Milbank's application. The judge cautioned JNL "to pick your fights carefully." He warned that he would take appropriate action "if it appears that what Jackson National Life is trying to do is just to stall the Court proceedings by filing an overwhelming number of motions." Eisenberg indicated that the law on conflicts of interest was "all over the map," and that he had "a general inclination not to remove lawyers from a case, particularly if [other parties] know about [potential conflicts]." He noted the special problems with disqualifying lawyers in Chapter 11 cases. Eisenberg also observed that the Seventh Circuit had suggested that a party who believed that a lawyer had a conflict of interest might pursue the matter through disciplinary channels, rather than attempting to remove the lawyer from the case.

Turning to the specific grounds for JNL's objection, the judge suggested that he might have little sympathy for either. First, with respect to dual representation of both the Bucyrus and the holding company, he said that "that happens all the time. And there are so many . . . cases that say that you could do that. And when you look at it from a practical perspective, I don't know why they would need different lawyers." With respect to Milbank's interest in obtaining a release, Eisenberg declared that "[g]iving a law firm a release is something that's really almost pro forma in so many cases. . . . And getting a release in the proposed plan in and of itself, to me, it is not sufficient reason—and I'll give JNL a clear message—that in and of itself is not sufficient reason to me to disqualify Milbank Tweed."

On March 2, Assistant U.S. Trustee John Byrnes also submitted an objection to Milbank's retention application. The objection stated that Gellene needed to provide more information about the firm's "representation of equity security holders and institutional creditors" that he had mentioned in his declaration. Byrnes was especially interested in further details about the relationship between Milbank and Goldman Sachs.

About three weeks later, at a March 17 hearing, Judge Eisenberg emphasized that whether Milbank had a conflict of interest "may be a very important side show," but that he didn't want it to "derail from what this case is about, and that's working down the path to get a plan confirmed." Even if there were reason to disqualify the firm, he observed, many judges were moving away from a standard of strict disinterest to one that weighed the likelihood that representation of other clients might influence a lawyer's judgment. As Eisenberg put it, these judges were essentially saying, "[I]t's okay if you're not disinterested, as long as you're not too [not] disinterested."

At a hearing on March 23, Eisenberg described the trustee's objections as relating to (1) avoiding duplication of services between Milbank and local counsel, and (2) possible conflict arising from the firm's "representation of equity security holders and institutional creditors." Andy Rahl indicated that JNL was willing to accept Milbank's retention, subject to Milbank's satisfactory response to the trustee's concerns. He noted that one subject in which his client was particularly interested was Milbank's representation of Goldman Sachs.

Gellene indicated that he would have no difficulty responding to Byrnes. The court gave him until March 28 to do so. Eisenberg preserved JNL's right to pose a new objection based on Milbank's response. Relying on the law in the Seventh Circuit, he suggested that Milbank might be able to represent Bucyrus creditors in other matters if it used a firewall. He asked that Gellene "state precisely" in his response what steps Milbank was taking to establish such an arrangement. Finally, Judge Eisenberg left Gellene with an admonition that may have indicated wariness about how bankruptcy lawyers from large New York firms tended to approach their ethical obligation to the bankruptcy court. "New York is different from Milwaukee," he warned Gellene. "[P]rofessional things like conflicts are taken very, very seriously. And for better or worse you're stuck in Wisconsin."

While appreciative of the judge's words, Gellene, on the basis of the hearing, believed that "we could just clean up our papers and that the retention issues would be behind us." He focused on the concerns

153

expressed by the trustee. Gellene recognized that the firm's connection with Goldman possibly could serve as the basis for disqualification. The judge had seemed to suggest, however, that an effective firewall might suffice. Gellene's sense was that Judge Eisenberg would be reluctant to require withdrawal based on the Goldman connection, given that Milbank had spent almost a year working with Bucyrus to prepare it for bankruptcy. He thus believed that ultimately there was little chance that Milbank would be disqualified on the basis of the objections on the table. Of course, none of those objections related to Salovaara and South Street, because Gellene had not brought these connections to anyone's attention.

Five days after the hearing, Gellene submitted a supplemental affidavit "to address the comments made by the United States Trustee in his objection" to Milbank's retention application. That objection, he said, "requested more detailed information regarding Milbank's past and current representation of equity security holders and institutional creditors." Gellene stated that Milbank in the past had represented in unrelated matters Cowen & Company, a member of the Bucyrus creditors' committee, and Mitsubishi International Corporation, a secured creditor of the company. Each representation had ended before Milbank began its work on the reorganization in February 1993.

Gellene's supplemental affidavit also listed five matters unrelated to Bucyrus in which Milbank currently was representing Goldman Sachs. Gellene indicated that the firm had established procedures to ensure that no firm lawyers working for Bucyrus worked for Goldman or vice versa. Lawyers working for one client would be precluded from access to information relating to the other. Noting the representations contained in the original February 18 affidavit, Gellene stated that "after due inquiry I am unaware of any other current representation by Milbank of an equity security holder or institutional creditor of the Debtors." In response to a request from the trustee, Gellene also disclosed in his second affidavit that his hourly billing rate was $415. Finally, he informed the court that Milbank would be representing Bucyrus while the Milwaukee firm of Howard, Solochek & Weber would be representing the holding company. This would avoid any potential conflict because of simultaneous representation of both companies by the same law firm.

Byrnes and Rahl were satisfied with Gellene's second affidavit. Judge Eisenberg therefore approved Milbank's retention application. That decision could not be appealed at the time. Both the trustee and JNL, however, still had the right to challenge it after the plan was confirmed, when Milbank eventually sought authorization from the court for compensation from Bucyrus. Furthermore, Gellene had an ongoing obligation during the bankruptcy proceeding to inform the court if the firm developed new ties with any claimant. In asserting that Milbank had no connections to any party in interest other than those listed in his affidavit, Gellene already had crossed a crucial divide. To put it bluntly, he had lied to the court.

AFTER GELLENE FILED his affidavit, Milbank continued its work for Salovaara in his dispute with Eckert and for South Street on the Busse matter. Lichstein continued to work on discovery in Salovaara's suit in New Jersey against Eckert, as well as on discovery in connection with the Bucyrus bankruptcy proceeding. As Bucyrus heated up, she met regularly with Goelzer to prepare company officials for depositions and to discuss document production. In the Salovaara case, Lichstein prepared for and attended a hearing in late February regarding Salovaara's request for a preliminary injunction against Eckert. She also was also involved in preparing the appeal from the denial of that motion.

In late March, at the request of Salovaara, Lichstein attended a meeting of South Street investors at the St. Regis Hotel in New York. Salovaara had asked Lichstein to come because he was afraid that the hostility surrounding the lawsuit against Eckert might spill over into the meeting. During the course of the meeting, there was some discussion of the fund's investment in Bucyrus. This made Lichstein uncomfortable in light of the intensified pace of the JNL suit against the company.

A week or two later, Lichstein again asked Gellene whether Milbank's representation of both Salovaara and Bucyrus was a potential conflict of interest. Gellene told her that Salovaara wasn't a creditor of Bucyrus, that the law firm had disclosed its connections with Goldman, and that Milbank had fully met all its disclosure obligations. Around this time, Lichstein belatedly learned of the firewall in place between lawyers working for Bucyrus and those representing Goldman. Gellene apologized for not having informed her earlier of this arrangement. There is no evidence that this lapse affected Milbank's representation of Bucyrus. Nonetheless, it suggests that firewalls intended to prevent conflicts are not always exactly airtight.

Right after talking to Gellene, Lichstein went to Lederman's office and reiterated her concern about a possible conflict. Lederman initially didn't share her view. Eventually, however, he told her to call the firm of Shereff, Friedman to arrange for someone there to represent Salovaara. As a result, Milbank's representation of Salovaara in the Eckert lawsuit began to wane. The last day on which Lichstein billed time to the case was April 22, a day after her time sheets reflect a conference with Lederman in his office. By then, Milbank had billed more than 478 hours on the matter. It billed only 12.5 scattered hours afterward, all but a quarter hour of which were by early June.

Ultimately, Milbank realized no fees from its representation of Salovaara in his dispute with Eckert. On December 23, 1994, Bob Reder, a Milbank lawyer who handled Lederman's billing, wrote a memo to Bob O'Hara, chair of the billings and collection committee. Reder indicated that, at O'Hara's request, he had asked Lederman whether any matters should be written off before the end of the year. Lederman instructed Reder to submit the bills for the Salovaara-Eckert dispute to O'Hara. Reder wrote, "Larry characterizes the results of this as a 'disaster' and does not believe that he can bill this individual for the significant time that was accrued." Attached to the memo was a form "Authorization for Write Off of Time Charges and/or Disbursements When Billing." This indicated that $291,564 in time from November 30, 1993, through June 10, 1994, was to be written off, as well as $32,922.30 in expenses.

The Busse matter in which Gellene represented South Street was less active during the time the Bucyrus bankruptcy plan was before the court. Lazard Frères, acting on behalf of South Street, had notified the bankruptcy court in Denver on April 9, 1994, that it had purchased from Fetzer a $19.9 million claim in the Gillett bankruptcy on January 26. The court sent notice to Fetzer on April 12 that its claim had been transferred. Gellene billed 5.9 hours on the case from the date of the Bucyrus bankruptcy filing to the end of 1994, none of which indicated any conversations with Salovaara.

A memo from Reder to O'Hara on November 8, 1994, said that the "Greycliffe/Busse" [sic] matter "was undertaken for Mikael Salovaara and billed prior to a conflict arising in connection with our representation of Bucyrus-Erie in bankruptcy. Accordingly, Larry Lederman has resigned this representation and has not asked for payment of this outstanding bill." The memo indicated that Lederman wished to write off the receivable of $15,752.81, reflecting 57.5 hours of attorney work through October 25, and $462.93 in expenses. There is no indication of the nature of the conflict that prompted the withdrawal of the firm. On July 6, 1995, however, billing for the Busse matter resumed and continued through May 7, 1997.

It's possible that Lederman concluded that Milbank should not be representing Salovaara in his purchase of the Busse note as long as the Bucyrus bankruptcy plan was still under consideration. Billing records indicate, however, that work was done at Milbank on the matter after October 24, 1994, until billing resumed in July 1995. The records don't indicate how many hours were spent, and each entry describing work is followed by the entry "Back Out" on the same day. This apparently ensured that Salovaara would not be billed for the work. During this period, Gellene had a phone conference with Lederman and Salovaara on December 16, 1994, and a phone conference with Salovaara, followed by a conference with Lederman about that phone call, on December 20. Both these events occurred after the Bucyrus bankruptcy plan was confirmed on December 2. Salovaara apparently wasn't billed for either. Reder never informed Gellene about the write-off or the reason for it; it's unclear whether Lederman ever did so.

At the time that John Gellene filed his affidavit with the court, Milbank thus was representing Salovaara in his dispute with Eckert, and

South Street in its claim on the Busse note. Before Bucyrus filed its Chapter II petition, Gellene had participated in a conference with Lederman and Lichstein about the first matter. He was the lead counsel on the second one. Milbank would cease most of its work on the Salovaara-Eckert dispute a couple of months after Bucyrus filed for bankruptcy. It would write off its fees and expenses for the Busse matter until after the court confirmed the Bucyrus bankruptcy plan. From the time that Bucyrus filed for Chapter II until its plan was confirmed, Gellene himself billed no time on the Salovaara-Eckert dispute and only 5.9 hours on the Busse claim.

Nonetheless, there could be no doubt that Milbank had "connections" with Salovaara and South Street that Gellene should have disclosed under Rule 2014. Had he made such a disclosure, Milbank almost certainly would have been disqualified from representing Bucyrus in the bankruptcy proceeding. Milbank's connection with Goldman Sachs didn't disqualify it because it would have been difficult to find a firm experienced in major Chapter II work that did no work for Goldman. By contrast, South Street was so small that it would have been relatively easy to find a firm with no ties to it. The court theoretically could have permitted Milbank to represent Bucyrus on matters other than those related to South Street, and appointed special counsel to handle South Street matters. The fund, however, was a key player in the bankruptcy negotiations. Not only was it the company's only secured creditor, its claim was in dispute. In the give-and-take of negotiations, it would be extremely difficult, if not impossible, to isolate issues that had no implications for South Street's claims.

Finally, JNL would be certain to protest Milbank's appointment with vehemence if it knew of the firm's connection to Salovaara and South Street. It would have liked nothing more than to remove from the case the lawyer who had concluded that Bucyrus should cram down a plan over JNL's objections. In proceedings already filled with acrimony, Judge Eisenberg likely would be wary of adding even more fuel to the fire. All this leads to one conclusion: had Gellene disclosed Milbank's connections to Salovaara and South Street, he and Milbank would no longer be working on the Bucyrus bankruptcy.

THE CONFLICT over Milbank's retention, of course, reflected JNL's broader and more intense dissatisfaction with the bankruptcy plan itself. Five days after Bucyrus filed its Chapter 11 petition, JNL filed a motion to terminate Bucyrus's exclusive right to propose a reorganization, and to submit its own plan. The creditor's primary vehicle for expressing its dissatisfaction was a motion claiming that the disclosure statement prepared and circulated by the company didn't contain enough information to permit creditors and shareholders to make an informed decision whether to accept the plan. JNL's opening attack thus was on the process by which Bucyrus had obtained agreement on the plan. Should it lose this battle, JNL almost certainly would then oppose confirmation of the plan by directly challenging its terms.

In a bankruptcy case in which there is not a prepackaged plan in advance of the petition, the company first puts together a plan. It then submits a disclosure statement for approval to the court. Only if the court rules that the statement is adequate may the debtor then solicit creditor acceptance of the plan. The court may, for instance, require the debtor to set forth parties' positions on various issues before it can solicit agreement. Once most creditors accept the plan, the court conducts a hearing on whether to confirm it.

By contrast, in a prepackaged bankruptcy the company sends out a disclosure statement to creditors and seeks their approval of the plan before any petition is filed with the court. Only after the Chapter 11 case begins does the court review the adequacy of the disclosure statement. If the court finds that the statement was inadequate, the debtor must amend it or file a new statement that is satisfactory to the court. In either case, those entitled to vote on the plan must be given another opportunity to do so once they receive a disclosure statement that the court regards as adequate. If enough parties accept the plan, the court must then hold a hearing to determine if it should be confirmed.

In challenging Bucyrus's disclosure statement, JNL lawyer Bruce Arnold argued that the statement "sweeps under the prepack rug anything concerning the leveraged buyout and its impact upon [Bucyrus]." Had disclosure been adequate, he claimed, the plan never would have been approved. JNL focused in particular on the description of the releases to all parties of any claims that Bucyrus might have against them. It asserted that the disclosure statement failed to indicate the minimal investigation that Gellene had conducted before recommending the releases. JNL also argued that the statement had not disclosed what, if any, consideration Bucyrus had received in return for the releases. Nor had it revealed that Milbank itself was a potential defendant in a suit challenging the LBO and sale-leaseback, and that Lederman was a potential defendant in attacks on those two deals as well as the exchange offer. If given this information, JNL maintained, creditors would have realized that Milbank could not be expected to perform a disinterested analysis of wisdom of granting releases. JNL's challenge thus drew on conflict-of-interest arguments that it had made in opposing Milbank's appointment.

JNL contended that a neutral analysis would establish the folly of granting releases. It would reveal that the series of Bucyrus financing transactions in which Goldman and Salovaara had been involved represented efforts by those parties to enrich themselves unfairly at the company's expense. JNL also saw the sale-leaseback arrangement as an attempt by Bucyrus and Salovaara to evade the debt restrictions connected with the $60 million sale of notes to JNL. The upshot of JNL's contentions was that had the disclosure statement contained all this information, creditors and shareholders would have concluded that the plan was defective—most significantly because it treated Goldman and South Street's claims in the bankruptcy as legitimate.

Bucyrus declined to respond to JNL's objections by amending the disclosure statement. That would require resolicitation of the creditors to gain renewed agreement to the plan, which would be expensive and time-consuming. Furthermore, the company believed that even if the disclosure statement were revised, JNL would still contend that the plan should not be confirmed. Judge Eisenberg expressed some concern that JNL was attacking the plan by challenging the disclosure statement, rather than presenting its objections at a confirmation hearing. At one point, the judge declared:

I think that the strategy of trying to cut off the war party at the pass, which is at the hearing on the disclosure statement, is very risky, because if it works, you're probably not going to have a plan confirmed by the end of the year, because you'll never be able to have another hearing on the disclosure statement and then renegotiate and then have a hearing on confirmation of the plan and get all that done by the end of the year. That's going to be very difficult.

JNL attorney Andy Rahl of Anderson, Kill responded to the judge's observation. "Our position," he said, "is that the interests of the creditors in this case would be—the debtor as well—would be promoted by rejecting this disclosure statement and therefore the plan that goes with it now rather than later." Rahl continued, "Our view is that that would promote negotiations. That would enhance the likelihood of something, having something confirmed by the end of the year." Eisenberg cautioned that a hearing on the disclosure statement need not be a hearing on the confirmation of the plan itself. There followed a colloquy between the judge and Rahl about the wisdom of focusing on the disclosure statement at that point:

> *The Court:* Let's go to what's really important. . . . Jackson National Life I don't think gives a hoot about the disclosure statement as such. What Jackson National Life wants is a financial deal in the case which is satisfactory to Jackson National Life. Isn't that right? . . . What you're trying to do in this case is get more and get a sum satisfactory to Jackson National Life. Isn't that your object?
>
> *Mr. Rahl:* Obviously. There is a financial goal in mind.
>
> *The Court:* Let's concentrate on the financial goal. . . . Let me put it, how do you get there?
>
> *Mr. Rahl:* Let me put it in the framework of the disclosure statement, Your Honor. It is our view that if the disclosure in this disclosure statement had been adequate, and by that, I mean that the notice that was available that we have found in discovery had been made available at the time, that this plan never would have been proposed in the first place.

The Court: Forget about that. The goal is to get more. The goal isn't who did what, whether the vote is right, whether the vote is wrong. What you're trying to do is get what you want to get.

Mr. Rahl: We understand that.

The Court: Then why not concentrate on that. In order to get more, you've got to be able to talk to the debtor, right? You've got to be able to talk to the creditors committee. You've got to be able to talk to the United States Trustee. . . .

Mr. Rahl: I think the ultimate party we really aren't able to talk to, and the one that controls the outcome of this as long as this plan is on the table, is Goldman Sachs, Your Honor. That just seems to be an impossible task. I think that the only way in our view to get negotiations rolling in a producti[ve] fashion is to get this plan off the table.

In other words, Rahl was arguing, Bucyrus was giving up claims against Goldman and South Street that could generate funds that would enhance the recovery of unsecured creditors. JNL undoubtedly was mindful of precisely what Judge Eisenberg had said—that disapproval of the plan risked delaying the case beyond the end of the year, which jeopardized the tax benefits available from a reorganization. This fact could give JNL some leverage in negotiations. At the same time, JNL couldn't press its position too far. It expected to have a significant stake in the reorganized company. It too would suffer if the plan were not confirmed in time for Bucyrus to obtain those same benefits. The negotiations therefore became a game of chicken, with $100 million at stake. Bucyrus professionals had to decide whether to make additional concessions to JNL before the disclosure statement trial, or to plunge ahead and hope that approval of the statement would ease the way to speedy confirmation of the plan. They decided to plunge ahead.

JUDGE EISENBERG set aside three days in June for a trial on the adequacy of the disclosure statement. In the weeks leading up to the trial, the parties conducted intensive, and often acrimonious, discovery. In general, the use of discovery in bankruptcy proceedings has expanded since more large law firms with their stable of litigators have become involved in Chapter II cases. The process in this case was designed to generate information relevant to the adequacy of the disclosure statement. It also, however, resulted in the production of much material that related to whether the plan should be confirmed. Toni Lichstein and Milbank associate David Gelfand had primary day-to-day responsibility for the litigation over discovery issues, with Gellene playing a general oversight role. At the same time, Gellene and one or two associates focused on core bankruptcy matters.

Prior to the Chapter 11 petition, Lederman had been the "relationship partner" for Bucyrus with respect to its reorganization. After the petition was filed, Gellene took over this role and the responsibility for billing the company. Lederman billed Bucyrus for a total of four hours for "advice" on bankruptcy-related matters in four separate meetings, with the last date billed on March 4, 1994. Otherwise, Gellene didn't share his duties on the reorganization itself with any other partners at Milbank. As former Bucyrus general counsel David Goelzer put it, Gellene "was just totally running the show."

Gellene's burdens increased when Cynthia Revesz, the associate most familiar with the case, transferred to another department at Milbank not long after the bankruptcy petition. She was replaced with a new associate not as familiar with the case. This gave Gellene virtually sole responsibility for the bankruptcy, in addition to the duties that he had on other major Chapter 11 cases. "He was always rushed," said Goelzer, "and he was always tired. He used to say that five hours sleep was a huge luxury for him." For Goelzer, this made all the more remarkable Gellene's high performance on the case. It also suggests, however, someone whose judgment might be clouded at times by fatigue and stress.

JNL served its discovery request on Bucyrus, South Street, Goldman, Houlihan, and various other parties on March 4. In addition to documents relating to the plan, JNL also requested documents concerning the LBO, the exchange offer, and the South Street sale-leaseback.

Bucyrus refused to produce any documents regarding the LBO or the exchange offer. It argued that such documents were "not relevant to the subject matter involved in this proceeding." Bucyrus's refusal was based on its contention that the statute of limitations had run with respect to any claims arising out of these transactions. One major concern of the company was that JNL would attempt to use discovery in the bankruptcy proceeding to obtain information for its lawsuit in New York. That suit had been stayed when Bucyrus filed for bankruptcy. This meant that JNL couldn't use the discovery process in that case to acquire information from the defendants. Goldman produced no documents concerning the LBO and the exchange offer in the bankruptcy proceeding as long as Bucyrus refused to do so.

Faced with Bucyrus's resistance, JNL filed a motion on April 7 to compel the company to provide material dealing with the LBO and the exchange offer. The creditors' committee voted on April 12 to support the motion. Bill Rochelle, attorney for the committee, had advised the creditors of his belief that the statute of limitations had not expired on claims arising out of these transactions. Rochelle called Gellene later that day to tell him about the committee's position and the reasoning behind it. They spoke for about an hour and a half. Gellene asked that the committee either reconsider its position on the statute of limitations, or that it take no position at all. There would be no need for the committee to take a position, Rochelle responded, if Bucyrus complied with JNL's discovery request.

Gellene spoke with Lichstein and Gelfand about his conversation with Rochelle. Eventually, they decided that Bucyrus would produce material to JNL relating to the LBO and the exchange offer. Gellene called Rochelle back later that evening and informed him of their decision. A few minutes before midnight, Gelfand faxed a letter to Tony Princi, Milwaukee counsel for JNL, indicating Bucyrus's willingness to produce these documents. Gellene informed Goldman of the company's change of position, and the investment bank likewise withdrew its objections to JNL's discovery request.

Lichstein, who was familiar with Chapter 11 proceedings, supervised the Bucyrus document production. Milbank lawyers found that documents were dispersed throughout the company in the files of various employees, rather than in any central location. The material was gathered in more than one hundred boxes and stored in a room at the company. Bucyrus lawyers and legal assistants eventually reviewed about three hundred thousand pages of documents and determined that sixty thousand of them were responsive to JNL's requests.

Discovery activity involved not only document production but depositions as well. A total of thirty-three depositions—thirty conducted by JNL—were taken during the period from April 27 to June 3. Among those deposed were Bucyrus officers Winter, Verville, and Mork; company lawyers Goelzer and Russell Hutchinson; Bucyrus financial advisors Werbalowsky and Eric Siegert; creditors' committee financial advisor Skip Victor; Salovaara and Eckert of South Street; and representatives of the various unsecured creditors. Bucyrus deposed John Stark and Melissa D'Arcambal of JNL, and JNL's financial advisor Joseph Radecki.

Lichstein coordinated the preparation and defense of the debtor's witnesses, and conducted the depositions of Stark and D'Arcambal. Gellene himself did not defend any depositions, but took one of Radecki. The intensity of the deposition schedule is reflected in the fact that several days featured multiple depositions: two on May 4, two on May 13, two on May 17, three on May 19, four on May 20, four on May 24, two on May 25, and two on May 27.

The hostility between the parties carried over into the depositions. The local court rule limited any single deposition to six hours; the attorneys wrangled over how stringently to apply this restriction. Most depositions were peppered with objections from opposing counsel. During one group of ten depositions, for instance, there were 1,288 objections to the form of the question. Assuming six hours per deposition, that's an average of more than 20 such objections per hour, or one every three minutes. Discovery, in other words, was just one more front in the warfare between Bucyrus and JNL.

IN THE MIDST of this activity, the creditors' committee continued to consider JNL's challenge to the disclosure statement as well as the terms of the reorganization plan. JNL lobbied hard to convince the rest of the committee that the disclosure statement was inadequate and the plan couldn't be confirmed. Rochelle invited Bucyrus to discuss its plan with the committee prior to the disclosure statement hearing. Gellene demurred on the ground that discovery was already in progress. That process, he said, provided a forum in which the committee could obtain the information that it wished. Gellene was concerned about letting Bucyrus officers be questioned about the LBO and other deals while those managers were defendants in the JNL lawsuit in New York. He also may have been wary because of a perception that the committee had become more adversarial to the company than the unofficial committee had been before the Chapter II petition.

On April 27, Rochelle prepared a memorandum for the committee on the confirmability of the plan, the adequacy of the disclosure statement, and the fraudulent conveyance claims. One question about confirmability, observed Rochelle, was why the plan allowed current holding company stockholders to share with creditors a portion of the value in the holding company. Those shareholders consisted of Goldman Sachs and the Bucyrus managers who had participated in the LBO. The amount of value that each party received would serve as the basis for calculating the portion of equity that each would receive in the new combined company.

Holding company creditors could have denied existing shareholders any portion of the value in the holding company, and thus in the reorganized company. Instead, those creditors had consented to the distribution of some value to holding company shareholders. As a result, the plan provided for equity holders to receive 43 percent of the value of the holding company, and debt holders to receive a little over 47 percent. In the latter group was the operating company, which was assigned about 9 percent of the value of the holding company in recognition of its claim against B-E Holdings.

The court would have to find that this allocation of value among shareholders and creditors in the holding company was made in good faith, said Rochelle. Bucyrus could argue that the distribution was necessary in order to obtain Goldman's consent to the plan, thereby avoiding the need for a cram-down of Goldman or litigation over the plan. At the same time, Rochelle noted, before the court accepted the propriety of an allocation to Goldman, it might want a more thorough explanation of why Bucyrus had concluded that fraudulent conveyance claims against the investment house were not viable. In short, one obstacle to confirmation might be the perception that the plan unduly benefited holding company shareholders at the expense of creditors. In particular, why had Goldman been assigned to receive so much value in B-E Holdings, and, ultimately, the new company?

Another issue in determining the good faith of the distribution of value in the holding company might be why the plan discounted the operating company claim against B-E Holdings by 75 percent. Creditors of the operating company—JNL was the largest—would be the ultimate beneficiaries of whatever value was assigned to this claim. They would receive a larger—and holding company shareholders a smaller—share of value the less this claim was discounted.

The viability of the fraudulent conveyance claims was another issue that might jeopardize confirmation of the plan. A key consideration with respect to the LBO and the exchange offer was Bucyrus's claim that the statute of limitations had expired for challenges to both. In an April 18 memo to the committee relating his conversation with Gellene, Rochelle noted that reasonable minds could differ on the legal question of the applicable statute of limitations. He stated, however, that he was "more than surprised by the major reason which John gave for opposing a six-year statute of limitations. Without exaggerating his words, *John said that the prepackaged plan was dead if the statute of limitations is six years.*" The reason, Gellene told Rochelle, was that the plan gave no value to any fraudulent conveyance claims because of the belief that they were time-barred. "As a result, if the claims are viable," said Gellene, "the prepackaged plan is deficient."

Rochelle continued:

In one of the few unqualified statements in the disclosure statement, the debtors state flat out that the fraudulent conveyance claims have no merit. . . . The disclosure statement does not say that the debtors' opinion is based on the statute of limitations. If the debtor's opinion was based largely on the statute of limitations, the disclosure statement may also be deficient in a material sense for not giving the reason for the conclusion.

If Gellene was not exaggerating, said Rochelle, "the debtors bet one year's effort and $5 million in expense on a legal opinion about the statute of limitations." Rochelle said that Gellene may have been overstating the case in order to convince the committee to reverse its position on the statute of limitations and JNL's motion to compel. Gellene himself remembered his comment as a lighthearted attempt to ease the tension near the end of a spirited and lengthy conversation. He recalled saying that if the statute of limitations hadn't expired, then the plan was dead "and we can all go home." In any event, the exchange between Gellene and Rochelle underscored the significance that the releases had assumed for approval of both the disclosure statement and the plan.

At a meeting on April 27, Rochelle expressed his view to the committee that the plan likely would not be confirmed in its present state. He repeated that conclusion in a May 17 conference call with the committee. If the company hoped to meet its end-of-year deadline, he suggested, the committee should propose a different plan with a greater chance of being confirmed. This was good news for JNL. It was less pleased, however, with Rochelle's statement that it was unlikely that the bondholders' claims would be extinguished or subordinated to JNL. Three days later, Rochelle met with Brian Rosen and Andy Rahl. They hoped to devise a compromise that would ensure that the bondholders received no less than what they would get under the proposed plan, while still affording JNL the opportunity to seek better treatment.

The committee had another conference call on May 23. Rochelle and David Rosenzweig reported on the information that was emerging from discovery. The discussion then turned once again to the adequacy of the disclosure statement and whether the plan could be confirmed. Rochelle suggested that the disclosure statement provided little discussion of why the debtors had concluded that the fraudulent conveyance claims lacked merit, or the nature of the investigation that had led to that conclusion. Some of the evidence, he felt, was of sufficient weight that it should have been included in the disclosure statement or disclosed to the creditors' committee in the prepetition negotiations.

The committee considered Rochelle's views over the next few days. JNL, of course, believed that the disclosure statement was inadequate and that the plan should be revised. The other members of the committee, however, concluded otherwise. By a vote of five to one, the committee instructed Rochelle to prepare a motion from the committee in support of the statement. He did so, and filed the motion with the court on May 31. The vote effectively confirmed what most people already knew: the war was between JNL and everyone else.

IN MID-MAY, Byrnes and JNL requested Judge Eisenberg appoint an examiner to analyze the most significant areas of disagreement about the plan and to assess the likelihood that it could be confirmed. Bucyrus opposed the motion. On May 23, Eisenberg appointed Salvatore Barbatano of the Chicago law firm of Rudnick & Wolfe to submit a report on these issues before the disclosure statement hearings began in mid-June. Barbatano met with JNL, the creditors' committee, and Byrnes over the course of about three weeks and issued his report on June 13, three days before the disclosure statement trial began.

Barbatano drew no definitive conclusion about the merits of JNL's claims of a fraudulent conveyance. Nonetheless, he was skeptical about either subordinating South Street's sale-leaseback claim or giving JNL priority over all other creditors. More defensible, he suggested, might be to subordinate the claims that Goldman and South Street had based on purchases of holding and operating company securities in the open market. Those claims could be subordinated in the interest of reaching agreement on a plan, even in the absence of misconduct. Goldman and South Street, he observed, had already profited significantly from transactions with Bucyrus through the receipt of fees, bond-trading profits, and unusually high interest payments.

Barbatano strongly urged that the court proceed to a hearing on confirmation of the plan as soon as possible. Whatever disagreement JNL had with the plan could be addressed in that setting. Moving ahead, he emphasized, was necessary both to prevent loss of possible tax benefits and to provide reassurance of the company's long-term business prospects. The examiner's report was limited by the qualified nature of its conclusions, and the narrow scope of the inquiry that Barbatano was able to conduct. It did, however, seem to echo Judge Eisenberg's suggestions that the parties might be better served by focusing on the issue of confirmation rather than on the disclosure statement. This may have provided some hope to Bucyrus that the court would give scant credence to JNL's complaints about the disclosure statement. On the other hand, it offered some encouragement to JNL that the plan as it stood could not be confirmed without concessions by the debtors.

On May 26, Judge Eisenberg directed JNL to submit a description of the specific changes that it proposed to the disclosure statement. On June 13, the same day that Barbatano submitted his report, JNL filed its "Disclosure Statement Amendment." The amendment was especially necessary, the creditor claimed, in light of significant new information that had emerged during recent discovery. The preface to the document stated, "Although Jackson believes that the disclosures contained in the Disclosure Statement are grossly inadequate and that the Holding Company Plan is facially unconfirmable, Jackson is prepared to withdraw its Disclosure Statement Motion if the Debtors agree to circulate this Disclosure Statement Amendment to creditors and interest holders."

The proposed amendment effectively requested that the disclosure statement set forth JNL's objections to the plan. JNL's first objection was that it had been improperly placed in a creditor class by itself in order to ensure that Bucyrus obtained the approval of two-thirds of the unsecured creditor class for the prepackaged plan. Had JNL been placed in a class with other unsecured creditors, its 40 percent share of unsecured debt would have blocked the plan. JNL was surely right in contending that this was why it had been placed in a separate class. The issue was whether there was otherwise a sufficient basis for doing so. Second, JNL argued that the operating company claims against the holding company were improperly discounted and undervalued. Third, it claimed that there should be no distribution to shareholders of the holding company without full payment of all holding company creditors. Fourth, the plan should not provide releases and indemnification of Bucyrus managers and representatives, South Street, and Goldman. Fifth, related to this, there was no provision for pursuing fraudulent conveyance and other claims on behalf of the company. Finally, JNL claimed that the proposed staggered board of directors would prevent JNL as the largest shareholder from immediately controlling the new company.

JNL's proposed amendment stated that JNL estimated the potential recovery against Goldman at $15 million, and against South Street at $15 million for avoidance or subordination of its claims against Bucyrus. In addition, JNL maintained that the company's obligations on bonds debt in connection with the LBO and exchange offer were avoidable as fraudulent conveyances. The proposed amendment noted that both Bucyrus and the holders of such bonds, who had three of the six seats on the creditors' committee, "strongly disagree with JNL's position on this issue."

JNL declared that it would not condition withdrawal of its disclosure statement motion on Bucyrus's willingness to circulate the amendment in the "*precise* form attached hereto." It was hard to imagine, however, that the company would agree to circulation of anything even remotely resembling the document that JNL had submitted. Even if the claims of inadequate investigation, conflict of interest, and bad faith were described as only JNL's allegations, Bucyrus regarded an elaborate recitation of those allegations as inappropriate for the disclosure statement. Furthermore, the company feared that the need to resolicit acceptance of the plan would doom any effort to get the plan confirmed by the end of the year.

Attempts to reach agreement on the plan in the period from mid-February to mid-June thus had come to no avail. If anything, the acrimony was even greater than before. Indeed, hostility even infected discussion of how the forthcoming trial would proceed. The court had given each side six hours to present its case. JNL designated twenty-eight persons as possible witnesses in the presentation of its case. Bucyrus regarded this as harassment, because it likely would require company lawyers to spend time preparing for ostensible witnesses who would never actually testify. The day before the hearing was to begin, John Byrnes moved for sanctions against JNL for its designation of an excessive number of witnesses. Judge Eisenberg reserved a ruling on the motion until the end of the hearing. With this final preliminary skirmish out of the way, the main event began on June 16.

CHAPTER SIX

Bankruptcy Trials

BOTH BUCYRUS AND JNL knew that the outcome of the disclosure statement trial would have a major impact on the company's ability to emerge from bankruptcy on the terms it wanted by the end of
the year. If Bucyrus won, the court would proceed to a confirmation
hearing in thirty days. Since many confirmation issues were intertwined with the question of whether the disclosure statement was adequate, Bucyrus felt that winning the trial would increase the chances
that the court would confirm its plan.

On the other hand, JNL would gain considerable bargaining power
if Judge Eisenberg ruled that the disclosure statement was deficient.
As a practical matter, Bucyrus would have to negotiate a new reorganization plan, resolicit acceptance after circulating a new disclosure
statement, and then gain confirmation of the plan—all by the end of
the year. With the clock ticking, JNL would be in a strong position to
press for the terms that it wanted. Given the intense hostility between
JNL and the other unsecured creditors, as well as between JNL and
South Street, would those creditors be willing to make enough concessions to reach an agreement before the clock ran out? In effect, the
proceedings would be a trial on the wisdom of Bucyrus's gamble that
it could get a reorganization plan confirmed that featured a cram-
down of JNL.

If Gellene had given any further thought to disclosure after he
moved for appointment as bankruptcy counsel, events between the
time the bankruptcy petition was filed and when the trial began likely
had only reinforced his reluctance to reveal Milbank's ties to Salo-

vaara and South Street. Clashes over Milbank's appointment application, the production of documents, the conduct of depositions, and the provisions in the disclosure statement had intensified hostilities between Milbank and JNL. The fact that JNL had challenged Milbank's claim to be disinterested made it clear that it would regard Milbank's ties to Salovaara and South Street as fatally compromising the firm's ability to represent Bucyrus. Conflict of interest, in other words, was a high-visibility issue that had attracted considerable attention in the proceedings thus far.

The clear salience of this issue might suggest that Gellene would feel some pressure to disclose. At the same time, however, his vigorous public defense of Milbank in those battles meant that revealing the connections to Salovaara and South Street would involve an enormous psychological reversal. Having decided to conceal the information, in other words, it became harder to reverse course the more time passed.

Furthermore, Gellene was in litigation mode by the time of the disclosure statement trial. As a formal matter, of course, JNL was not an adversary. It was a member of the bankruptcy estate. Bucyrus therefore had an obligation to look after JNL's interest as much as possible. Given how things had proceeded thus, far, however, it was more natural for Bucyrus, its creditors, and Gellene all to think of JNL as a foe. The stylized combat of the upcoming trial would only reinforce that tendency. For Gellene, who began his career as a litigator, it would evoke adversarial norms against providing any advantage to one's opponent. Disclosure of Milbank's connections to Salovaara and South Street certainly fell into that category.

OPENING ARGUMENTS in the trial began on June 16 at 9:00 A.M. in Judge Eisenberg's courtroom. John Gellene was up first on behalf of the debtors. He laid out the standard for the adequacy of the disclosure statement: that it contain all information that a reasonable investor in the proposed new stock would regard as material to the decision whether to accept the company's proposed plan. JNL's objections, said Gellene, relate essentially to whether the plan should be confirmed. Its challenge to the disclosure statement is "a technical exercise which is intended to delay and deter the progress of this case from its conclusion."

Bruce Arnold countered on behalf of JNL that the disclosure plan "sweeps under the prepack rug" any issues regarding the LBO, which was the event that led the company down the path to bankruptcy. The estimated value of Bucyrus's litigation claims in connection with the LBO and subsequent transactions is $40 million, he asserted. That fact is nowhere disclosed in the statement. These and other omissions had prevented the creditors from making an informed decision to accept the plan.

The first witness for Bucyrus was David Goelzer, the company's general counsel. Goelzer had been the primary contact with the Bucyrus advisors during the preparation of the disclosure statement. Goelzer's testimony mainly focused on the expense and risk that the company would incur if it were forced to revise the disclosure statement and resolicit votes on the plan. The financial costs of resolicitation, Goelzer estimated, would be between $150,000 and $200,000.

Of even more concern, he suggested, would be the effect on the company's competitive position. When Bucyrus filed its petition on February 18, it advised customers and suppliers that it would be done with the Chapter 11 proceedings in 120 days. Customer confidence in the long-term viability of the company was crucial, he said, because the large and expensive machinery that Bucyrus manufactures takes a long time to produce and erect. Furthermore, the company's suppliers provide specially designed and manufactured materials. They needed assurance that when the company placed an order with a long lead time, it would eventually accept and pay for it. Their patience, he noted, was wearing thin. In addition, competitors had been circulating material on the troubles of the company, in an effort to steal business while Bucyrus's future was being decided.

On cross-examination, Byrnes asked Goelzer, "Did you inquire of Jackson National Life as to whether or not they had any objections to the disclosure you were going to submit to the SEC?" asked Byrnes. "No," Goelzer said. The company at that time felt "that any input from Jackson would be with a view to delay and impede the process itself rather than an attempt to make a constructive contribution to the disclosure statement."

Gellene then sought to make clear that JNL had an opportunity to present objections to the statement. "Did representatives of Jackson National Life receive a draft of the disclosure statement?" he asked Goelzer. They did, responded Goelzer, sometime in September. JNL counsel Tony Princi then asked Goelzer, "That was a mistake, right?" "To the best of my knowledge, it was," acknowledged Goelzer. "You didn't want to send Jackson National Life Insurance Company the disclosure statement, did you?" Princi pressed. "That's correct," said Goelzer. Byrnes then offered Goelzer an opportunity to elaborate on his answer. Goelzer explained that he understood that drafts of the document should be sent only to parties who agreed to keep them confidential and refrain from trading based on the information contained in the statement. "So when you say it was a mistake sending to JNL," asked Byrnes, "was it your position at the time that you weren't going to send it to anybody who hadn't agreed to confidentiality?" "Yes," answered Goelzer.

Byrnes then turned to the discussion of the releases in the disclosure statement. He asked if Bucyrus had received any "financial consideration" in return for the releases. "We received concessions from South Street in connection with the current South Street claims," said Goelzer. "As far as I know, that's the only financial consideration received." When Byrnes finished shortly thereafter, Judge Eisenberg asked the Bucyrus general counsel, "Was the counsel who gave the advice [on the releases] Milbank Tweed?" Goelzer answered that it was. "And the fraudulent transfer matters pertaining to Goldman, Sachs [was] a part [of that advice]?" asked the judge. "Yes, sir," said Goelzer. "Where you said there was no financial consideration for the releases except from South Street, is that indicated in the disclosure statement?" "I don't recall that it is, Your Honor," replied Goelzer.

The next witness was Jeff Werbalowsky. After Gellene's direct examination, Princi asked Werbalowsky on cross-examination what the basis was for his conclusion that the claims against South Street had no merit. Werbalowsky replied that he had formed that opinion after reading the JNL draft complaint and the material connected with the South Street financing transaction, as well as engaging in discussions with the company in the context of working on the restructuring. Since he didn't believe those claims were viable, he said, he didn't discuss them in the course of his negotiations with Salovaara.

Before the parties broke for lunch, Andy Rahl informed the judge that JNL was still willing to withdraw its objections to the disclosure statement if the parties could work out an amendment to the statement that could be circulated in order to conduct a new vote on the plan. If that occurs, asked Werbalowsky, "[W]ould you then agree to confirm the plan?" "Whether the plan is confirmable or not isn't your decision yet," said Eisenberg. He then asked Werbalowsky whether he was satisfied that there was no possibility of resolving the debtors' differences with JNL. "Your Honor," replied Werbalowsky, "if I had a scintilla of hope that there was any potential for an amicable resolution, we wouldn't be here today." "So you believe then it was not possible to resolve the problems with JNL?" asked the judge. "In a way that would allow the consensual restructuring of these companies, absolutely not, Your Honor," said Werbalowsky. With that, the parties adjourned for lunch.

After the lunch break, Gellene called the final Bucyrus witness, Skip Victor of Chanin & Company, who served as the financial advisor to the creditors' committee both before and after the Chapter II petition. The committee, he said, "tried to initiate a dialogue with Jackson National consistently throughout." There were, however, several meetings among creditors to which JNL had been invited in which it didn't participate. Bruce Arnold objected to the line of questioning as irrelevant. Eisenberg overruled his objection, saying that "the apparent refusal . . . of JNL to cooperate in sitting and negotiating goes to the heart of JNL's request that it be granted specific equitable relief. I think this is very important testimony." Arnold responded, "[I]f the Court wants testimony along those lines, I will tell you now that I will elicit extensive testimony from Mr. Radecki regarding the cold shoulder that Jackson received."

Arnold also asked Victor whether he had been asked to analyze the

South Street financing transaction, and specifically whether the interest rate on that deal was above market rate. Gellene objected, arguing that the question was relevant to confirmation of the plan, not to the adequacy of the disclosure statement. Judge Eisenberg overruled his objection, saying, "It's an important point if it's not in the disclosure statement." Victor then testified that, consistent with his earlier deposition testimony, he had concluded that the South Street financing was one thousand basis points (ten percentage points) above the market rate.

Arnold then asked the witness if the staggered board provided for in the plan was adopted because the committee "did not want Jackson National Life Insurance Company to be able to control the constituencies of the board of directors following any confirmation of a plan of reorganization." Victor disagreed. Arnold then directed Victor to his prior deposition testimony, in which Victor had said that "one of the reasons" that the committee had endorsed a staggered board was its concern about JNL. Victor agreed with that statement. "And sir," asked Arnold, "if you could just point to the section of the disclosure statement that has that in there as to the reasons why the staggered board provisions are in the disclosure statement." Gellene objected that Victor had not written the document; Eisenberg said that Victor could answer if he knows. "I don't know," replied Victor.

With that, Bucyrus rested its case. The parties took a break at 3:00 P.M. They resumed at 3:15 with the presentation of JNL's witnesses.

ARNOLD CALLED as his first witness JNL financial advisor Joseph Radecki of Jeffries & Company. Radecki testified that he agreed with Victor's opinion that the effective interest rate for the South Street financing transaction was one thousand basis points over market rate. This difference, he stated, came to about $8 million in interest payments in fiscal years 1992 and 1993. With respect to the intercompany claim, Radecki set forth the calculations that formed the basis for his conclusion that the claim of the operating company against the holding company had been discounted by 75 percent. Had there been no discount, he said, operating company creditors would have received about $3.2 million in equity instead of $1.2 million. This was not discussed in the disclosure statement.

Gellene objected that the amount by which the intercompany claim was discounted could be calculated by the figures set forth in the statement. The statement "does show numbers," conceded Eisenberg. But, he said, JNL's contention is that "it's very difficult to pull them out and put them in a meaningful form."

Arnold continued his direct examination of Radecki the next morning. Radecki sought to establish that JNL had negotiated in good faith throughout the prepetition period. He himself had begun participating in negotiations in mid-May 1993, he said, and meetings were held involving the debtor, the creditors' committee, and JNL through the first week in June. Werbalowsky, however, had then declared that the discussions were not fruitful and that they would be broken off. Nonetheless, Radecki said, he continued thereafter to contact Werbalowsky in an effort to reach an agreement. Those efforts were ongoing throughout the remainder of 1993 up until the company filed its material with the SEC in January 1994.

Gellene then began his cross-examination of Radecki. He pressed the witness about the basis for his contention that the rate of interest for the sale-leaseback transaction was ten percentage points higher than the market rate. Gellene suggested that there was no transaction with the specific components of that deal that could be used to establish a market rate with which the deal could be compared.

Shortly thereafter, the court declared a brief recess, which lasted about ten minutes. When Gellene resumed, the tension in the courtroom moved up a notch. "Mr. Radecki," Gellene inquired, "could you tell the Court the substance of the conversation you had with Mr. Rahl and Mr. Stark during the break?" Radecki replied, "I discussed with them what the questions had been and my impressions of them and my impression of where the questions were going." Gellene then asked the court to strike all of Radecki's testimony, on the ground that "the discussions that this witness has while under oath while in the middle of cross-examination with counsel for Jackson National Life is an abuse of the evidentiary process."

Eisenberg demurred. He acknowledged that it would be an abuse of process if Radecki had been coached during the break in any way. The solution for that, however, would not be to strike the testimony that Radecki had already given. "But as a certainty," he said, "I will think through very carefully the weight to be given to any testimony that he'll give from this point on." Eisenberg continued, "Discussing testimony between a lawyer and a witness during a break is something that really makes you wonder a little bit." He then asked Radecki whether there had been any discussion of the testimony that Radecki had given. No, Radecki said. "I gave my impressions to Andy Rahl and to John Stark. I don't think they gave me any impressions back."

Gellene's cross-examination then continued, but Judge Eisenberg twice broke in to express impatience with Radecki. When the witness testified about his presentation to JNL and its lawyers in applying to be hired as an advisor for the Bucyrus case, Gellene suggested that Radecki had done no independent investigation to verify if JNL's charges against the various parties were well founded. Radecki responded that he had simply taken those allegations from the draft JNL complaint and incorporated them into his presentation. As Gellene began a follow-up question, Judge Eisenberg interjected, "You weren't uncomfortable doing all of this, giving opinions based on a draft of a complaint that may or may not have been filed and going in and making a presentation thinking that all these people are going to be sued and your time in going through all of this, none of that bothered you?" Radecki replied that the presentation simply contained a recital of the defendants named in the complaint. Eisenberg then asked if there were any industry-wide canons of ethics for investment bankers. Not that I'm aware of, said Radecki.

Shortly afterward, Eisenberg broke in again to note that Radecki was looking out into the audience while he was testifying. "You were clearly looking up and looking at a person in the courtroom. Have you done that consistently? Why do you do that? Are you looking for instructions or feedback?" "No," replied Radecki, "I'm just looking out." The judge then stated, "I just want the record to be clear that I've noticed that you have a habit of looking in the direction of Mr.

Stark after you make a statement." Stark, he noted, was providing no reaction to Radecki and often was not even looking at him. Nonetheless, Eisenberg said, "I think the record should be clear that you do that."

Albert Solochek, counsel for the holding company, then asked Radecki if he thought that JNL would vote for the plan if the disclosure statement contained all the amendments that it had proposed. "No," replied Radecki. John Byrnes followed up on this line of questioning, clearly skeptical of JNL's professed concern about the deficiencies in the disclosure statement as opposed to the plan itself.

Later in Byrnes's cross-examination, Radecki gave an indication of the gap between the positions of JNL and the other parties. The plan provided JNL with 38 percent of the equity in the new company. Based on its portion of the Bucyrus debt, Radecki testified, JNL should be entitled to 80–85 percent of the equity. Radecki said that he probably would advise the creditor to settle for something less than that. However, he said, "I've not yet done the analysis to determine the spot between 38 and 80 percent where I would tell JNL please settle this case." Eisenberg interjected, "If that doesn't go a long way in explaining what the problem in this case is, I don't know what does."

The judge expressed his irritation at Radecki yet again a moment later. The witness said that since the Chapter II petition had been filed he had not been invited by the creditors' committee to participate in any negotiations. "Mr. Radecki," said Judge Eisenberg, "in all fairness to you, hearing your testimony for much of the morning, it's easy to see why. I'm waiting for you to say something conciliatory." Princi objected to what he regarded as the court's suggestion that JNL was the source of the problem in reaching an agreement. "JNL is one of the problems," replied Eisenberg, and "It's fair to say that the approach of the Debtors is another one of the problems." He went on, "I've said that before and I'm saying that again. And it's painful to me to sit through all of this and to really get a pretty clear picture on what's happening and to think what's going to happen to the debtor, to the company as a result of all of this."

Bucyrus officer Norbert Verville then took the stand, called by JNL as an adverse witness. Princi's questioning suggested that the company believed that the success of a prepack hinged on JNL's acceptance of a plan. Bucyrus therefore had been imprudent in presenting the court with a proposed cram-down of the creditor. The implication, of course, was that it was Bucyrus, not JNL, who was being unreasonable. "Are you faulting the companies for giving this a shot?" asked Eisenberg. "Yes, Your Honor, I am," replied Princi. The judge then offered a comment on confirmation that could not have been comforting to Bucyrus. "So much of these are confirmation issues," said the judge. "Confirmation is not going to be easy, you know that, I know that, the debtors know that."

A little while later, Judge Eisenberg attempted to focus the proceedings more sharply on the disclosure statement by himself calling John Stark to testify. This turned out to be a crucial moment in the case. Tell me, the judge said, what information should have been in the disclosure statement that wasn't. Stark replied that he had been jotting down notes on that topic and had a list that he would be happy to recite. He then proceeded to tick off thirteen items that he said should have been described in the disclosure statement as JNL's allegations.

Five matters were especially significant: (1) that Goldman had earned more than $10 million in trades allegedly using inside information about Bucyrus; (2) that the sale-leaseback had been structured to get around the debt restriction covenants that accompanied the sale of reset notes to JNL; (3) that the holding company actually owed $106 million rather than $26 million to the operating company; (4) that prior to the LBO, Bucyrus and Goldman had discussed the probable need for a Chapter 11 filing by the operating company after the LBO; and (5) that there had been insufficient investigation of fraudulent conveyance claims regarding the LBO, exchange offer, and the sale-leaseback financing. The judge's belief that Stark had significantly helped frame the issues was expressed in his comment a few minutes later that "what this trial really was all about was what Mr. Stark testified to in ten minutes."

Gellene asked Stark during cross-examination why JNL believed that there would be enough time to develop and confirm a new plan by the end of the year if the prepackaged plan were defeated. Stark replied that the other creditors were embarrassed to have participated in an "ill-fated attempt to craft a prepackaged plan over the objection of JNL." As a result, he said, they feel it necessary to stand by the plan. Only if the plan is defeated would they be willing to negotiate with JNL.

Judge Eisenberg later gave an indication that Stark's testimony may have inclined him to be more tolerant of JNL's choice at that point to contest the disclosure statement rather than the plan itself. Albert Solochek asked Stark what difference it would make to send out a disclosure statement amended as JNL wished if the plan remained the same. Solocheck asked whether JNL would accept the plan if the disclosure statement were amended and other creditors voted for the plan. Eisenberg cut in:

> The answer is "No, Jackson won't vote for the plan." But that's Jackson's right. They have the right not to vote for the plan.
>
> What Jackson is doing is very clear; that I think Jackson believes that . . . the treatment is unfair. That's a confirmation issue, and it may be right or wrong. It believes the plan is not confirmable, and that may be right or wrong.
>
> But Jackson believes, also, that now that additional facts are available, other people, if given the opportunity to ballot, to reballot, would vote against the plan. The only way that Jackson can do that is by utilizing the disclosure statement as the vehicle.

Princi and Rahl then read into the record excerpts from the deposition of Mikael Salovaara, which had been taken about a month earlier as part of the disclosure statement discovery. The excerpts dealt with Goldman's role in the LBO and its purchase of operating company notes in anticipation of the Bucyrus exchange offer. With respect to the LBO, Salovaara was asked whether prior to the LBO he had ever considered whether the operating company "would need to raise additional capital or refinance once the LBO was consummated in order for it to be able to operate its businesses and pay its debts?" Salovaara had replied, "I concluded that it would need to and that it would be able to."

Princi and Rahl presumably sought to use this statement to bolster Stark's earlier contention that Bucyrus should have revealed in the disclosure statement that before the LBO the company and Goldman had discussed the likelihood that the company would need to file for Chapter II after the LBO. Salovaara's deposition testimony, however, related not to the probability of a bankruptcy filing, but to the likely need for Bucyrus-Erie to refinance its obligations—a significant difference. No one, however, called attention to this.

After the last witness stepped down on Friday, Judge Eisenberg scheduled final arguments in the case to begin at 9:15 the following Monday morning. As he concluded the proceedings, he advised the parties that his chambers had been "following two separate tracks as we have done our research." The first, he said, "is basically ruling for the companies. The other is basically ruling for JNL. The final argument will be very important, because if ever there were a matter which is not prejudged, that certainly is . . . this." With that, the lawyers on both sides hunkered down over the weekend to prepare for their last shot to persuade the judge that their clients should prevail.

JOHN GELLENE PRESENTED the main closing argument for the debtors on Monday morning. The disclosure statement, he said was adequate to allow impaired creditors to make an informed decision on the plan. JNL's challenge to it was simply one more example of its effort to thwart the plan by "pursuing litigation as a first resort." JNL had attempted to undermine Bucyrus's reorganization, without regard to the effect on the debtor's business. This was all prompted by its extreme position on the share that it should receive in the new company.

In summing up his argument, Gellene asked the court to consider that

[n]ot a single bondholder has responded to [JNL's] publicity campaign, not a single bondholder has responded to the attempts

by Jackson National Life to create some kind of rallying cry regarding substantive positions which they have put before everyone in this case for a considerable period of time. Only Jackson National Life stands before you today as an objector.

JNL's challenge to the disclosure statement, argued Gellene, "is tactical, not substantive." Revising the statement and resoliciting agreement to the plan from the creditors would cost between $150,000 and $200,000, but would produce no outcome different from what has already happened. It is time, Gellene said, to focus on the goal of confirming the reorganization plan.

Bruce Arnold presented the closing argument on behalf of JNL. He described the alleged shortcomings of the disclosure statement. While the statement concludes that there is no merit to JNL's claims of fraudulent conveyance, he said, it doesn't contain any estimate of the value of those claims and the amount that Bucyrus would forgo by granting releases. It indicates that Milbank Tweed investigated the viability of these claims, but doesn't disclose that one of Gellene's partners at Milbank, Larry Lederman, represented the buyout group in the LBO. Nor does the statement indicate that Milbank continues to represent Goldman Sachs on an ongoing basis in various matters. These omissions, argued Arnold, render suspect the advice that Milbank gave the company regarding the claims of fraudulent conveyance.

Arnold concluded by saying that the plan "anesthetizes all of the debtor's claims against third parties and insiders, compromises multimillion dollar intercompany claims and attempts to cram down its largest unsecured creditor, Jackson, by gerrymandering the classification of the unsecured debt." He declared, "The time to stop this plan is now, and the way to do it is not to approve the disclosure statement."

John Byrnes then addressed the court on behalf of the U.S. Trustee's Office. The standard for determining the adequacy of a disclosure statement, he stated, is relatively low, and the statement in this case satisfies it. He closed by voicing a concern about the case as it went forward. JNL may have some colorable claims at the confirmation stage, he said. If, however, the process of considering those claims resembles the disclosure statement trial, he warned, "we're going to be here for weeks if not months and spend millions rather than hundreds of thousands of dollars of other people's money to get those issues resolved."

At the end of the morning, Judge Eisenberg thanked the parties for their presentations. He said that he would definitely be able to read a decision into the record later that afternoon. After some discussion, he asked the parties to return to the courtroom at 2:30 P.M. With that, he repaired to his chambers to make a decision, while everyone else headed out of the courtroom for lunch. Lawyers and their clients speculated over lunch about what the judge would do. Each could take comfort from Eisenberg's comments at different times during the proceedings, but it was hard to infer how he might come out. The mood in the Bucyrus contingent was anxious, but mixed with a slight dose of optimism. The view seemed to be that the company's chance of prevailing was somewhat better than even, but no one was confidently predicting victory.

ONCE THE PARTIES reassembled in the courtroom after lunch, Judge Eisenberg wasted little time in announcing his conclusion. The disclosure statement, he ruled, is inadequate. Reballoting of creditors would be necessary, but he would approve a new statement without another trial if it contained certain specified information. He then read his decision into the record; a more formal version would be made available later. The process of reciting the grounds for his decision to the court reporter took about an hour and a half.

Eisenberg began by noting that the driving force behind the challenge to the statement was JNL's belief that "it is getting the short end of the stick." What it really wants, he said, in one word, is "more." Its criticism of the disclosure statement "is the legal mechanism selected by JNL to try to get more . . . the court believes that JNL doesn't care what happens with the disclosure statement. If it got what it wanted, it would pack up its tent and go away. But JNL is entitled to pursue its right and it cannot be criticized" for doing so.

Eisenberg then moved on to elaborate the ways in which the disclosure statement was deficient. Stark, he said had "zeroed in on that nicely in his testimony." The judge then ticked off the items that Stark had listed, and found most of them significant. First, he said, "it was negligence and perhaps recklessness of the debtors . . . not to have made inquiry of Goldman Sachs and its activities." Goldman had earned millions in fees and was a major shareholder dealing in the company's securities. Yet there was no indication of any consideration that the company received for releasing Goldman from potential liability. "JNL needed only one deadly arrow in its quiver," the judge said. This defect was "the arrow more than any other arrow that shot down the disclosure statement."

A second problem was the failure to disclose that there had been a discussion between Goldman and the company prior to the LBO of the probable need to file for Chapter II protection after the buyout. Here, Eisenberg accepted Stark's characterization of Salovaara's deposition testimony, rather than Salovaara's own language referring to the need to "refinance" the operating company's debt after the LBO. Third, said the judge, the disclosure statement should have indicated that the sale-leaseback financing rate may have been substantially over the market rate. Furthermore, the statement should have made clear Salovaara's history of involvement with the debtor so that a creditor could fairly assess the terms of that transaction. In addition, the statement should have disclosed that the deal was "structured in a manner solely or principally to get around the covenants in the JNL-owned securities." Next, Bucyrus should have explained more clearly how it had calculated the intercompany claim.

Eisenberg then declared that there should have been greater disclosure about the investigation of JNL's charges concerning the LBO. Milbank was a potential defendant in legal action challenging the LBO because it had represented the company in connection with it. Goldman, with whom Milbank had an ongoing attorney-client relationship, also was a potential defendant. Given these facts, the statement should have made clear that it was Milbank that had conducted this investigation and advised the company not to pursue any claims. This would have allowed the creditors to make a more informed decision about whether Bucyrus should grant releases to potential defendants.

Bucyrus officials and representatives sat in stunned silence as Eisenberg read his remarks into the record. Their worst fears had materialized. They had anticipated the possibility that the judge might rule against them. What they had not expected was that the judge would rely so heavily on John Stark's testimony in reaching his decision. Stark had lost credibility with those in the Bucyrus camp because of what they perceived as his outrageous and irresponsible demands. As one person put it, "I wouldn't trust him to hold my wallet while I went swimming." As a result, it was especially galling to them that Judge Eisenberg had so thoroughly adopted Stark's view of the situation. By contrast, Stark surely felt vindicated that his long campaign to prevent a reorganization in which JNL was treated unfairly had finally borne fruit.

The judge extended until mid-October the period in which Bucyrus had the exclusive right to propose a plan. He said that he would approve a disclosure statement with the changes he specified. There was no doubt, however, that his decision was a huge victory for JNL. It was clear that Bucyrus would have to placate Stark in order to reach agreement on a plan. The Bucyrus team members went back to an office about a block from the courthouse. They had suffered a terrible defeat, they agreed, but there was nothing they could do that day. Judge Eisenberg's decision was not even available yet for their review. They needed to go home and think about what to do next. When a transcript of the decision became available, Goelzer began to create a summary of the points that Eisenberg had made.

More than a year's work on putting together a proposed plan had just been reduced to ashes. There was little time, however, to dwell on that. If the company hoped to obtain tax benefits important to its recovery, it had less than six months to negotiate the terms of a new plan and get it confirmed.

Jeff Werbalowsky called John Stark to discuss how the parties would now proceed in light of Eisenberg's ruling. "Congratulations, John," he said. "You're the dog that caught the truck. Now what do you do with it? . . . The other unsecured creditors aren't simply going to agree that all their claims should be subordinated to JNL," said Werbalowsky. "Salovaara isn't going to say that he no longer has a secured claim. How are we going to get this company out of bankruptcy? What do you want?" Werbalowsky was concerned that there was little that Bucyrus could offer that it hadn't already proposed. The important thing that might propel the parties toward a deal, he thought, was the possible loss of millions in tax benefits if the company's reorganization plan were not confirmed before the end of the year. His pitch to the parties was that if they didn't come to a timely agreement, they would blow the chance of enjoying that benefit.

Stark met with Bucyrus officials and advisors several times in July to discuss possible revisions to the reorganization plan and JNL's proposals to provide financing to the company. Two provisions of the plan were of particular concern to the creditor. First, JNL believed that the intercompany claim should allocate more value to the operating company and, thus, its creditors. JNL, of course, was one of those creditors. Second, JNL wanted Bucyrus to assign to it any claims the debtor might have against Goldman and South Street.

Bucyrus was able to use the possibility of JNL's financing to induce South Street to modify its claim. Progress on other issues, however, was slower. With respect to the releases, Bucyrus was concerned that leaving open the possibility of claims against Goldman and South Street would undermine the finality of the reorganization and complicate relationships with these parties. On the intercompany claim, the court hadn't appointed a separate financial advisor for the holding company until July 28. The advisor, Seymour Preston, was wary about making concessions immediately after being appointed to protect the holding company's interests.

The outlook for an agreement finally began to improve in mid-August. On Friday, August 12, Werbalowsky called Rahl to propose that JNL take assignment of Bucyrus's fraudulent conveyance claims against Goldman and South Street as part of an overall resolution of differences between JNL and the company. He told Rahl that he planned to be in New York the following Monday for a meeting with Bucyrus officials and Milbank. He said that he would like some idea of JNL's reaction in advance of that meeting. Rahl responded that the idea was worth pursuing. "Since Stark was going to be in New York on Monday as well," he said, "why don't we get together with you before your other meeting?"

Werbalowsky, Eric Siegert of Houlihan, Rahl, and Stark met for lunch in New York the following Monday, August 15. They continued their discussion afterward at Anderson, Kill's offices. Stark and Rahl indicated that JNL would seriously consider accepting assignment of the claims against Goldman and South Street. The larger part of the discussion, however, was devoted to another issue about which JNL had concerns: the board of directors of the reorganized company. A consensus emerged for a seven-person board. JNL would nominate two of the directors, as would the remainder of the creditors' committee. These four would agree on two additional members. Company management would nominate the seventh director. Finally, Werbalowsky told Rahl that Bucyrus would acquiesce in whatever agreement JNL reached with Preston on the intercompany claim.

After his lunch with Werbalowsky on the fifteenth, Rahl attended a large meeting at Milbank at which Preston was present. He told Preston that JNL believed that the holding company was not entitled to any allocation of value under the plan, since JNL maintained that B-E Holdings owed the operating company around $100 million. Preston insisted that the holding company's subsidiaries were of considerable value to the reorganized combined company. He also said that he could push for substantive consolidation of the companies in one bankruptcy if Rahl did not back off. This would have placed the assets of both companies and the combined claims against them in one pot, a structure that would reduce the share of the combined company that operating company creditors such as JNL would receive.

Nonetheless, negotiations on the issue continued over the next couple of weeks. Preston told Rahl that he didn't believe that JNL was willing to torpedo the plan over this one issue because it had too much at stake. Rahl responded that he believed that the committee would support JNL on the intercompany claim issue. Eventually, Preston agreed to reduce the value assigned to the holding company from 12.9 percent to 8.5 percent.

Discussions on the plan continued into September. They culminated in a lengthy session that began on September 18. In the early morning hours of September 19, Stark finally told Gellene that the amended plan on the table was acceptable to Bucyrus. The plan gave JNL an increase from 38 percent to 40 percent in the percentage of stock it would hold in the reorganized company. This reflected slightly more equity than JNL would have received as a creditor of the operating company on a ratable basis.

At the time, the principal and accrued interest on the South Street 1992 financing was $54.6 million. Under the new plan, that obligation would be paid through the issuance of five-year notes issued to South Street. The original plan provided that South Street's claims were to be refinanced though 13.5 percent notes, payable in cash. The revised plan provided that interest on the five-year notes would be 10.5 percent for the first year. In successive years, the rate would be 10.5 percent if paid in cash and 13.5 percent if paid in notes, at the discretion of Bucyrus. Furthermore, South Street agreed to reduce its claim based on the sale-leaseback by $2.5 million, and to forgo interest it was due under a default provision in the terms of that transaction.

With respect to the releases, Bucyrus told Stark that the company had no choice but to give South Street a release for the sale-leaseback if it hoped to gain any concessions from Salovaara on that claim. JNL eventually acquiesced in this. JNL received the right to pursue fraud claims in connection with South Street's purchase of Bucyrus bonds in the open market. JNL also would have the right to pursue any potential claims that Bucyrus might have against Goldman. It agreed to indemnify Bucyrus for losses arising from any lawsuits it filed in pursuit of such claims. Goldman's counsel had asked Gellene several times to advise Bucyrus to settle the claims with Goldman, so that the investment firm would not be subject to suit by JNL. Gellene, however, recommended against such a course. Goldman was dismayed by the transfer of claims to JNL and expressed its intention to oppose the amended plan.

All bondholders except South Street thus would become owners of the new corporation, entitled to a voice in its governance. Corporate governance changes that JNL had desired also were included in the amended plan. Board members would not serve staggered terms. Instead, there would be a single class of directors, which initially would number seven. JNL would later gain a majority of the board when additional directors were appointed. Stark would eventually become chairman of the board of the newly reorganized company, Bucyrus International.

The parties notified Judge Eisenberg later in the day on September 19 that all creditors but Goldman had agreed to an amended plan. On September 23, the debtors distributed solicitation material to the creditors. All but Goldman voted in favor. On November 10, Goldman filed its objection to the plan. It claimed that JNL had acted in bad faith in pressing for the right to sue Goldman, because JNL had relied on discovery in the Chapter 11 proceeding to bolster its claims that Goldman was liable in the New York lawsuit. Goldman withdrew its objection, however, after it reached a settlement with JNL. Bucyrus agreed to indemnify Goldman for the prepetition expenses it had incurred in defending itself in the action by JNL.

As a result, the confirmation hearings began November 30 with all parties in support of the plan. Judge Eisenberg confirmed the plan on December 2, and it went into effect on December 14. The company had just met its end-of-year deadline for confirmation. As Gellene put it, the company was "reorganized, reconstituted, and was free to go forward and do its business outside bankruptcy."

AT THE END of 1994, the Milbank compensation committee memo reflected Gellene's immersion during the year in the Bucyrus bankruptcy. "John has again worked fiendishly hard," it said. The memo indicated that Gellene had billed more than 2,700 hours through November 30, and had spent a total of almost 2,850 hours by that point on activities for the firm. Gellene stated that he had "another extremely busy year," even though a year earlier he had not known what work would emerge to replace the Maxwell case. The Bucyrus and U.S. Brass bankruptcies had kept him occupied throughout the year. Gellene told the committee, "I think we are getting a little crazed here; a high volume of work, fewer people to do it, some resulting tension among the Partners." He noted that he had spent over a quarter of his time on the road in the past year.

As usual, comments from partners were laudatory about the quality of Gellene's work. Lederman said, "He is wonderful; he has done a great job for us." Jerome quoted one client as saying that Gellene "is the best bankruptcy lawyer in the U.S." "He is exiting my orbit," said Jerome, "which is good." At the same time, other comments painted a more complex portrait. One partner said that Gellene was a "madman; sometimes he does things he doesn't know about; but he is absolutely brilliant, extremely impressive, and a team player." Al Lilley described him as "overworked." Barry Radick, cohead of the bankruptcy practice, said that "[h]e is a control freak and a loner. He refuses help; we are concerned that he may get himself into trouble because he is working so hard." The head of the summer associate program reported that Gellene was no longer asked to help with recruiting or interviewing, since "he generally refuses or, if he agrees he then cancels." Finally, Bob O'Hara indicated that Gellene remained one of the most delinquent half-dozen partners in submitting his daynotes, at one point being fifty-six days late. "Last year," O'Hara said, "he attempted to enter unmeaningful daynotes (which is particularly a problem on bankruptcy matters). He comes into compliance just enough to get paid."

Despite his busy schedule, Gellene reiterated a theme that he had sounded in previous meetings with the committee: the prospect of a serious slowdown in work. There is "less business and more competition" in the representation of lenders, he observed. The bankruptcy group was having trouble keeping good people: "The business has shrunk so much that our people do not see the upside potential for them" in remaining in bankruptcy practice. Gellene noted some personal tension among some of the senior bankruptcy partners. More generally, he maintained, "The Firm is now a collection of businesses and the [executive committee] cannot really manage the practices beyond setting overall administrative policies. . . . It is hard for a partnership to run itself as a business."

Gellene earlier had offered to rejoin the Litigation Department. The executive committee, however, was attempting instead to attract lateral recruits to that practice. He thus had little time to savor confirmation of the Bucyrus reorganization plan. He foresaw that the U.S. Brass matter would keep him occupied much of the upcoming year. After that, however, the longer-term outlook was far less clear.

Gellene had one last opportunity to disclose Milbank's ties with Salovaara and South Street when he applied to Judge Eisenberg for compensation for his representation of Bucyrus. He didn't take advantage of it.

CONTENTION IN the Bucyrus bankruptcy didn't end with court approval of the Chapter 11 plan. The next battleground was a trial on the amount of compensation that professionals should receive for their work on the bankruptcy. Gellene's actions in this trial would later serve as the basis for one of the criminal charges against him.

Milbank applied in spring 1995 for court authorization of $1.96 million in fees and a little over $370,000 in expenses. The firm already had received a substantial portion of this in two interim awards in August 1994 and April 1995. The money was still subject to return to Bucyrus, however, pending Judge Eisenberg's final decision on the amount to which Milbank was entitled. Among other reasons, the judge could deny Milbank's request if he found that the firm had not been eligible to represent the DIP because of a conflict, or had failed to make full disclosure to the court. In other words, if Judge Eisenberg learned at the fee trial of Milbank's ties to Salovaara and South Street, he could deny Milbank any compensation and order it to return to Bucyrus the fees that it had received.

JNL also filed a request for a little over $3 million in compensation, which it indicated that it would accept in the form of stock in Bucyrus International. It claimed that its opposition to the disclosure statement and the prepackaged plan had benefited the estate by preventing the release of valuable claims against Goldman and South Street. Bucyrus and John Byrnes objected, arguing that JNL's efforts had benefited only itself. Byrnes also claimed that Milbank should receive somewhat less than it requested.

In keeping with the battle lines during the bankruptcy, JNL objected to most other parties' requests for fees. It asserted that Milbank should receive $1.5 million less than it was seeking. Most of the firm's work, it maintained, was on behalf of a prepackaged plan that could not be confirmed and a disclosure statement that the court had ruled was inadequate. Furthermore, Milbank's investigation of Bucyrus's potential claims had been deficient. "In the end," alleged JNL, "Milbank's entire strategy was to sacrifice value for speed."

Milbank litigator David Gelfand arrived in Milwaukee on Sunday, November 28, 1995, to help prepare Gellene for his testimony in the fee trial the following day. Gelfand had assisted Toni Lichstein in discovery matters in preparation for the disclosure statement trial. He also had worked with Gellene on the firm's earlier requests for interim compensation.

A few days before flying to Milwaukee, Gelfand received Gellene's outline of the testimony that he planned to give. Gelfand converted Gellene's outline into a question-and-answer format. The outline didn't indicate the use of any exhibits, but the parties had agreed that all the pleadings they had submitted during the bankruptcy would be part of the record in the fee trial. Gelfand identified certain exhibits that would be introduced at the hearing in connection with various lines of questioning. Among the exhibits he designated were Gellene's original and amended affidavits in support of Milbank's application to represent Bucyrus, dated February 18 and March 28, 1994, respectively. Gelfand and Gellene had only a brief time to go over the outline the day before Gellene testified.

The fee trial began on the morning of November 29. Much of the trial turned out to be essentially a relitigation of the bankruptcy, with

Milbank and JNL contending that the other was entitled to little or no compensation because it had acted so unreasonably that it had jeopardized the interest of the estate.

Gellene was Milbank's first witness, with Gelfand conducting direct examination. Following Gellene's original outline, Gelfand asked whether Gellene currently was engaged in representing any parties in bankruptcy other than Bucyrus. Gellene responded by stating that he was lead counsel for United States Brass Corporation, a Chapter 11 debtor in a Texas proceeding. His outline had also listed three other companies that he did not mention at the hearing. In addition, at the time of the hearing, Gellene continued to represent South Street in its claim on the Busse note in the Gillett bankruptcy in Colorado. That representation had begun in December 1993. Neither Gellene's outline nor his testimony at the fee trial, however, mentioned this.

Shortly before the lunch break, Gelfand sought to address JNL's objection that Milbank should not be awarded any fees because it had represented Goldman in other matters during the Bucyrus bankruptcy. Gelfand had Gellene confirm that he had disclosed Milbank's relationship to Goldman Sachs in two documents filed with the court and distributed to all the parties. The first was Gellene's February 1993 affidavit in support of his application to represent Bucyrus, which named Goldman as a client of Milbank's. The second was his March affidavit that described in more detail the firewall that Milbank had established to segregate its work for Bucyrus from its work for Goldman.

Gellene testified that the March supplemental affidavit was filed as a response to the objections of the trustee and JNL to his first affidavit. Both the February and March submissions had stated that Gellene was unaware of Milbank's representation of parties with any interest in the bankruptcy other than those listed in the relevant affidavit. He could not know it when he testified, but Gellene's reliance on his March 28, 1994, affidavit would later serve as one of the bases for his criminal prosecution.

Gelfand later returned to the issue of Milbank's disclosure of its relationship with Goldman. "Mr. Gellene," he asked, "do you believe that Milbank Tweed's relationship with Goldman Sachs was adequately disclosed to all parties and the Court?" "Yes, I do," said Gellene. Gelfand then asked the witness to describe the steps that he had taken "to ensure there would not be any conflict of interest between Milbank's representation of Bucyrus-Erie and Milbank's representation of Goldman Sachs on other matters." Gellene described the procedures that Milbank had put in place. Gelfand asked if at any time during the Chapter 11 proceedings Gellene was "representing the interests of any creditor or creditor group over the interests of the debtors?" Gellene replied that he was not.

In response to a question from Gelfand, Gellene stated that Milbank had received about $3.3 million in legal fees from Goldman from January 1991 through February 1994. That constituted, he said, about 0.6 percent of Milbank's $565 million fees during the same period. "Come on," interjected Judge Eisenberg, "you know that with a client like Goldman Sachs there are other considerations as well . . . what work do they bring in, who might refer and what connections did you get and [so] on. So the information was interesting but not all encompassing."

Byrnes's cross-examination of Gellene followed up on the Goldman theme. Gellene told him that no Milbank lawyers who worked on the Bucyrus bankruptcy did any work for Goldman during that period. He acknowledged that he knew that Goldman had done work on the LBO, but said that he had never discussed that transaction with Larry Lederman. Byrnes asked if Lederman had ever discussed the Bucyrus case with Gellene. Gellene replied, "[D]uring the course of 1993, from time to time, I would brief him on developments that were occurring in our attempts to obtain a consensual restructuring. At the time we commenced the Chapter 11 case, I . . . did not have any substantive discussions with him about the matter." Gellene told Byrnes that Lederman was the "client relationship" partner with Bucyrus, but that this responsibility shifted to Gellene after the company filed for bankruptcy.

A couple of exchanges during the examination of Gellene suggested that Judge Eisenberg saw New York law firm practice as excessively driven and quite different from practice in Wisconsin. On his redirect examination of Gellene, Gelfand noted that a Milbank attorney had worked 18.5 hours one day reviewing JNL's proposed exhibits for the disclosure statement hearing. Eisenberg asked, "Is it something to be proud of if you work 18 and a half hours a day? Out of curiosity, in New York do you get a button if you work hours like that saying, 'I am proud I worked 18 and a half hours today?'" Gelfand replied, "No, Your Honor." Eisenberg continued, "Okay. It certainly can't help people's personalities if they work like that day after day after day. As I see more of this, it sheds more light on perhaps why in New York there tends to be so much more acrimony than here in Milwaukee." Later, told during his own examination of Gellene that witness preparation had occurred on Father's Day, Eisenberg remarked, "I don't know why lawyers do that on Father's Day, but that's up to you. That's your decision."

A colloquy somewhat more embarrassing to Milbank occurred on the morning of Gellene's last day of testimony. Eisenberg said that he had been reviewing the various components of Milbank's fee and reimbursement request. "[O]ne of the things that . . . just sort of pop out and hit you in the eye is Lotus Cab Company, Lotus Cab Company, Lotus Cab Company, Lotus Cab Company," he remarked. Eisenberg said that he visited New York fairly often and had never seen a cab from Lotus. "Is there anything special about Lotus Cab Company?" he asked Gelfand.

Gellene interjected, "May I respond to that?" Gellene explained that Lotus was one of two sedan companies that Milbank used that did not cruise the city for passengers. Possibly primed by information that he had received from someone in New York beforehand, Eisenberg asked, "Does Milbank, Tweed have an interest in Lotus Cab Company?" "No, Your Honor," replied Gellene. "I wish the firm did, but it doesn't." Eisenberg pressed further: "Do any of the partners have an ownership interest in Lotus Cab Company?" Gellene answered, "I believe some of them do, Your Honor." Eisenberg asked if Gellene thought that this should have been disclosed to the court; Gellene said that it had not occurred to him. The judge inquired whether this issue had been raised in any court in New York. Gellene told him that as far as he knew it had not. Later, after the lunch break, Gellene informed the court that he had inquired at Milbank whether Lotus Cab Company had ever been disclosed in fee applications in New York. There had been such disclosure, he said, in the Maxwell Communication bankruptcy before Judge Brozman.

The other main witness for Bucyrus was David Goelzer, who began his testimony on the morning of December 4 after Gellene's testimony ended. Gellene conducted the direct examination. In response to a question, Goelzer expressed his belief that Milbank had used its lawyers efficiently during the bankruptcy. Indeed, he said, he occasionally had a mild concern, which was not "particularly significant," that Gellene was shouldering too much of the burden of the case:

> There were times, when I had some concern that you, Mr. Gellene, were spread a bit too thin and that the staffing in support of you could have been greater. I would say that surveying the whole history of the proceedings, possibly the only negative impact of that was at times we had to bide our time for a day or two or three while you were engaged in other matters and there didn't seem to be a complete sort of a staff available to pinch hit for you. And there were points where that was a little bit vexing to me.

Goelzer acknowledged that this also had a "positive side," which was that "by doing a great amount of the work yourself, you maintained a very good grasp at all times, not only of the broad strategy, but of the details of the engagement." The court later noted during Princi's cross-examination of Goelzer that of the 1,744 hours billed by Milbank on the case, Gellene accounted for almost 1,120 of them, with Lichstein billing another 545.

Later in the trial, Gellene brought to the judge's attention additional information about Milbank's relationship with the Lotus Cab Company. He told Eisenberg that in 1994 some twenty-three partners in the firm had investments in the company. None of the partners who worked on the Bucyrus case had any such investments, he said. He said that lawyers in the firm were free to use whichever company they chose. Eisenberg responded, "[Y]ou are saying that with a straight face, too. I am sure they would never select a company . . . in which they had an interest because they would always be happy with the service of that company." He continued:

> But my point is really simple. I think if you do business with a business owned by you or your family or your partners, I think it's—that is sort of a red flag and you should give notice, let people know what you are doing. In Milwaukee that's—we are just talking about a little pimple on the tail of a dog, so to speak. The irritation only was with disclosure.

Testimony in the case ended on January 29, 1996. Judge Eisenberg scheduled final arguments in the case for April 18, two years and two months after Bucyrus had originally filed for bankruptcy. The fee trial had made clear that Bucyrus and JNL representatives were still bitter at what each regarded as obstreperous conduct by the other during the reorganization process. The final arguments continued in that vein.

John Byrnes's closing remarks reflected irritation at both sides. It was a "gross misnomer," he said, to call this case a prepackaged bankruptcy and to request the customary expedited process afforded such reorganizations. Milbank knew that it would face maximum resistance from the company's largest creditor. Milbank also was unreasonable to resist discovery as it did, especially in light of the fact that it was seeking expedited treatment of Bucyrus's petition.

Furthermore, said Byrnes, the matter of Milbank's relationship with Goldman was not handled entirely satisfactorily. Gellene's supplement to the retention application was tardy. It came at a point when it would have been extremely difficult for Bucyrus to obtain new counsel and complete the Chapter II process on schedule. Details about the firm's representation of Goldman should have been disclosed in its original application and the accompanying affidavit. While Byrnes didn't oppose compensation for Milbank, he did suggest that it not receive the full amount for which it had asked.

With respect to JNL, Byrnes stated that "[t]hey did everything for their own benefit." JNL was the only creditor dissatisfied with its share in the prepackaged plan. It couldn't expect the other creditors to begin meaningful negotiations with it by telling them at the outset that all their claims should be subordinated to those of JNL. Furthermore, it was hard for JNL to say that Bucyrus was unwilling to negotiate when JNL had begun discussions by proposing to name Bucyrus directors in a lawsuit.

Finally, Byrnes commented on the contentious nature of the bankruptcy. There had been, he said, little effort at negotiation, compromise, or even civility between the parties. Professionals need not be enthusiastic about dealing with each other, but they shouldn't assume that "they all hate each other."

Judge Eisenberg took the parties' presentations under advisement and deliberated for more than a month on the fee applications. On May 31, he announced his decision. The application of JNL was denied, said Eisenberg, with the exception of reimbursement of $500 for a Chinese interpreter who had explained the bankruptcy proceedings to a Chinese customer of Bucyrus. Milbank Tweed was entitled to what it had received in fees and expenses to date, but no more. This left the firm with about $1.86 million in fees. Judge Eisenberg observed:

> The Court is satisfied, but not overly enthusiastic, with the explanation given by Attorney John Gellene as to how Milbank Tweed dealt with the internal conflict in representing both Goldman, Sachs in certain matters and handling matters in these two jointly administered cases which may have been adverse to Goldman, Sachs. . . .
>
> Milbank Tweed was forthright in disclosing its relationship with Goldman, Sachs, and it gave details including detailed financial information. Milbank Tweed did not try to hide its relationship with Goldman, Sachs. The Court does not view the Milbank Tweed relationship with Goldman, Sachs as a relevant matter under the facts of these cases.

Much of the judge's opinion expressed his considerable exasperation with the conduct of the parties in the proceedings. "The animosity, anger, distrust, and at time downright hatred of the parties was something to behold," he observed: "Neither side would make a concession regarding even the most obvious substantive matters until, and unless, necessary." The debtors had thrown up "every conceivable roadblock to discovery. JNL wanted everything in sight and everything which was not in sight." The cost of Milbank's fight to resist JNL's discovery demands, he suggested, was "exorbitant." Furthermore, Milbank knew the difficulty of obtaining confirmation of a nonconsensual prepackaged plan, and the "practical impossibility of getting such a plan confirmed under the facts of these cases."

JNL, declared Eisenberg, "was at all times acting in its self-interest. Any benefit to anyone else was both accidental and incidental." JNL was the only party that improved its position from the date of filing until confirmation of the plan. The creditor "chose to pursue a scorched earth policy. That was its right. It is not its right to compel the debtors to pay for that policy." Furthermore, some of JNL's discovery demands were intended primarily to assist it in its New York litigation, not the Chapter 11 proceeding.

The judge concluded on a sober note. The proceedings, he said, "were probably the most litigious, angry, and bitter cases in the history of the Eastern District of Wisconsin." They were characterized, he declared, by "a fury never before seen in this district, on any court level. . . . That's not something that we should all be proud of."

Judge Eisenberg had no idea when he spoke these words that the proceedings in the Bucyrus bankruptcy were far from over.

PART III

THE FALL

CHAPTER SEVEN

Nowhere to Hide

WHEN TONI LICHSTEIN came into her office at Milbank Tweed on the morning of Monday, February 24, 1997, she received disturbing news from her colleague Scott Edelman. Edelman had just spoken with a *Wall Street Journal* reporter. The reporter had called him to ask why Milbank was risking the loss of almost $2 million by not responding to a motion filed by Jackson National Life in federal bankruptcy court in Milwaukee. Edelman said he knew nothing about the motion. The reporter told him that JNL was claiming that in the Bucyrus bankruptcy John Gellene had hidden from the court the fact that Milbank was representing Mikael Salovaara's interests at the same time that it was counsel to Bucyrus. JNL was requesting that Judge Eisenberg order Milbank to return the $1.86 million it had earned in the bankruptcy. Milbank had not replied to JNL's accusation by the February 14 deadline. This gave the judge the authority to rule automatically against the firm. Lichstein immediately picked up the phone to call Gellene about this. From that moment on, John Gellene's world began to unravel with relentless and unforgiving speed.

ABOUT THE SAME TIME as Judge Eisenberg awarded Milbank its fees at the end of May 1996, Gellene was approached by John Jerome about relocating within the firm. Jerome had been head of Milbank's bankruptcy group for many years and Gellene's mentor within the firm. He encouraged Gellene to move to the firm's mergers and acquisitions (M&A) practice. A Milbank lawyer had left the M&A group for a job as a company general counsel. Jerome told Gellene that

Milbank partners felt that Gellene was the best available lawyer to take his place.

It is possible that a decline in Gellene's bankruptcy workload prompted the firm's request. His billable hours for 1995 through November were 1,981, a figure almost 1,250 less than for the same period in 1994. Perhaps Gellene's repeated warning of a slowdown in bankruptcy matters was finally coming true. Stories in the press over the previous year about a downturn in bankruptcy practice seemed to indicate that this was the case. One observer commented, "The big LBOs are flushed out of the system."[1] Another report stated, "Many law firms that only a few years ago earned millions from mega-bankruptcies have shifted associates back to litigation, corporate, or real estate work."[2] Weil, Gotshal's bankruptcy department, for instance, was twelve to thirteen lawyers smaller in 1995 than it had been in 1993.[3]

In any event, Gellene was ambivalent about the request. "It was a strange thing," he reflected, "to have somebody you worked with for 12 years say would you like to go somewhere else." He interpreted the suggestion as an indication that he could either practice bankruptcy at another firm or do M&A work at Milbank. Milbank was the only place Gellene had worked since his judicial clerkship in the year following law school. He had already left the firm once and didn't want to do so again. Moreover, the move could be a challenge for him, an opportunity to retool. As a result, he agreed to move to the fifty-fifth floor to join the M&A lawyers.

The change proved far more stressful than Gellene had anticipated. One reason was that he took his pending bankruptcy work with him rather than handing it off to someone else. This meant that he was "carrying a double burden": traveling extensively on bankruptcy matters while coming to grips with the new demands of representing clients involved in buying and selling companies.

The strain was exacerbated by the fact that he found it difficult to get enough help from other bankruptcy lawyers in the firm. He was ten floors above the bankruptcy practice group, and could no longer just go down the hall and enlist the aid of a colleague or draw on his or her advice. Furthermore, as Gellene put it, younger bankruptcy lawyers "were ambitious like lots of young lawyers and they knew that I wasn't going to be the one to sort of bring them along." As an M&A lawyer, Gellene would not be conducting their performance reviews, nor would he be in an effective position to lobby for them when the firm was considering them for partner.

In the past, Gellene would have been able to go to John Jerome and ask for more support. Jerome, however, was no longer head of the bankruptcy practice. He had been replaced by two lawyers, one of whom was in the Los Angeles office and had been with the firm only four years. Adding to the difficulty, as Gellene himself admitted, was the fact that he was the sort of person who, when he needed help, "wouldn't necessarily reach out for it." The result was that Gellene just vowed to work harder, to do whatever it took to carry his workload. He felt increasingly isolated, unable to gain the support of bankruptcy lawyers, while finding it hard to fit in with the M&A group. He had made the move because he wanted to stay with the people with whom he had worked for the last dozen years. Now, however, he found that he had little contact with them or anyone else in the firm.

A couple of months after moving to the M&A department, activity in the Busse matter picked up. Gellene had begun work in the case on behalf of South Street in December 1993. After a flurry of activity in summer 1995, the proceedings had been dormant for several months. In April 1996, however, the bankruptcy trustee in Denver served South Street with a request for documents in order to bolster his argument that the court should deny South Street's claim to collect on the Fetzer note in the Gillett bankruptcy. When Gellene failed to respond, the trustee filed a motion to compel production of the documents. On the eve of a hearing on that motion, Gellene reached an agreement with the trustee to produce the documents within a couple of weeks or so. When that deadline passed, the trustee filed another motion to compel. In addition, he asked that South Street be sanctioned by having its claim disallowed. The court granted that request on August 2, 1996.

When Gellene received the court's order, he sent an August 8 letter to the trustee enclosing the requested documents. The following day, he submitted a motion asking the court to reconsider its order denying South Street's claim. The motion stated that "[t]he delay in responding to the document requests was the result of the winding up of the South Street Funds and an ongoing dispute between the managing partner of the South Street Funds and the fund's portfolio advisor, Greycliff Partners, Ltd., regarding control of the funds and other matters. This dispute is the result of ongoing litigation between the parties and their principals." The court denied Gellene's motion. This meant that South Street could not recover on the $19.9 million note that it had purchased.

The corporate secretary of South Street Fund, Gary Hindes, later stated that Gellene did not even inform him of the document request until Hindes called Gellene in late July for general information about the status of the Gillett bankruptcy proceeding. Hindes had been frustrated about Salovaara's secretiveness concerning the Fetzer note. He had learned of it only in May 1996 at a South Street investors meeting. His call to Gellene was prompted by the fact that Salovaara refused to give him any information that would allow Hindes and the partnership's auditors to ascribe a value to the claim for bookkeeping purposes.

In the course of the conversation, Gellene mentioned the trustee's request for documents and asked Hindes to provide him with the relevant material. Hindes, who was preparing for a deposition in one of several lawsuits that Salovaara had filed against him, asked if he could get to it the following week. Gellene responded that he needed the documents in the next day or so. When Hindes reiterated his difficulty in gathering the material on such short notice, Gellene told him that all that was really necessary were the documents creating the South Street Fund and the entities associated with them.

Hindes promptly sent this material to Gellene, who must have received it right around the time that the court in Colorado entered its order disallowing South Street's claim. The litigation involving South Street, Hindes made clear, did not affect the company's ability to meet any document request from the Denver trustee. Hindes says that Gellene told him in December of that year that Salovaara had never provided Gellene with any documents relating to the Fetzer claim. Whether because of Salovaara's secrecy, Gellene's workload, or a combination of the two, the failure to respond to the request for documents resulted in a death blow to South Street's claim of almost $20 million. This sequence of events would later come back to haunt Gellene in his criminal trial.

IN DECEMBER 1996, John Stark was on a flight from New York to Chicago. He was reviewing trial transcripts in an effort to locate funds that Mikael Salovaara would have available if JNL prevailed in its lawsuit against South Street. Salovaara's dispute with Eckert, Stark thought, might reveal something about South Street's financial condition that Stark could use to his advantage. As he perused the papers in that case, he found much more than he had bargained for. He was shocked to read Salovaara's testimony that Larry Lederman and Toni Lichstein of Milbank had represented Salovaara in the dispute with Eckert since December 1993. Salovaara also stated that Lichstein had appeared at his deposition in that case in February 1994, and that Milbank previously had represented Eckert in a trust and estate matter. Milbank, in other words, had been representing the key partner of Bucyrus's secured creditor at the same time that the firm was counsel to Bucyrus. Yet Gellene had never disclosed this to the court or to any of the parties in the bankruptcy.

As soon as his plane touched ground, Stark called Andy Rahl with this news. They agreed that JNL should immediately call it to Judge Eisenberg's attention. On December 12, 1996, JNL filed a motion that did so. The motion stated that JNL recently had learned that Larry Lederman and Toni Lichstein were representing Mikael Salovaara in December 1993 in his dispute with Fred Eckert, at the same time that Lederman and Milbank were representing Bucyrus. JNL noted that the Form S-4 that had been filed with the SEC late in the year regarding the proposed Chapter 11 plan had Lederman's name on its cover. Furthermore, Gellene had stated in his declaration to the court that he periodically briefed Lederman during 1993 on the progress of negotiations concerning a financial restructuring of Bucyrus. In addition, alleged JNL, Toni Lichstein, who was the Milbank partner in charge of litigation matters in the Bucyrus bankruptcy, represented Salovaara at his February 1994 deposition in his lawsuit against Eckert. Finally, Salovaara had testified that Milbank in the past had served Eckert as trust and estate counsel.

JNL also indicated that Salovaara had testified about what JNL described as the "close personal relationship between himself and Mr. Lederman of Milbank." Salovaara had discussed a trip that the two men took "to a bicycle camp in March 1993 and the Thanksgiving holiday in 1993 that Mr. Lederman spent with both Eckert and Salovaara at Salovaara's house." At that same time, Bucyrus was involved in negotiations with South Street about whether to release it from any claims that Bucyrus might have against it.

JNL maintained that Milbank's failure to disclose its representation of Salovaara and Eckert was especially egregious in the circumstances of the Bucyrus bankruptcy:

> [T]he critical importance of Salovaara (and Eckert) as parties in interest in the bankruptcy case—and Milbank's indisputable knowledge of Salovaara's role—cannot be overemphasized. Milbank knew that Jackson believed that Salovaara and Eckert were liable to the debtors for millions of dollars of damages for fraudulent conveyances and other claims. Throughout the bankruptcy case, Salovaara's involvement in the 1988 LBO, the 1989 Exchange Offer and the 1992 sale leaseback transaction was at the heart of the disputed issues that needed to be resolved for a plan to be confirmed. Perhaps even more so than Goldman, the worst conflict that could have existed for counsel for these debtors was to represent Salovaara.

Bankruptcy Rule 2014, the motion argued, is intended to aid the court in ensuring that an attorney for the debtor is disinterested. This makes strict compliance with the rule essential to the integrity of the bankruptcy system. A lawyer applying for retention has no discretion to decide which connections to disclose. The court must receive complete information about any connection, no matter how trivial it might seem. Only the court is authorized to make the determination whether debtor's counsel might be compromised by his relationship with other interested parties. Milbank's interference with the court's ability to fulfill this obligation, claimed JNL, warranted that the firm disgorge all the compensation it had received during the course of the bankruptcy. This came to $1.86 million.

Upon receiving JNL's motion papers, Gellene sat at his desk in shock. He had the feeling that what he had accomplished in the Bucyrus bankruptcy "had just become dust." He was stunned to learn from the JNL papers that Lederman and Salovaara were close enough friends to have had Thanksgiving dinner together. "What don't I know about this?" he wondered to himself.

Gellene made three sets of copies of the motion papers, one each for himself, Lederman, and Lichstein. He did the same when Bucyrus, represented by Forrest Lammiman of Chicago's Lord, Bissell & Brook, filed its own disgorgement motion a short time later. JNL, of course, was now the controlling shareholder of the company as a result of the bankruptcy. It therefore was no surprise that Bucyrus would file a motion similar to JNL's. The papers sat on his desk as he tried to figure out how to cope with the crisis that suddenly confronted him. He told no one as he wrestled with how to account for what he had done—and had not done—more than two years earlier.

As Gellene remained paralyzed by distress, the deadline to respond to the disgorgement motions loomed near and then passed. Gellene was roused from his immobility by Lichstein's phone call on February 24 after Scott Edelman told her about the call from the *Wall Street Journal.* Had JNL filed such a motion? she asked Gellene. He confirmed that it had. When? she inquired. Gellene gave her only a vague answer. Lichstein asked Gellene for a copy of the papers, and he agreed to send them to her. She had to follow up with more calls to Gellene during the day before she finally received anything.

What Gellene finally sent her late in the day, however, was only the memorandum of law in support of JNL's motion. The memo was unusual in that it had no date on the signature page. Lichstein then called Gellene to ask him for the other papers connected with the motion, such as the motion itself and the accompanying affidavit. By the end of the day on Monday the twenty-fourth, she still had not received them.

Meanwhile, the inquiry by the *Journal* prompted a meeting the next day between Gellene and several high-level partners in the firm. The meeting was called by Milbank chair Mel Immerglut. Present were Gellene; Immerglut; Lederman; Lichstein; John Jerome; Geoffrey Barist, the head of the litigation practice; and Trayton Davis, a member of Milbank's executive committee. Lichstein was piqued that Lederman and Gellene had downplayed her earlier inquiries about a potential conflict. She suggested to Lederman that perhaps they should have taken her more seriously. Gellene nonetheless appeared composed during the meeting. He did not talk about the specifics of the JNL motion. He intimated, however, that the *Wall Street Journal* was incorrect about the deadline to respond. A response to the motion, he said, was due that coming Friday, February 28. He gave no indication of any problems with the response. The other Milbank partners apparently left the meeting feeling reassured that Gellene was on top of the situation, and that there was no danger to the firm.

After the meeting, Lichstein continued to ask Gellene for the full set of papers associated with the motion. She would be happy, she said, to help with the response. Gellene said that he would prepare a draft response the next day, which she could then review before it was filed on Friday. As the day went on, Lichstein's exasperation mounted as her repeated calls to Gellene failed to result in receipt of the papers. At one point, Lichstein enlisted Barist and asked for his help. Barist called Gellene, but the latter was not in his office.

Finally, late that afternoon Lichstein sat down to read closely the only document she had, the memorandum of law. She was surprised by the fact that it referred to an accompanying affidavit of Andy Rahl dated December 12, 1996. That's odd, she thought. Why would a motion that had been filed in February be accompanied by an affidavit executed two months earlier? Lichstein then asked David Gelfand to go up to Gellene's office to get a copy of the full set of papers. Gelfand had no more luck than she had, and came back empty-handed.

Finally, early that evening, Lichstein phoned Gellene in his office and asked why the Rahl affidavit was dated in December. Gellene said that he would come down to talk to Lichstein and Gelfand.

Gellene was quite distraught when he entered Lichstein's office. As Gelfand put it, "[W]hat happened next was a very difficult thing to witness." Gellene broke down in front of his colleagues. He felt terrible, he said, but he couldn't lie to Lichstein and Gelfand any longer. He said that the JNL motion papers had actually been served on him in December 1996, and that he had later received a second set of papers filed on behalf of Bucyrus. He explained why the memorandum that he had given Lichstein had no date on the signature page: Gellene had whited it out. The motions, he said, had come at the end of a very difficult year for him both professionally and personally. The movement to the M&A practice had been "very disruptive," and his father-in-law had died suddenly. Gellene said that he had been immobilized by the two motions. He had sought an extension of time to file a response to them. The court, however, had denied his request. As a result, he had missed the deadline by about two weeks. Milbank thus faced the prospect that Judge Eisenberg would rule that the firm had to return almost $2 million to Bucyrus.

As Lichstein and Gelfand listened, their concern about the two motions was eclipsed by their alarm at Gellene's state of mind. They had never seen Gellene in such a condition, and had no idea what he might do next. They sought to reassure him that they would do whatever they could to help him deal with the situation. Gellene pulled together the motion papers for Gelfand shortly afterward in his office, but it was obvious that he was extremely distraught. Gelfand asked Gellene if he could take him out for a beer, and Gellene accepted. Lichstein spent all her time the next day with Gellene because she was concerned about what he might do if he were left alone. Gellene attended a meeting with a client outside the office that morning. He then went back to Milbank and was put on paid leave by the firm for "serious problems requiring medical attention."

Stephen Blauner, cochair of Milbank's bankruptcy practice, announced that the firm had become belatedly aware of JNL's claim.

We take the allegations "very seriously," he said, "and we intend to thoroughly and completely respond." The disgorgement motion, he suggested, was simply a continuation of JNL's efforts to reduce Milbank's fees, now that Jackson owned a controlling interest in Bucyrus. Stark retorted, "The conflict is incredible, and it may be the reason that Salovaara got too much and everyone else too little."

David Gelfand undertook a preliminary investigation of the matter on behalf of the firm. Milbank eventually called in the law firm of Sidley & Austin to handle the matter. The February 14 deadline for responding to the JNL and Bucyrus motions had passed. Gelfand, however, prepared an affidavit stating that no one at the firm other than Gellene had been aware of the motions. The court then granted Milbank an extension of the time to reply until March 21.

Meanwhile, Milbank lawyers interviewed Gellene as they gathered information about the Bucyrus matter. Later in March, Gellene submitted an affidavit to the bankruptcy court concerning his motion for appointment as Bucyrus counsel. In it, he accepted "full and complete responsibility" for the failure to inform the court of Milbank's representation of Salovaara. "At no time," he said, "during or before the bankruptcy cases did I ask Mr. Lederman, Ms. Lichstein or any other of my partners to review the disclosures submitted to the court." He stated that he had explained to Lederman his thinking on disclosure at the time he filed the retention application. "Lederman," he said, had "accepted my judgment." Gellene declared that his errors "were entirely my own," and reflected "a mistake in judgment." Gellene did maintain, however, that Bucyrus management "was well aware" that Lederman "had a long-standing attorney-client relationship with Goldman, Sachs, as well as a personal relationship with Mr. Salovaara." Furthermore, stated Gellene, Milbank's "involvement in unrelated matters had no impact on the quality, loyalty, or zealousness of our representation."

Milbank echoed the latter theme in papers filed April 30 in response to the disgorgement motions. The response revealed for the first time that Gellene himself had worked briefly on behalf of Salovaara in his dispute with Eckert. "Milbank acknowledges and profoundly regrets its failures; and it recognizes that the consequences for these failures are properly within the discretion of this court," the firm declared. "Milbank is also convinced, however," the pleading went on to say, "that its errors caused no economic injury to any party in interest in this case." Indeed, claimed the firm, "there can be no question that Milbank delivered exceptional value to Bucyrus' estate."

Citing Gellene's most recent statement to the court, the firm argued that Gellene alone was responsible for the failure to make proper disclosure in the bankruptcy proceeding. JNL's attack on Milbank, claimed the firm, was an attempt simply to relitigate the "long, bitter and contentious battle" between JNL and all the other parties in interest.

Bucyrus and JNL did not see it that way, however. Bucyrus's brief in response said that "the hear no evil, see no evil approach simply does not explain [Milbank's] failure to disclose multiple representations" of Salovaara. Two Milbank lawyers "were covertly representing" Salovaara, wrote Lammiman, in a dispute over assets that included rights to payment from the South Street Fund's investments in Bucyrus. JNL contended that the firm was attempting to avoid responsibility through the "disgraceful self-serving sacrifice of John Gellene by using his confession that was signed, no doubt under great personal pressure." In the same vein, trustee John Byrnes added, "Both legally and factually, it's somewhat simplistic to attribute it all to a misjudgment by one partner."

Both Rahl and Stark voiced their conviction to the press that Milbank's failure to disclose was part of a broader scheme to benefit Salovaara. "We believe," said Rahl, "that this was a deliberate strategy/conspiracy; that some individuals in this law firm were trying to aid Salovaara. When you piece together all of the unexplained things that happened in the case, it is the only rational explanation for what happened."

Similarly, Stark said, "I think there were probably three or four partners involved. The partner who was the architect of the scheme was Larry Lederman. Then he involved Gellene, Lichstein and Gelfand." The problem, suggested Stark was the "star system" established when Milbank recruited Lederman from Wachtell, Lipton. "[T]hat was a big deal when they got him and I think, basically, he was allowed to operate in an unsupervised manner . . . [I]n lots of organizations, if you let one person establish themselves as superior to the others, that is a recipe for disaster." "The conspiracy theory is absolute rubbish," retorted Blauner. The *Wall Street Journal*, however, was not sympathetic to the idea that Milbank's sanction should be limited to its expression of regret. "[I]f an apology after the fact were sufficient penalty for one caught out," it said, "why would anyone disclose at all?"

On June 4, Judge Eisenberg ruled that Milbank had violated Bankruptcy Rule 2014. He scheduled a nine-day hearing in February on the disgorgement request by Bucyrus and JNL. Byrnes later filed a motion for sanctions, disgorgement, and revocation of the order approving Milbank as counsel for Bucyrus during the Chapter 11 proceedings, on the ground that the firm had obtained its position through fraud. At least one of the lawyers involved speculated that the judge had set such an extensive schedule in order to encourage the parties to settle the case.

Former Bucyrus general counsel David Goelzer probably had worked more closely with Gellene during the bankruptcy than had any other company official. He learned of Gellene's secret while on a ski trip in Michigan's Upper Peninsula with Norbert Verville and Bucyrus controller Craig Mackus. Goelzer called into his office for messages and received word that David Gelfand of Milbank had called with an urgent request to speak to him. When he called Gelfand back, the Milbank lawyer described what had occurred in Lichstein's office. Gellene, he said, had basically broken down and was in terrible shape. Goelzer was shocked, as were Verville and Mackus when he told them. They couldn't imagine that Gellene would do this, especially since it seemed so unlikely that he would be able to hide for long the fact of Milbank's representation of Salovaara.

As summer began, Forrest Lammiman contacted Goelzer for assistance in JNL's claim against Milbank. Lammiman asked if Goelzer would sign an affidavit refuting Milbank's contention that it was immune from any claim by Bucyrus against it by virtue of releases contained in the amended bankruptcy plan. Goelzer signed a short statement, which expressed his disapproval of Gellene's failure to comply with Rule 2014. He then spent considerable time with Lammiman reconstructing the events surrounding the bankruptcy.

Lammiman also told Goelzer that the company would help him and other current or former Bucyrus officials retain criminal defense counsel to deal with any investigation that might occur. Milwaukee attorney Steven Epstein took on the representation of Goelzer for this purpose. Hiring criminal defense counsel was necessary because the stakes in the Gellene matter had gone well beyond simply disgorgement of bankruptcy fees. In early May, the United States Attorney's Office in Milwaukee had begun to investigate whether Gellene's breach of Rule 2014 had violated federal criminal law.

A MAJOR IMPETUS for the criminal investigation was trustee John Byrnes. Byrnes had familiarity with criminal matters by virtue of his former service as U.S. attorney in Milwaukee. His and the federal prosecutor's office were both located downtown in the federal courthouse. Byrnes called Assistant U.S. Attorney Steven Biskupic when the Gellene story broke and suggested that he come down to talk to Byrnes about Gellene's misconduct. "This is a big deal," he told Biskupic. He recommended that the U.S. Attorney's Office consider bringing charges against Gellene for making false statements to the court in connection with Gellene's appointment application. Byrnes reportedly "laid out the paper trail to make the task more enticing."

The arguments for prosecution may have had force also because of a sense that, as one publication put it, "a venerable local company claimed it had been betrayed by its New York attorneys." Concern that New York law firms might try to cut corners in Milwaukee had been voiced by Judge Eisenberg earlier in the bankruptcy proceedings, when he informed Gellene at a hearing on Gellene's application that "New York is different from Milwaukee. . . . [P]rofessional things like conflicts are taken very, very seriously. And for better or worse you're stuck in Wisconsin." Biskupic swung into action in late May, when the

federal grand jury in Milwaukee began to subpoena documents in connection with a criminal investigation.

Biskupic was a thirty-five-year-old prosecutor who had been in the
office since March 1989. He had grown up in the Chicago suburbs, but
attended Marquette University in Milwaukee for both his undergraduate and law school education. He came from a family of lawyers: his
father and sister were lawyers, as was a brother who was the district
attorney for Appleton, Wisconsin. Biskupic had clerked after law
school for Chief Federal District Court Judge Robert Warren in Milwaukee from 1987 to 1989. He was a dark-haired, lanky, six-feet, four-
inch man who looked more like an earnest student government representative than a federal prosecutor. His demeanor was low-key and
serious.

Working with Biskupic was Joseph Wall, who had been in the office
about four years longer. Wall was a certified public accountant who
also had been an assistant district attorney. As the investigation proceeded, he took responsibility for preparing charts of the various
financial transactions in which Bucyrus had been involved that had
been at issue in its bankruptcy.

Partly at the instigation of Byrnes, the Milwaukee U.S. Attorney's
Office in recent years had focused more on bankruptcy matters. It had
obtained convictions under the bankruptcy fraud statute primarily for
concealing assets and for embezzlement from bankruptcy estates. At
the time he began the Gellene investigation, Biskupic was working on
a case involving a developer's lawyer who had hidden in a trust
account funds that he should have disclosed to the bankruptcy court
as part of his fees. Given his familiarity with the Bankruptcy Code and
his experience in working with Byrnes, Biskupic regarded a possible
prosecution of Gellene for bankruptcy fraud as well within the scope
of the type of cases he had pursued.

From the outset, Biskupic deliberately sought to put to one side the
complications of the bankruptcy proceeding and the animosities that
had permeated it. His focus was simply on what had happened in the
courtroom: had Gellene intentionally lied to Judge Eisenberg when he
filed his Rule 2014 declarations? Biskupic did eventually learn the

intricacies of the LBO and the various transactions that were at issue in the Chapter II case. He also checked out Larry Lederman's book *Tombstones* from the library to gain some insight into the Milbank partner. He found both the deals and the book interesting, but Biskupic regarded them as ultimately irrelevant to whether the office should prosecute Gellene.

In Biskupic's mind, the salient issues were the truthfulness of Gellene's representations to the court and his state of mind when he made them. He thus limited his contact with JNL to efforts to obtain certain documents, and is adamant that JNL had no influence on the decision to prosecute Gellene. Biskupic also determined at an early point that neither Lederman nor Lichstein were subjects or targets of the investigation, since they had not submitted any sworn statements to the bankruptcy court.

Biskupic and Wall worked with the FBI over the summer to put together the pieces of the case. They contacted Sidley & Austin to obtain Milbank's billing records, and got copies of the depositions in the civil proceedings against the firm. They consulted Byrnes on occasion for an explanation of the Bucyrus Chapter II proceeding and the context in which Gellene's statements were made. The prosecutors obtained facts from Byrnes and discussed possible legal theories with him, but remained prepared not to pursue an indictment if they concluded that the case would not be supportable. Biskupic and Wall also had to be careful not to give Byrnes too much information, since he would be a witness subject to cross-examination in any criminal trial.

Eventually, prosecutors came to rely heavily on David Goelzer for information. Goelzer's precise notes and his memory were valuable to the prosecutors, and made him an excellent prospective witness at trial. They were confident that he would say nothing unexpected or surprising on the witness stand. Furthermore, while Goelzer was insistent that Gellene should have disclosed Milbank's representation of Salovaara, he had no personal grudge against Gellene. In fact, he believed that Gellene had done an excellent job during the bankruptcy. Goelzer ended up testifying before the grand jury as well as at trial. He and Biskupic developed a good working relationship. After the trial, they learned that they attended the same Catholic church at Marquette University.

The prosecutors believed that, unlike most investigations of perjury or false statements, the case got stronger as they went along. They regarded Gellene's earlier misrepresentation of his New York state bar membership as relevant to his state of mind when he submitted his Rule 2014 declarations, undercutting any claim that his failure to disclose was unintentional. This led Biskupic to wonder what representations Gellene had made when he had applied to practice before the federal bankruptcy court in Milwaukee.

Biskupic walked down to the clerk of the court's office and asked what the office did with the records that accompany lawyers being sworn in to practice before the court. The clerk led him to a large box filled with papers. Biskupic and the clerk waded through the papers looking for Gellene's application from 1994. Eventually, they found it. Gellene had stated under oath that he was a member of the bar for the federal court in the southern district of New York, which included Manhattan. Gellene in fact wasn't a member of this bar, even though he practiced regularly there in federal court. He hadn't taken the simple steps to gain admission to it even after finally being admitted to the New York state bar. In fact, Gellene didn't need to be a member of the federal bar in order to be admitted to practice before the court in Milwaukee. He needed only to be a member in good standing of his state bar. His misrepresentation therefore was unnecessary.

Awareness that Gellene also had worked for South Street on the Busse matter led Biskupic to interview Gary Hindes. Hindes had managed South Street for a period, although he currently was embroiled in a dispute with Salovaara over his performance of that duty. Hindes refuted Gellene's assertion to the Gillett bankruptcy court that South Street's failure to respond to the trustee's request for documents was due to the litigation between Salovaara and Eckert. In Biskupic's eyes, all these events tipped the scales toward prosecution. They were additional occasions on which Gellene had lied to a court. They strongly suggested that Gellene's failure to disclose Milbank's ties to Salovaara and South Street was not an honest mistake, but was intentional.

Meanwhile, Mark Rotert of the Chicago law firm of Winston & Strawn had agreed to represent John Gellene in the criminal investigation. Rotert, a bearded, stocky, down-to-earth man in his mid-forties, was a South Dakota native who had attended law school at Loyola in Chicago. He had spent ten years as an assistant state attorney general in Illinois, then seven years as an assistant United States attorney in Chicago, where he was director of the white-collar crime unit. As a prosecutor, he had concentrated on fraud cases, and had overseen a major undercover project that uncovered commodities fraud at the Chicago Board of Trade and the Chicago Mercantile Exchange. He had joined Winston & Strawn in 1994.

Rotert's partner Dan Webb, a noted white-collar criminal defense lawyer, had received a call from Milbank Tweed in the early summer of 1997. The firm was interviewing possible lawyers to represent it in connection with the criminal investigation in Milwaukee. Webb himself was too busy to take on the matter, but recommended that Rotert meet with Milbank.

Rotert went to the O'Hare Airport Conference Center to discuss the case with Milbank chair Mel Immerglut and Milbank litigation partner Geoffrey Barist. Rotert was not a regular reader of the business press. When the Milbank partners prefaced their discussion with the remark that Rotert undoubtedly had read about the matter in the *Wall Street Journal*, Rotert thought that assumption doomed his chance to get the case. He hadn't read about the Bucyrus controversy and had no idea what it involved. Immerglut and Barist summarized the facts for him and Rotert gave them his impressions. He left the meeting doubting that the firm would be interested in hiring him because he had no experience in bankruptcy and wasn't sure how much they were looking for white-collar criminal expertise.

A few days afterward, the firm called and asked Rotert if he would represent John Gellene in the criminal matter. Milbank would pay Gellene's legal costs. Rotert had just finished an arduous trial in Texarkana, Texas. The call came the Thursday before the Saturday Rotert planned to leave on a vacation with his family to Cancún, Mexico. Rotert said that he would take on the case if it didn't interfere with his vacation. Gellene called later that afternoon and asked if he and Rotert could get together. Rotert told him that they would have to meet the next day because Rotert would be leaving at 4:00 P.M. Friday afternoon to begin a ten-day vacation. Gellene flew in the next morning, and the two discussed the broad outlines of the case before Rotert left town.

When he returned, Rotert spent a considerable amount of time learning the complexities of the case. Unlike Biskupic, he sought to focus on the dynamics of the Bucyrus bankruptcy and the transactions that had led up to it. This context might offer the best perspective from which to argue that, in the wider scheme of things, Gellene did not deserve to face criminal prosecution. Aside from notifying the U.S. Attorney's Office that he was representing Gellene, Rotert was in no particular hurry to be in contact with the prosecutors. He wanted time to get his arms around the case, and figured that Biskupic was probably at the same fact-finding stage.

In the midst of all this turmoil, Bucyrus continued not only to operate but to thrive. In 1996, the company now known as Bucyrus International had turned a profit for the first time in seven years, with earnings of $2.88 million on sales of almost $265 million. In early spring, Bucyrus had announced that it planned to acquire the Marion Power Shovel Co. This prompted an increase of 59 percent in the company's share price by the end of July. On July 31, Bucyrus agreed to be purchased by American Industrial Partners Capital Fund II L.P., a private investment partnership that makes equity investments in companies located mostly in the United States. Bucyrus stock rose 26 percent upon announcement of the agreement, resulting in a purchase price of about $190 million.

Officials associated with the company praised the move, emphasizing the partnership's track record of patient investment. JNL, Bucyrus's largest shareholder with some 43 percent of its equity, expressed its approval through Stark, the chairman of the company's board. "The people at American Industrial Partners invested a lot in the management team as well as the company," he said. Stark went on to say, "We've been involved with this company for seven years, and it hasn't always been a happy experience. It's time to redeploy our capital." He said that JNL would receive $76 million from the takeover, representing an annualized rate of return of 3.4 percent. Stark also claimed that JNL would have had an even greater stake in Bucyrus after the bankruptcy if not for the machinations of Salovaara.

DURING THE SUMMER of 1997, Milbank filed a motion in the disgorgement action for a protective order that would prohibit both depositions and the production of documents. Among other things, Milbank contended that the documents regarding the bankruptcy in its possession were its, not Bucyrus's, property. On August 21, Judge Eisenberg denied Milbank's motion. He authorized Bucyrus to begin deposing Gellene, Lederman, Lichstein, and Gelfand in early September. At the same time, he cautioned Bucyrus to limit questions to those directly relevant to the disgorgement motion. Steven Biskupic had assured the judge at the hearing on that day that discovery proceedings in the disgorgement action would not interfere with the government's criminal investigation.

Around the same time, Rotert arranged to have Gellene finally meet Biskupic and tell his story. He and Gellene made the two-hour drive together from Chicago to Milwaukee one morning. They met with Biskupic around nine o'clock. Although Gellene was not under oath and made no formal presentation, he answered Biskupic's questions for the better part of the day. The situation was immensely stressful, but Rotert was struck by Gellene's enormous self-control throughout the interview. When he finished his questioning, Biskupic asked Gellene to leave the room so that he could talk privately with Rotert.

As he discussed the case with Biskupic, Rotert could see Gellene through the window, pacing on the street opposite the courthouse as his fate was being decided. Gellene's life was already in shambles, Rotert emphasized to the prosecutor. His reputation had been destroyed, and he would never be hired again by a major law firm. In light of the punishment he had already suffered, Rotert argued, prosecuting Gellene for a felony would provide little additional deterrent. Furthermore, it would bar him from voting, would deprive him of his license to practice law, and could result in a prison sentence—injuries far out of proportion to any harm he had caused.

Having assessed the case, Biskupic was prepared to permit Gellene to plead guilty to a misdemeanor for contempt of court, with no recommendation on a sentence. Gellene would have to cooperate in all further investigations by the U.S. Attorney's Office. His law license would be automatically suspended, although he would have the right to apply for readmission to the bar at a later time. Rotert said that he would get back to Biskupic within twenty-four hours.

Biskupic's proposal had some appeal to Gellene. Ideally, of course, he must have hoped that the prosecutor would simply decide not to pursue criminal charges. Short of that, however, pleading guilty to a misdemeanor would preserve the possibility that he might one day practice law again, and would eliminate the chance that he might have to serve time in prison. After speaking with Gellene, Rotert called Biskupic the next morning and agreed to his proposal.

Rotert and Biskupic then began negotiation over the next several days on a statement of facts that would serve as the foundation for the plea. Determining precisely how to describe in the plea Gellene's state of mind when he had submitted his disclosure affidavits to the bankruptcy court was a tricky matter. There had to be sufficient culpability to support a criminal charge, but not so egregious as to trigger a felony prosecution.

About ten days later, Rotert was downstate in Bloomington on a white-collar matter. He contacted his office for messages, and learned that Biskupic had called and asked him to get in touch right away. Rotert called the prosecutor. He could tell by Biskupic's tone of voice that something was wrong. U.S. Attorney Thomas Schneider had rejected the plea agreement, insisting that the office seek a felony conviction. Rotert inferred from Biskupic's tone of voice that the prosecutor was distressed at this turn of events. From his own prosecution experience, of course, Rotert knew that an assistant U.S. attorney could never have the final word on plea bargains. He was aware that Biskupic's superiors might override his decision. At the same time, the parties had been involved in intense negotiations about the factual

basis for the misdemeanor plea. Those dynamics had fostered Rotert
and Gellene's expectation that Gellene no longer needed to fear exposure to a felony charge. Heartsick, Rotert broke the news to Gellene.
The stakes were now much higher. They would be fighting for Gellene's liberty and his ability to practice law.

Rotert was furious over Schneider's decision to reject the plea bargain. If the case had been in New York, Chicago, or Los Angeles, he
believed, there would have been no prosecution at all. He couldn't
help wondering if the U.S. attorney wanted a high-profile prosecution
because of public reaction to the events surrounding the Bucyrus
bankruptcy. The theme of much of the press coverage of the case had
been that rich people were scooping money out of the company while
blue-collar workers faced the possibility of losing their jobs. Bringing
charges against a wealthy Wall Street lawyer who had not been forthright with the company could be a way of playing to that sentiment.
All other cases involving Rule 2014 violations had resulted in fines or
disgorgement of fees. Why single out Gellene for criminal sanctions?

Biskupic understood Rotert's frustration at the ultimate decision.
He maintained, however, that it was based on concerns that went
beyond Gellene's particular case. Gellene's insistence that he had not
intentionally done anything wrong, he said, made it difficult to establish a factual foundation for a criminal contempt charge. The U.S.
Attorney's Office simply could not enter into plea agreements "with
that kind of disconnect" between the required elements of the offense
and the defendant's admissions about his state of mind. Furthermore,
the office kept discovering new evidence of Gellene's past dishonesty
that seriously called into question any claim that Gellene had not
acted intentionally. The harm that Gellene inflicted, Biskupic said,
was to the bankruptcy court and trustee, by thwarting their ability to
ensure the integrity of the proceedings. Given that, the office didn't
believe that a felony prosecution would be disproportionate to the
wrongdoing that Gellene had committed.

All this ultimately convinced prosecutors that proceeding on the
felony charges "wasn't a close call." They knew that a judge might not
allow them to admit the evidence of Gellene's prior deceptions on the

ground that it was more prejudicial than probative. Nonetheless, they were prepared to argue that these incidents provided a powerful rebuttal to Gellene's claim that his failure to meet his Rule 2014 disclosure obligation was not intentional.

On September 25, Bucyrus turned up the heat on Milbank by filing a lawsuit against the firm in Wisconsin state court in Milwaukee for fraud, breach of contract, malpractice, and breach of fiduciary responsibility. The company sought $100 million in damages. It claimed that it could have recovered at least that amount if Milbank had disclosed its representation of both Bucyrus and Salovaara, or properly advised Bucyrus of the company's true interests.

The complaint asserted that Milbank "dissuaded Bucyrus from filing bankruptcy in early 1992 in order to enable the Salovaara parties to benefit from a $35 million financing with Bucyrus," whom Milbank represented. Bucyrus then entered into a transaction with South Street on terms that were "highly disadvantageous" to the company. Bucyrus claimed that Salovaara had leased the company's equipment back to it "at exorbitant lease financing rates." Milbank thus allegedly conspired with Salovaara to strip Bucyrus of its assets. The complaint claimed that Bucyrus was especially vulnerable to such a conspiracy because its senior officials had "relied heavily on Milbank and Salovaara for business advice as well as legal advice" in the company's bankruptcy and its financing decisions from 1991 through 1995.

Furthermore, Bucyrus maintained, Milbank's ties to Salovaara during the bankruptcy prevented the firm from providing disinterested advice to Bucyrus about the possibility of pursuing a fraudulent conveyance action against South Street for the sale-leaseback. Bucyrus claimed that Milbank had accepted engagements to represent Salovaara and South Street in late 1993 and early 1994 knowing that those engagements would have to be concealed in order for Milbank "to obtain the lucrative representation of Bucyrus in the bankruptcy proceedings, thus giving Salovaara an enormous degree of leverage and control over Milbank's actions throughout the bankruptcy proceedings and thereby making Milbank Salovaara's agent in pursuing his interests."

In sum, Bucyrus alleged, "The contemporaneous representation of the Salovaara parties during the bankruptcy proceedings—by the same attorneys at Milbank who represented Bucyrus—were [*sic*] in knowing contravention of Milbank's duty to provide full disclosure to the bankruptcy court and all interested parties, as well as in direct violation of Milbank's ethical and professional responsibilities." JNL financed the suit by Bucyrus against Milbank, claiming that it had suffered $60 million in damages of its own. If the company won, JNL would receive the fee reimbursement from Milbank and the first $8.69 million recovered in the malpractice suit. The two companies would split anything above that figure.

As discovery proceeded in the disgorgement action, Milbank filed a motion to seal all documents that it produced, as well as the depositions of Gellene, Lederman, Lichstein, and Gelfand. The firm argued that this was necessary in order to prevent the disclosure of confidential information. The Milbank partners were represented by their own lawyers at the depositions, but Milbank paid the legal fees of each. On October 1, Judge Eisenberg denied Milbank's motion, thus freeing the material for disclosure to the public. "I can't imagine in my wildest dreams," said Eisenberg, "how each of 20,000 documents can all be confidential."

The depositions indicated that Gellene and Salovaara offered different accounts of the investor's role in the decision not to disclose Milbank's representation of Salovaara. Gellene testified that Salovaara had told Milbank that he didn't want the firm to reveal its representation of Salovaara in matters unrelated to the Bucyrus bankruptcy. Lederman, said Gellene, had told him that Salovaara "wished to maintain the representation as confidential."

Salovaara denied this in his own deposition. He said that Milbank had no actual conflict because of its representation of him. A report in the *Wall Street Journal* stated that "[d]epositions of Milbank lawyers reveal that Mr. Lederman . . . let it be known within the firm that he didn't see a problem with the dual representation." Lederman and Lichstein, however, placed responsibility for the disclosure decision squarely on Gellene's shoulders. They testified that they were unfamiliar with bankruptcy procedures. Therefore they didn't know whether those rules required Gellene to disclose the firm's representation of Salovaara.

Meanwhile, Milbank's troubles were attracting wide national attention. The firm pointed out that it could find no case in which any firm earning more than six hundred thousand dollars in bankruptcy fees had been required to disgorge its entire compensation. Not surprisingly, John Stark was not shy about informing the press of his view that large New York firms too often were accustomed to lenient treatment. There is "too much deference paid to the large firms" in New York courts, he asserted. Stark pointed to the *Leslie Fay* bankruptcy case in late 1994, in which the court explicitly found that Weil, Gotshal had violated Rule 2014 by failing to disclose potential conflicts of interests. The judge had declined, however, to disqualify the firm from continuing to represent the debtor, and levied against it the cost of the special investigation that had been necessary, which came to about $1 million. Weil, Gotshal still earned several times that much from the engagement. This decision, argued Stark, "was damaging. [The judge] let those guys off with a slap on the wrist. This judge and others need to send a message so that this does not happen again." In the Bucyrus case, he said, "John Gellene was running the company. . . . Management didn't do anything without talking to John Gellene. . . . You've got to make sure that the bankruptcy lawyers clean up their act."

Responding to Milbank's argument that the disclosure violation had not caused any harm, one lawyer connected to the case said, "There is no way to turn back the clocks and get inside every Milbank lawyer's mind to find out if decisions they made throughout the entire prepack and ensuing representation were tainted by the firm's representation of this creditor." Bankruptcy professor Jay Westbrook suggested that "disclosure should be like voting in Chicago—early and often. Disclose, disclose, disclose. It is hard to get in trouble if you follow that rule."

One major bankruptcy publication framed the disgorgement dispute as hinging on whether Milbank had a conflict that "was a blatant scheme to cover up and curry favor with a hot shot vulture investor or, as Milbank contends, just a conflict on the surface—the matters of the two clients weren't related." This reflected the view that the gravity of the disclosure violation ultimately depended on the significance of the conflict that had not been disclosed.

On November 1, Gellene learned that the Milbank executive committee had decided to remove him as a partner. In a November 18 memo announcing Gellene's expulsion to persons in the firm, the committee stated that Milbank "will not tolerate any breach of either the profession's ethical code or our own standards of conduct." There was some speculation that Rotert and Gellene might have preferred this instead of having Gellene resign, on the ground that it would permit them to argue in any criminal trial that Gellene had already suffered severe punishment. At the same time, it made clear that Milbank assigned blame exclusively to Gellene and had no intention of standing behind him.

On December 3, however, Gellene expressed second thoughts about his earlier assumption of sole responsibility for the violation of Rule 2014. On that day he executed an affidavit, which he submitted to the bankruptcy court the next day. Gellene's affidavit said that he had recently come across important information of which he previously had been unaware, in connection with rendering assistance to Milbank in preparing for depositions of Winter, Goelzer, and Stark. Specifically, he had been given copies of Goelzer's notes that were gathered during the discovery phase of the disclosure statement hearings, as to which Bucyrus had claimed attorney-client privilege. Gellene maintained that the notes revealed that the relationship between Salovaara and Lederman was much closer than he had realized. They also indicated that Salovaara had been more heavily involved than Gellene had known in advising Bucyrus on its financing options in the period leading up to the sale-leaseback transaction.

Goelzer's notes set forth discussions within the company about whether it should continue to retain Wachtell as main outside counsel after Lederman left the firm. Gellene pointed out that the notes described Salovaara's vigorous lobbying of Bucyrus officials, especially Winter, on behalf of Lederman. Stated Gellene, "My review of Mr. Goelzer's notes had led me to conclude that pressure from Mr. Salovaara and the strength of his relationship with Bucyrus, and particularly Mr. Winter . . . played a primary role in the company's decision in 1991 to replace its counsel and retain Milbank when Lawrence Lederman departed his former law firm and joined Milbank."

Gellene declared that the Goelzer material also made clear that Salovaara had advised Bucyrus against both a sale of the company and an exchange offer as Bucyrus officials sought to deal with a mounting financial crisis. Salovaara suggested instead that Bucyrus obtain financing from his new South Street Fund. Goelzer's notes shortly before that transaction closed set forth several possible concerns about entering into a deal with the vulture fund. Salovaara would have considerable influence over the company, Goelzer observed, "from priority position on all necessary assets; ownership of large position in our debt; inside knowledge." He also noted, "It appears to be in Mikael's interest that we are *not* able to refinance. The more it looks as though we'll fail, the further down our bond prices will go, and that creates opportunities for him." Inability to refinance also might attract other vulture investors, Goelzer speculated, which would make it even more difficult to restructure the company.

Gellene maintained that this information would have affected his preparation of the opinion that Goelzer had requested for insurance purposes on the good faith of the Bucyrus directors in the sale-lease-back. He declared, "I believe that I would not have been able to deliver the requested opinion if I had been provided with access to the foregoing notes of Mr. Goelzer, or if the directors of the company, Mr. Goelzer or anyone else had informed me of the events set forth in those notes. I further believe that if I had received this information in 1993, I would have been sufficiently sensitive to Mr. Salovaara's dealings and relationship with the company so that I would not have committed the errors regarding disclosure that this Court is now reviewing."

On December 9, Gellene was indicted by a grand jury in Milwaukee on three counts of violating federal criminal law. The first two counts alleged that Gellene had violated 18 U.S.C. Section 152, which prohibits false oaths or declarations in a bankruptcy proceeding. The first count charged that Gellene had made a false declaration in his February 18, 1994, affidavit in support of his appointment application. In violation of Bankruptcy Rule 2014, the indictment stated, Gellene "knowingly failed to state that Milbank Tweed represented Salovaara, Greycliff and South Street Funds." The second count was based on the same failure in Gellene's March 28, 1994, amended declaration in support of his application. The third count alleged that Gellene had violated 18 U.S.C. Section 1623, which forbids, among other things, the use of a materially false document in a federal legal proceeding. This was based on the claim that on November 29, 1995, Gellene under oath used the false March 28 document in his testimony in the Bucyrus fee trial.

Each count carried a maximum sentence of up to five years in prison and a fine up to $250,000. Federal sentencing guidelines required that the sentences be concurrent, so as not to exceed a total of five years. After the indictment was announced, Rotert declared, "It certainly was a mistake [Gellene] regrets, but it was just that, a mistake. To say it was deliberate and with fraudulent intent is simply absurd." Gellene was arraigned on December 12 and pleaded not guilty to all three charges.

Upon Gellene's indictment, Milbank's executive committee once again emphasized that the bankruptcy lawyer had acted on his own. In a statement distributed to all lawyers in the firm, the committee said that it had fully cooperated with the prosecution's investigation. "Mr. Gellene's sworn testimony," declared the statement, "was that he took sole and full responsibility for his failure to disclose certain information to the bankruptcy court. Milbank does not tolerate this or any breach of either the profession's ethical code or our own standards of conduct. . . . Each of us is ultimately responsible for his or her actions."

A little more than a week after Gellene's indictment, Milbank agreed to settle the disgorgement lawsuit by returning the entire $1.86 million bankruptcy fee. Hearings on the motions had been set for February 3, and it was likely that several Milbank partners would be

called as witnesses. Bucyrus and JNL agreed to drop their requests
that the bankruptcy court sanction Milbank any further. The parties
also agreed to submit to mediation the pending state fraud and malpractice suit against the firm. Former federal appellate judge John
Gibbons eventually agreed to serve as mediator for these claims.

William Conlon of Sidley & Austin, outside counsel for Milbank,
said that "[w]hile the firm fully and firmly believes it provided outstanding legal services to Bucyrus . . . certain representations by Mr.
Gellene to the court were not accurate or complete and were far below
the standards maintained at Milbank." An internal memo circulated
at Milbank stated, "It is in the best interests of the firm to put this matter to rest." JNL was entitled to receive 90 percent of the $1.86 million,
which Milbank agreed to return by December 30.

Milbank emphasized that it would "continue to vigorously oppose"
the fraud and malpractice claim, which is characterized as "completely baseless" because Bucyrus could identify no harm that it had
suffered due to the disclosure violation. The firm eventually settled
this lawsuit as well. The terms of the settlement were not disclosed.
One report pegged the settlement at $50 million, quoting "a lawyer
who asked for anonymity." Another report, however, placed the figure
at $27 million.

At the December 18 hearing on the proposed disgorgement settlement, Judge Eisenberg indicated that he had given considerable
thought to whether he should approve it without a trial on the merits.
"Something went terribly wrong at a major international law firm," he
said. "What was it that went wrong and why? Milbank Tweed knows
how to do things correctly. Was somebody asleep on the job or was it
purposeful?" A trial might produce the answers to these questions, the
judge remarked. While he ultimately decided to accept the settlement,
he said that he would not have done so had it called for less than complete disgorgement of all Milbank's fees.[4]

John Stark created a stir in early February 1998 when he sent an e-
mail to all Milbank partners urging them to prevail upon Milbank
chair Mel Immerglut to settle the fraud and malpractice case. The e-
mail read: "Attention Milbank, Tweed Partners: After you have had

an opportunity to read the attached article, you should convey any thoughts that you may have with respect to the wisdom of settling this matter to the chairman of your firm, Mr. Mel Immerglut." The attached article was a *Wall Street Journal* account of the court proceedings relating to Milbank and Gellene. Stark's message also included the index to a seventy-five-page compilation of news stories prepared by Stark entitled "Why Milbank, Tweed Has Deep Regret." Copies of an earlier version of the compendium had been placed on tables outside meeting rooms at the National Conference of Bankruptcy Judges in Philadelphia the preceding October.

Milbank management was furious, contending that Stark was trying to bully the firm into settling by spreading negative information about it. Others hinted that the compendium was intended to be a threat to other entities that did not negotiate to JNL's satisfaction. Stark responded, "All the articles have already been published. There is no commentary by us." He suggested that the packet of articles satisfied the public's natural curiosity about other's misfortune. "Why do people slow down for an accident?" he asked rhetorically.

Conlon filed a complaint a few months later with the bar disciplinary committee of Minnesota, in which Stark was licensed to practice. He charged that ethical rules prohibited Stark from directly contacting Milbank without notice to its attorney, who was Conlon. The complaint alleged that "there can be little doubt that Mr. Stark's e-mail was designed to create discord among Milbank's partners and create pressure for a monetary settlement." Stark's rejoinder was that in sending the information he was acting not as a lawyer, but in his business capacity as an officer of JNL. The Minnesota Office of Lawyers' Professional Responsibility eventually sided with Stark and dismissed the complaint.

As the disgorgement action and civil lawsuit against Milbank neared resolution, most eyes turned to Judge J. P. Stadtmueller's courtroom in Milwaukee. It was there that John Gellene's criminal trial would begin in late February. "The question that many attorneys are asking," reported the *Wall Street Journal* on the eve of the trial, is "what transformed the Gellene episode into a criminal matter that could end up with an established attorney serving prison time and being banned from the profession?"5

The paper noted the active involvement in the case of Assistant Trustee John Byrnes, a former federal prosecutor. It suggested that "Milbank's efforts to pin responsibility on Mr. Gellene also made his prosecution more likely."6 It speculated that had the firm collectively accepted blame and sought to protect Gellene, the relatively small U.S. Attorney's Office in Milwaukee likely wouldn't have gone after the firm as a whole. Gellene, however, had taken full responsibility for the violation shortly after it became public. "In making this declaration," the *Journal* said, "Mr. Gellene is said to have assumed—however unrealistically—that the firm would try to insulate him from criminal liability. He was wrong."7 Milbank cooperated with prosecutors and eventually terminated Gellene because it "felt twice burned" by him in light of his earlier bar membership problem.8 The *Journal* also noted the opinion of some lawyers that officials in Milwaukee were determined to press for punishment because this was a case in which a "famous New York law firm thought it could cut corners in a Milwaukee courtroom."9

Gellene's trial would determine if he would be the first lawyer ever convicted for failing to disclose a potential conflict of interest in a bankruptcy case. "Disputes over conflicts and when they must be disclosed," said the *Wall Street Journal*, "have become the bane of big law firms, which juggle hundreds of clients." As a result, "[L]awyers around the country are watching the Gellene case with an acute sense of fear and pity."10

CHAPTER EIGHT

Gellene on Trial

ON THE MORNING of February 23, 1998, the criminal trial of John Gellene began in Milwaukee. Presiding over the case was Federal District Judge J. P. Stadtmueller, fifty-six, a former assistant United States attorney. Gellene was represented by Rotert and Jeffrey Crane of Winston and Strawn, and local counsel Pamela Pepper of Milwaukee. Steven Biskupic and Joseph Wall would prosecute the case on behalf of the government. Six men and six women would ultimately comprise the jury. Two had a college degree, and six had some post-secondary education. Their professions ranged from vice president of information services to journeyman sheet metal worker. By midmorning, they had been sworn in to decide the fate of John Gellene.

JUDGE STADTMUELLER dismissed the jury after it was chosen until 1:15 P.M. He then turned to a dispute over what information the government could introduce into evidence. Biskupic and Wall planned to inform jurors that Gellene had falsely represented that he was a member of the New York bar from 1980 to 1989. Rotert had objected, and filed a motion to exclude this evidence. He argued that this event occurred too long ago to be relevant to the current charges against Gellene. He noted that the New York bar disciplinary committee had concluded that Gellene was fit to practice law despite this prior misrepresentation. Finally, Rotert maintained, any intent to deceive with respect to bar membership was quite different from the intent necessary to prove criminal fraud in a bankruptcy case. He argued that Gel-

235

lene therefore would be unfairly prejudiced by evidence that bore only a tenuous relationship to the crime with which he was charged.

Wall responded that Gellene himself had put his intent at issue by claiming that his failure to disclose was an accident or oversight. That deception was relevant to whether that claim was credible. Gellene's deceit regarding his bar membership reflected his continuing dishonesty and lack of candor to the courts before he practiced. It relates to misrepresentation to the court, Wall said, which is precisely what's at issue in the criminal case.

Stadtmueller ruled for the prosecution. The government could introduce the evidence at trial. "It is abundantly clear," the judge said, "that Mr. Gellene has put the issue of his own intent" before the jury. Gellene's past misrepresentations about his bar membership were relevant to that issue. The judge indicated that he would provide a more detailed record of the basis for his decision at a later time, but his conclusion was final: the jury would hear about Gellene's past misrepresentations of his bar membership.

After a break for lunch, Biskupic and Rotert each laid out for the jury the case that he planned to present. This case, Biskupic told the jury, involves the bankruptcy proceeding of Bucyrus, a company in south Milwaukee that employed a thousand persons in 1994. Gellene applied to the court to represent Bucyrus in that case. He failed to disclose, however, that Milbank Tweed, and Gellene himself, were doing work on behalf of a Bucyrus creditor at the same time. This was not just any creditor. It was Mikael Salovaara. Salovaara had been giving the company financial advice for several years, and had arranged several transactions that resulted in the company's profits being "sucked off to pay the debt." Furthermore, he had arranged a deal that made him first in line among Bucyrus creditors. By not making full disclosure, Gellene never gave the bankruptcy judge the chance to decide whether Milbank might have loyalties to Salovaara that would affect his work for Bucyrus.

Biskupic told the jury that another creditor, Jackson National Life, believed that Salovaara had taken advantage of Bucyrus. Jackson urged Gellene to sue Salovaara on behalf of the company. Gellene said no. He never told anyone, however, that Salovaara was a client of his law firm. When Gellene later applied to the court for attorney's fees, said Biskupic, he relied upon his earlier representation that he had no "divided loyalty." As a result, Milbank received almost $2 million for his work on the bankruptcy.

Biskupic declared that Gellene's claim that he didn't intentionally deceive the court about Milbank's connections to Salovaara was not credible. When Bucyrus and Jackson learned that Salovaara was a Milbank client and sued for return of the bankruptcy fees, Gellene lied to his partners about the lawsuit, and altered documents to conceal the truth. Furthermore, Gellene had practiced law in New York for nine years while falsely representing himself as a member of the bar. This case involves complicated financial transactions, Biskupic said, but the prosecution's claim is a simple one: Gellene intentionally lied to the bankruptcy court in violation of federal law.

Rotert agreed that the issue the jury would have to decide was whether Gellene lied. John Gellene himself would testify and establish that he didn't intend to lie, to deceive anyone, or commit fraud. We need to focus, argued Rotert, not only on communications *by* Gellene, but on communications *to* Gellene. What was he told and not told, and by whom?

The judge in the Bucyrus bankruptcy, Rotert noted, had described it as the most contentious and bitter case in the history of the court. The company was already in a big financial mess because of cash flow problems. "Nobody would run a personal account the way this company is run," said Rotert. "These guys are debt junkies." There was bad blood between Goldman Sachs, who had set up deals that had created much of this debt, and Jackson National Life, who had bought some of it. The prosecution, Rotert contended, said that Gellene was brought in to develop a bankruptcy plan. In fact, however, that plan was already mostly in place by the time Gellene came on the scene. It was not Gellene's job to negotiate over who got what in the reorganization. Rather, that job fell to financial advisor Jeff Werbalowsky.

Jackson carried its animosity toward Goldman so far as to suggest that Bucyrus sue everyone connected with the company's earlier financial transactions. Gellene, however, said that Bucyrus "won't knuckle under" to pressure from Jackson. Every creditor but Jackson agreed to an initial plan. Jackson disagreed because it wanted to elbow its way to the head of the line by convincing Bucyrus to ignore everyone else's claims. When Gellene applied to represent Bucyrus, he disclosed to the judge that Milbank had ties to the two most bitter rivals in the case, Goldman and Jackson National Life. Nonetheless, the judge said, "I don't see the problem."

Gellene believed that he didn't need to mention the firm's connection to Salovaara because Salovaara already had agreed to the proposed bankruptcy plan. Salovaara and Bucyrus therefore had a common interest in gaining court approval of the plan. This turned out to be "bad judgment" on Gellene's part, but was not a crime—just like his failure to complete the paperwork for bar admission even though he had passed the bar exam. If we look at the big picture, Gellene did an excellent job of representing Bucyrus under difficult circumstances.

Rotert closed by saying, "[I]f you're waiting in this trial to find admirable characters, you will wait and wait. This is a story of sharp elbows, hard dealings, bare knuckles meetings. . . . The question in this case is not whether . . . any of the people you're going to hear from or about are wonderful people. The question in this case is much more serious. Is this man guilty of a crime?" He asked that the jury suspend its judgment on this question before hearing Gellene himself testify.

Biskupic thus had made clear that the prosecution planned to focus on one thing only: did Gellene intentionally lie to the bankruptcy court? Whether his lie caused any harm to anyone, and whether Gellene provided valuable legal services to Bucyrus, was irrelevant under the law. Swearing to false information in a federal bankruptcy proceeding constitutes a crime, and Gellene was guilty of it.

By contrast, Rotert signaled in his opening statement his claim that the focus should be broader. He intimated that Gellene may not have been fully informed about the significance of both Bucyrus's and Milbank's relationships with Salovaara. He suggested that Gellene's disclosures were being attacked because he had refused to let Jackson skew the bankruptcy proceeding to its own benefit. Rotert hoped to create sympathy for Gellene as someone who did the best he could under extremely trying circumstances, and was now being pilloried for a technical violation that, in the scheme of things, was ultimately of no consequence. It was Rotert who had asked the jury not to be swayed by admiration or distaste for all the other parties involved. In fact, however, it was the government who hoped that the jury would disregard such reactions and ask itself only a single narrow question: had Gellene intentionally failed to disclose Milbank's ties to Salovaara and South Street?

THE PROSECUTION began to present its case around 3:30 P.M. Its first witness was former Bucyrus general counsel David Goelzer. In response to questioning, Goelzer described the history of the company and its financial dealings from the LBO forward. How to deal with Salovaara, he testified, was a major concern looming over the bankruptcy negotiations—made even more difficult by the fact that the company's bondholders were quite hostile toward him. "They seemed to feel," he said, "that he had gotten a better deal in July 1992 than he should have, that the terms of this transaction were richer than they should have been." The company feared that South Street might foreclose on its security interest because of concern about Bucyrus's future. Since that security interest consisted of the company's production machinery, such a course of action would effectively put the company out of business. Goelzer also spent some time describing the claims in JNL's draft complaint. Gellene, he said, told the company that it should not pursue the suit because the claims in it were groundless.

Much of the remainder of Goelzer's testimony related to two matters. The first was the significant role that Gellene played in the bankruptcy. The second was the fact that on several occasions Gellene served as a conduit for information between Bucyrus and Salovaara. On the first point, Goelzer said that Bucyrus "was in Mr. Gellene's hands legally. We relied on his advice in numerous, many, many decisions, large and small, relied on his guidance and on his ability as our lawyer to see us through this and get us reorganized. . . . So we were totally relying on Mr. Gellene as our lawyer for a matter that was life and death for the companies." Goelzer testified that he "was pretty much in constant contact with John," sometimes talking to him several times a day and attending dozens of meetings with him.

In the course of this ongoing contact, Gellene periodically described to Goelzer his conversations with Salovaara or Salovaara's lawyer on various matters. At a May 1993 meeting, for instance, Gellene agreed to contact Salovaara "to discuss how the South Street Funds would participate in a restructuring." On occasion, Goelzer testified, Gellene conveyed to him information about Salovaara's thinking that he had obtained from Larry Lederman.

Near the end of his direct examination, Wall asked Goelzer whether, had he known on February 18, 1994, that Milbank was representing Salovaara on another matter, "would that have raised any concerns in you?" "Objection," interjected Rotert, "speculative nature of the question, Your Honor." Stadtmueller overruled Rotert's objection. "This would have been an extremely serious and significant thing for me to have known at that time," answered Goelzer. Salovaara, said Goelzer, was the company's largest secured creditor and owner of its production machinery. There had been ongoing discussion of how that debt would be handled in a reorganization. It's true that South Street had agreed to a proposed plan. That plan, however, had not yet been approved and "there was no telling what would happen in the future."

Goelzer elaborated: "[W]hen I'm in a situation where a lawyer is representing the company that I work for, it's important to me—it's essential to me that the lawyer give us his complete loyalty, that he be motivated only by his interest in our affairs, and that any information that we give him be held in total confidence and that he not have . . . any other party involved in the same issue to whom he also has loyalty." In this particular case, the question is, "Would we have Mr. Gellene's complete loyalty or, in some discussion, negotiation with South Street Funds or Mikael Salovaara, his other client, might he be tempted to favor them?"

The gist of Goelzer's testimony was thus that Gellene was a central player in the bankruptcy negotiations, that a major focus of those negotiations was how to deal with Salovaara, and that Gellene himself had had contact with Salovaara about matters critical to the ability of the company to conduct a successful reorganization. All this occurred even as Milbank represented Salovaara's interests in other matters. This supported the prosecution's claim that Gellene's failure to make adequate disclosure deprived Bucyrus, the court, and other parties in the bankruptcy of information that was vital in assessing the propriety of Milbank's appointment as the debtor's counsel.

Rotert began his cross-examination of Goelzer around ten-thirty on the morning of February 24. His first theme was that Gellene's incomplete disclosure had caused no harm. His opening question was blunt: "Are you aware of any evidence, do you have any information that demonstrates to you that John Gellene favored the interests of South Street Funds or Mikael Salovaara over the interests of the Bucyrus-Erie Company in 1993 and 1994?" Goelzer replied, "No, sir."

Rotert then moved on to the second of his themes: that Goelzer and Bucyrus were well aware of the close relationship between Larry Lederman and Mikael Salovaara. Goelzer admitted that he knew that Lederman was a "social contact" of Salovaara, and that the two were "close personal friends."

Rotert then pointed Goelzer to the latter's notes of July 19, 1991. They indicated that after Lederman had left Wachtell, Bucyrus CEO William Winter told Goelzer that "Mikael called him at home last night and said that Bill should just tell Ray [Olander, to whom Goelzer reported] to deal with Larry." Goelzer acknowledged that he knew that Winter had Salovaara's number on his telephone speed dial. Goelzer's notes stated that Salovaara pressed Bucyrus to use Lederman for its legal work. Goelzer acknowledged that the reason that Bucyrus had changed law firms from Wachtell to Milbank was because Lederman had left the former for the latter.

Rotert also underscored that Goelzer was aware that some of Gellene's information about Salovaara was coming from Lederman:

Rotert: And throughout the summer of '93 or at least the summer of '93 Mr. Gellene indicated to you that communications were

coming to Mr. Gellene from Larry Lederman about what
Mikael Salovaara was thinking. Do you recall that?

Goelzer: I recall it happening, yes.

Rotert: Okay. So there was nothing in that context that troubled
you to know that Larry Lederman was getting insights from
Mikael Salovaara about how the bankruptcy should work?

Goelzer: Well, again, that's a broad characterization. The fact
that Mr. Gellene was telling me that Mr. Lederman had some
comment from Mr. Salovaara did not bother me, no.

Rotert's third theme was that Bucyrus saw no problem in other situations in which Milbank's involvement posed a potential conflict of
interest. He focused in particular on Milbank's representation of Goldman Sachs in matters unrelated to the Bucyrus bankruptcy. Once you
learned of Milbank's representation of Goldman through Gellene's
disclosures in February and March 1993, Rotert asked, "as long as that
was unrelated to the debtors, that wasn't a reason for you to fire Milbank, Tweed; was it?" Goelzer replied that it was not. Rotert asked
Goelzer if the gist of his earlier testimony was that "to the extent that
you knew that Milbank, Tweed had any attorney-client relationship
with Goldman, Sachs, you didn't think that it was of a dimension that
was sufficient to cause a problem, that it wasn't a big enough client; is
that fair to say?" "Something like that, yes," replied Goelzer. Indeed,
if Milbank had not been able to represent Bucyrus because of the
Goldman connection, said Goelzer, it would have been "cataclysmic"
and "disastrous" for the company.

Rotert also pressed Goelzer about his request for an opinion from
Milbank whether the Bucyrus board of directors had acted in good
faith in entering into the transactions that JNL was challenging in its
lawsuit. Is it your testimony, asked Rotert, that "you did not know at
the time you made that choice that Larry Lederman could be sued on
the same theories that were potentially available against Mr. Winter
and the others on the board?" Goelzer replied, "[A]s you know, Jackson National . . . [was] threatening everybody that conceivably could
be a viable defendant. They did not mention anything about lawyers
in that target range."

Rotert's final theme in his cross-examination of Goelzer was that Jeff Werbalowsky, not Gellene, had primary responsibility for negotiating with South Street and the other creditors. Werbalowsky was "in the picture and advising the company before John Gellene had been sent from Milbank, Tweed to South Milwaukee, am I correct?" asked Rotert. Goelzer agreed.

Goelzer was less accommodating, however, when Rotert tried to get him to acknowledge that Werbalowsky was the primary person charged with negotiating South Street's concessions in the bankruptcy proceeding. Wasn't it true, asked Rotert, that you assigned Werbalowsky the primary responsibility for dealing with South Street and the other creditors? Goelzer replied, "I'm really not sure I can agree with that characterization . . . [O]urselves and our advisers, including Mr. Werbalowsky and Mr. Gellene, had conversations with various creditor groups at various times to try to facilitate [the creditors] coming together. I do not specifically recall saying, Jeff, I'm telling you you are the primary negotiator."

Rotert drew Goelzer's attention to his deposition of December 1997, taken in connection with the Bucyrus disgorgement suit. He asked him to focus on a colloquy relating to the division of labor between Milbank and Houlihan, Lokey. Rotert read from the deposition transcript:

Rotert:
> Q. During 1993 who was responsible for negotiating the financial terms of the restructuring with creditors?
> A. Primarily Houlihan.
> Q. And that would have been true for Jackson; correct?
> A. Yes.
> Q. For the bondholder committee?
> A. Yes.
> Q. For South Street and Mikael Salovaara?
> A. Yes.

Did you give those answers in response to those questions?
Goelzer: Yes, sir, I did.

Rotert's cross-examination of Goelzer thus sought to make four points. First, Gellene's failure to disclose Milbank's representation of Salovaara didn't compromise the bankruptcy proceeding. Second, Bucyrus was well aware of the close relationship between Lederman and Salovaara. It thus could hardly have been a surprise to anyone at Bucyrus that Milbank was representing Salovaara on other matters. Third, Bucyrus had not been concerned with potential conflicts of interest involving Milbank in other instances. Finally, the tie between Milbank and Salovaara didn't taint the negotiations with South Street because Werbalowsky, not Gellene, was the point person in those discussions.

The prosecution, of course, regarded all this as beside the point. For Biskupic and Wall, the jury needed to consider only one issue: what was Gellene's intent when he filed his disclosure papers? Gellene's fate would depend on whether the government could convince the jury to maintain this narrow focus, or whether the jurors would conclude that Gellene's failure to make full disclosure was insignificant in the larger scheme of things.

THE NEXT PROSECUTION witness was Cynthia Revesz, who was a fourth-year associate at Milbank at the time of the Bucyrus bankruptcy. Between February 1993 and February 1994, Revesz had worked under Gellene's supervision both on the Bucyrus case and on the Busse matter for South Street. She had since left legal practice and now was a producer of television documentaries. Revesz was testifying under a grant of immunity from the government.

The prosecutors used Revesz's direct examination to introduce into evidence billing records establishing that Gellene, Revesz, and Lichstein all had worked on matters for both Bucyrus and Salovaara during the bankruptcy. Ms. Revesz also testified to the intense competition to make partner at Milbank, as well as the fierce competition for clients among law firms. Those comments suggested why Gellene might have a motive to conceal the firm's connection to Salovaara: he feared that disclosure would disqualify him from representing Bucyrus in the bankruptcy, which might disadvantage him within the firm.

On cross-examination, Rotert pursued a line of questioning intended to imply that Larry Lederman had some influence on the decision not to disclose the representation of Salovaara:

Rotert: And do you recall what you told the FBI about Lawrence Lederman when they asked you about him?
Revesz: I do.
Rotert: And what did you say?
Revesz: It will make the jury smile. I said that he was the 800 pound gorilla.
Rotert: And he can sit anyplace he wants at Milbank; right?
Revesz: I guess that's right.
Rotert: And he can sit on anybody he wants to at Milbank if the mood moves him; is that right?
Revesz: He had a lot of power.

Revesz testified that Gellene was not a "rainmaker"—that is, not someone who brought in new clients, as Lederman did.

Revesz then agreed with Rotert that Mikael Salovaara was notable for acting "like a vulture" in bankruptcy cases, not wishing to reveal that he was buying up the debt of companies in financial distress. She also accepted Rotert's suggestion that Jeff Werbalowsky was "primarily responsible" for negotiating with South Street. Rotert's cross-examination thus was intended primarily to convince the jury that Lederman was the lawyer who should be held responsible for deciding what Milbank should disclose during the Bucyrus bankruptcy. The decision not to disclose the firm's representation of Salovaara, his questions implied, was consistent with the investor's wishes to conceal information about his investment holdings.

The next witness, Milbank partner Robert Reder, was the person chiefly responsible for handling Lederman's billing of clients. He testified about the write-offs that Lederman had asked Reder to effect for the Busse and Eckert matters. On cross-examination, Reder acknowledged that he didn't ask Lederman about the nature of the conflict that caused the write-off of Busse fees. Nor did he inform Gellene that such a write-off was being made for that rea-

245

son. Similarly, he didn't notify Lichstein that the firm decided to swallow more than three hundred thousand dollars in fees on the Eckert matter because the efforts on behalf of Salovaara had been a "disaster."

In response to a question from the judge, Reder said that he didn't know if Lederman had told Gellene and Lichstein about these matters. He did say, however, that there was no policy of advising lawyers that their time had been written off at the direction of a senior lawyer.

The prosecution presumably had called Reder to confirm that Lederman knew that representing Salovaara posed a conflict with the firm's representation of Bucyrus. If Lederman perceived a conflict, surely Gellene did in light of his extensive bankruptcy experience. The main thrust of Rotert's cross-examination, however, was again that Lederman was the one pulling the strings at the firm. Gellene had not even known that the more senior partner regarded the firm's representation of Busse and Bucyrus as a conflict.

ALFRED ECKERT, Salovaara's former colleague at Goldman and partner in South Street, was the next witness for the prosecution. He made clear that the Bucyrus bankruptcy would necessarily have an impact on South Street. He then discussed his falling out with Salovaara, precipitated by Eckert's plans to move to Travelers Insurance.

The fact that Lederman had taken Salovaara's side in the dispute with Eckert "was extremely disappointing and annoying to me," Eckert said. He and Lederman had worked together on many transactions over the years, and he had considered Lederman a personal friend. Even though a New Jersey firm was counsel of record for Salovaara in his suit against Eckert, it was clear that Milbank was "the puppeteer" who was really in charge. Toni Lichstein, he testified, had sat in on his deposition for the entire day.

On cross-examination, Rotert sought to foster the impression that Milbank was casual at best about conflicts of interest. The firm had worked with Eckert in preparing his will, thus acquiring intimate knowledge of his financial situation. Yet no one at Milbank, said Eckert, had ever contacted him to seek permission to represent Salovaara against him. Instead, Milbank arranged for New Jersey counsel formally to represent Salovaara, trying to conceal its involvement because "[i]t didn't look very good to do that to a former client." Rotert didn't make the point directly, but the implication of his line of questioning was clear: Gellene was a middle-level attorney who took orders from more senior lawyers at Milbank who were used to cutting corners.

Even though Eckert was on the stand for a relatively brief period, Biskupic felt that his testimony was an important moment in the trial. First, Eckert was the first nonlawyer to testify. He didn't try to parse questions finely as lawyers tend to do. Instead, he "spoke English to the jury." Second, Eckert suggested that it was unrealistic to treat representation of Bucyrus as completely unrelated to representation of Salovaara. The bankruptcy plan would determine the amount that South Street received on its claim; the dispute between Eckert and Salovaara would affect how that claim would be divided between the two. Finally, Eckert put in personal terms the impact of a conflict of interest. Milbank had prepared his will, yet, as Eckert testified, "I go to this deposition and there they are sitting across the table from me." Biskupic thought that this made clear the sense of both hurt and outrage that results when a client feels that a lawyer has been disloyal.

Douglas Jessop then testified briefly for the prosecution. Jessop had been the trustee in the Gillett bankruptcy, and had dealt with Gellene regarding South Street's claim in that proceeding. His office had filed an objection to the claim and then sought discovery from South Street in connection with the objection. Jessop said that South Street had not responded even after a motion to compel. As a sanction, the court entered a judgment against the fund. Gellene had filed a motion for reconsideration that stated that the South Street response had been delayed because litigation between Salovaara and Eckert had made it difficult to obtain the necessary documents.

The next witness shed more light on Gellene's failure to respond to Jessop's discovery request. Gary Hindes had been corporate secretary of South Street, and had assumed a more prominent role in day-to-day operations after the Salovaara-Eckert dispute. He testified that he called Gellene in late July 1996 for an update on the Busse matter. Gellene then told him for the first time that Hindes needed to compile several documents in response to a discovery request in the case. When Hindes asked to put off the task for a bit in order to attend to other pressing matters, Gellene told him that the response was due in the next day or so. The two men agreed that Hindes would assemble the basic documents that had created South Street and send them to Gellene.

Hindes testified that Gellene had not mentioned the document request before that phone call. Even more important, he said that the litigation between Salovaara and Eckert created no obstacle to complying with any document request. The prosecution's purpose clearly was to reinforce the view of Gellene as someone who was willing to lie when it suited his purposes.

On cross-examination, Hindes described his frustration in being unable to obtain meaningful information from Salovaara about both the Fetzer note and other investments of South Street. He said that Gellene had told him in December 1996 that Salovaara had never provided Gellene with any documents relating to that note. The portrait of Salovaara that Rotert sought to present was of an intensely secretive person, who denied even those ostensibly working closely with him all the information that they needed. The implication was that he, and perhaps his close friend Lederman as well, had done the same with Gellene, thus depriving the attorney of the facts he needed for an accurate assessment of his disclosure obligations.

The next witness, John Jerome, had been subpoenaed by the prosecution. Jerome had been head of the bankruptcy practice at Milbank for twenty years, and had served as Gellene's mentor in the firm. While he had been called by the government to testify, Biskupic and Wall regarded him as only minimally cooperative and as defensive about both Milbank and Gellene. Now retired and of counsel to Milbank, Jerome said that he had had an "extremely close" working relationship with Gellene.

The government had called him primarily to testify about a paper that he had written with Gellene on the ethical issues involved in bankruptcies of firms that had been through LBOs. The paper observed that fraudulent conveyance claims were common in such situations. As a result, a lawyer who had represented the acquirer in an LBO might later have to defend that earlier deal in the company's bankruptcy. The bankruptcy judge would then have to decide whether this potential conflict of interest disqualified the lawyer from representing the debtor in bankruptcy. The prosecution thus sought to use Jerome's testimony to emphasize that Gellene was intimately familiar with the kinds of ethical issues that were likely to arise in the circumstances involved in the Bucyrus case.

On cross-examination, Jerome confirmed that John Stark had approached Milbank in late 1993 to express unhappiness about how the firm was handling the Bucyrus bankruptcy. Shortly thereafter, Stark had fired Milbank as its counsel in another bankruptcy. Rotert then asked Jerome to expand on the contentious nature of bankruptcy and the complexity of ethical issues that arise within it. Everyone is "jockeying for position in bankruptcy," said Jerome. "How many times," asked Rotert, "in your experience and to your knowledge, is there a successful fraudulent conveyance claim?" "I don't know of any," replied Jerome. "It's posturing, for the most part."

Rotert thus sought to present Gellene as someone attempting to navigate around fiercely contending parties to arrive at agreement on a reorganization plan that would be in Bucyrus's best interest. He had not been deterred from this path even when it cost Milbank his mentor's client.

The parties then entered a stipulation that a recordkeeper for the New York state bar would testify that Gellene was not licensed in that state until 1990. A similar official for the Southern District of New York federal court was prepared to testify that Gellene had never been a member of that bar. This information thereby became part of the record in the trial without the need for either person to take the stand. Rotert's hope, of course, was that agreeing to a stipulation would have a less forceful impact on the jury than hearing the live testimony of these witnesses.

THE NEXT PERSON to testify for the prosecution was Milbank partner Toni Lichstein. Lichstein was testifying under a grant of immunity from the prosecution. Wall conducted the examination. He focused mainly on two matters. The first was Lichstein's discussions about whether the firm had a potential conflict arising from its representations of Bucyrus and Salovaara. The second was Gellene's actions in regard to the disgorgement motions. On the first, Lichstein said that at the December 22, 1993, meeting among Lederman, Lichstein, and Gellene in Lederman's office, she asked both men whether they saw any potential conflict of interest. Gellene, she testified, responded that "it was a pre-packaged bankruptcy case and he did not perceive that there was a conflict." Lederman, she said, told her that "it was not a problem because the matters were unrelated." Lichstein stated, "At that time I was satisfied by what I heard at the meeting."

Lichstein described another instance in early spring 1994 when she raised questions about a conflict. After attending a South Street investors meeting at which the fund's investment in Bucyrus was one of the topics of discussion, she spoke separately with Gellene and Lederman. She conveyed her concern that the "bankruptcy case had really heated up and become acrimonious," and that there might be potential for a conflict. Gellene told her that "Mr. Salovaara was not a creditor of Bucyrus-Erie, that Milbank had undertaken all of its disclosure obligations, and he pointed out that Milbank had fully disclosed all of its representations of Goldman, Sachs." When she spoke with Lederman, he initially reiterated his opinion that there was no conflicts issue that needed attention. When Lichstein raised the issue again shortly afterward, however, he told her to get Salovaara "additional counsel." After that, Milbank's representation of Salovaara in the Eckert dispute gradually tapered off

Lichstein then described the events of Monday, February 24, and Tuesday, February 25, 1997. On Monday, she and other members of the firm learned from the *Wall Street Journal* that JNL had filed a motion to require that Milbank return all of the fees it earned in the Bucyrus bankruptcy. When Lichstein called Gellene about the *Wall Street Journal* story, he confirmed that he had received a motion. He was vague, however, about when Milbank's response was due. The next day, Gellene assured a meeting of several senior partners that the motion was not due for another three days.

Lichstein said that Gellene nonetheless didn't give her the full set of motion papers despite her request for it. She eventually examined the document that Gellene had given her, which was a copy of the disgorgement motion. She noticed that the affidavit that accompanied the motion was dated in December 1996. This struck her as odd for a motion that Gellene said had been filed in February 1997. When she called Gellene to ask him about this anomaly, he asked if he could come down to her office and talk to her. When Gellene arrived at Lichstein's office, Gelfand also was there. Gellene told them that he felt terrible "because he had not been truthful or candid to us about when the motion had been filed." Wall asked, "Is that the phrase he used?" Lichstein replied, "Well, I believe he probably said that he had lied to us." "He admitted lying to you and David, didn't he?" pressed Wall. "Yes," Lichstein answered.

Wall sought to drive home two points with Lichstein's testimony. The first was that Gellene had been given ample opportunity to reflect upon whether the firm's simultaneous representation of Bucyrus and Salovaara was a potential conflict that should be disclosed to the bankruptcy court. Second, hard on the heels of the stipulation about Gellene's misrepresentations of his bar memberships, the prosecution sought to portray Gellene as someone who would lie even to his own partners if he felt it were necessary.

Rotert spent some time on cross-examination trying to rebut the prosecution's claim that Gellene's disclosure failure was motivated by his desire to gain the bankruptcy fee. Lichstein, who sat on Milbank's compensation committee, testified that the committee had recommended at the end of 1992 that Gellene advance to the salary "plateau" for someone with his experience in the firm. The plateau, explained Lichstein, was the maximum compensation that a partner could expect unless he or she was a "rainmaker" who brought in significant business or assumed an important leadership position in the firm. Of the one hundred partners at Milbank, some sixteen or seventeen received compensation above the plateau. Gellene, Lichstein acknowledged, was not considered a rainmaker. "And so," Rotert asked, "for Mr. Gellene in terms of finances, once he has worked himself hard enough to be put in the plateau, he's doing as well financially as he can hope to do at Milbank, Tweed; correct?" Lichstein replied, "Based upon my understanding of Mr. Gellene and the type of work he was doing, yes."

Rotert then turned to the December 22, 1993, meeting in Lederman's office. "At the beginning of this case," he said, "the jury was told that you warned John that there was a conflict of interest. Is that your testimony, that on this occasion you warned John?" "No, it's not my testimony," Lichstein responded. She acknowledged that she believed that Gellene was satisfied that there was no conflict-of-interest problem. Lichstein testified that she never told Gellene that Lederman had arranged for other counsel to represent Salovaara in his dispute with Eckert after she had renewed her question whether Milbank had a conflict.

Finally, Rotert elicited from Lichstein more detail about Gellene's distraught state when knowledge of JNL's disgorgement motion became public:

> *Lichstein:* . . . He essentially said that he had been unable to function, that his movement from the bankruptcy department to the mergers and acquisitions department had been very disruptive, that there had been a very tragic event in his family life, [the sudden death] of his father-in-law, and that he really wasn't able to function.
> *Rotert:* How would you describe his demeanor?
> *Lichstein:* I was scared . . . The following day I stayed with John the whole day.
> *Rotert:* Was that because you were concerned?
> *Lichstein:* Absolutely, concerned about John.

Wall was sharp with Lichstein on redirect. It was clear that, while she was a prosecution witness, she had no wish to incriminate Gellene any more than was necessary. Wall referred to Lichstein's statement, in response to Rotert's question, that she had not meant to deceive anyone when she was simultaneously working on Bucyrus and Salovaara matters. Wall asked rhetorically, "Mr. Rotert . . . left out a real important fact; didn't he? . . . [D]idn't he leave out the fact that you weren't here swearing out declarations under oath that you had no connections with parties that were in the B-E bankruptcy case?" Lichstein acknowledged that she had sworn no oath before the bankruptcy court. Lichstein also admitted that when she asked Gellene whether the firm should be concerned about conflicts, he never told her that he was also representing Salovaara in the Busse matter.

Things got even more heated when Wall asked Lichstein about her conversation with Gellene regarding the disgorgement motion:

> *Wall:* When John Gellene got all upset and broke down and talked about the JNL memorandum [in support of the motion] . . . when he's giving his confession, does he tell you and Gelfand that, hey, you know another thing I should tell you was I was representing South Street Funds in a whole [other] bankruptcy?
> *Lichstein:* Not that I recall.
> *Wall:* In this confession of his.
> *Lichstein:* Not that I recall.

At this point Rotert rose to object:

> Your Honor, I don't mind that Wall is cross-examining his own witnesses, but I'm not going to sit here and talk about confessions because he knows that that's not an accurate statement and it's objectionable and he's experienced enough not to do that sort of stuff.
> *Mr. Wall:* Well, Mr. Rotert knows when he lies and says I lied—
> *Mr. Rotert:* Judge, can we go to sidebar?

"No," Stadtmueller replied, "perhaps a better idea is to adjourn for the day." When Rotert and Wall stated that they thought the testimony would continue for only a brief period, the judge agreed to go another two minutes. He admonished Wall, however:

And eliminate all the editorial comment. I think you would have
   been finished without all the editorial comment.
Mr. Wall: Judge, I'm just responding to Mr. Rotert.
The Court: No, questions like confessions are not responding to
   Mr. Rotert.
Mr. Wall: I understand.

The next morning, the prosecution called Milbank partner David
Gelfand to the stand. Gelfand, who had become a partner at Milbank
in 1996, had worked with Gellene and Lichstein on discovery in the
disclosure statement trial. He also had assisted Gellene at the fee trial
in November 1995. The third count in the indictment was based on
Gellene's reliance in his testimony in that trial on the March 28, 1994,
affidavit he had filed in connection with his appointment application.

   Gelfand confirmed that during Gellene's testimony at the November
29 hearing, he had presented the bankruptcy lawyer with this document. The affidavit purported to list Milbank's connections with all
parties with interests in the Bucyrus bankruptcy. Gellene's use of that
document, Gelfand said, was prompted by JNL's objection that Milbank's request for compensation should be denied because of the
firm's representation of Goldman Sachs in various matters. Gellene's
testimony, stated Gelfand, was to "establish that John had disclosed to
the court and the court had already passed on the issue of Milbank's
relationship with Goldman, Sachs." "The purpose was to get Milbank's fees granted?" asked Wall. "Yes," replied Gelfand.

   Wall then turned to another incident that was meant to demonstrate
Gellene's lack of candor with courts. Gelfand confirmed that at a
December 4, 1995, hearing in the fee trial, Judge Eisenberg commented
on the number of expenses for Milbank lawyers attributed to the Lotus
Cab Company service. He asked Gelfand if Milbank had a financial
interest in the company. Gellene asked if he could answer the question. He then replied that the firm did not. When Judge Eisenberg
asked if any partners at the firm had any interest in Lotus, however,
Gellene admitted that some of them did.

   Wall then asked Gelfand about the difficulties that he and Toni

Lichstein had encountered in trying to get the JNL disgorgement motion papers from Gellene. He confirmed Lichstein's testimony that Gellene was extremely upset when he revealed to them that the motion papers had been filed in December. Gellene told them, "I can't lie to the two of you anymore." He said that he had been so upset upon receiving the disgorgement request that "[h]e wasn't able to respond to the motion papers and deal with them."

Wall then asked Gelfand to compare the copy of the JNL motion that he and Lichstein had originally received from Gellene with the one that they obtained after the meeting with Gellene. They are "identical except for one aspect, correct?" asked Wall. "Correct," replied Gelfand. "And what is that one difference?" "The date on [the first] has been whited-out and the date appears on [the second]." Finally, Wall presented Gelfand with a copy of Gellene's entry in the legal directory Martindale-Hubbell. Among other things, the entry states that Gellene was admitted to the bar in New York in 1982. "Is that line correct?" asked Wall. "Not to my knowledge," said Gelfand.

On cross-examination, Rotert first focused on Gellene's misrepresentation that he was a member of the New York bar. He elicited from Gelfand that Milbank had reinstated Gellene as a partner after initially removing him from the firm. But now, Rotert observed, Milbank had terminated Gellene: "[W]e can say with assurance, can we not, that you can envision no set of circumstances whereunder Mr. Gellene would be invited to rejoin the partnership at Milbank, Tweed Hadley & McCloy?" "I believe that's correct," Gelfand replied.

Rotert then pursued questions regarding the November 29 fee hearing in which Gelfand assisted Gellene. Gelfand agreed with Rotert that it was difficult to get Gellene's time and attention because the latter was preparing several other witnesses for their testimony, as well as developing cross-examinations of JNL witnesses. Rotert asked if it were true that "you did not have the luxury of sitting with Mr. Gellene, your prospective witness, and going through with him what was going to be said and in what order and why; correct?" Gelfand responded, "Not in any detail, no; very briefly." Gelfand then acknowledged that it was Gelfand's idea, not Gellene's, to include a reference to the retention affidavits in Gellene's testimony.

Gelfand agreed with Rotert that Gellene had been asked two questions about Lotus Cab by Judge Eisenberg at the fee hearing and had answered both truthfully. Rotert then read from Eisenberg's fee decision: "The Lotus Cab situation was very mildly disconcerting. The Lotus Cab caper has not been taken into account in this decision as it is de minimis." "Is that Latin for ain't nothing to worry about?" asked Rotert. "Of minimal concern," said Gelfand.

Rotert continued to hammer away at the government's claim that Gellene had violated his disclosure obligation in order to receive a fee of almost $2 million. Gelfand testified that Gellene would not receive any direct specific percentage of the Bucyrus bankruptcy fee, nor would he receive any bonus as a result of the firm obtaining it. Rather, the fees would be added to the pool of money comprised of all other fees earned by the firm. This would then be distributed among the partners according to criteria that Milbank had established at the beginning of the year.

On redirect, Wall asked Gelfand what his answer would have been had he been able to answer Eisenberg's question about Lotus Cab. "I think my answer would have been: no, some of its partners do," replied Gelfand. Wall pressed him whether he would have said "yes" in answer to the judge, but Gelfand persisted in his original answer. Wall then referred Gelfand to the transcript of the Milbank lawyer's interview with the U.S. Attorney's Office and the FBI:

Wall: Did you or did you not tell the agent and others there during that interview that you were going to answer that question, quote, 'yes'? Did you or did you not, Mr. Gelfand? . . .

Gelfand: Yes, I did say that.

Wall: Why don't you read the line.

Gelfand: "Gelfand stated that he was ready to tell Judge Eisenberg yes. However, Gellene stated, I will answer this question."

Wall: Okay. And you didn't—This is the first time you've said that you were going to answer that question, "no, but some of the partners do"; correct?

Gelfand: Yes.

Wall and Rotert continued to use Gelfand's testimony to wrangle on the question of Gellene's financial motivation for his failure to disclose. Gelfand acknowledged to Wall on redirect that winning the Bucyrus fee award would be a factor in setting the following year's partner compensation. He also responded to Rotert on recross, however, that Milbank would not have penalized Gellene if he had been disqualified from representing Bucyrus.

AFTER A BREAK for lunch, Assistant U.S. Trustee John Byrnes took the stand for the prosecution. Byrnes emphasized that reliance on the accuracy of sworn statements is crucial to the operation of the bankruptcy system "[b]ecause we have so many cases that it's impossible to conduct a detailed examination as to the truth and accuracy of everyone . . . [T]he entire system would bog down if you had to go through and do a detailed review of each one." Biskupic then walked Byrnes through the text of Bankruptcy Rule 2014. Byrnes stated that the term *connections* in the rule is broader than the term *conflict* that is used in conflict-of-interest analysis. He also emphasized that all connections with interested parties must be disclosed, even those unrelated to the bankruptcy.

Byrnes said that had he been aware at the time of Milbank's appointment application that the firm also represented Salovaara in other matters, it would have "raised a very serious issue" whether the application should be approved. South Street was more important than even Goldman Sachs in the bankruptcy, said Byrnes, because it was a secured creditor that owned Bucyrus's production equipment. Furthermore, disclosure of the representation for the first time at the fee hearing "would have been like a major bombshell . . . [B]oth I and everyone else would have rung the alarm bell." Biskupic intended the import of Byrnes's testimony to be straightforward: Rule 2014 clearly called for Gellene to disclose Milbank's representation of South Street. Had he done so, his application to represent Bucyrus would have received close scrutiny and might well have been denied.

On cross-examination, Rotert directed attention to Byrnes's request that Gellene provide "more specific information" about Milbank's reference in its appointment application to "representation of equity security holders and institutional creditors." Rotert noted that Judge Eisenberg had asked Gellene if there would be any problem submitting this information. Gellene said there would not be.

Rotert then moved on to discussion of Gellene's second affidavit. Byrnes agreed with him that the affidavit said that it was intended to "address the comments made by the United States Trustee on Milbank's first affidavit." Byrnes had requested "more detailed information regarding Milbank's past and current representation of equity security holders and institutional creditors." The second affidavit listed additional clients that had not been named in the first, and provided more information about the work that Milbank was doing for Goldman. It also described steps the firm was taking to prevent the exchange of information between attorneys working on the Bucyrus bankruptcy and on Goldman matters. Rotert then asked:

> Did this amount of detail further inform you as to whether you wished to object to Milbank Tweed being retained?
> *Byrnes:* Yes. It was more information than was in the original declaration.
> *Rotert:* And what did you file after you got this second declaration? Did you file a renewed objection to Milbank, Tweed's retention?
> *Byrnes:* No.

Rotert thus hoped to use his cross-examination of Byrnes implicitly to make two points. First, Gellene may not have disclosed the connection to Salovaara because he didn't regard South Street as either an equity security holder or an institutional creditor. Second, Gellene didn't start from scratch in preparing his second affidavit. Rather, he submitted it to address the specific questions raised by the trustee at the earlier hearing, and did so to Byrnes's satisfaction.

Rotert's final question to Byrnes returned to the theme of larger forces at work in the case. When word of the JNL disgorgement motion got out, Rotert asked Byrnes, had he been contacted by "various media organizations" about the case? That's true, said Byrnes.

Rotert then asked Byrnes to read a comment that he acknowledged he had made: "Both legally and factually it's somewhat simplistic to attribute it all to a misjudgment by one partner."

The prosecution rested its case with the completion of Byrnes's testimony around 10:45 on the morning of February 27. The judge then temporarily excused the jury. Judge Stadtmueller told Rotert that he believed that the government had made out a case that was sufficient to go to the jury, but gave Rotert an opportunity to file a motion for a directed verdict.

Rotert did so, expressing particular concern about the charge that Gellene had used a false document during the fee trial. Gellene, he said, had testified at that trial only about Milbank's prior disclosure of its work for Goldman and had said nothing on the subject of other potential conflicts. Stadtmueller wasted little time in denying Rotert's motion. Gellene had a continuing duty to disclose, he said. The affidavits that he had filed earlier "carried the same significance and the same weight at the time [Milbank's] application for fees was under consideration by the court."

THE JUDGE'S DENIAL of Rotert's motion set the stage for the appearance of John Gellene, the defense's only witness. The slim former Milbank partner took the stand a little after 11:00 A.M. Rotert immediately asked Gellene about his misrepresentation that he had been a member of the New York bar. Gellene said that he had not taken the time to fill out the required forms containing personal information and employment history, or to solicit affidavits from character references. This failure, he insisted, was not because he feared the disclosure of any information about his background. Rather, it reflected his preoccupation with work demands. Gellene testified that he typically worked ten to twelve hours a day five days a week, and several hours on Saturday and sometimes Sunday.

Some five months after he was made partner at the beginning of 1989, he said, the firm learned of his misrepresentation and asked him to leave. He then took steps to meet the bar's requirements. Those testifying to his fitness to practice law included prestigious judges and lawyers. Rotert's questions were intended to convey the message that Gellene had made a minor mistake by not completing all the paperwork for bar admission. Despite this mistake, prominent members of the bar had vouched for his fitness to practice law, and New York had agreed to admit him.

Rotert then sought to eliminate any suggestion that Gellene had recommended that Bucyrus provide a release to South Street because it was a client of Milbank. Gellene testified that releases such as this are common in bankruptcy as a way to "bring everything to a close so that the company doesn't have to look back on its recent history." Such closure assures creditors that what they receive will not be subject to challenge after the bankruptcy plan is confirmed. "And at the time you made that recommendation [to release South Street]," Rotert inquired, "did you have any reason to believe that the South Street Funds or any principals of the funds were clients of Milbank, Tweed?" "No," answered Gellene.

Rotert asked Gellene about his conversation with Lederman the morning Gellene flew out to Milwaukee to finish preparing the papers for the bankruptcy filing. "What did you tell [Lederman] about disclosures?" asked Rotert. Gellene responded:

> I said, look, you need to know that we're disclosing that we represent Goldman, Sachs in unrelated matters and that we represent Jackson National Life—we used to but we were fired, and I'm going to say that. And I also said that I don't believe that we have to disclose that we represent Salovaara because he's not a creditor.

Rotert asked when Gellene had reached his conclusion about Salovaara. Probably the weekend before he flew out to Milwaukee, replied Gellene. In going through the process of preparing his affidavit to accompany the retention application, "Salovaara occurred to me. I said, well, it's not related and he's not even a creditor. And then I moved on to the rest of the document." Rotert pressed Gellene, "John, how could you think that Salovaara was not a creditor?" Gellene haltingly replied:

Well, I—it was wrong. He wasn't—actually, he was a creditor. It was not because he was somebody that the company owed money to personally but he did have, as I later understood, he did have the potential for becoming a creditor. But the Salovaara—you know, whether Salovaara was a creditor or not really isn't the issue. I just wouldn't say that was the only issue. That was—that was what I was doing that weekend but that wasn't the issue. He managed a fund. He was—however you want to look at it, technically or, you know, stepping back, he was just too close, he was just too close to what was going on at Bucyrus-Erie, and I think you could say that, you know, from a—from a narrow point of view that Salovaara wasn't, on the day that I thought, wasn't a creditor, but that should not have ended my thinking on it. It should not have—it should not have ended what I should have wrote or what I should have said.

"You made a bad judgment, didn't you, John?" asked Rotert. Gellene answered, "Yes, it was—yes. Yes, I did."

Rotert continued, "[T]he government's assertion here, as I understand it, John, is that you thought that you should disclose Salovaara and that you formed a decision in your mind not to disclose him. Is that true?" "No, it is not," said Gellene. The defense's argument thus was that Gellene may have been careless, but he hadn't intended to deceive anyone. As Gellene's rambling response to Rotert's question reflected, even this concession must have been extremely difficult for someone who had been constantly praised for his high intelligence and keen legal judgment. It was necessary, however, if he had any hope of avoiding criminal conviction.

Rotert then turned to the trustee's objections to Gellene's original retention application. Gellene agreed that the trustee had asked for more information about Milbank's representation of equity security holders and institutional creditors. Then Rotert asked about South Street:

Rotert: At any point in February or March of 1994, in your mind, did you consider the South Street Funds to be an institutional creditor of this company?

Gellene: I didn't then and I don't now.

Rotert: At any point in time in history, in your mind or any other mind that can look at this issue, was South Street Funds an equity security holder of Bucyrus-Erie?

Gellene: They definitely were not.

Gellene testified that as he prepared his second affidavit, his understanding was that "we could just clean up our papers" by addressing the trustee's concerns. The implication was that Byrnes had requested additional information only about equity security holders and institutional creditors. South Street fell into neither of these categories. The second affidavit therefore didn't fail to disclose any information that Gellene had been asked to provide. As a result, Gellene had committed no fraud by failing to include South Street in it.

At the conclusion of his direct examination, Rotert asked Gellene why the jury should believe him. After all, he had misrepresented his bar membership and had misled his partners about the JNL disgorgement motion. Gellene offered a lengthy reply. In large measure, he threw himself on the mercy of the court even as he denied any intentional wrongdoing:

> I think I have two things to say. First, is that I have not just for my adult life but before that I've been recognized as a person with gifts in terms of my intellect and my ability to deal with problems, and I've been very good and very competent at the kinds of problems presented [by] my clients in the practice of law and in academics and so on.
>
> And that is I think such a part of me and who I hold myself out to be and who I am that when I am confronted with mistake, an act of inadvertence that is stupid that I'm—it is very difficult for me to stand up and say I did a stupid thing.
>
> When I was a young lawyer, I did a very stupid thing. I got caught up in my work and I didn't fill out the forms, and as time went on it got more and more absurd and I could not stand up and say, I did something stupid. And when that first happened in my life in a traumatic way, I could not say it to myself and I could not say it to others so I hid it. I lied, and when it was discovered,

I set about to repair it. It was a long process. Nine years ago it would have taken three weeks and it took almost a year later but I fixed it and moved on.

When I did that with the state court, I didn't do it with the federal court, the other major court in New York City and I should have done that. And it would have been—certainly after the year that went on in my life with the New York bar, it would have been a very simple thing to do, but I was confronted again with the absurd stupidity of not filling out forms that thousands of lawyers fill out year in and year out and I couldn't stand up and say, I did this. I did something stupid so I didn't do it.

Gellene then turned to the disgorgement motion that JNL had filed in late 1996 and his difficulty in responding to it:

When I saw the papers in December, the same crushing weight of what I had experienced in May occurred again and it occurred at the culmination of a year that was personally and professionally very difficult and had created a sense of isolation from my colleagues, from my work, from things that I had invested thousands of hours in trying to give meaning to myself and to my life and I could not deal with it. I just fell apart during the month of December. I didn't work. I didn't do anything. I would sit at my desk.

And only when I absolutely had to did I zip up all of that and for whatever time it took put a face before the world that didn't reveal what was going on with me. I did that and I've done that because through my adult life I have not been able to deal in a responsible and mature and forthright way with the imperfections that I like anyone else have and the shortcomings that I think any man or woman has in a world that's not perfect.

And that is my history and that is why I am here today. But I am charged with defrauding a court about a matter that didn't involve me. It involved clients of my firm. It involved their relationships, their adversary nature, and that mistake began with a mistake that was made—for me it began with a mistake that was made in Lawrence Lederman's office on December 22, 1993. It was a mistake I never saw. It was a mistake I never appreciated until Jackson's papers, even stripped of all their rhetoric, said, you've done something very wrong.

Gellene concluded by suggesting that these personal shortcomings were at the root of his violation of his disclosure obligations:

> I've had a year to contemplate that and I've had help and counseling to appreciate that, and I don't think I could say this with even the clarity that I'm trying to express it today a year ago, but I'm somebody who or have been somebody who feels that he had to be perfect because that is where I've gotten my view of myself. That is where I've gotten satisfaction. That's where I've tried for better or worse to have meaning in my life and it was not right.
>
> And as a result I've, I've hurt myself immeasurably. I've—there is no question that I have—fell down in my responsibilities as a lawyer, as an officer of the court, and as someone who by profession is supposed to put the interests of others over the interests of self.
>
> But on the one hand, you can see this pattern of behavior. On the other hand, you can't—I could not acknowledge that I did it for the money. I could not acknowledge that I did it because I didn't have enough to do. I can't acknowledge that I did it because I was trying to reach some milestone in my career.
>
> *Rotert:* Why can't you acknowledge those things?
>
> *Gellene:* Because they are not true. Because that's not why this happened.

On cross-examination, Biskupic wasted no time in trying to counter any sympathy that Gellene may have evoked. He referred Gellene to the Milbank compensation committee report for 1992. "You were quite upset about the salary you received in 1991; weren't you?" asked the prosecutor. Gellene answered, "I was until I understood what the basis was for the salary that was set by the compensation committee." Biskupic pointed out that Gellene was quoted in the report as saying that he was "shocked" at his salary. Gellene acknowledged that he had been upset. He said, "I was concerned that I had been treated differently than another partner who was my age in seniority for reasons I didn't understand, and the reasons were explained to me and I accepted them." By raising the issue, Biskupic sought to refute Rotert's claim that Gellene had no financial motive to mislead the court.

Biskupic also questioned Gellene about why he told Toni Lichstein that there was no problem when she raised the issue of a potential conflict at the meeting in Lederman's office on December 22, 1993. "I formed the view that it was unrelated," answered Gellene. The other reason, he said, was that

> [t]here was in connection with the Bucyrus-Erie matter no adversity between Mr. Salovaara on the one hand and Bucyrus-Erie on the other. They were on the same team. They had agreed to the terms of the plan. We were moving forward with getting the plan through the SEC, and the only party that was opposing the plan and was opposing both Bucyrus and South Street and Mr. Salovaara was Jackson National Life.

"Well," Biskupic asked, "Goldman, Sachs also was on your same team, wasn't it?" "Yes," replied Gellene. "But you disclosed Goldman, Sachs," said Biskupic. The inference was plain: if Gellene assumed that he didn't have to disclose Milbank's ties to any party that had agreed to the prepackaged plan, then why disclose the representation of Goldman?

Biskupic then asked Gellene about his claim that he hadn't disclosed his representation of Salovaara because it was unrelated to the Bucyrus bankruptcy. "You disclosed Milbank's representation of Bucyrus creditors Cowen & Company and Mitsubishi in unrelated matters," he said. "Why disclose these clients but not Salovaara?" Gellene responded:

> Well, the analysis that I had made, flawed as it was, really dealt with three points. First, that Salovaara and Bucyrus-Erie were not adverse to each other with respect to Bucyrus' reorganization. That was something that was discussed—
> *Biskupic:* Were Cowen & Company and Mitsubishi adverse?
> *Gellene:* —in December of 1993.

Rotert then objected that Biskupic had not allowed Gellene to finish his answer. Judge Stadtmueller agreed. The prosecutor then moved on to another subject. His point had been made, however. Gellene claimed that he had seen no need to disclose Milbank's representation of Salovaara because South Street had agreed to the prepack and the matter was unrelated to Bucyrus. Yet Gellene *had* disclosed the firm's representation of other companies that had the same characteristics.

With the completion of Gellene's testimony, the defense rested its case. The two sides had battled for six days over how broad a perspective the jury should take in judging Gellene's conduct. Biskupic and Wall had argued that jurors should focus only on whether Gellene intentionally submitted sworn documents to the court that omitted material information. Rotert had asked that the jury consider that Gellene's omission had caused no harm to anyone. He had suggested that Gellene was a middle-level functionary compared to powerful and influential actors such as Salovaara and Lederman.

Which approach the jury would take appeared to be crucial to the outcome at this point. Gellene's claim that his failure to disclose that Salovaara was a Milbank client was an unintentional mistake seemed unpersuasive. His bankruptcy experience and his weak efforts to distinguish Salovaara and South Street from the other clients he had disclosed to the court undermined that claim. Gellene's only hope appeared to be that the jury would not consider his conduct egregious in the larger scheme of things.

THE FOLLOWING MORNING, March 2, the lawyers met with Judge Stadtmueller to discuss jury instructions. Rotert's main objection was to the government's proposed instruction concerning the definition of bankruptcy fraud. That instruction stated that "[a] statement is fraudulent if known to be untrue, and made with intent to deceive." Rotert claimed that the instruction should say that fraudulent intent requires deception for the purpose of obtaining pecuniary gain. The prosecution, argued Rotert, had explicitly claimed that Gellene violated his disclosure obligation in order to obtain bankruptcy fees. The defense's proposed instruction therefore was consistent with the case as the government had presented it.

Stadtmueller, however, held otherwise. Pecuniary gain need not be a necessary element of the offense, he ruled. Courts that have spoken about financial gain in the context of bankruptcy fraud have done so, he acknowledged, in cases involving deceit for this purpose. They don't suggest, however, that such a purpose must be proven in all cases under the bankruptcy fraud statute. The jury therefore would not be instructed that Gellene's guilt depended on whether he had violated Rule 2014 because he was motivated by financial gain.

The two sides then began their final arguments to the jury. Wall would speak first, followed by Rotert. Biskupic would then address the jury in response to the points that Rotert had made. Wall began by declaring, "This case is about the integrity of the legal system." Lawyers who appear before a court, he said, are officers of that court and have a responsibility to help the judge pursue justice. In this case, the defendant was a lawyer who had been described as brilliant and intimately familiar with bankruptcy practice.

It was apparent, Wall said, that South Street and Salovaara "[were] the most important parties in this bankruptcy because Salovaara and the South Street Funds hold the company's assets. . . . Very little [could] happen without [their] approval." David Goelzer had testified that he would have been concerned had he known that Milbank and Gellene were representing Salovaara at the same time as they were representing Bucyrus. In addition, Trustee John Byrnes had testified that South Street was a more important entity in the bankruptcy than was Goldman. Byrnes, Wall reminded the jury, had said that if Gellene had disclosed at the fee trial that Milbank was representing South Street, that revelation would have been a "major bombshell." Wall noted throughout his argument the numerous conversations that Gellene had both with and about Salovaara during the course of negotiations.

At the time that Gellene filed his declarations, Wall said, he was representing South Street in the Busse matter. He also knew that Toni Lichstein was representing Salovaara in his dispute with Eckert. Nonetheless, he disclosed neither representation. Gellene continued in his deception, despite the fact that Lichstein twice questioned him whether the firm had a conflicts problem. Furthermore, Wall argued, Eckert had been asked whether South Street's interest was affected by the Bucyrus bankruptcy and replied, "Yes, it certainly was."

Wall then emphasized Gellene's willingness to stretch the truth. Gellene had lied to the Colorado court about why he had missed the deadline in the Busse case. Similarly, Gellene had missed the deadline for filing a response to the Bucyrus and JNL motions for disgorgement. He then had lied to his partners about when the response was due. Earlier in his career, he had misrepresented that he was a member of the New York bar. Furthermore, in the Bucyrus case itself he had filed an application for admission to practice before the federal bankruptcy court in Milwaukee, in which he falsely claimed that he was a member of the bar of the federal district court in the Southern District of New York. In sum, Wall concluded, "John Gellene has shown a total disregard of his obligations, his ethical obligations as an attorney."

After a break for lunch, Rotert began his closing argument on behalf of Gellene. The central issue in the case, he said, was, "what was in this man's mind?" In order to answer this question, he argued, the jury must ask itself, "why would he lie?" Rotert then stepped back and attempted to place the events involving Gellene in broader context. We must begin, he said, with the very close relationship between Larry Lederman and Mikael Salovaara. That relationship was both social and professional; it "was one of these, I'll scratch your back, you scratch . . . my back kind of relationships." When Lederman left Wachtell, Salovaara called the CEO of Bucyrus and urged him to use Lederman's legal services. When Bucyrus asked Lederman about its options, he suggested that the company consult Salovaara. These two have a "long-standing, professional and social mutual admiration society."

In addition, "Salovaara has for whatever reasons extraordinary influence over the people who run Bucyrus-Erie Company." William Winter, the company CEO, got calls from Salovaara at home and had private conversations with him. Bucyrus officers worked with Salovaara five years before John Gellene ever arrived on the scene. Furthermore, no one ever told Gellene that Salovaara had argued to the board of directors that Bucyrus should obtain financing with South Street rather than follow Goldman Sachs's advice to file bankruptcy.

There thus was an intricate set of connections among Bucyrus, Salovaara, and Lederman long before John Gellene ever began his work for the company. How does Gellene fit into this larger picture? "He's a bankruptcy grunt," said Rotert. "He's real bright and he also works too many hours. Works like a fiend somebody said. Works like a dog somebody else said. Indeed, he works so hard that he regularly doesn't take the time to fill out his timesheets, and Milbank docks him thousands of dollars for this failure." When Gellene first arrives in Milwaukee, the company already has prepared a draft release stating that it is suspending payment on its debts. Jeff Werbalowsky has already been working for months with the company devising a financial reorganization strategy. Gellene becomes involved, in other words, in a project whose basic outlines have already been filled in.

Gellene, maintained Rotert, was completely loyal to Bucyrus when he served as its counsel. He refused to bend to JNL's pressure to sue other parties, even though this resulted in Stark firing John Jerome, Gellene's mentor at Milbank, as its counsel in another matter. That decision, as well as his decisions about the terms of a prepackaged bankruptcy plan, occurred before Gellene ever became aware in December 1993 that Milbank was representing Salovaara in any other matters. Afterward, he worked only minimally on the Busse matter until the time that Bucyrus filed its bankruptcy petition.

David Goelzer, said Rotert, had testified that he would have been concerned had he been aware that Milbank was representing Salovaara in other matters during the bankruptcy. Yet when Goelzer needed an outside opinion about the good faith of the Bucyrus officers in the 1988 LBO, he turned to Larry Lederman—someone who had represented the buyout team and himself could be a defendant in any lawsuit challenging it. Therefore, argued Rotert, when Goelzer "tells you that he vigilantly worries about issues regarding conflicts of interest, please evaluate his credibility in light of what he decided he should do with Larry Lederman."

Gellene, asserted Rotert, had no reason to believe that he would be disqualified if he disclosed Milbank's representation of Salovaara. Judge Eisenberg had already indicated that the firm's representation of Goldman, and the possibility that Milbank might obtain a release from Bucyrus, were insufficient to remove Milbank from the case. Gellene had already disclosed "things that are explosive enough to get him fired," and that hadn't happened. Nor did Gellene have to fear that if he were not hired as Bucyrus counsel he would receive no fees for his work, said Rotert. Judge Eisenberg ruled on March 23, 1993, that Gellene could be paid for his efforts thus far on behalf of Bucyrus. That compensation came to $1.6 million. Rotert argued:

> He's got a boot full of money to show for fees; and if somebody comes up to him and says, hey, John Gellene, we heard you didn't get hired by the bankruptcy court in Milwaukee, he can say, yeah, talk to Larry Lederman. It's his client relationships that screw it up. These aren't John Gellene's clients. He's absolutely immune to any criticism if the judge rejects the retention application.

Contrary to the prosecution's contention, Rotert maintained, Toni Lichstein never gave any warning to Gellene that the firm faced a potential conflict. Rather, she asked whether there was a conflict, and Gellene told her no. Eventually, she went to Lederman and prevailed upon him to arrange for new counsel for Salovaara in his dispute with Eckert. She never, however, told Gellene that this had occurred. Similarly, Milbank partner Robert Reder charged off the fees the firm had earned from the Salovaara case at the direction of Lederman, but never told Gellene that this was done because of a conflict of interest.

Rotert also voiced his objection to the government's references to Gellene's prior misrepresentation of his New York bar membership, the annual income of Milbank partners, and Judge Eisenberg's admonition to Gellene that he was no longer in court in New York but in Wisconsin. Have the prosecutors mentioned these topics, he asked, "because they are appealing to your higher sensibilities or are they asking questions designed to make you think, you know, who cares? They are all rich, east coast snobs." The real issue, said Rotert in closing, is whether the prosecution has proven "that [Gellene] lied in order to get fees." If the government has not met this burden of proof, he said, the jury's responsibility is to acquit.

Consistent with the prosecution's strategy, Biskupic's rebuttal charged that Rotert had introduced a wide range of evidence that was designed to deflect the jury's attention from the essence of the prosecution's case. Gellene intentionally never told his client that Milbank was representing Salovaara and South Street. The question was not whether there was a conflict of interest; it was whether Gellene had engaged in "the intentional omission of required information."

No one can seriously contend, argued Biskupic, that Gellene was not required to disclose the information in question, nor that his failure to do so was not intentional. Gellene was an expert in bankruptcy who was intimately familiar with Rule 2014. He himself had worked on the matters for Salovaara and South Street that should have been disclosed. Furthermore, the evidence indicated that Gellene had misled courts in the past—including as recently as when he represented to the bankruptcy court in Milwaukee that he was a member of the bar of the Southern District of New York. Finally, the fact that Gellene disclosed Milbank's representation of Goldman is no indication of his truthfulness. JNL already knew of this representation, so Gellene couldn't have gotten away with concealing it.

It is undisputed, said Biskupic, that Gellene earned almost $2 million in fees for Milbank by virtue of representing Bucyrus. Nonetheless, he stated, "We don't have to prove motive. It's not a required element because it's almost impossible to know what really motivates someone. Their intent, however, is another thing. Intent to deceive versus honest mistake, that's the issue before you." Gellene's lies in the past, Biskupic asserted, constitute evidence of his intent to lie in this case.

In his concluding remarks, Biskupic argued that Gellene was someone who "throughout his legal career has lied," but has never been punished for it:

Lies about his bar membership for nine years. What happens to him? Keeps his job, half-million dollar salary. Nobody seems to mind. Everyone keeps giving him clients. Then he lies again. He lies about his federal bar membership, and he lies again and he practices law in federal court. Nobody complains about anything. His partners certainly didn't mind. He lies again and again because he's never been stopped.

BISKUPIC WARNED the jury, "Don't be fooled by this defendant. Don't be letting him do to you what he did to the bar association in 1990, promising this is all a mistake and it won't happen again, because you know better than that bar association in 1990. This is a defendant who lies about big things and he lies about small things. . . . Ladies and gentlemen, hold him accountable."

With that, the argument was over and the deliberation began. The case went to the jury shortly before 5:00 P.M. The jury had sent a message to the judge indicating that it didn't wish to deliberate past 5:30 P.M. Judge Stadtmueller authorized the jury members to leave for the day at that point, and to report at 8:30 A.M. the next morning to continue their deliberations.

SHORTLY BEFORE 11:00 A.M. the following morning, March 3, the jury reported to the bailiff that it had reached a verdict on all three counts of the indictment. By 11:20, the judge, the attorneys, and the defendant had assembled in the courtroom. The foreman passed the envelope containing the verdict to the bailiff.

At the request of the judge, the bailiff read the verdict in open court: "We the jury, duly impaneled and sworn, for our verdict . . . find the defendant, John G. Gellene, guilty of the offense charged in Count 1 of the indictment, guilty of the offense charged in Count 2 of the indictment, and guilty of the offense charged in Count 3 of the indictment." Rotert asked that the jurors be individually polled. They were, and all indicated their assent to the verdict. Judge Stadtmueller acknowledged to Rotert Gellene's right to challenge the verdict in a motion to the court. He advised him, however, that it was "going to be pretty much an uphill travel to convince the court that the jury did not in this case do the right thing."

A little more than five years after he had first heard of Bucyrus-Erie, and a little more than four years after he had filed the company's petition for bankruptcy, John Gellene was a convicted felon. He had been found guilty of a federal crime in the same courthouse in which he had helped gain approval of the Chapter 11 plan that had brought Bucyrus out of bankruptcy. William Conlon, Milbank's outside counsel, told the press, "The firm respects the jury's decision but is, of course, saddened by the outcome."

THE JURY'S CONVICTION of Gellene sent shock waves through the legal community in general and bankruptcy practice in particular. One prominent bankruptcy law publication, for instance, declared: "If this ruling stands, it will forever change the way bankruptcy law is practiced."[1] If we look at the case simply in terms of whether the prosecution proved the charges brought against him, however, the verdict is not surprising.

Gellene was charged on two counts of violating 18 U.S.C. Section 152. That proscribes "knowingly and fraudulently" making a "false declaration . . . under penalty of perjury" in any Chapter 11 case. He was charged on one count of violating 18 U.S.C. Section 1623. That section prohibits using under oath any document "knowing the same to contain any false material declaration." The court instructed the jury that a statement is fraudulent if a person "knows that it is untrue and is made with an intent to deceive."

The evidence strongly indicated that Gellene knew that he should have disclosed Milbank's ties to Salovaara and South Street and chose not to. This choice reflected his intent to deceive the bankruptcy court in order to obtain appointment as Bucyrus's Chapter 11 counsel. His two affidavits in connection with his application thus contained false material declarations. They each stated that Gellene was aware of no connections that Milbank had with any party in interest other than those listed in the affidavit even though the affidavit made no mention of Milbank's representation of South Street and Salovaara. This constituted a violation of Section 152. Gellene relied on his second affidavit when he testified under oath at the fee hearing. This brought his conduct within Section 1623. A jury that followed the prosecution's suggestion to ignore the contention surrounding Bucyrus's bankruptcy, and to focus only on what Gellene did when he submitted his affidavits, could find fairly easily that the prosecution had proved its case.

The question that has generated the most controversy, however, is whether Gellene should have been prosecuted in the first place. Prosecutors don't bring charges against every person who violates a criminal statute. They take into account a variety of factors in the process of determining whether a prosecution would be in the interests of justice. Critics argue that Gellene's prosecution didn't satisfy this standard, and therefore was a flawed exercise of prosecutorial discretion.

"I don't believe that there's any criminal intent," said Harvey Miller, at the time head of Weil, Gotshal's bankruptcy practice.[2] *Bankruptcy Court Decisions* informed its readers that "you might want to remember that Gellene didn't actually lie. His life, liberty, and chosen career are all in jeopardy because he didn't volunteer information (sound like anybody you know?)."[3] Law professor Bruce Markell, who advises bankruptcy firms on conflicts issues, declared, "I think what Gellene did was dumb. But it's these kinds of cases that are going to make it increasingly difficult to adequately and zealously represent debtors."[4]

Probably the most intuitively appealing criticism is that Gellene's false statements caused no harm to any party in the bankruptcy. David Goelzer could point to no instance in which he believed that Gellene's representation of Bucyrus had been compromised in any way by Milbank's ties to Salovaara and South Street. Indeed, he believed that Gellene did an excellent job on behalf of his client. JNL claimed that Gellene favored South Street at the expense of other creditors. South Street, however, was in a powerful bargaining position because of its status as a secured creditor. It acquired this status in a transaction that preceded Gellene's involvement with Bucyrus. South Street thus had no compelling need to look to Gellene for favoritism, especially with the hard-nosed Mikael Salovaara negotiating on its behalf.

In addition, South Street's receipt of a release in the plan was hardly unusual. Salovaara agreed to concessions that reduced South Street's recovery. It's customary for a creditor, especially one that's secured, to condition such concessions on a release of any claims that the debtor may have against it. Furthermore, by all accounts the reorganization was a success. Bucyrus emerged from bankruptcy as a viable entity, and eventually was acquired by a larger company because of its profitable potential. In the larger scheme of things, one can argue, Gellene's disclosure violation was of no real significance—and certainly not something that should send him to jail.

Prosecutors, however, can point to a long line of cases holding that criminal liability for violating Section 152 does not require a showing that a false statement harmed creditors or affected the distribution of assets in any way. A debtor may, for instance, falsify records in an effort to make it appear that someone else, not he, is the owner of a business. Even if the business is worthless, and his failure to list it therefore doesn't deprive creditors of any assets, his omission of it on his list of assets is a violation of Section 152. This is because truthful disclosure is necessary to enable the court and trustee to trace the debtor's assets and determine if any have been fraudulently transferred.[5] The false statement, in other words, impedes the functioning of the bankruptcy process even if ultimately it has no tangible effect on what parties receive.

Similarly, courts have held that when a debtor intentionally fails to list an asset,[6] or falsely states that he doesn't know its whereabouts,[7] he can be guilty of violating Section 152 regardless of whether the asset in question ultimately is determined to be part of the estate. Courts also have emphasized that it's unnecessary to prove an impact on creditors, or on the allocation of assets, for convictions under Section 152 to stand when debtors have submitted false information on a variety of other matters.[8] Misrepresentations and omissions can make it more difficult to determine whether a petitioner is eligible for bankruptcy and what assets it has, regardless of whether they ultimately affect distribution of the estate.

All these decisions were on the books at the time that the U.S. Attorney's Office considered whether to prosecute Gellene. The fact that Gellene's false statement didn't harm any of the creditors or affect the distribution of assets in the bankruptcy thus didn't distinguish his case from many others in which prosecutors sought convictions for violations of Section 152.

A more subtle criticism of the prosecution is that all those other cases involved debtors who provided false information about themselves, their assets, or their financial history. In such cases, it's easy to infer that the debtor's motivation is to evade his obligations to his creditors. His false statements thus reflect disregard for the moral underpinning of bankruptcy, which is to achieve a fair distribution of the estate. Whether the misstatements or omissions actually impede that distribution is immaterial; the important thing is that the debtor has acted in bad faith by attempting to corrupt the core function of bankruptcy.

By contrast, one might argue that Gellene's case is one in which the motivation for providing false information is to affect the appointment of counsel, not the fair distribution of assets. One can imagine that a lawyer might want to represent a DIP in order to manipulate the bankruptcy process to the advantage or disadvantage of different parties. In such a case, his motivation would be the same as that of a debtor who provides false information in the hope of thwarting the legitimate expectations of creditors.

One can also imagine, however, that a lawyer would want to represent a DIP for a different reason: in order to obtain the fees for doing so. In that case, he violates Rule 2014 in order to prevent the court from making an informed decision on his application, not to thwart the legitimate claims of creditors.

As a result, one might argue that Gellene's case is distinguishable from others in which prosecutions for violations of Section 152 were brought against debtors even when there was no harm to creditors or the estate. Those cases involved falsehoods intended to frustrate the fair distribution of assets. They were, in other words, part of a scheme to defraud. Gellene's untruth, however, was not part of such a scheme. Critics can argue that the law permits prosecutors to bring charges under Section 152 if they wish when no such scheme exists, but they should exercise their discretion not to.

There are a few responses to this argument. The first is that Gellene was in fact engaged in a scheme to defraud. At trial the prosecution suggested that Gellene failed to disclose Milbank's connections to Salovaara and South Street because he sought to obtain bankruptcy fees that eventually came to almost $2 million. These fees were paid out of the Bucyrus estate, and were disbursed on the assumption that Judge Eisenberg had made an informed decision that Gellene met the requirements of Section 327. From this perspective, the estate was defrauded of almost $2 million because Gellene obtained this money under false pretenses. In this sense, Gellene's falsehood was comparable to debtors who made false statements to the court in an effort to exert corrupt influence on distributions by the estate.

Second, it can be hard to determine if a lawyer's Rule 2014 violation was part of a scheme to affect the distribution of assets to creditors or an effort to secure appointment as counsel. The best evidence of the former would be that the lawyer acted so as to favor some creditors unfairly to the disadvantage of others. It can be extremely difficult, if not impossible, however, to trace the numerous decisions that an attorney for the debtor makes on a daily basis and to determine if they should have been made differently. Furthermore, how can we know how the parties would have exercised their bargaining power if the lawyer had made different decisions or chosen other courses of action? Requiring evidence of a scheme to defraud in order to bring a prosecution thus might have the practical effect of immunizing most Rule 2014 violations from criminal prosecution.

Third, one might argue, it's not appropriate to try to segment bankruptcy proceedings into core and peripheral elements. The laws establishing those proceedings are intended to function as an integrated whole that ensures the fair distribution of a debtor's assets. The appointment process is an important part of this system, especially in light of historical concerns about the potential for favoritism and corruption in bankruptcy. Counsel for the DIP wields considerable influence over the debtor's operations and in the negotiations with various parties in interest. The requirement that he be disinterested thus serves as important protection for the integrity of the overall bankruptcy process. Falsehoods that compromise this protection are no less deserving of prosecution than those that deprive the court of information that it needs to oversee the distribution of assets.

Biskupic and Trustee John Byrnes have suggested that at least some of the outcry over Gellene's prosecution stems from the implicit belief that lawyers should not be subject to criminal prosecution for statements made during the bankruptcy process. As Byrnes has put it, "Lying under oath in bankruptcy is a crime. . . . I refer for prosecution Joe Schmo who doesn't have a pot to piss in when he conceals his '67 Mustang in his brother-in-law's garage, and how is it that I refer dozens of cases like him and when a Wall Street guy comes in and lies for money, it's something different? Well, it's not something different to me."

Similarly, Biskupic has stated, "Gellene was prosecuted because the evidence against him overwhelmingly showed that he had repeatedly lied while under oath. Since debtors are routinely prosecuted for similar conduct, no great leap was needed in the decision to prosecute a lawyer."[9] Gellene lied to the court, despite frequent reminders of the importance of being free of any potential conflicts. In the prosecutor's and the trustee's view, this in itself was enough to justify prosecution. Whether Gellene was a debtor who lied because he hoped to evade creditors, or a lawyer who lied because he wanted to be appointed DIP counsel, simply was immaterial.

One can acknowledge that it may be appropriate to prosecute lawyers for violating Rule 2014 per se, and still claim that Gellene did not have fair notice that nondisclosure could subject him to criminal liability. First, no lawyer had ever been prosecuted, much less convicted, for violating the rule. Second, even the noncriminal penalties that courts tend to impose for Rule 2014 infractions are not necessarily severe. Indeed, some regard them as relatively lenient.

Courts weigh various equities in determining appropriate sanctions for violations of Rule 2014. These include the harm from the nondisclosure, the quality and scope of the representation that the lawyer has provided, and whether the debtor would be prejudiced by having to hire new counsel. Law firms that have violated Rule 2014 will not necessarily forfeit all bankruptcy fees they have earned,[10] and may be able to continue representing the debtor even if full disclosure of all their connections would have led to denial of their original application. Thus, even if nothing in Section 152 excluded the possibility that a professional might be prosecuted for violating Rule 2014, that possibility hardly could have been on Gellene's radar screen.

Any novel prosecution, of course, can be subjected to the criticism that there is no precedent for it. As Biskupic has written, "The lack of a prior criminal case under Rule 2014 does not mean there should never be one."[11] The combination of novelty and a pattern of flexible noncriminal sanctions, however, raises more concern. Consider, for example, the *Leslie Fay* case dealing with Weil, Gotshal's failure to disclose. Judge Brozman began her opinion by declaring: "Rarely am I faced with a motion as troubling as this one." An examiner concluded that the firm should not have been appointed had the appropriate disclosures originally been made. Yet, citing both equitable and practical considerations, the judge did not require Weil to return all of its fees and permitted it to continue as DIP counsel.

Bankruptcy lawyers understandably might take from the *Leslie Fay* case the view that Rule 2014 violations should be avoided, but not that they carry the kind of substantial moral stigma that characterizes the criminal law. The decision was handed down as Judge Eisenberg confirmed the Bucyrus reorganization plan, but before Gellene submitted his fee request to the court. It should have prompted him to reconsider his compliance with Rule 2014. It contained nothing, however, that would alert him to the possibility that failing to do so would be treated as a crime. Indeed, it indirectly may have suggested just the opposite.

There is an argument that Gellene *was* on notice that he might be prosecuted for submitting a false affidavit: the case against him in substance, although not completely in form, was for perjury. Gellene was indicted for making a "false material declaration" under penalty of perjury in his first two affidavits by virtue of his knowing failure to state that Milbank represented Salovaara–South Street. He also was indicted for using his second affidavit while under oath in the fee hearing, knowing that it contained a false material declaration. The notion that lying to a court was a crime, the argument goes, could hardly have been news to him. As Byrnes has declared, "[I]s it news to you that lawyers ought to be careful about what they sign under penalty of perjury? That's not a novel concept."

The question then is whether Gellene's experience with bankruptcy practice—perhaps especially in New York—led him to believe that this principle wouldn't be invoked for violations of Rule 2014. If his experience created this expectation, the strongest prosecution response is that it shouldn't have—that bankruptcy lawyers were wrong in thinking that they weren't subject to criminal penalties for make false statements to a court. From this perspective, prosecution of Gellene served as a wake-up call for the bankruptcy bar, providing a deterrent to future Rule 2014 violations. The deterrent argument also addresses claims that prosecution was inadvisable because Gellene already had suffered enough punishment. If prosecution was intended to serve a larger social purpose, then Gellene's individual ledger wasn't the only consideration.

Biskupic, however, expressly disclaims any attempt to use the Gellene prosecution as a deterrent aimed at the bankruptcy bar. "Prior to the prosecution of John Gellene," he says, "bankruptcy lawyers (especially those in large firms) may well have needed their attention drawn to the strict requirements of Rule 2014. That factor, however, simply was not an issue in the decision of the U.S. Attorney to criminally charge John Gellene."[12] Biskupic says that he wasn't intimately familiar with bankruptcy practice, and thus didn't know "whether or not 2014 was out of control." For him, the crucial consideration was the weight of the evidence that Gellene had intentionally lied to the bankruptcy court.

While Byrnes also felt that prosecution was warranted because of the strength of the case, he likely was more attuned to the broader ramifications of the prosecution. He had been stressing the importance of full disclosure under Rule 2014 for some time. Proceeding against Gellene certainly was a way to bring his message home to bankruptcy lawyers in a powerful way.

Furthermore, the Department of Justice became increasingly aggressive in the mid-1990s in its prosecution of misconduct related to bankruptcy.[13] Attorney General Reno announced that prosecuting bankruptcy fraud was one of her top priorities.[14] The Department of Justice had announced in early spring 1996 that "Operation Total Disclosure" had been formed to assemble teams of members from different agencies to crack down on such fraud.[15] By April 1998, there had been 134 defendants charged and convicted of bankruptcy fraud.[16]

One former prosecutor in Chicago noted "the strongly-felt view that the prosecution of the people who become involved as professionals in bankruptcy and who are criminally liable will have more of a deterrent effect than just focusing on the prosecution of individual debtors."[17] Thus, it has been increasingly common for prosecutors to apply criminal law to bankruptcy, and to regard professionals as potential targets. The U.S. Attorney's Office in Milwaukee reflected this trend in its heightened attention to bankruptcy cases and the close cooperation between the office and John Byrnes.

Just about any prosecution, of course, will have at least some deterrent effect for those aware of it. Biskupic certainly hoped that Gellene's prosecution would create a strong incentive for lawyers to be truthful in bankruptcy proceedings. What he likely means in saying that deterrence was not a basis for the prosecution is that this objective alone would not have led him to bring charges against Gellene if the evidence had not been so strong. Biskupic and Byrnes regarded that evidence as so overwhelming that they felt they had little choice but to bring charges. Indeed, they felt it was one of the rare perjury cases that got stronger with more investigation.

In light of this, the prosecutor maintains that Gellene's misconduct was so blatant that if charges were not brought against him the office would have a hard time ever justifying prosecuting anyone else for lying to a bankruptcy court. As Biskupic puts it, the case was not simply an example of trying to vindicate "kind of a quaint Midwestern value of honesty." Had Judge Eisenberg given him any indication that Gellene's actions were not significant, says Biskupic, he would not have proceeded with the case. "He's the neutral and detached magistrate of bankruptcy proceedings," Biskupic observes. "He thought it was a big deal and so I'm going to protect his courtroom."

The decision whether to prosecute Gellene thus highlights the existence of contrasting legal cultures. Prosecutors in Milwaukee were accustomed to applying criminal concepts to the conduct of parties in bankruptcy proceedings. In their view, lying to obtain fees was just as corrosive to the integrity of the bankruptcy process as lying to evade creditors. Treating them as different, they believed, would unfairly protect lawyers while leaving penniless debtors open to prosecution. From their perspective, evidence of intentional perjury was rarely if ever as strong as it was against Gellene. As a result, the fact that no one had ever been prosecuted for violating Rule 2014 was no reason not to bring charges against him.

For large-firm bankruptcy lawyers, however—especially those who practice regularly in New York and Delaware—the norms of practice were that the bankruptcy court, not prosecutors, monitored Rule 2014 and imposed sanctions for violating it. For these practitioners, bankruptcy conflict and disclosure rules don't always serve the high moral purpose that the prosecutors believe they do. Too often, they believe, disclosure can lead to strategic use of disqualification motions by adversaries, as well as disqualification for an ostensibly technical conflict that raises no substantive concern.

This skepticism about the moral status of the rules can make criminal prosecution for violating them seem an unduly harsh penalty. While Milbank's ties to Salovaara and South Street hardly constituted a mere "technical" conflict, many lawyers in large firms tend to believe that failing to disclose it should have exposed Gellene to criminal liability only if that failure was part of a larger scheme to manipulate distribution of the estate.

The difference between the two legal cultures doesn't mean that Wisconsin residents are more naive or upright than those in New York or Delaware, or that bankruptcy courts are less sophisticated. Rather, the Chapter 11 caseload in Wisconsin contains a much lower proportion of large corporate bankruptcies involving the nation's largest law firms. As a result, there is less occasion in Wisconsin to confront on a regular basis the problems with bankruptcy conflict and disclosure rules that large law firms present more frequently in these other states. Lawyers and judges in Wisconsin therefore may see less reason to doubt that the rules serve important moral purposes in every instance, and that criminal prosecution is appropriate for those who violate them. In other words, lawyers and judges in Wisconsin may have a different "mental model" of bankruptcy conflicts and disclosure law from that of large-firm bankruptcy lawyers who frequently practice in New York and Delaware.

If there is disagreement about the wisdom of prosecuting Gellene, there is less about the impact of the case. In the aftermath of the conviction, large law firms began to scrutinize their bankruptcy conflict and disclosure procedures more closely. Six months after the verdict, Jones, Day, Reavis & Pogue returned $230,000 in fees to settle claims by the U.S. trustee that it may have held interests adverse to a debtor whom it represented in bankruptcy. The firm admitted no wrongdoing, but said that it was "very influenced" by the Gellene conviction and other recent cases in which firms had been required to return bankruptcy fees.[18] Jones, Day also adopted a comprehensive conflict-of-interest policy for all its bankruptcy attorneys. As part of that policy, the firm indicated its intention to supplement its disclosure every 120 days.

Similarly, *Crain's New York Business* reported that "[t]o protect themselves from future liability, some big Manhattan firms are trying to learn from others' mistakes." As part of this effort, they

> have begun reviewing their internal procedures for spotting potential conflicts of interest. Some have even sought out the U.S. Trustee for Bankruptcy Court for advice on how to protect themselves. And firms are making more candid disclosures to bankruptcy judges than ever before.[19]

As the head of bankruptcy practice at Skadden, Arps put it, "I think big firms are sort of in a transition. We are now all hypersensitive." Ironically, then, the one rationale for prosecution on which Biskupic says he didn't rely may have turned out to be the most significant of all.

ON THE MORNING of July 24, 1998, the parties gathered in Judge Stadtmueller's courtroom for Gellene's sentencing hearing. Prior to that date, the court's probation office had submitted a presentencing report containing recommendations on the sentence that Gellene should receive under the federal sentencing guidelines. Gellene's "base offense level" under the guidelines was based on the crime of fraud and perjury. The report had recommended "enhancements," or increases, to this level based on aggravating features of his crime.

These features were that the crime had involved "more than minimal planning," had been an abuse of a position of trust, and had constituted "substantial interference with the administration of justice." As a result, the report recommended a prison term of twenty-four to thirty months, between two and three years of supervised release for each count of the conviction, a fine of between five thousand and fifty thousand dollars, and a special assessment of one hundred dollars for each count.

Several persons had written to Judge Stadtmueller urging that he be lenient in his sentencing of Gellene. "The ruination of his career . . . is, in a real sense, a life sentence," wrote John Jerome. Frank Musselman, former Milbank managing partner, asked the judge to consider "the very sad ending of the legal career of a very young man." Former Milbank lawyer George Brandon declared that Gellene was "simply not a dishonest or venal person," while Elliott Gewirtz of the firm said that Gellene "was absolutely committed to obtaining the best result for his client."[20]

The judge gave Rotert an opportunity to comment on the presentencing report. Rotert argued that the court should depart downward from the base offense level under the sentencing guidelines in order to give Gellene a lighter sentence. "There is a heartland of perjury cases," Rotert said. Gellene's case did not fall within it. The drafters of the guidelines could not have had conduct such as Gellene's in mind, since no one else had ever been charged with a crime for a violation of Rule 2014. There was "no pecuniary gain, no showing of pecuniary motive, no showing that he had an intent to do harm to the client he represented, [and] no showing that he inflicted any harm on that client." Departing from the guidelines would help avoid a rigidly inappropriate punishment in this case and promote overall respect for the guidelines and the sentencing process. Biskupic acknowledged that there were no other criminal cases under Rule 2014. However, he said, "if you define it as a fraud case, then it becomes much more common."

Judge Stadtmueller then set forth his reasoning about the sentence that Gellene should receive. He rejected the probation office's recommendation that the sentence be enhanced because the crime involved "substantial interference with the administration of justice." That enhancement, he said, was reserved primarily for conduct that affected the outcome of a civil or criminal trial.

He did, however, agree that enhancements for more than minimal planning and for the abuse of a position of trust were appropriate. The first was based on Gellene's continuing duty to disclose throughout the bankruptcy proceedings. The second, said the judge, was based on Gellene's obligations to the court, to his partners at Milbank to act ethically, and to Bucyrus "to be free from all of the intrusions that surround potential conflicts of interest."

Stadtmueller then made clear that he did not accept Rotert's argument that the court should depart downward from the sentencing guidelines on the ground that this was an unusual case that did not raise the core concerns involved in a perjury case. Such a step, he said, "sends the wrong message." He elaborated:

> I think we who are involved in the legal profession, whether it be judges, lawyers, paralegals, investigators, are in a very, very stringent strait jacket these days to, quote, get our house in order, particularly as it relates to the matter of relationships with clients, conflicts of interest, whether the professional interest of the lawyer is truly driven by the interest of the client or driven more by interest in terms of protecting his or her own situation within a law firm.

He continued:

I have substantial amount of contact with my colleagues in law
firms to appreciate that there are incredible pressures in this area
that, frankly, sooner rather than later are going to have to be
addressed or we are going to see more cases of this nature being
prosecuted for criminal conduct because lawyers are so focused
on other matters . . . [W]hen they become so focused to the exclu-
sion of ethical considerations, that is when the entire system
breaks down, the public at large is ever more distrustful.

As a result, he said, "I conclude that it would not be in anyone's
interest to depart . . . from the otherwise applicable sentences that
[are] presently before the court."

That left the range of the penalty for Gellene as a prison sentence
between fifteen and twenty-one months, a fine between four thousand
and forty thousand dollars, and a special assessment of three hundred
dollars. Rotert and Biskupic made their presentations on what the
penalties should be within those parameters. Rotert noted that the
objective of deterrence had already been largely achieved because of
the considerable publicity that the case had generated. He said that he
had seen a lot of "bad guys" in his seventeen years as a prosecutor,
and that "John Gellene isn't a bad guy." Gellene, he said, was someone who was "overstressed and overworked." "I saw the amount of
time this man was billing," Rotert said, "and it made me nauseous."
He has three young children, Rotert reminded the judge. The longer
the separation from them, the more strain would be placed on his relationship with them. Rotert asked the court to select a sentence of
fifteen months, at the lowest end of the applicable range.

Gellene himself then addressed the court. He acknowledged that he
had been given many advantages and opportunities, but for many
years "had acted on the basis that somehow those gifts and those
opportunities were something that were an affliction, something that I
had to reject, something that I suppose I wasn't worthy of. And in
some ways I stand here today as—in effect, as a self-fulfilling
prophecy to that view that I've held about myself." However deserving

he may be of punishment, Gellene said, the one sanction that would be visited not only on him but on his family was the separation imposed by imprisonment. For that reason, he asked the judge to accept the sentence that Rotert had proposed.

Biskupic agreed that a fifteen-month sentence for Gellene would be appropriate. He did remind the court, however, that Gellene's plea of mitigation based on his family responsibilities, the pressures of his workload, and his psychological traits had also been made during the 1990 proceedings in connection with his misrepresentation of New York bar membership. Nonetheless, he argued, Gellene continued with his pattern of deceptions. "This case," he said, "will have specific deterrence to those in the legal profession."

Judge Stadtmueller then delivered his sentencing decision. The case, he noted, rightly had received much publicity. This reflected the fact that leaders of law firms need to give more attention to ethical issues. In general, he said, young lawyers have "a very unhappy lot indeed because of the enormous pressures that are brought to bear within the firms' hierarchy in terms of compensation, billable hours, collecting fees, attracting clients, keeping clients, who controls the client within the firm and so on and so forth." This reflects the fact that lawyers tend to be "more concerned about all of the things that relate to the business side of the practice of law as opposed to the professional side of the practice of law." Gellene had many opportunities along the way to set matters straight but didn't avail himself of them.

Taking all considerations into account, Stadtmueller concluded, he was imposing a fifteen-month sentence for each count, to be served concurrently, and a fine of fifteen thousand dollars. Gellene would be eligible for two months credit for good behavior, which could reduce his eventual sentence to thirteen months. Upon completing his sentence, he would be on supervised release for two years. This required him to report when released to the probation office near the prison in which he had been in custody.

During the two-year probation period, Gellene could own no firearm or other dangerous weapon. He would be subjected to a drug test within fifteen days of release, and to two periodic tests thereafter.

He could not use existing credit or open new lines of credit without the approval of his probation officer. He also was required to participate in a mental health treatment program. Stadtmueller delayed Gellene's entry into prison until on or after September 15, so that he could be home until his daughters began the new school year.

John Gellene had stood triumphant in this courthouse in Milwaukee less than four years before, as Judge Eisenberg approved a plan that would bring Bucyrus out of bankruptcy. He left that courthouse in July 1998 with fewer than two months of freedom remaining. In September 1998, he said goodbye to his wife and three young daughters and entered federal prison in Fort Dix, New Jersey. On July 20, 1999, the United States Court of Appeals for the Seventh Circuit unanimously upheld his conviction.

PART IV

WHAT HAPPENED?

CHAPTER NINE

Feeling Pressure

IN FEBRUARY 1994, John Gellene was a thirty-seven-year-old partner at a prestigious Wall Street law firm. He made half a million dollars a year. He was regarded both within his firm and by members of the bankruptcy bar as a brilliant and accomplished lawyer. He was married, had three young daughters, and lived on the Upper East Side of Manhattan. By most standards, he had a successful and rewarding life. A little over four and a half years later, he was in federal prison.

What happened? Why would Gellene risk all he had by withholding information about Milbank Tweed's connections to Mikael Salovaara and South Street Funds? To answer these questions we have to go beyond the explanations offered by Gellene, his detractors, and critics of Milbank Tweed. We need to explore the ways in which Gellene's personality and the circumstances that he faced combined to bring him down. In addition, we must be attentive to the broader implications of his experience for lawyers in modern large firms. Gellene's story may be unique, but its broad outlines suggest that other lawyers may be at risk of meeting the same fate.

Gellene's explanation was that his violation of Rule 2014 was not intentional, but was the result of mistaken judgment on his part. This explanation is unconvincing, however, if we look closely at the facts. Gellene was, of course, an experienced bankruptcy lawyer who was familiar with Rule 2014. His argument that he didn't disclose the ties because he didn't view Salovaara himself as a creditor is unpersuasive. Everyone involved in the negotiations with creditors treated Salovaara as the person who spoke on South Street's behalf. By all accounts, it was Salovaara who took the lead in discussions with Bucyrus and the creditors' committee. Even if Salovaara were not formally a creditor, his central role in negotiations clearly made him a party in interest under Rule 2014. Gellene himself acknowledged at his trial that Salovaara "was one of the major participants in the restructuring that we were trying to put together."

Even if Gellene distinguished Salovaara from South Street, at the time he submitted his retention application he was also working on the Busse matter on behalf of South Street itself. At a minimum, he could not have been mistaken about the need to disclose that connection. He contended that it was a minor matter, on which only about thirteen thousand dollars had been billed at the time of the bankruptcy petition. That made no difference, however. He was required to disclose Milbank's ties to any party in interest, regardless of the size of the matter. This was especially important in light of South Street's critical role in the bankruptcy.

Gellene also contended that he didn't see the need for disclosure in light of the fact that Salovaara had consented to the proposed plan. This doesn't explain, however, why he disclosed Milbank's connections with other, less significant, creditors who also had accepted the plan. Furthermore, with a contested bankruptcy proceeding on the horizon, there might well arise the need to engage in further negotiations with South Street and other creditors in order to gain confirmation of the plan. Gellene's decisions on what concessions to seek from South Street in those negotiations potentially could be influenced by the fact that South Street was a current Milbank client.

Finally, even if Gellene initially made a mistake, he had numerous opportunities to rectify it as the bankruptcy proceeded. Potential conflict of interest was a recurring and highly visible issue in the case. Gellene had to file a second affidavit when JNL and the trustee refused to accept his first one at face value. JNL maintained that Milbank had not adequately investigated the merits of suing Goldman and South Street because the firm's involvement in the transactions at issue tainted its judgment. Even after the plan was confirmed, JNL contested Milbank's right to compensation in part because of alleged conflicts of interest.

Gellene himself took steps to avoid a potential conflict even in the midst of intense negotiations that followed Judge Eisenberg's rejection of the disclosure statement. On August 2, 1994, he requested that the firm write off about thirteen thousand dollars in fees and expenses due from Bucyrus for work done by Milbank prior to the bankruptcy petition. He explained that "[u]nder bankruptcy law, retaining these amounts as a receivable would cause the firm to be a creditor of Bucyrus-Erie, creating both a potential conflict of interest and potential grounds for disqualification and denial of post-bankruptcy fees." In sum, it was not the case that Gellene filed his affidavits and then had no further reason to think about conflicts and disclosure as he became immersed in the bankruptcy.

Two explanations have tended to dominate observers' commentary on Gellene's behavior. Gellene's detractors claim that he was habitually dishonest. He misrepresented that he was a member of the New York bar for eight years. He lied to the Wisconsin court about being a member of the federal bar in New York City. Evidence at his trial indicated that he had cut corners on other occasions. In light of this behavior, it should not be surprising that he would conceal Milbank's ties to Salovaara if he thought he could get away with it.

Critics of Milbank Tweed offer a second explanation: that Gellene was simply the fall guy for the law firm. There have been accusations or insinuations that Larry Lederman masterminded a plan to protect his old friend and client Salovaara in the Bucyrus bankruptcy.[1] Since disclosing Milbank's work for Salovaara probably would disqualify the firm from representing Bucyrus, Lederman pressured Gellene to keep quiet. When the scandal broke, Milbank protected Lederman and threw Gellene overboard.

These two explanations may have some plausibility, but at best are incomplete. It's reasonable to think that we should examine closely Gellene's character, his relationship with Lederman, and the environment at Milbank Tweed when trying to piece together what happened.

Attributing blame solely to flawed individuals or corrupt organizations rarely captures the subtleties of how ethical misconduct occurs. Furthermore, it offers false reassurance that only moral deviants, not ordinary people, engage in such behavior.

A striking amount of wrongdoing can occur in settings populated by people who are generally decent and well intentioned. Complex features of individual and social psychology can interact in ways that can't always be anticipated, leading to behavior that individuals wouldn't engage in on their own. In the case of John Gellene, there is enough information to sketch out at least the outlines of a plausible explanation that is more complex than the prevailing theories. This explanation acknowledges the need to consider Gellene's personality and character, but also takes account of crucial features of modern large law firm practice. These features include the continuation of a competitive tournament among lawyers after they are promoted to partner, the norms and culture of specialized fields of practice, and the tendency of lawyers to work on teams that handle high-stakes projects for corporate clients. In Gellene's case, this directs attention to Gellene's status in the partner tournament at Milbank Tweed, the approach of elite corporate transactional lawyers to conflicts of interest, large-firm bankruptcy lawyers' views of conflict and disclosure rules, and the particular dynamics of the Bucyrus bankruptcy.

Once we take these considerations into account, we can construct a story in which some of these factors provided motivation for Gellene's behavior, while others helped him rationalize it. This chapter explores the pressures that may have led Gellene to conceal Milbank's representation of Salovaara's interests. The next chapter suggests how Gellene may have convinced himself that such concealment was not a serious ethical breach—and in fact may have been the right thing to do under the circumstances.

The insights we gain from approaching events in this way suggest that Gellene's story may be less lurid but more sobering than standard explanations imply. Gellene's personality is not dramatically different from that of other lawyers, and may in fact be functional for succeeding in highly competitive law practices. Furthermore, the tournament deciding who wins partnerships in a law firm, the influence of specialized practice norms, and membership on high-stakes project teams are pervasive features of practice in modern large firms. In other words, neither Gellene's personality nor the circumstances in which he practiced are unique.

CONSIDER FIRST John Gellene the individual. Throughout his academic and professional career, Gellene was widely regarded as brilliant. He skipped two grades in school, finished high school at age sixteen, graduated summa cum laude and Phi Beta Kappa from Georgetown, and cum laude from Harvard Law School. He served as a clerk on the prestigious New Jersey Supreme Court. He made partner at Milbank against the high odds facing any incoming young lawyer. Comments from other lawyers in the firm regularly praised his work in the highest terms. Larry Lederman, an especially demanding high-profile partner in the firm, described Gellene's work as "absolutely brilliant." One partner noted the view of a client that Gellene was the best bankruptcy lawyer in the United States.

Gellene was well aware of this perception of his intellectual ability. He admitted that it was a crucial element of his sense of self-worth. "[N]ot just for my adult life but before that," he has said, "I've been recognized as a person with gifts of my intellect and my ability to deal with problems." Gellene was not alone among lawyers in the importance of intellectual achievement to his self-image. Some studies suggest that those who attend law school have a particularly high need for academic accomplishment, and come from families in which performance in school is strongly valued.[2] Lawyers thus may have an especially pronounced "need to compete against an internal or external standard of excellence."[3]

An intense orientation toward intellectual achievement can lead to significant professional success. It also, however, can be a burden. Gellene acknowledged that he was afraid to admit that he had made any errors, out of fear that this esteem for him would evaporate. "When I am confronted with a mistake," he said, "it is very difficult for me to stand up and say I did a stupid thing." He was, he acknowledged, someone "who feels that he had to be perfect because that is where I've gotten my view of myself. That is where I've gotten satisfaction. That's where I've tried for better or worse to have meaning in my life." Adding to the burden was a sense that perhaps Gellene did not deserve the admiration that he seemed to evoke. "For many years before I even learned that Bucyrus-Erie existed," he observed, he had acted as if his supposed gift was "an affliction, something that I had to reject, something that I suppose I wasn't worthy of."

Such anxiety about his stature prompted Gellene to be extraordinarily hard-working. Those who knew him in law school recall someone who seemed driven to prove himself, who put in exceptionally long hours even in a universe of unusually prodigious students. This compulsiveness may have been fueled by the fear that he might someday reveal that he was not as smart as others had been led to believe.

Consider, for instance, Gellene's desire to hide the fact that he hadn't completed his New York bar application. Someone in his situation might be concerned that if his failure came to light, others would think that he was unethical or sloppy, or that he feared some revelation about his character. Gellene, however, expressed the fear that his failure would be taken as evidence of stupidity—as an intellectual, not a moral, delinquency. Similarly, he described the nondisclosure of Milbank's connections to Salovaara as an act that was "incredibly stupid." This suggests that Gellene regarded aspersions on his intellect as the most devastating form of personal criticism.

Gellene's work habits continued when he joined Milbank Tweed. In an environment of high achievers who spent most of their waking hours at the firm, he stood out as someone who "works like a dog." Gellene described his typical work week as "being in the office ten, twelve, sometimes more hours a day five days a week and then a number of hours in the office on Saturday or Sunday or both." He adopted this schedule, he said, soon after he joined the firm. The desire to make partner in a very competitive environment no doubt intensified any predilection he had for immersing himself in his work. He continued these habits, however, even after making partner. In 1993 and 1994, for instance, he billed about three thousand hours each year while immersed in the Bucyrus bankruptcy and other matters.

Gellene's compulsiveness compounded his stress, because it left him unwilling to turn down assignments and unable to delegate significant tasks to anyone else. His partners counseled him to share his duties more and to use associates more effectively. His failure to do so left him typically juggling several matters at once, responsible for major decisions on each.

Gellene himself admitted that he was the sort of person who "if I needed help, I wouldn't necessarily reach out for it." During the Bucyrus case, for instance, he was the sole partner responsible for the bankruptcy negotiations, simultaneously handling major responsibilities in other matters. As a result, much of the time he was in crisis mode, rushing from one meeting to another, to and from the airport, going down to the wire in getting papers filed on time, and calling from other locations to check on progress in the various matters. In the forty-eight hours leading up to the Bucyrus Chapter 11 filing, he worked straight through without any sleep.

Although he felt that Gellene did a superb job, Bucyrus general counsel David Goelzer acknowledged at the bankruptcy fee hearings that he had some concerns during the bankruptcy that Gellene was trying to balance too many tasks at once. Goelzer many times was not quite sure where Gellene would be on a given day, or how easy it would be to get in touch with him if an emergency arose. Similarly, when Gellene moved to the corporate department at Milbank in 1996, he didn't asked to be relieved of any of the bankruptcy matters in which he was involved. He thus had to take on new work in a field with which he wasn't completely familiar, while still meeting the extensive demands of his bankruptcy cases.

Gellene's reluctance to share responsibility, his difficulty in seeking help from others, and his insistence on handling several intensive matters at once are consistent with the portrait of perfectionism and anxiety that emerges from his own comments. Perhaps he feared that if others worked closely with him they would come to question his reputation for brilliance. In any event, his approach to his work posed the constant threat of isolation. He ran the risk of cutting himself off from valuable second opinions, and of depriving himself of the sounding board that colleagues can provide.

These tendencies may be especially prevalent in the legal profession. Some research suggests that those who choose this career path may be especially prone to be highly self-critical and anxious about performance, as well as to project an image of self-containment that eschews assistance from others.[4] The result is that many lawyers may be propelled by a "never-satisfied drive for success"[5] that places a premium on controlling one's environment. Yet, as we've seen, law practice in modern large firms is perhaps more competitive and turbulent than ever before. Those for whom this drive is a crucial component of identity may channel their insecurity into even greater efforts at control, rather than rely on others for support.

Pursuing this course can lead to a kind of myopia, in which anything not immediately relevant to the task at hand receives short shrift. Gellene, for instance, repeatedly failed to submit his billing records on time, and shunned any involvement in the firm's summer associates program. These delinquencies obviously were frustrating to Milbank's partners in charge of these activities. They reflect a lack of consideration for others, and blindness to the importance of the prosaic tasks that keep a firm running. Few, however, would regard them as freighted with grave moral significance.

More disturbing than these failures was Gellene's tendency on occasion to cut corners—to flirt with dishonesty by being less than forthright or actually engaging in misrepresentations. This happened three times before he filed his Bucyrus affidavit: his misrepresentation that he was a member of the New York state bar, his false statement that he was a member of the federal bar in Manhattan, and his retroactive reconstruction of his daynotes. It happened three times afterward: his colloquy with Judge Eisenberg about Lotus Cab, his falsehood to the Colorado bankruptcy court about why he had not responded to the trustee's discovery request in the Busse matter, and his document alteration and lies within Milbank after receiving the JNL disgorgement motion.

How much do these incidents support the claim that Gellene's flawed character was the main reason for his disclosure violation? If we examine these episodes closely, they generally are different in nature from Gellene's misconduct in the Bucyrus case, and arguably are less serious. With the exception of the exchange about Lotus Cab, they have a common pattern: negligence, followed by dishonesty to cover it up. Indeed, all the incidents prior to the Bucyrus bankruptcy fit this pattern.

Consider Gellene's misrepresentation of his bar membership. Gellene passed the New Jersey and New York bars the summer before he began his clerkship on the New Jersey Supreme Court. One can imagine that, wanting to prove himself in his first job out of law school, he put off filing the paperwork and making the trip to Albany to complete the New York application process.

When he finished his clerkship, the partnership competition at Milbank Tweed required an even more demanding commitment. As a delay of weeks and months turned into years, it became even harder to rectify his earlier omission. Given the embarrassment of admitting that he was not really a member of the New York bar, the time necessary to complete his application, and the apparent lack of risk to any client, it may well have been simpler to say that he was a member of the bar. As Gellene acknowledged:

> I did a very stupid thing. I got caught up in my work and I didn't fill out the forms, and as time went on it got more and more absurd and I could not stand up and say, I did something stupid. And when that first happened in my life in a traumatic way, I could not say it to myself and I could not say it to others so I hid it.

Thus, what began with minor procrastination due to work demands eventually evolved into misrepresentation, which in turn made it difficult to change course as the years went on. This clearly was dishonest. At the same time, putting off completing the application process after passing the bar exam was common enough that a partner at a major New York law firm described it as a "long tradition." The character and fitness committee to which Gellene eventually submitted his material had compiled a list the previous year of almost one hundred individuals in practice who fell into this category, some at prestigious law firms. The committee's secretary said that he was unaware of any case in which a person had ever been denied admission because he or she had performed legal work without completing the application process. This policy of leniency, reported the *New York Law Journal*, "may reflect a recognition of the unintentional hole that some young lawyers dug for themselves when, in the race to pile up billable hours, they failed to complete the paperwork required for admission."[6]

Surprisingly, given that bankruptcy lawyers practice in federal court, when Gellene took the steps to gain admission to the state bar, he didn't also submit an application to be admitted to the federal bar in New York City. He may have simply focused at the time on clearing the one obstacle to his ability to practice in New York. With that out of the way, he was able to return to Milbank as of counsel and begin working again. At that point, he may have felt even more pressure to prove himself to the firm. He may have had little patience for any task, however minor, that diverted him from that mission.

In 1994, of course, this led him to misrepresent that he was a member of the federal bar in New York. He believed that this was necessary for him to practice before the federal bankruptcy court in the Bucyrus case. Eventually, there would be discovery of this misrepresentation as prosecutors began to investigate disclosures in that case. As Gellene has said of gaining admission to the federal bar, "[I]t would have been a very simple thing to do, but I was confronted with the absurd stupidity of not filling out forms that thousands of lawyers fill out year in and year out and I couldn't stand up and say, I did this. I did something stupid so I didn't do it."

Gellene's delinquency with his daynotes led to another incident in which he tried to cover the tracks of an earlier omission. "At one point," said Bob O'Hara in the 1993 Milbank compensation committee report on Gellene, "he was retroactively putting in incomplete daynotes; we caught him on it and he has corrected the problem." That is, Gellene was submitting billing hours that were reconstructions from memory some time after the fact. Gellene was not necessarily lying about the number of billable hours that he had worked. Given that Milbank lawyers were required to bill in tenths of an hour, however, at a minimum he was misrepresenting the precision with which these figures had been calculated.

After the Bucyrus bankruptcy, Gellene failed to respond to the trustee's discovery request in connection with the Busse matter in Colorado. When the court penalized this failure by entering a default judgment against South Street, Gellene falsely told the court that his delay in responding was due to the conflict between Salovaara and Eckert. It's not hard to imagine that Gellene had been swamped by his move to the corporate department earlier in the year, especially since he had kept the bankruptcy cases on which he had been working. These demands may well have led him to put off responding to the trustee's request and eventually miss the deadline. When the court imposed the sanction of denying South Street's claim, Gellene then tried to avoid the embarrassment of having to tell his client that it had lost $19.9 million because of his neglect.

Finally, of course, Gellene panicked when he received JNL's disgorgement motion in December 1996. He became paralyzed and unable to act as the deadline to respond came and went. By the time his partners asked him about his apparent responsibility for an imminent default judgment against Milbank, he obviously had painted himself into another corner. In his eyes, the only way to avoid a catastrophe was denial. This led him to lie to his partners and alter the affidavit accompanying JNL's motion. That, of course, only postponed the inevitable.

Each of these episodes represent an instance in which Gellene put off dealing with an obligation for an unreasonably long period of time. He then lied in order to conceal his earlier omission. In other words, if Gellene had a character flaw, it was that he tended to lie when he wanted to avoid the consequences of his own negligence. That surely is not admirable, but it is understandable.

Gellene's disclosure violation in the Bucyrus case, however, doesn't seem attributable to this flaw. He lied at the outset to deceive the court, not to save himself criticism or embarrassment. That was a different, and arguably more serious, ethical breach. Certainly none of his transgressions before the Bucyrus case was comparable.

Gellene's only instance of dishonesty that doesn't fit the pattern of negligence followed by cover-up occurred after he filed his disclosure affidavit. This was his response to Judge Eisenberg's question whether Milbank owned an interest in Lotus Cab. "No, Your Honor," Gellene replied. "I wish the firm did, but it doesn't." When Eisenberg asked if any Milbank partners had an interest in Lotus, Gellene conceded that some did. Gellene's first response was literally true. It was not, however, completely honest. He knew that what prompted the judge's question was the desire to ensure that Milbank's transportation expenses had been incurred for legitimate work reasons, rather than to benefit anyone at the firm.

At the same time, Gellene took pains not to lie to the court. In addition, the amount in question was relatively trivial in light of Milbank's total fees and expenses. Judge Eisenberg said in his fee decision that, while Gellene's response was "very mildly disconcerting," the judge did not take it into account in his decision because it was "de minimis." The magnitude of Gellene's fudging on Lotus Cab thus is much smaller and less significant than his Bucyrus disclosure violation.

On balance, therefore, it seems unpersuasive to claim that Gellene's misconduct in the Bucyrus case was simply the product of a dishonest character with an impaired moral compass. Gellene had a tendency to cut corners when his inattention got him into a bind. Lying to a court on a material issue at the beginning of a case, however, was not simply one more instance of this tendency. With that, he moved from defensive dishonesty to more assertive deceit.

At the same time, the fact that Gellene tended to engage in petty transgressions may have left him at risk for the commission of more egregious ones. Moral behavior to some degree is a matter of habit. The ways people routinely approach and react to circumstances shape them in subtle ways over time, much as continuous incremental changes in the course of a river can eventually shift its course. The fact that Gellene tended to cut corners on occasion may have eroded some of his resistance to dishonesty, leaving him with dwindling ethical resources to withstand temptation. Each small misstep may have pushed him further down the ethical slippery slope, so that lying to the court in the Bucyrus case seemed like an incremental, not a momentous step to take.

A sobering possibility is that these personality traits may be increasingly functional in highly competitive corporate and professional life. Research suggests that those who advance in the tournament-like environment of large organizations tend to share certain characteristics.[7] They are able quickly to grasp the rules of the game—to "get a sense of the prevailing metric and outperform their peers on it."[8] They tend to be adept at rationalizing questionable behavior when it's necessary to accomplish their objectives. Their skill in doing so is enhanced by an ability to minimize or bracket the moral significance of the situations that they encounter. This enables them to approach decisions pragmatically, less fettered by a sense of categorical constraints. Tournament survivors thus exhibit the flexibility necessary to move from one competition to another with a minimum of psychological friction.

In sum, as Donald Langevoort has put it, success in highly competitive organizations "is skewed in the direction of rewarding those who are highly focused at the business of competing, which of necessity means the cognitive ability to block out concerns—like difficult ethical problems—that are likely to be distracting."[9]

Appreciating that these attributes can be adaptive underscores that individual personality is only part of the equation. Character traits express themselves in concrete actions in specific environments, and reflect the reward systems that operate in particular settings. For many lawyers, an especially influential environment in which they operate is the large law firm.

ORGANIZATIONS SUCH AS law firms can exert a significant influence on how people within them deal with ethical issues.[10] Formal procedures, lines of authority, and informal norms all combine to create an organizational culture. That culture can affect how individuals approach ethical rules, as well as provide guidance in ambiguous situations. The culture of the large law firm is shaped by three especially notable features: a tournament among partners, the presence of specialized practice groups, and the creation of teams of lawyers to handle high-stakes projects for clients. Understanding what happened in John Gellene's case therefore requires examining the partner tournament at Milbank Tweed, the norms of elite transactional and bankruptcy specialists in large firms, and the moral universe that Gellene may have inhabited as a member of the Bucyrus bankruptcy team.

Milbank Tweed established its partner tournament shortly before John Gellene was promoted to partner. Gellene had joined Milbank as an associate in the fall of 1980. For many years the firm had a reputation as a genteel "white shoe" Wall Street firm, with longtime ties to the Rockefeller family interests. By the mid-1980s, however, the firm was concerned that it had fallen behind in the new entrepreneurial world of law practice. Milbank therefore took steps to transform itself into a more efficient business enterprise. Partners modified the compensation system to place more emphasis on revenue and business generation. As a result, some partners suffered a reduction in earnings. More dramatically, the firm asked some partners to leave because they lagged behind their colleagues in hours billed and revenue generated. The firm also set about to lure partners from other law firms to Milbank, such as Larry Lederman, who could increase its visibility in more profitable practice areas.

These changes were instituted beginning in late 1986, when Gellene was still an associate. By the time that Gellene was named a partner at the end of 1988, the new rules for success at the firm were clear. A lag in productivity could result in lower compensation, and a serious deficiency would lead to expulsion from the partnership. Thus, whatever workaholic tendencies that Gellene brought to Milbank were reinforced by a firm that felt it was crucial to spur productivity and profitability in order to survive. Gellene operated within a law firm culture in which his drive to prove himself would be encouraged and rewarded. In this respect, of course, Milbank was similar to other elite corporate law firms that perceived the need to change in light of market conditions.

This was also a milieu, however, that could reinforce whatever anxiety Gellene felt about whether he was doing enough to keep up. Past performance was no guarantee of future security. He may also have felt an especially strong need to reestablish his credentials at Milbank after the revelation that he had misrepresented his New York bar status. The firm had terminated him when it first became aware of the problem. After Gellene completed the steps necessary to gain bar admission, Milbank had not welcomed him back right away. Instead, it had first employed him in an of counsel capacity.

Even when he rejoined the firm as a partner, Gellene was not placed back in his class, but was treated as if he had just been made a partner. This put him two years behind the class of partners who had been named with him at the beginning of 1989. This apparently was the source of some displeasure on Gellene's part. Such displeasure reflects the fact that compensation is significant in Milbank and other such firms not simply in absolute terms, but as a measure of one's standing in the partner tournament. Gellene's awareness that his tenure as partner at the firm had been clouded virtually from the start may have intensified his already strong desire to prove himself worthy of a Milbank partnership. This may have exacerbated his tendency to take on large amounts of work with little assistance from others.

As his comments to the Milbank compensation committee indicated, Gellene had ongoing concern about having enough work. Recall that he complained that in bankruptcy practice there were "too many lawyers for the available business," and that bankruptcy work was in danger of becoming a "commodity," with low profit margins. Especially notable was his statement in late 1993, two months before he filed Bucyrus's bankruptcy petition and his own appointment application with Judge Eisenberg. Beginning in mid-1994, he said, "[T]he challenge . . . will be to find adequate new work." In light of these concerns, Gellene argued that compensation decisions at Milbank needed to take account of the fact that some downturns in business might be beyond a partner's control.

Gellene thus was keenly aware that Milbank had followed many other large firms in adopting a partner tournament. This appeared to create some anxiety about the future of his practice. He already likely felt pressure to keep pushing hard because of his own personal tendencies. The more aggressive entrepreneurial culture at Milbank reinforced this pressure. It could make Gellene feel especially vulnerable because of his earlier problem over bar membership, and uncertainty about whether the bankruptcy practice group would continue to generate enough work.

By others' accounts, and by his own admission, Gellene wasn't and apparently didn't expect to become a rainmaker who brought clients to the firm. That meant that his success in the Milbank partner tournament depended on developing good relationships with rainmakers who could provide him with regular work for clients. The arrival of Larry Lederman at the firm provided an opportunity to do just that. Lederman offered the potential for access to a large roster of corporations and investment banks that could provide a steady stream of work for Gellene, especially on behalf of debtors. This could ease Gellene's concerns about building a stable practice.

Lederman, of course, was the partner who tapped Gellene to work on the Bucyrus bankruptcy. Gellene may have been loath at that point to risk losing the opportunity to work for the client of such an important rainmaker. Might Lederman have relied on that reluctance to press Gellene not to disclose Milbank's work for Salovaara and South Street? Exploring the influence of the Milbank partner tournament on Gellene's fateful decision thus requires looking more closely at the interaction between Gellene and Lederman on the Bucyrus bankruptcy.

GELLENE SUBMITTED an affidavit to Judge Eisenberg in March 1997 shortly after revelation of his disclosure violation. It said that he took "full and complete responsibility" for the failure, and that he hadn't consulted any of his partners about whether to disclose the relationship with Salovaara–South Street. Lederman, he said, had accepted Gellene's judgment about whether disclosure of these ties was necessary.

Press accounts of depositions in the disgorgement suit later in 1997, however, present a different story. They reported that Gellene testified that Lederman had told him that Salovaara wanted Milbank to keep its representation of him confidential. In his own deposition, Salovaara denied expressing any such wish. An article in the *Wall Street Journal* also declared that the depositions indicated that Lederman "let it be known within the firm that he didn't see a problem with the dual representation." For his part, Lederman testified that he had relied on Gellene to make the decision about what to disclose to the court, since he was not a bankruptcy expert.

Both John Stark and JNL's attorney Andrew Rahl have suggested that Lederman was the person who controlled the decision whether to disclose Milbank's representation of South Street and Salovaara. "We believe that this was a deliberate strategy/conspiracy," said Rahl a few months after Gellene's Rule 2014 violation was discovered. "[S]ome individuals in this law firm were trying to aid Salovaara." Who might those individuals be? Stark argued that "the partner who was the architect of the scheme was Larry Lederman. Then he involved Gellene, Lichstein, and Gelfand." The problem, said Stark, was "the star system," in which Lederman was "allowed to operate in an unsupervised manner" after he joined Milbank.

Others have rejected the notion that Gellene would act alone on such a significant decision in light of Lederman's strong personality, his critical role in Milbank's effort to become a major player in corporate practice, and his close relationship with Salovaara. As the only secured creditor of Bucyrus, South Street might be vulnerable to challenges from unsecured creditors and other parties in interest. Having Gellene handle the bankruptcy would be a way to minimize the chance that Salovaara's interests would be jeopardized in the reorganization.

Of course, having Milbank perform the legal work for the bankruptcy wasn't a step that Lederman had to force on an unwilling client. Given Lederman's close involvement in discussions of Bucyrus's financial condition and options, it would have been natural for the company to look to him for guidance. From the time that Chapter 11 was on the table as an option, Bucyrus officials and representatives appear to have assumed that Milbank would work on the legal aspects of a reorganization. At the November 1992 meeting with Goldman and Houlihan, which Lederman apparently did not attend, someone mentioned that if the company filed a Chapter 11 petition, Lederman would need to designate someone at Milbank to handle the bankruptcy.

Furthermore, Bucyrus officials were aware of Lederman's history of working with Salovaara, the likelihood of that continuing, and the close relationship between the two men. When Lederman left Wachtell, Salovaara had repeatedly urged Bucyrus to use Lederman for its legal work. The company eventually followed this suggestion by replacing Wachtell with Milbank as its main outside counsel. It seems implausible to claim that Lederman sought to conceal from Bucyrus Milbank's ties to Salovaara. Because of Lederman's familiarity with the company, Bucyrus may have preferred that Milbank handle the Chapter 11 proceedings even if that created a potential conflict. Indeed, Bucyrus officials might take some comfort in the connection between Milbank and Salovaara, since it could provide an avenue for persuading South Street to make some concessions. That's not to say, of course, that Milbank didn't have the legal obligation to disclose to Bucyrus the specific work that it was doing for Salovaara–South Street.

Bucyrus, however, wasn't the only party in interest in the bankruptcy. Unsecured creditors and shareholders stood most directly to lose at Salovaara's expense. They would want to know if Milbank had any ties to him. They especially would want to know if Gellene himself had any connection to Salovaara, since Gellene was the legal advisor to Bucyrus. If it's true that Lederman desired to put Milbank in a position to look after Salovaara's interests, disclosure to other creditors and to shareholders of the firm's relationship to the investor could threaten this objective. Those parties might insist that Milbank be disqualified, in order to eliminate any possibility of favoritism. For this reason, Lederman might have an incentive to direct that Gellene not mention Salovaara and South Street in his affidavit.

The record indicates only two discussions between Lederman and Gellene about whether Milbank's simultaneous ties to Salovaara and Bucyrus were a problem. The first occurred in Lederman's office on December 22, 1993. Lederman, Gellene, and Toni Lichstein were discussing Salovaara's dispute with Fred Eckert. Gellene then briefed Lederman on the status of the Bucyrus bankruptcy. At that point, a proposed disclosure statement and plan had been submitted for approval to the SEC. Lichstein asked if Milbank had a conflict as a result of its simultaneous work for both Bucyrus and Salovaara. Both Gellene and Lederman replied that it didn't. Salovaara, said Gellene, had already agreed to the terms in the proposed Chapter 11 plan. His interests and those of Bucyrus thus were aligned. Lederman said that there was no problem because the two matters were unrelated.

Both comments were responsive to the question whether Milbank might have a *conflict of interest* because of its dual representation. They weren't dispositive, however, of whether the firm had an obligation to *disclose* that representation when Bucyrus filed for bankruptcy two months later. Bankruptcy Rule 2014 requires disclosure of connections with any party in interest, not simply those that might constitute a conflict. It is intended to bestow upon the court, not the applicant, the authority to determine whether any relationship presents a disabling conflict of interest.

The second conversation between Lederman and Gellene was on the morning that Gellene flew out to Milwaukee shortly before Bucyrus filed its Chapter 11 petition. Gellene testified that he told Lederman that he would be disclosing the firm's ties to Goldman. Those ties wouldn't be a problem in a bankruptcy court in New York, he said, but he wasn't sure how the Wisconsin court would react. Gellene also said that he didn't believe that the firm's connection to Salovaara needed to be disclosed because the investor was not a creditor. Lederman, he said, accepted his conclusion.

How likely is it that Lederman told Gellene that Milbank should conceal its representation of Salovaara and South Street? By the time that Gellene was preparing to file his application in February 1994, all parties except JNL had signed off on the proposed Chapter 11 plan. The parties that had agreed to the plan may well not have opposed Milbank's application if Gellene had disclosed the connection to Salovaara and South Street.

JNL, however, was a different story. The creditor had aggressively pursued its claims. It had challenged Bucyrus and the other creditors every step of the way. The plan contained a cram-down of JNL, which the creditor fiercely contested. Gellene had kept Lederman briefed on developments in the case, and Lederman's, rather than Gellene's, name was on the S-4 filed with the SEC. Lederman thus would have been well aware of JNL's obstinacy. He could anticipate that the creditor would use information about Milbank's dual representation to object both to the firm's application and to the releases for South Street in the bankruptcy plan. If Lederman wanted Milbank to stay on the case to protect Salovaara, he had to be nervous about how JNL would react to full disclosure.

In addition, Salovaara's general secretiveness may have prompted Lederman to prefer that Milbank not disclose that it was representing him. For instance, Salovaara apparently refused to disclose the amount of his holdings in Bucyrus. He also allegedly wouldn't disclose to South Street's own fund manager the amount of his claim in the Busse matter.

Furthermore, Salovaara was reported to have engaged in a more questionable form of secrecy after the Bucyrus bankruptcy. When he and Eckert were winding up South Street in late 1994, among the last investments remaining in the fund were Bucyrus notes with a face value of $54 million. Gary Hindes was then administering the fund. When he sold most of the notes at a price of 94.67 cents on the dollar, Salovaara accused him of conspiring with Eckert to sell the notes at a price below their actual value. He sued Hindes for breach of fiduciary duty. As evidence in support of his claim, Salovaara stated that he had been able to sell the remaining $1.6 million in Bucyrus notes for 98 cents on the dollar shortly after Hindes' sale.

Hindes, however, alleged that the sale of the $1.6 million notes was a charade arranged by Salovaara, not an arms-length transaction. As the *New York Times* verified, the person who purchased the notes from Salovaara was the roommate of his wife's sister. The funds that she used came from Salovaara's mother-in-law, who had recently received a transfer of $1.5 million from Mikael Salovaara. Hindes wrote to South Street investors: "We have been able to conclusively determine that Mr. Salovaara's sale of the offshore fund's B-E Securities at 98 was [a] sham transaction orchestrated and engineered by him in furtherance of his lawsuit."[11] Salovaara denied any wrongdoing in the matter. Hindes eventually prevailed in the lawsuit. The allegation against Salovaara, however, lends some plausibility to the theory that he may have asked Lederman quietly to look after his interests in the Bucyrus bankruptcy.

Lederman maintained that he relied on Gellene to make the appropriate disclosure because he wasn't intimately familiar with bankruptcy practice. Lederman, however, had extensive experience in corporate financial restructuring, which can eventually shade into a Chapter 11 filing. He may have been aware of at least the general terms of the bankruptcy disclosure requirement. In addition, given his strong personality, is it likely that Lederman would have been content to rely completely on Gellene's judgment on a matter that was sensitive to Salovaara?

On the other hand, there is evidence that undermines the claim that Lederman orchestrated the disclosure violation. Lederman offered comments on Gellene in late 1993 to the Milbank compensation committee that seem inconsistent with an intention to conceal the firm's dual representation. The remarks are attributed to "Larry Lederman/Al Lilley." Certain of the statements, however, are about matters in which Lederman was involved, and about which he logically would have been the person to comment. They state that Gellene "is managing the Bucyrus-Erie matter, which is highly contested—we have billed over $1 million, and they will not do anything without talking to Gellene; he is an absolutely brilliant strategist." Immediately after this, the comments read: "Also handling brilliantly a matter for Salavano." This likely was a reference to Salovaara, simply transcribed incorrectly by the person conducting the interview. There is no entry for a "Salavano" matter in Gellene's billing records any time near then. The matter in question presumably was the Busse case.

Given what had happened in the Busse case thus far, it seems rather extravagant to characterize Gellene's work in that matter at that point as brilliant. A bit of hyperbole, however, would not be unusual for someone who regarded Gellene so highly. If the reference is indeed to Gellene's work for Salovaara, it seems unlikely that Lederman would have offered this unsolicited comment if he were intent on keeping quiet the firm's simultaneous work for Bucyrus and Salovaara.

It is not clear whether the December 22 meeting in Lederman's office had occurred by the time that Lederman made these comments to the compensation committee. If it had, Lederman's and Gellene's assurance to Lichstein that there was no conflict could have provided him enough comfort that he felt no qualms about mentioning the dual representation to the compensation committee. In addition, keep in mind that the question of disclosure didn't arise until mid-February of the following year. The December 22 meeting instead focused on whether there was a potential conflict. Gellene and Lederman briefly argued to Lichstein that there was not, and she apparently accepted their conclusion.

Even if there had been a potential conflict, state ethical rules permit the representation if both parties consent to it. The relevant parties in December 1993, before Bucyrus filed its Chapter 11 petition, were Salovaara and Bucyrus. There seems little doubt that Salovaara knew that Gellene was representing Bucyrus in the negotiations preceding its Chapter 11 filing. Top Bucyrus management probably didn't know specifically of Gellene's representation of South Street in the Busse matter, or of Lichstein's work on Salovaara's dispute with Eckert. They probably were generally aware, however, of the close relationship between Lederman and Salovaara. They had some reason to believe that Milbank would provide ongoing legal services to the investor after Lederman arrived at the firm. Thus, while they may not have known of the Eckert and Busse matters in particular, they likely would not have been surprised to learn about them—and may well not have objected.

This wouldn't necessarily be adequate to support a claim that Milbank had fulfilled its disclosure obligation to Bucyrus sufficiently to cure a potential conflict. It may have been enough, however, for Lederman and Gellene to conclude that the dual representation presented no problem at the time of the December discussion. Even if there were a potential conflict, both parties involved arguably had no problem with it.

If this is correct, Lederman would have no reason to conceal Milbank's representation of Salovaara when he made his comments to the compensation committee. Lederman's reference in December to the work for Salovaara therefore wouldn't necessarily be inconsistent with advising Gellene in mid-February to conceal it. By then the issue had shifted from conflict to disclosure. Lederman, however, probably wouldn't have drawn such a fine distinction. The S-4 had been filed with the SEC in October. It could be approved at any moment. That would lead to filing the Chapter 11 petition and Milbank's application within a month or so. Revealing the dual representation at any time therefore could jeopardize the ability to conceal it from the court.

Informing other partners at Milbank, of course, is not the same as broadcasting it to the world at large. Nonetheless, it still increased the risk of disclosure. Furthermore, it was a completely gratuitous comment, not called for by the interview and relating to a very small matter on which Gellene had spent relatively little time.

There is thus some evidence that can be used both to support and to question each claim—that Lederman prevailed upon Gellene not to disclose Milbank's ties to Salovaara–South Street, and that he relied on Gellene to determine whether those ties should be disclosed. There is, however, a third possibility. This is that Lederman dealt with the Bucyrus matter in a way that Gellene construed as implicitly signaling that Milbank should not disclose its representation of Salovaara to the bankruptcy court. Exploring this possibility requires attention to the influence of practice specialties on lawyers' perceptions and behavior.

Large law firms typically contain specialists in several different fields of practice. These lawyers deal with questions that are unique to their fields and distinct from issues that their other colleagues in the firm confront. The collective process of resolving these questions generates shared understandings of those aspects of practice that can't be fully captured in formal rules. This process of socialization is captured by John Gellene's description of Milbank bankruptcy partner John Jerome: "He taught me how to be a lawyer." Appreciating the norms and culture of elite corporate transactional lawyers sheds light on how Lederman may have viewed any potential conflict of interest in the Bucyrus case. It suggests the possibility that Lederman could have influenced Gellene in ways more subtle than direct pressure or instruction.

AS AN EXPERIENCED corporate lawyer, Lederman may have regarded Milbank's dual representation as unexceptional. For various reasons, transactional lawyers tend to regard potential conflicts of interest as a less urgent concern than do litigators. This is because conflicts rules speak more explicitly to litigation than to transactional work, transactional clients tend to be fairly tolerant of potential conflicts, and transactional lawyers work closely with investment bankers who are subject to relatively lenient conflicts constraints.

From this perspective, the issue with respect to Lederman is not whether he explicitly directed Gellene to conceal Milbank's dual representation. Rather, it's whether he was sufficiently sensitive to the potential for conflict inherent in that representation when he dealt with Gellene. Either unreflectively or deliberately, Lederman may have applied a transactional lawyer's perspective to a situation in which reliance on it wasn't appropriate. Sensitive to implicit cues from Lederman, Gellene may have then concluded that he should not make full disclosure to the court. Exploring this possibility requires that we examine why many corporate transactional lawyers tend to have a distinctive approach to conflicts issues.

First, ethical rules on conflicts of interest are geared primarily to litigators, and provide little direct guidance to transactional lawyers.[12] Most states have adopted some version of American Bar Association

Model Rule 1.7 to deal with possible conflicts arising from concurrent representation of clients. Section 1.7(a)(1) says that a lawyer generally shall not represent a client if doing so would be "directly adverse" to another client.[13]

The comments to the rule reflect the fact that 1.7(a)(1) is most easily applied to litigation. They observe, for instance, that a lawyer ordinarily may not act as an "advocate" against a client, even in an unrelated matter. Is a lawyer an "advocate" against a client if he represents a party in negotiations with that client about a possible transaction between the two? Does it make a difference if, say, the two parties are seeking to establish a joint venture?

The comments also state that directly adverse conflicts may arise in transactional matters, such as when a lawyer is asked to represent someone in negotiating the sale of a business to another party who is a client in a different matter. The comments provide no guidance, however, on scenarios that fall short of this. By contrast, it's easy to determine whether a lawyer is acting as an "advocate" against another client in the context of litigation.

Section 1.7(a)(2) contains a prohibition whose application to transactional practice also can be ambiguous. It provides that a lawyer generally may not represent a client if her work for that client may be "materially limited" by the lawyer's obligations to another client or person, or her own interests.[14] Suppose that a lawyer represents a bank on various matters, and then seeks to represent a company in negotiating a financing agreement from the same bank. Is his work for the bank likely to compromise his ability to obtain favorable terms for the company?

The comments to Rule 1.7 acknowledge that the question whether a conflict under Rule 1.7(a)(2) exists in the nonlitigation context is "often one of proximity and degree."[15] Factors to consider, they suggest, are the nature of the lawyer's relationship with the clients, the kind of work the lawyer is doing for each, the likelihood that a conflict will arise, and the prejudice likely to arise from that conflict. The comments go on to say that "a lawyer may not represent multiple parties to a negotiation whose interests are fundamentally antagonistic to each other, but common representation is permissible where the clients are generally aligned in interest even though there is some difference of interest among them." Determining whether a conflict exists in a transactional setting thus requires making quite subtle judgments.

In sum, conflicts rules generally provide clearer guidance to litigators than to transactional lawyers. The litigator operates in a milieu in which the adversity between or among parties is fairly evident. By contrast, the transactional lawyer's work involves matters in which there can be both adversity and cooperation between parties. On the one hand, a business deal reflects a situation in which parties are expected to act in self-interested fashion, as they seek to maximize their rewards and minimize their risks. On the other hand, each party hopes that entering into a transaction will achieve benefits from cooperative activity that it couldn't enjoy by acting alone. They know that such a transaction won't occur unless it's beneficial to both parties. Transactional negotiations in which the interests of the parties are "fundamentally antagonistic" to each other thus may be rare, which means that transactional lawyers may seem less needed than litigators to devote close attention to conflicts.

A second reason that transactional lawyers tend to have a distinctive approach to potential conflicts is that corporate clients often prefer representation by lawyers with the multiple ties that create such conflicts. Clients can benefit from lawyers' relationships with lenders, underwriters, commercial banks, potential merger or joint venture partners, suppliers, and even competitors. The most able lawyers tend to have the widest network of connections. The existence of this network can lower transaction costs for a client. The lawyer may serve as a reputational intermediary who makes negotiations go more smoothly because the other parties know and trust him. He may have an especially good understanding of those parties' needs and interests, and thereby be able to devise mutually beneficial terms. The lawyer's set of connections may reduce the client's search costs for financing assistance, and permit it to move more swiftly on time-sensitive matters. Furthermore, the transactional lawyer's location in a web of interconnected relationships can heighten the importance of reputation, and make informal sanctions an effective deterrent to opportunism or disloyalty.

All these potential benefits flow from the fact that a lawyer has relationships with parties who have interests that could potentially conflict with those of the client. Many business clients are willing to take this risk, however, in the belief that the lawyer will instead be adept at finding common ground. They desire the opportunity to draw on the lawyer's stock of "relational capital" to derive benefits that might be unavailable from lawyers with fewer potential conflicts.

The most desirable transactional lawyers thus tend to possess the most potential conflicts of interest. Indeed, the existence of such conflicts is an indication of how much their services are in demand. A corporation could use another lawyer with fewer connections, but that may promise fewer rewards. As Susan Shapiro puts it, "[I]ndependence often comes at the price of inexperience." Shapiro goes on to suggest that in a process akin to natural selection, the fittest fiduciary organizations "evolve by assuming or orchestrating greater conflicts." The survivors are those who can recruit members who "come from central nodes in large well-heeled social networks." As a result,

> Principals and clients gravitate to these tangled webs where they find more trustworthy agents, greater expertise and talent, vicarious access to positions of power and influence, economies of scale, greater profit, protection from risk, and all manner of exceptional service. The attractions of role conflict on both sides of the fiduciary relationship are quite compelling.[16]

This leads to a third influence on transactional lawyers' views of potential conflicts. Client waiver of conflicts is more common in transactional than in litigation settings. Indeed, client consent to conflicts has been described as "routine" in corporate deal work.[17] The transactional lawyer often can anticipate that a client's consent to a conflict will be forthcoming. This makes its existence a much less urgent matter. He thus may have no great incentive to focus on whether a conflict exists, because he assumes that even if it does, it ultimately will not pose a problem.

Other factors may lead transactional lawyers not to spend as much time as litigators in detailed conflict analysis absent an obvious concern. Whether a corporate lawyer in a large firm asks for a waiver likely will be driven by practical rather than legal concerns. Even if there arguably is no conflict, for instance, a firm may still seek permission from an important client to take on a representation to which it thinks the client may be sensitive. By contrast, with other less significant clients, the firm may be less solicitous even if the issue is closer to the line.

Furthermore, many discussions with clients about possible waivers tend to be oral rather than written. Goldman's waiver of objection to Milbank's representation of Bucyrus, for instance, was provided orally rather than in writing. Written requests for waivers may inject an awkward and even adversarial tone into client relationships. In addition, a formal written request may imply that the firm has concluded that there is a conflict, while an oral discussion can fudge the issue. The matter can be introduced casually in conversation, in a manner that suggests that there really is no conflict but that the firm wants to check with the client out of a sense of courtesy and an excess of caution. Oral descriptions of the potential conflict also may not be as detailed as written requests for a waiver. Inside general counsel's legal training will incline her to read a waiver request closely, while she may not be as inclined in a conversation to press for as many details.

Reinforcing this tendency for informality is the fact that transactional lawyers are accustomed to the idea that informal practices constitute "the law." Litigators obviously shape the law through their advocacy. It's clear, however, that the parties who make the law in the litigation context are judges. By contrast, the terms that transactional lawyers negotiate and the structures that they establish create rights and obligations that courts will enforce with relatively minimal review of their substance. In this sense, transactional lawyers act more as lawmakers than do litigators. For them, it may be natural to assume that the "law" of conflicts in transactional legal work is comprised of the relatively relaxed practices of corporate lawyers and clients, rather than the formal conflict of interest rules.

Finally, the ambiguity of conflicts in the transactional context creates considerable opportunities for self-serving rationalization. Under conditions of uncertainty, even well-intentioned individuals tend to interpret events consistent with their own self-interest. Lawyers whose compensation and prestige depend largely on keeping clients will naturally be disposed to conclude in a given situation that there is no problematic conflict unless it's unmistakably clear.

Transactional lawyers thus tend more than litigators to see rules on conflicts not as unqualified commands but as default rules—rules subject to bargaining that apply only if parties don't agree on another arrangement. As a formal matter, litigators are free to take the same approach to the rules. The fact that adversity can be more clearly identified in the litigation context, however, tends to make those rules seem more categorical in that setting.

With such an orientation to issues of conflicts, transactional lawyers may look implicitly to the investment bankers with whom they work as models of how to approach potential conflicts—especially since such bankers enjoy greater power, prestige, and income than do lawyers. Investment bankers are of course ubiquitous in corporate transactions, playing a variety of roles on deals, sometimes simultaneously: underwriter, financial advisor, trader, principal, fair value opinion provider, and others limited only by the fertile imaginations of those who work in such institutions. They thus are immersed even more than transactional lawyers in intricate networks of commercial relationships.

Since the mid-1970s, both investment banks and corporate law firms have seen the evaporation of long-term relationships with clients and the emergence of fiercer competition.[18] Many corporate lawyers tend to perceive investment bankers as having been far more forceful and innovative than law firms in responding to such market changes. Successful banks create a complex network of ties with numerous market actors that enable them to identify and respond quickly to opportunities for profitable transactions that can involve billions of dollars.

Investment banks have been able to promote this aggressive culture in part because of conflict-of-interest restrictions less stringent than those that govern lawyers. For instance, a bank may underwrite bonds for companies, purchase bonds for its own account, advise investors on bond purchases, and manage bond portfolios.

Consider the potential conflicts that could arise from these multiple roles. A bank's desire to minimize underwriting risk could influence its recommendations to investors on bond purchases. Its interest as a bondholder in sustaining a market for the bonds could affect its decisions to buy and sell securities in the portfolios that it manages. Its desire to cultivate a relationship with an influential investment fund could have an impact on the terms that it recommends for the bonds that it underwrites.

Similarly, to the extent that an investment bank becomes active in the market to acquire corporations, it may compete with its own clients. It also is not uncommon for investment banks to represent both sides in a "merger of equals," which creates the potential for conflict in negotiating the terms of the transaction. In addition, as Goldman Sachs did with Bucyrus, a bank may both represent a buyout group in an LBO and be a member of that same group.

Investment banks have more latitude than lawyers in playing these multiple roles because, unlike lawyers, they are not regarded in all cases as fiduciaries for clients. Courts generally will impose fiduciary duties on banks only when a bank is in a "superior position to exert influence or control" over a party.[19] Otherwise, the relationships between investment banks and their clients are governed by the rules that apply to parties involved in arms-length market relationships. By contrast, attorneys are treated as fiduciaries for their clients under all circumstances.

Elite corporate lawyers thus may chafe at conflicts rules that can prevent them from representing new clients or moving easily into new areas of practice. They may regard fiduciary restrictions as anachronistic obstacles to building a successful entrepreneurial law firm. Conflict constraints may seem to rest on an outdated notion that a tie of loyalty binds lawyer and client, when in reality both corporate clients and law firms are involved in multiple relationships. Further-more, many corporate clients hardly fit the model of the vulnerable party that is the foundation of the fiduciary paradigm. If only subcon-sciously, transactional lawyers in large firms may seek to emulate investment bankers in their approach to conflicts of interest.

Consider how these dynamics may have influenced John Gellene's decision on disclosure. The man who got Gellene involved in the Bucyrus bankruptcy was of course Larry Lederman. Lederman was a prominent corporate lawyer who had been involved in major transac-tions over the years at Wachtell, Lipton that had helped transform corporate America. In so doing, he had worked closely with invest-ment banks. Lederman for some time had extolled the ability of investment banks to capitalize on market opportunities more rapidly than law firms. He had suggested in his book *Tombstones* that this edge was due to the tendency of investment bankers to retire relatively early. This meant that "[i]mportant responsibilities were necessarily given to young people, all ready to embrace change."[20] By contrast, there were a greater number of older partners in positions of leader-ship in law firms, who were overly constrained by traditional notions of law practice. As a result, investment banks moved quickly and aggressively to seize competitive advantage in emerging areas of busi-ness, while law firms lagged far behind.

It therefore would not be surprising if Lederman found the invest-ment bank approach to conflicts congenial. Lederman and others who aspired to top-tier corporate status for Milbank might implicitly regard the constraints that limit law firms but not investment banks as obsolete relics of a bygone era. One perhaps unintentional indication of Lederman's belief in the need for an aggressive approach to busi-ness opportunities is the page following the table of contents in his book. On it is a single sentence: "It's hard to see the line if you're standing on it."

For a variety of reasons, Lederman therefore may have been inclined to regard Milbank's simultaneous representation of Bucyrus and Salovaara on unrelated matters as unremarkable. It was simply

another opportunity to reinforce the web of connections that constituted the relational capital of his corporate practice. That capital
could work in the bankruptcy to the advantage of both parties.

As an experienced bankruptcy lawyer, however, Gellene knew better. Unlike in the transactional context, bankruptcy conflicts rules
aren't simply default rules. Courts generally don't permit waiver of
conflicts in bankruptcy proceedings. The debtor-in-possession is not
authorized to pursue only its own narrow objectives. Rather, it's a
fiduciary for all parties with an interest in the estate. Bucyrus and
Salovaara weren't the only parties who might care about Milbank's
potential conflict of interest.

Bankruptcy conflicts rules therefore are meant not simply to protect
self-interested clients, but to ensure the integrity of the bankruptcy
process as a whole. For this reason, they have a more categorical status than do conflict rules applicable in a transactional setting. Gellene
also knew that Rule 2014 required disclosure of all "connections" with
parties in interest—not simply potential conflicts of interest. Thus,
even if he were satisfied that the firm's ties to Salovaara represented no
conflict, he still had to disclose them.

Gellene, however, likely was extremely sensitive to any signal from
Lederman about how to handle disclosure. Lederman was the most
powerful partner at Milbank, the main catalyst of a transformation of
the firm into an entrepreneurial business enterprise. Gellene was
among a relatively select group of lawyers teamed to work regularly
with Lederman in a effort to capitalize on Lederman's contacts and
expertise. It was in furtherance of this plan that Lederman had gotten
Gellene involved in the Bucyrus bankruptcy. Gellene therefore had an
interest in maintaining strong ties to Lederman.

Indeed, the manner in which Gellene became involved in the Busse
matter shows that he didn't simply passively accept assignments from
Lederman. Instead, he actively embraced opportunities for work.
When Lederman called Gellene to discuss the Busse claim, Lederman
asked him whether the corporate or the bankruptcy group should handle it. In either case, Milbank's representation of South Street in the
matter would create a potential conflict of interest because of the

simultaneous work for Bucyrus. Beyond this, it clearly was a "connection" under Rule 2014 that would have to be disclosed.

Nonetheless, the potential conflict would be more acute, and the connection even more likely to disqualify Milbank, if Gellene himself were representing Busse rather than a lawyer in Milbank's corporate group. Despite this, Gellene recommended that lawyers in the bankruptcy group do the work under his supervision. This suggests that Gellene's desire to sustain his relationship with Lederman was a major influence on his thinking, even to the point of clouding his judgment about the risks to which he was exposing himself.

For Gellene to conclude that Lederman wanted him to withhold information, the older lawyer need not have explicitly advised Gellene to that effect. Lederman may have instinctively relied on a transactional lawyer's approach to conflicts and assumed that the dual representation was not problem. As a result, he may have given disclosure little sustained thought. Alternatively, he may have known that the transactional approach was inappropriate for bankruptcy, but implicitly conveyed the view that bankruptcy rules should not stand in the way of Milbank's dual representation. In either case, Gellene would be bright enough to infer that he should not disclose the firm's relationship to Salovaara. He may have acquiesced in this tacit message rather than press for a more sharply focused discussion of the issue.

Certain tendencies of subordinates in large organizations may have reinforced Gellene's willingness to defer to what he regarded as Lederman's wishes. First, it's common for such persons to attribute highly positive qualities to those on whom they are dependent. Lederman, of course, was not a bankruptcy lawyer. Gellene, however, may have rationalized that Lederman's vast experience with financially distressed corporations engaged in capital restructuring made him better qualified than even Gellene to decide how best to approach issues of conflicts and disclosure. Lederman could see the big picture in a way that Gellene could not. He was a rainmaker and Gellene was not. It might be easy, therefore, for Gellene to conclude that Lederman possessed more wisdom than he on how to proceed.

Second, ambitious subordinates often seek to anticipate what their superiors wish them to do rather than wait for explicit direction. Waiting to act until one has received explicit instructions can be seen as a lack of initiative, which can be fatal to prospects for advancement. Many individuals "can be expected to intuit what orders they would be given and 'follow them in advance.' "[21]

Lederman already had indicated to Gellene and Lichstein that he saw no problem with Milbank's representation of both Bucyrus and Salovaara. Relying on this and perhaps other implicit signals, Gellene may have felt that he could anticipate what Lederman's position would be on disclosure. He might fear that if he concluded that disclosure was necessary, or if he waited to act until after consulting Lederman, the senior lawyer might regard him as too cautious to play an important role in future major corporate matters. The best way to carry out what Gellene believed were Lederman's wishes would be to tell him that Milbank would not be disclosing its ties to Salovaara and South Street to the bankruptcy court. In this way, Gellene may have drifted slowly toward nondisclosure without giving the matter in-depth consideration. At the same time, Lederman could maintain that he relied on Gellene to make the appropriate disclosure.

In sum, Gellene's personality, the pressures at Milbank Tweed, and the importance of Lederman to Gellene's career may all have inclined Gellene to withhold information from Judge Eisenberg. Each of these factors is a specific instance of more general influences that shape the experiences of many lawyers in large firms. Together, they could have motivated him to violate Rule 2014. They would not necessarily have been enough, however, to move him to act on that motivation. What information there is about Gellene suggests that he was not indifferent to moral concerns. As with most of us, he needed to rationalize his actions as morally defensible. Two influences may have helped him do this. The first is the culture of corporate bankruptcy practice in large firms, especially in cases in New York and Delaware. The second is the dynamics of the Bucyrus bankruptcy. We turn now to how these factors may have helped Gellene justify his behavior.

CHAPTER TEN

Justifying Concealment

MOST PEOPLE are not indifferent to moral concerns. A person's self-esteem usually rests in fundamental ways on the belief that he is a good person who tries to do right and avoid wrong. We know that people are strongly motivated to maintain this self-image even in the face of what might seem to be evidence of misconduct. This motivation leads individuals in many cases to interpret their own behavior in self-serving ways that allow them to believe that they have acted morally, or at least not immorally. Even many whom we think of as moral monsters have been able to convince themselves in the face of widespread condemnation that they acted in the service of noble ends.[1] It is rare for a person to acknowledge to himself or others that he perceived a clear choice between right and wrong and deliberately chose the latter.

John Gellene was motivated for various reasons to conceal Milbank Tweed's representation of Mikael Salovaara's interests from the bankruptcy court in Milwaukee. Those reasons rested on personal concerns that aren't conventionally regarded as justifications for violating an ethical rule. If Gellene wanted to avoid admitting to himself that he was prepared to act unethically, he needed a way to frame the situation in different terms. At a minimum, he had to neutralize the moral significance of his choice so that he could convince himself that he wasn't acting unethically. Perhaps he could even fashion an interpretation of the situation that allowed him to conclude that he was acting virtuously.

In order to act on his motives and maintain a sense of himself as a good person, Gellene therefore needed to draw on moral universes different from the one expressed in Rule 2014. Two such universes were available to him. One was the world of large law firm bankruptcy practice. The other was the Bucyrus bankruptcy project. By invoking the norms contained in these moral universes, Gellene could act on his motives without having to admit that he was being unethical. This chapter explores how that process may have unfolded.

BANKRUPTCY LAW is a distinct practice specialty. It is governed by an explicit federal statutory and regulatory scheme and is practiced before special tribunals. Until the late 1970s, bankruptcy was practiced mostly by lawyers in relatively small firms who tended to represent only creditors or debtors. That began to change with passage of the Bankruptcy Act of 1978, which made Chapter 11 much more attractive to large corporations. The recession of the late 1970s and early 1980s then generated considerable bankruptcy work. A decade later, bankruptcies by companies burdened by debt that they had acquired in leveraged deals in the 1980s created even greater opportunities. Large law firms subject to heightened competition for business began to realize that there were lucrative prospects in bankruptcy practice. They started acquiring smaller bankruptcy firms in the hope of capitalizing on this promise.

Large firms entering bankruptcy practice, however, began to encounter difficulties with potentially disqualifying conflicts of interest. Large law firms have hundreds if not thousands of clients, many of which are major corporations and financial institutions. Any large corporate bankruptcy may involve thousands of parties with claims on the debtor. It's almost certain that clients of large law firms will be among them. These clients can be characterized as having an interest adverse to the debtor under Section 327 of the Bankruptcy Code. The debtor would like to minimize payouts, while claimants seek to maximize them. Even if a law firm represents these clients in matters unrelated to the bankruptcy, it still might be in a position to favor them over other claimants if it also represents the debtor. As a result, the firm would not meet Section 327's requirement that it be disinterested. Thus, if the Bankruptcy Code is applied literally, it would prevent large law firms from representing the debtor in the vast majority of major corporate bankruptcies.

Large law firms naturally are disturbed by this prospect. Major corporate bankruptcies can bring in millions of dollars in fees, all of which have priority over payments to creditors. Large firms argue that the multitude and dispersion of their offices and clients means that the likelihood that a firm will try to play favorites in bankruptcy is remote in many cases. For example, they suggest, a partner representing a debtor in possession in Seattle may well be unaffected by the fact that a partner he doesn't even know in Frankfurt is representing in a merger a German client that also happens to be one of the DIP's creditors.

Firms maintain that disqualification in such cases would serve no real purpose, and would deprive DIPs of the benefit of the firms' expertise in bankruptcy. As was the case with Milbank and Bucyrus, for instance, many law firms begin representing companies in the period preceding bankruptcy. They help the company in its effort to avoid bankruptcy by restructuring its debt, or they participate in negotiations designed to produce consensus on a prepackaged plan. Forcing a firm to withdraw once the company files its bankruptcy petition thus can deprive the debtor of counsel that is familiar with the company and all the other parties in interest. In such circumstances, having to hire new counsel and bring it up to speed can be both expensive and disruptive.

More generally, large firms argue, enforcing Section 327 literally would prevent corporations in complex bankruptcies from hiring the law firms best qualified to handle such reorganizations. Since the Bankruptcy Act made Chapter 11 more attractive to corporations, major companies now use bankruptcy as a business tool. Expertise in business planning, recapitalization, mergers and acquisitions, tax, labor law, environmental regulation, intellectual property, pensions, employee benefits, and other fields thus has become more important in corporate bankruptcies. Large firms claim that it's more efficient for a debtor to retain a firm with all these capabilities than to hire separate firms to deal with each area of the law. If Section 327 is interpreted literally, they argue, this will be impossible.

Lawyers in large firms thus tend to be skeptical that strict application of the bankruptcy conflict rule serves important ethical purposes. That skepticism is reinforced by the inconsistent ways in which bankruptcy courts and experts have interpreted Section 327. As one leading legal ethics scholar puts it, "[T]here is widespread disagreement about starting point, not to mention finish line, with respect to lawyer conflicts in bankruptcy. Judicial decisions on the subject sometimes reflect what may charitably be called as chaos." Much of this confusion results from unique features of bankruptcy that make it difficult to apply conventional conflict-of-interest principles.

RULES GOVERNING CONFLICTS of interest don't map easily onto corporate bankruptcy practice for several reasons. First, large bankruptcies involve thousands of parties. Prospective counsel for the debtor may represent some of these parties in other matters. Does the fact that those clients are creditors of the debtor automatically make them adverse to the debtor, regardless of the size of their claim? What if the debtor is not contesting a creditor's claim? What if the debtor and creditor have reached agreement on a prepackaged bankruptcy before the Chapter 11 petition? What if the debtor and creditor are allied against another creditor? Does only the second creditor have an interest adverse to the debtor, or do all creditors?

Section 327(c) says that an applicant for DIP counsel can't be rejected solely because she has a client who is a creditor, unless there is an actual conflict and the trustee or another creditor objects. This suggests that simply representing a creditor in another matter isn't necessarily an actual conflict. The Bankruptcy Code doesn't define, however, what is an actual and a potential conflict. If courts look to state ethics rules for guidance, they'll see that those rules say that a lawyer who represents Client A in one matter may not represent Client B against Client A in any lawsuit, even if it deals with an unrelated matter. Involvement in litigation thus seems to be the paradigm of an actual conflict. Whether the lawyer has an actual conflict outside this setting generally is a matter of "proximity and degree."

The problem, unfortunately, is that there is disagreement on the extent to which bankruptcy should be characterized as litigation. Some claim that litigation doesn't begin until the Chapter II petition is filed, while others argue that prepetition negotiation often is adversarial and crucial, especially over the terms of a prepackaged plan.[2] Still others maintain that only when specific disputes arise during the bankruptcy case are the parties engaged in litigation.[3]

Another feature of bankruptcy makes actual conflicts difficult to identify: it involves multiple, shifting alliances and rivalries that arise and dissipate as particular issues come to the fore. Nancy Rapoport describes this process as the generation of conflicts that are dormant, temporary, and actual. They are dormant, she observes, because "the potential for conflict lies in wait unless and until the right combination of strategy decisions (by several parties) comes into play."[4] Conflicts are temporary because they are issue-specific: once the underlying issue has been resolved, the conflict also is resolved. They are actual in that as long as the triggering issue is active, two or more parties are adversaries toward one another.

This makes it very difficult for a lawyer, and a court, to know at the outset of a case which interests now aligned will diverge, and which interests now opposed will converge. Must a court wait and entertain a series of disqualification motions as different issues arise on which parties become adversaries? Should it rescind a disqualification once the adversity disappears? Or should it try to anticipate which actual conflicts are likely to arise? Adding to the complexity is the fact that creditors often sell their claims to other parties during bankruptcy. This means that creditors that could create conflicts of interest for DIP counsel may be constantly entering or exiting the bankruptcy.

This state of affairs has led courts to take a variety of positions on when prospective counsel for the DIP can be disqualified for a conflict of interest. Some courts have held that either an actual or a potential conflict will serve to disqualify counsel.[5] Other courts have ruled that a potential conflict may serve as the basis for disqualification in some cases.[6] Still another court has created a rebuttable presumption that counsel should be disqualified because of a potential conflict.[7] Some courts will disqualify an applicant only if there is an actual conflict.[8]

Finally, one court has suggested that the distinction itself is not very useful as a guide to disqualification decisions.[9]

There has been substantial criticism of Section 327's requirement that counsel be disinterested. Critics charge that this provision made sense when the law directed that management be replaced by a neutral trustee when a company filed for bankruptcy. The Bankruptcy Act of 1978, however, provided that in most instances management may continue to run the company during the bankruptcy. While managers in that position are fiduciaries for the estate, their involvement with the corporation means they're not completely neutral or disinterested. Section 327 thus purports to impose a higher standard on the debtor's counsel than on the debtor itself.

As one court has noted, strict application of this standard would mean that a law firm representing the DIP that bills the client for its services is not disinterested, because it has become a creditor of the estate. Another problem critics see is that the disinterested requirement can authorize disqualification based on an appearance of impropriety, even when no conflict exists. This is inconsistent with the American Bar Association's model ethical rules, which dropped the appearance-of-impropriety standard on the ground that it is too subjective.

Dissatisfaction with the directive that DIP counsel be disinterested has led to attempts to eliminate it. The fact that these efforts have been unsuccessful indicates that the requirement has its defenders. Nonetheless, the conviction, held by a substantial portion of those who work on bankruptcy, that the provision is misguided—and perhaps reflects simply a drafting error by Congress—may promote skepticism that it expresses a strong ethical principle.

The distinctive character of bankruptcy thus presents a potent challenge to straightforward application of conflict-of-interest concepts. This has led to the claim that bankruptcy law provides "inconsistent, incoherent, and incomplete guidance" about whether an applicant is eligible for appointment as DIP counsel. Such criticism undermines the claim that strict adherence to Section 327 is an ethical imperative, because it suggests that there is little consensus on how it should be interpreted. Large law firms complain that the fate of a firm's application may depend not on whether there is a serious risk that the firm's loyalty will be compromised, but on which court reviews the application.

Lawyers in big firms believe that this state of affairs creates too much opportunity for the strategic use of disqualification motions or objections to appointment. The Bankruptcy Code says that a law firm can't be disqualified from representing a DIP solely because it also represents creditors of the debtor, unless another creditor or the trustee objects and the court finds that there is an actual conflict. A large corporate law firm that wishes to represent a DIP thus to some extent is at the mercy of the other creditors. If negotiations have proceeded relatively smoothly, those creditors may not file an objection to the firm's application. If negotiations have been acrimonious, or creditors are not completely happy with their proposed treatment, they may object. The same underlying connection between the law firm and its creditor client therefore may pose no problem to representing the DIP in one case and serve to bar it in another, based on factors that have nothing to do with substantive conflicts of interest.

HOWEVER CONFUSING or unfair a lawyer may regard Section 327, it is supposed to be irrelevant to his disclosure duty under Rule 2014. A lawyer must disclose "all" of his "connections with the debtor, creditors, and any party in interest." He has no discretion to decide that some connections create only "technical" conflicts that raise no substantive ethical concern. That is for the court to decide, since "[a]n attorney's interest in being employed by the estate could cloud the attorney's judgment regarding what should be disclosed."[10]

Nonetheless, it's easy to imagine that a lawyer's sense of the gravity of his disclosure obligation under Rule 2014 will be influenced by his perception of the fairness and legitimacy of the conflict provisions of Section 327. The purpose of disclosure, of course, is to provide information that can be used in determining whether an applicant has a conflict of interest that would disqualify him from representing the DIP. If the applicant believes that those rules sometimes lead to arbitrary or unrealistic disqualification, he may not treat compliance with Rule 2014 as a categorical duty.

When negotiations among the parties have not been amicable—a situation hardly unprecedented in the annals of bankruptcy—disclosing all connections may not be seen as essential to the integrity of the bankruptcy process. Rather, a lawyer may believe that it simply provides ammunition for an adversary to use in bad faith against the firm. The requirement that the court find an actual conflict of interest may not be seen as affording significant protection from such behavior, given the variety of viewpoints on what constitutes such a conflict. Furthermore, a lawyer may fear that the court will be disposed to grant a disqualification motion in the hope that this will avoid any future controversy about DIP counsel's performance in the bankruptcy. Counsel thus may convince himself that the requirement of full disclosure is not justified in all cases.

A lawyer may find support for such a rationalization in court decisions that don't apply Section 327 according to its literal terms. These decisions highlight the role that different local bankruptcy cultures may play in creating shared mental models of the rules. The strongest empirical research supporting the existence of such local bankruptcy cultures has focused on consumer bankruptcies. That research suggests that consumer bankruptcy law bestows considerable discretion on actors within the system because of fear that debtors will abuse the right of discharge. This discretion in turn gives rise to "systematic and persistent variation in local legal practices," even when those localities are subject to the same law.[11]

While the empirical evidence is less robust, observers commonly note differences in local corporate bankruptcy cultures as well. For instance, New York and Delaware bankruptcy courts hear the largest proportion of major Chapter 11 cases. Research suggests that bankruptcy courts in these states are more lenient than other jurisdictions in their willingness to confirm reorganization plans.[12]

More directly relevant, those courts are perceived as rejecting a "literalist" reading of conflicts provisions in favor of a "realistic" approach that takes account of the practicalities of large-firm practice to avoid disqualification. Even when a potentially disabling conflict exists, these courts are amenable to resolving it by appointing special counsel to handle matters as to which DIP counsel has a conflict, or by requiring a law firm to establish a firewall between lawyers working on the bankruptcy and those working for interested parties in other matters. Neither measure is explicitly permitted in the Bankruptcy Code, but each appears to be a part of the rules in those jurisdictions.

Large firms regard this approach as based on a more realistic view of bankruptcy conflicts. They claim that it reflects appreciation that large corporations in Chapter 11 need the services of large firms. Critics, however, argue that courts that accommodate large firms in this way virtually read conflicts restrictions out of the Bankruptcy Code. Lawyers and judges in different jurisdictions thus may operate on the basis of different mental models of bankruptcy conflicts law.

As a result, a bankruptcy lawyer in a large firm may conclude that there is less risk in New York and Delaware than in other courts that full disclosure will result in what he regards as an unwarranted disqualification. This may incline him to be more forthcoming with disclosure in, say, New York than he is willing to be in Milwaukee. If he believes that a bankruptcy court in Milwaukee is likely to take a "literalist" approach to the conflicts rules, he may be inclined to rationalize to himself that a potentially troublesome connection is merely a "technical" conflict that need not be disclosed.

The evidence suggests that John Gellene was well aware of this possible difference in local bankruptcy cultures. On the morning he left for Milwaukee to finish the work necessary to file the Bucyrus bankruptcy petition, Gellene spoke with Larry Lederman about what he would be disclosing to the court. The disclosure of Milbank's ties to Goldman, he said, would create no problems in a New York bankruptcy court. He told Lederman, however, that he could not be certain how a bankruptcy judge in Wisconsin would react. In addition, of course, Judge Eisenberg pointedly admonished Gellene at one of the hearings on Milbank's application: "New York is different from Milwaukee . . . [P]rofessional things like conflicts are taken very, very seriously. And for better or worse, you're stuck in Wisconsin." As a result, Gellene may have suspected that he faced a greater chance of being disqualified in Milwaukee than in New York or Delaware for what he saw as merely a technical conflict.

There were at least three reasons that Gellene might have convinced himself that the conflict was a technical one that posed no threat to his loyalty or independence. First, Jeff Werbalowsky and the creditors' committee, not he, had done most of the prepetition negotiations with Salovaara regarding possible concessions by South Street. Second, Gellene had not undertaken his work for Salovaara–South Street until after Salovaara had signed on to the prepackaged plan on behalf of his investment fund. Thus, Gellene might tell himself, there was no way that his ties to Salovaara–South Street could have affected whatever discussions he had with that creditor about the terms of the reorganization plan. Finally, because he had agreed to the plan, Salovaara's interests were aligned with, not adversarial to, those of Bucyrus. Gellene's work as DIP counsel to obtain confirmation of the plan therefore would be in the best interests of both parties.

Gellene's possible belief that Milbank's ties to Salovaara–South Street gave rise only to a technical conflict of interest in turn would permit him to rationalize that withholding information about these connections was not freighted with moral significance. Gellene on occasion had neglected to fulfill obligations that he may have regarded as mere technicalities devoid of major moral importance. To the extent that Gellene believed that disclosure would lead to disqualification for a technical conflict, he could more easily rationalize his failure to make full disclosure as he had earlier transgressions—as compliance with the substantive requirements of Rule 2014 even if not with the letter of the rule.

From this perspective, disclosure would serve no meaningful purpose. Rather, it would simply reflect compliance with a formalistic regulatory requirement that was out of step with the realities of Chapter 11 practice in large law firms. In light of the motives Gellene may have had not to disclose Milbank's representation of Salovaara–South Street, he could have been especially receptive to this rationalization.

It's easy, of course, to see this rationalization as self-serving. Furthermore, to suggest that it may be available in some cases is not to say that bankruptcy lawyers in large firms frequently rely on it. Many bankruptcy lawyers regard a strong norm of disclosure as a necessary precondition for establishing trust among the parties in bankruptcy negotiations. The important point, however, is that corporate bankruptcy culture may make this rationalization seem plausible in situations in which a lawyer would prefer not to make full disclosure. As such, it represents one of the cognitive "resources" on which Gellene might have drawn to justify acting on his motivation.

GELLENE MAY HAVE suspected that, because Salovaara was such a central figure in the bankruptcy, even courts in New York and Delaware would rule that Milbank's ties to him and South Street created a substantive, not simply technical, conflict. Nonetheless, he may have morally neutralized failing to make full disclosure by noting that courts tend not to impose significant sanctions for disclosure violations—at least not on large law firms.

If a lawyer has violated Rule 2014, the court is authorized to terminate his employment for the debtor, deny compensation for work performed, and require him to disgorge any fees he already has received. Most courts, however, hold that the Bankruptcy Code permits, but does not require, the court to deny compensation or require disgorgement. It's rare for a court to deny or force disgorgement of all fees for a violation of Rule 2014 in the absence of some underlying violation of Section 327.[13] In addition, when a failure to comply with Rule 2014 is discovered at a late date in the Chapter 11 case, a court may be reluctant to disqualify counsel. Disqualification could penalize the client by jeopardizing the reorganization and requiring the DIP to incur the expense of hiring new counsel and helping it become familiar with the company.

One expert criticizes courts' unwillingness to impose more stringent penalties for violations of Rule 2014, lamenting that "[t]he signals sent by this approach are distressing. It rewards counsel who fail to disclose all connections."[14] Some counsel therefore may be willing to risk not providing full disclosure under Rule 2014 because of the "low likelihood of detection and the mild nature of the sanctions which might result from failure to disclose."

Events around the time that Gellene filed his appointment application may have reinforced a sense that one could gamble on less than full disclosure under Rule 2014 without drastic consequences. These events involved the large New York corporate law firm Weil, Gotshal & Manges, which has probably the most prominent bankruptcy practice in the country.

In the first case, Weil represented R.H. Macy & Company when it filed for bankruptcy in January 1992. At the time it applied to the court for appointment as counsel for the DIP, the law firm disclosed that it represented on other matters G.E. Capital and Prudential Life Insurance Co. of America. G.E. Capital was both a preferred shareholder and secured creditor of Macy, while Prudential was the company's most senior creditor.

After the filing, the mutual funds giant Fidelity Investments purchased claims against Macy, eventually becoming a creditor in the amount of $500 million. Fidelity took an active role in trying to shape the bankruptcy case to its advantage. Shortly before Macy filed its reorganization plan for approval on March 23, 1994, Fidelity retained Weil to represent it in another bankruptcy. At the time, the law firm did not file a supplemental disclosure revealing this fact to the court.

When Macy's bondholders learned of Weil's connection to Fidelity, Robert M. Miller, counsel for the bondholders, complained both to the law firm and to the court-appointed mediator. He stated that his clients "remain extremely concerned that the plan process has been potentially tainted by Weil, Gotshal's representation of Fidelity."[15] Harvey Miller, head of the bankruptcy practice at Weil and counsel for Macy, maintained that the law firm had erected a firewall shielding lawyers who were working on the Macy matter from those representing Fidelity.

In April, Weil amended its disclosure to refer to its representation of Fidelity. It included in this filing copies of acrimonious correspondence between Robert Miller and Harvey Miller. This raised the visibility of the controversy. The bondholders' counsel suggested that, because of its representation of Fidelity in the other matter, Weil might be tempted to favor the class of creditors of which Fidelity was a member. One Macy director solicited advice from Milbank Tweed about the situation. That firm suggested that the board might want to consider hiring new legal and financial advisors. John Jerome of Milbank sent a copy of this letter to Harvey Miller at Weil. Two directors then wrote letters to the other directors urging the board to hire new outside counsel and financial advisors. Ultimately, however, the bondholders never moved to disqualify Weil, Gotshal, nor did Macy's board seek new counsel.

Nonetheless, the case prompted criticism from several bankruptcy experts and highlighted two other incidents in which "bankruptcy judges recently slapped Weil's hand by withholding fees" because of the firm's failure to meet its disclosure obligations.[16] In the National Gypsum bankruptcy, Weil represented the company's bondholders. The law firm also was representing a creditor of National Gypsum in another bankruptcy, but didn't inform the court of this. In March 1993, Judge Steven Felsenthal found that the relationship did not constitute a conflict. He still, however, reduced Weil's compensation by $10,000 for its failure to disclose this representation. In the Colt Manufacturing Company's bankruptcy, in which Weil represented the DIP, Judge Robert Krechevsky withheld $250,000 of Weil's fees in January 1994 for failing to disclose that the estate's outside accountant had a financial interest in a company that was bidding to acquire Colt.

What might Gellene make of these events when preparing a disclosure affidavit in February 1994? On the one hand, Weil, Gotshal's disclosure failures exposed it to criticism and adverse publicity. On the other hand, in the Macy's case ultimately neither the bondholders nor the U.S. trustee moved for the firm's disqualification, even though Weil had not informed that court that it had begun representing a major creditor of the debtor at a crucial point in the case. In National Gypsum, the firm's failure to meet its disclosure obligation resulted only in a $10,000 penalty out of a $5.5 million fee, since the court found that Weil had no conflict. In Colt, the firm had $250,000 of its fees disallowed, but still earned $2.2 million for its work on the case.

Furthermore, Arthur Gonzalez, the U.S. trustee in the case, had traveled from New York to Hartford to argue before Judge Krechevsky that Weil should not be penalized for its disclosure violation.[17]

Someone who was motivated not to make full disclosure in a Rule 2014 affidavit might draw support for his inclination from these events. He might conclude that the law in action deals more leniently with prominent firms than does the law in the books. Weil, Gotshal was the envy of the corporate bankruptcy bar. The firm had booked $318 million in revenues in 1991, the fourth largest of any United States law firm. In the eyes of some, both admirers and detractors, its success was due in part to a willingness to push the limits of rules on bankruptcy conflicts—rejecting the idea that its extensive list of financial clients should preclude it from reaping the rewards of an increasingly lucrative field of practice. From this perspective, an occasional limited financial penalty was simply a cost of gaining access to the profitable world of debtor representation in corporate bankruptcy.

A lawyer confronting Rule 2014 thus might treat his decision as a calculated gamble. If the probability of objection and disqualification as a result of disclosure seems high, it may be preferable not to disclose. That is, the lawyer may believe that the fees the firm will obtain ultimately will exceed the penalty it would suffer if the failure to disclose is discovered. The likelihood that a lawyer will take such an instrumental approach to disclosure will be enhanced by his perception that the conflict that he is concealing is merely a "technical" one, which poses no real threat to his independence. There is a substantial danger, of course, that this assessment will be colored by self-interest. Nonetheless, to the extent that bankruptcy lawyers regard Section 327 as insensitive to the realities of practice in a large law firm and to the unique features of bankruptcy, there may be a respectable number of cases in which such lawyers find this rationalization plausible. It may well be that Gellene convinced himself that the Bucyrus bankruptcy was such a case.

Gellene's obligation to make full disclosure continued after his appointment applications in February and March 1994. On December 15, 1994, the day after the Bucyrus plan went into effect, Judge Tina

Brozman announced her decision in the Leslie Fay bankruptcy case in New York. At the time that Gellene had filed his retention application earlier in the year, Judge Brozman had just appointed an examiner to determine whether Leslie Fay counsel Weil, Gotshal had failed to disclose connections that rendered the firm not "disinterested" under the Bankruptcy Code. The case had been watched with great interest by the bankruptcy bar, and had the potential to have a significant impact on disclosure practices under Rule 2014.

Weil had been hired by Leslie Fay's audit committee to investigate accounting irregularities by company officials. Nine weeks into the investigation, revelations of fraud pushed the company into bankruptcy. Weil filed the Chapter 11 petition on Leslie Fay's behalf, and successfully applied for retention as bankruptcy counsel to the company. After the audit committee completed its inquiry, it came to light that the law firm had not disclosed that it had ties to three potential targets of the investigation: board members Michael L. Tarnapol and Steven Friedman, and Leslie Fay outside auditor BDO Seidman. Weil also had not disclosed that it represented in other matters Forstmann & Co., the seventh largest Leslie Fay creditor. Tarnapol and Friedman were high-ranking officials in Bear Stearns and Odyssey Partners, L.P., which the court described as "large and valuable" Weil, Gotshal clients.

The examiner found that Weil was not "disinterested" and had violated Rule 2014 in failing to disclose its representation of these parties. He concluded, however, that there was no evidence that Weil's investigation on behalf of the audit committee was affected in any way by these connections. There was no evidence that supported any claims by Leslie Fay against Tarnapol, Friedman, or BDO Seidman. Weil, Gotshal, the examiner recommended, should have to pay the fees and expenses occasioned by the examiner's report, which came to about $800,000. It should not, however, be disqualified from continuing to represent Leslie Fay in the bankruptcy.

U.S. Trustee Arthur Gonzalez, however, moved to have Weil disqualified from the Chapter 11 proceedings. "A court," he argued, "should not be required to rummage through files or conduct independent investigations to determine whether prospective attorneys are involved in actual or potential conflicts of interest." Furthermore, the firm should be fined an amount equal not only to the costs of the examiner's investigation, but the full costs to the estate arising from the controversy.

Weil, Gotshal opposed the motion. Not disclosing the organizational affiliations of Tarnapol and Friedman, it claimed, "conformed to the standard of disclosure found in large Chapter II cases." With respect to the Forstmann connection, disclosure was effected by notifying the court that the firm may represent "claimants of the debtors in matters totally unrelated" to the bankruptcy. Finally, Weil had stated that it represented in unrelated matters "accountants" that represented parties with interests in the bankruptcy, but that none of those relationships were adverse to Leslie Fay. That disclosure, it argued, covered BDO Seidman. "Sanctions for disclosure," Weil asserted, "should be meted out in proportion to the resultant harm." Disqualification would be a "draconian" penalty not warranted by the impact on the company, and would seriously disrupt Leslie Fay's bankruptcy proceedings.

Judge Brozman began by saying that "rarely am I faced with a motion as troubling as this one."[18] Weil, Gotshal's ties to Bear Stearns, Odyssey, and BDO Seidman meant that the firm did not meet the requirement of being "disinterested" debtor's counsel under the Bankruptcy Code. The firm had a "perceptible economic incentive" not to pursue a vigorous investigation of Tarnapol and Friedman because their companies were major clients.[19] Furthermore, as Weil told the audit committee but neither the court nor the U.S. trustee, it would not have sued BDO Seidman because of its policy against suing accounting firms.[20]

Judge Brozman also found that Weil, Gotshal had violated Rule 2014 by not disclosing its ties to Bear Stearns, Odyssey, BDO Seidman, and Forstmann. It may be true, she said, that the corporate affiliations of board members are not routinely disclosed under the rule. However, "[C]onnections with entities affiliated with board members that could cause pressure on investigating counsel must be disclosed."[21] Furthermore, the boilerplate disclosure of possible representation of accountants did not suffice to put the court on notice of a key party such as BDO Seidman. Similarly, the boilerplate disclosure of possible representation of creditors may cover "inadvertent failures to disclose insignificant connections; it is not an adequate substitute for disclosure of representation of known and significant creditors" such as Forstmann.[22]

Weil's violation, said Judge Brozman, "caused Leslie Fay very real harm."[23] In essence, the company had to hire an examiner to investigate the prior investigation, at considerable cost to the estate. Ultimately, however, the judge ruled that the law firm should not be disqualified from continuing to represent Leslie Fay in the bankruptcy proceedings. The company had already been in Chapter 11 for twenty months, and the costs of remaining in it "were enormous."[24] It would not be able to withstand the delay and cost resulting from "the departure of counsel with whom it had worked so long."[25] New counsel would be appointed to handle new matters such as litigation arising out of the accounting fraud. Finally, Judge Brozman ruled that Weil, Gotshal would be liable for the $800,000 in fees and expenses incurred in the examiner's investigation, as well as costs incurred by the creditors' committees. Shortly after her decision, she fixed the final figure at $1 million.

It's impossible to say for certain what, if any, impact, the *Leslie Fay* decision had on John Gellene's assessment of his disclosure obligations at that point. Judge Eisenberg's recent confirmation of the Bucyrus plan did not eliminate those obligations. Gellene was under a continuing duty of disclosure. The upcoming proceedings in which the judge would award compensation to Milbank and other professionals who had worked on the reorganization would afford an opportunity for any party to challenge Milbank's claim that it had been disinterested during its representation of Bucyrus. Even if the judge awarded Milbank compensation, the court could reopen that determination if information later came to light that brought disinterestedness into question.

On the one hand, the stern language and tone of Judge Brozman's decision in such a high-visibility case underscored the importance of full disclosure under Rule 2014. If Gellene had rationalized to himself that boilerplate language in his affidavits effectively served to disclose Milbank's representation of Salovaara, he could no longer credibly hold that view after *Leslie Fay*. South Street clearly was a creditor that was both "known and significant."

Furthermore, even though Weil, Gotshal's disclosure violation had had no impact on the quality of the representation that it had provided, the judge found that it had harmed Leslie Fay. By calling into question the integrity of the audit committee investigation, Weil's failure had made it necessary for the estate to hire an examiner to provide assurance that the original investigation had not been tainted. Weil thus effectively was fined $1 million because of the need to preserve public confidence in the integrity of the proceedings surrounding Leslie Fay's bankruptcy.

This suggested that even if Milbank's representation of Bucyrus were found to be above reproach, that would not necessarily insulate the firm from being subject to sanction. Gellene therefore could not reasonably assume that the absence of any tangible harm to the estate meant that Judge Eisenberg would regard Milbank's representation of Salovaara as inconsequential and not worthy of disclosure. In short, even if he had consciously avoided dwelling on his inadequate disclosure up to this point, the *Leslie Fay* decision could have served as a wake-up call that prompted him to redress his earlier failure.

On the other hand, one also might conclude that Weil, Gotshal had gotten off relatively easily. Judge Brozman had refused the trustee's request that the firm be removed from the case. She had not denied Weil entitlement to any of the fees it claimed up to that point, which came to more than $5 million. Projections were that the firm ultimately would gain more than $7 million from its representation of Leslie Fay. A $1 million fine was not peanuts. In cost-benefit terms, however, it could be seen as a risk worth taking in light of the overall rewards of being able to undertake the representation rather than being disqualified at the outset. Indeed, critics might argue that the longer a firm withheld potentially disqualifying information, the more likely it would be able to continue on the case because of the high cost of replacing it.

All this led some observers to claim that, despite its language, the *Leslie Fay* decision conveyed the impression that disclosure was not a very serious concern. The decision "does not come down very hard" on Weil, Gotshal, said bankruptcy professor Elizabeth Warren. "It's obvious that the court is not taking a very aggressive stand on the issue of disclosure," she suggested.

Gellene might seize upon this perception to convince himself that he need not disclose Milbank's ties to Salovaara and South Street because the court probably wouldn't care much about them anyway. He may have convinced himself that with respect to nondisclosure, the implicit standard was akin to "no harm, no foul." It wouldn't have been hard for Gellene to tell himself that he was rendering extremely valuable service to Bucyrus, or that his work was unaffected by Milbank's ties to Salovaara's interests. Under these circumstances, failure to disclose the firm's connections was no real moral transgression.

Of course, one could argue that if he expected the court to be lenient about nondisclosure, he should decide to correct his earlier affidavits. It likely would have been psychologically stressful for Gellene to do so at this point, however. He had made a prior decision not to disclose the Salovaara and South Street connections. He had publicly proclaimed Milbank's fitness for the job in the face of an attack. He likely had rationalized his conduct in a way that permitted him to deny that he had done anything unethical. It would be hard at this point to disavow those representations and to reassess that rationalization.[26]

In addition, it would have been hard enough at the time he submitted his affidavits to maintain that failing to list Salovaara and South Street was an inadvertent mistake made in the heat of the moment. As more time went on, nondisclosure would seem even less defensible and more deliberate. Finally, Gellene must have known that full disclosure would have given JNL more ammunition against Milbank. JNL would be out for blood, and would be an aggressive antagonist who was likely to claim that Milbank's representation of Bucyrus had been tainted and that the firm should return all the compensation it had received.

Finally, even if Gellene had construed *Leslie Fay* as a strict decision, he may have concluded that its significance was only prospective. There was considerable sentiment within the New York bankruptcy bar that Judge Brozman's decision was a "landmark" event that imposed a more stringent standard for compliance with Rule 2014. Many large firms with multiple institutional clients apparently began to rely less on boilerplate disclosures, and to expand the list of specific connections that they disclosed. Weil, Gotshal, for example, "restructured the manner and level of disclosure of potential conflicts in bankruptcies."[27] As a result, it disclosed previously unrevealed potential conflicts in a bankruptcy proceeding in Houston, thereby avoiding sanctions by the judge for not earlier disclosing them. Whether the *Leslie Fay* decision had changed the rules, or had simply served to align disclosure more closely with the requirements of the rules, many large bankruptcy firms regarded it as heralding a new, more stringent era in Rule 2014 disclosure.

Since Gellene was under an ongoing duty of disclosure at the time *Leslie Fay* was decided, the decision could have prompted him at that time to disclose Milbank's ties to Salovaara and South Street. His disinclination to do so, however, could be reinforced by convincing himself that the *Leslie Fay* decision had been rendered after the Bucyrus bankruptcy was over. At the time of the decision, Gellene was on to other matters, and likely was as immersed in them as deeply as he had been in the Bucyrus case. Placing Bucyrus in the past could allow him to conclude that he had abided by the rules as they had been understood at the time of his retention application. *Leslie Fay* may have changed the rules, but that was relevant only to future engagements.

In these ways, John Gellene may have been able to rationalize to himself that concealing Milbank's work for Salovaara's interests was not unethical. There is one final piece of the puzzle worth considering: that Gellene thought nondisclosure not only was not morally blameworthy, but under the circumstances was morally justified. In order to appreciate how this may have happened, we need to examine one additional influence on him: the specific dynamics of the Bucyrus bankruptcy negotiations.

BUCYRUS WAS A major assignment for Gellene from the time he began working on the matter in February 1993. He was the only Milbank partner with day-to-day responsibility for the project. As such, he served as the primary legal advisor for the company. Along with Jeff Werbalowsky, he represented Bucyrus in its negotiations with various interested parties. He was deeply involved in most everything that went on: discussions with most of the creditors and shareholders, analysis of JNL's fraudulent conveyance complaint, creation of the strategy to impose a cram-down on JNL, formulation of the bankruptcy plan, and preparation of the disclosure statement.

As Goelzer testified, he sometimes worried that Gellene had taken on too much responsibility without any significant backup. This appears to have been characteristic of his work style. He tended not to reach out at Milbank to others for help, but to shoulder burdens by himself. Under these circumstances, it would have been natural for him to identify closely with Bucyrus, and not to seek broader perspectives from his colleagues in the firm.

The course of the bankruptcy negotiations may have reinforced that identification and provided Gellene with the sense that he was operating in a relatively stark moral landscape. Two aspects of the negotiations were especially prominent. The first was a sense of urgency: the plan had to be confirmed and Bucyrus emerge from bankruptcy as soon as possible. If the company were to enjoy potentially substantial tax benefits, it had to file its plan by the end of 1993 or have it confirmed by the end of 1994.

Added time pressure came from company officials' fears that a protracted bankruptcy process would undermine Bucyrus's position in the market. Because of the long lead time necessary for heavy machinery orders, customers and suppliers had to have confidence that the company would be viable in the long run. Competitors evidently were already taking advantage of the bankruptcy filing to raise doubts about Bucyrus's condition. The attempt to put together a prepackaged

plan reflected the hope that the company could emerge from Chapter
11 in 90–120 days.

A second notable feature of the negotiations was the perceived hostility of JNL and John Stark virtually from the moment that Bucyrus
announced that it would be suspending interest payments on its debt.
Despite the company's invitation, JNL refused to join the unsecured
creditors' committee, insisting that Bucyrus negotiate with it separately. Furthermore, the insurance company demanded that all other
creditors' claims should be subordinated to its own because those
claims allegedly had been acquired in fraudulent conveyances.

JNL fired a major salvo about two months after the Bucyrus press
release by sending a draft complaint to the company. Gellene was
especially perturbed that JNL had included four individual Bucyrus
directors in its complaint. He saw this as an effort to intimidate company officials who would be involved in negotiations over the bankruptcy plan. Gellene and others associated with Bucyrus believed that
Stark didn't bargain in good faith, was grossly unreasonable in his
demands, and was simply an obstructionist. Eventually, efforts to con-
vene a meeting with JNL and other creditors to discuss a proposed
plan came to naught. By summer of 1993, the company had concluded
that attempts to negotiate with JNL were at an impasse. It turned its
attention to hammering out an agreement among the other interested
parties, and eventually concluded that the best way to proceed was to
cram down a plan for JNL.

Once a plan was devised, JNL learned of its terms when the printer
sent a copy of the solicitation materials to it by mistake. The creditor
was incensed at the cram-down effort. JNL amended its complaint to
add Bucyrus directors and creditors, and agitated for the opportunity
to present its own plan. It also urged the company to file bankruptcy
before the end of 1993 without a plan in place. This would result in a
"free fall" bankruptcy, which Bucyrus feared would severely harm the
company because of the uncertainty that it would create. As the date
approached to file the bankruptcy petition, it was clear that JNL felt
aggrieved. It intended to do all it could to derail the plan to which
Bucyrus and the other parties had agreed.

JUSTIFYING CONCEALMENT

By the time that Bucyrus prepared to file its petition and Gellene was ready to submit his appointment application, sharp battle lines therefore had formed: JNL versus everyone else. The company, other creditors, and shareholders regarded JNL as uncooperative and unreasonable. Confirmation of the plan would be significant not only as the vehicle for giving Bucyrus a fresh start, but as a vindication of this view of JNL.

In these circumstances, how might Gellene regard the prospect of disclosing that Milbank also was representing Salovaara–South Street in unrelated matters? Gellene probably already expected that JNL would oppose his appointment because of Milbank's well-known ties to Goldman Sachs.

Disclosure of the firm's representation of Salovaara and South Street would provide even more potent ammunition to JNL. As Bucyrus's major secured creditor, and thus the creditor first in line in bankruptcy, South Street was a potential target for anyone who hoped to increase its share under the plan. Furthermore, unlike Goldman, South Street wasn't so large, nor its connections to large law firms so pervasive, that it would be difficult to find another qualified firm to replace Milbank. Finally, the fact that Gellene himself had done work for Salovaara and currently represented South Street would weigh heavily against his application. For these reasons, JNL was certain to oppose Milbank's appointment with vehemence if Gellene disclosed the firm's ties to Salovaara and South Street—and probably would prevail.

In the moral calculus that likely had emerged for Gellene during those negotiations, this would mean that the party that had behaved so unreasonably during the past year would gain the upper hand. The debtor would have to hire new counsel. That counsel would have to spend valuable time becoming familiar with Bucyrus, the other parties, and the plan. Furthermore, JNL undoubtedly would use this disruption as an opportunity to push for drastic changes in the plan. The more time passed, and the closer the deadline for obtaining tax benefits loomed, the more leverage JNL would have in pushing for concessions. Given the hostility of other parties to JNL, the result might be a bloody mess that would leave Bucyrus beyond repair.

For these reasons, Gellene may have convinced himself that nondisclosure not only was not morally blameworthy, but that it was morally justified. Milbank's ties to Salovaara, he might claim, posed no real threat to his ability to represent Bucyrus effectively. The company and all its creditors aside from JNL wanted the court to confirm the plan as soon as possible. Nonetheless, JNL would seize upon those ties to demand that Milbank be disqualified, with potentially disastrous consequences for Bucyrus. On balance, therefore, Gellene might conclude that disclosing the connection to Salovaara–South Street would not be in the best interest of the estate. Disclosure would do little to add to the integrity of the bankruptcy process, but could seriously undermine the chance for a timely and successful reorganization.

This psychological dynamic could have offset any advantage there otherwise might have been from having another bankruptcy partner work with Gellene on the Bucyrus case. Unlike Gellene, that partner might not have had as strong a sense of the importance of Lederman to his career. This could have eliminated, or reduced, one motive for rationalizing that withholding information was necessary to avoid a technical disqualification. Like Gellene, however, that partner would be a team member who probably identified strongly with Bucyrus and was hostile to JNL. That could well be enough to lead him to accept this rationalization.

The circumstances that may have led Gellene to treat JNL as an adversary reflect the potentially powerful influence of project teams in modern large-firm practice. The movement of more routine legal work to corporate legal departments has meant that clients now look to outside firms for more specialized services on projects too large and complex for in-house counsel to handle on a regular basis. In addition to major corporate bankruptcies, such projects may include transactional work involving merger with, or acquisition of, a major competitor, a lucrative joint venture, or development of an innovative financing instrument. They may also involve "bet your company" litigation, such as defending of a large class-action suit, contesting a major antitrust action, or fending off a hostile takeover.

The fact that law firm lawyers increasingly work on such large intensive project teams enhances the potential role of group influence on perception and behavior. In particular, teams involved in bargaining or litigation may assume a competitive posture that both builds cohesion among group members and generates hostility toward outsiders. This makes it more likely that the group will construct a distinctive moral universe that guides its members' judgments about right and wrong in the context of the project. That universe will have especially powerful influence to the extent that high stakes and tight deadlines create a sense of crisis. Under these circumstances, team members are especially likely to develop a sense of mission that prompts self-serving justifications of behavior.

ANY EFFORT TO construct a sufficiently rich explanation of how John Gellene came to destroy his legal career thus needs to take account of a variety of factors, including Gellene's own personality, the law firm in which he practiced, the tendency of corporate transactional lawyers to cultivate ties to multiple parties whose interests potentially may conflict, the bankruptcy bar's views on conflicts and disclosure rules, and the dynamics of the particular case on which he was working.

A plausible narrative of how these factors interacted is one in which Gellene was motivated not to make full disclosure and then rationalized that this was the best choice under the circumstances. Gellene wanted to avoid disclosure because it would lead to disqualification. He wanted to avoid disqualification because he was anxious about his future in a competitive law firm, and he wanted to cultivate a relationship with an important partner who he anticipated would prefer that he not disclose the connection to Salovaara.

Gellene thus was motivated not to treat Rule 2014 as an absolute ethical command, but as a rule that called for the exercise of his discretion. He was able to rationalize this approach to the rule because he believed that strictly applying the bankruptcy conflict rule to large law firms was unfair and did not always serve ethical purposes.

Once Gellene justified weighing the costs and benefits of disclosure rather than automatically disclosing all connections, he was able to reach the conclusion that he preferred. He could convince himself that Milbank's ties to Salovaara were only a "technical" conflict that raised no serious concern. The benefit of disclosure thus would be negligible. At most it would serve the abstract purpose of promoting the integrity of the bankruptcy process, while resulting in a disqualification that served no significant ethical end. The cost of disclosure, however, would be substantial. Disqualification would be highly disruptive to Bucyrus, threatening its ability to emerge successfully from bankruptcy. It also, of course, would mean the loss of fees for Milbank, deprive Gellene of a client, and perhaps strain his relationship with Lederman.

Given his motivation not to disclose, Gellene may have underestimated the likelihood that his violation would be detected. Even if it were, however, he could rationalize that courts tended to be lenient about disclosure violations. Nondisclosure thus was a calculated risk that could pay off even if it were discovered.

None of this necessarily occurred on the level of conscious thought. Indeed, rationalizations generally are effective to the extent that they aren't recognized as such. Furthermore, while it may be useful to portray the process as relatively linear, in reality it is much less systematic. Nevertheless, the phenomenon of relying on self-serving biases in making judgments is well established. People strongly motivated to reach a certain outcome often are able to rationalize why that outcome is the most reasonable under the circumstances. In Gellene's case, there were several reasons why he might prefer to conceal Milbank's ties to Salovaara, and plausible ways that he could justify doing so.

To the extent that this scenario captures the dynamics of what occurred, it offers an account that is more sobering than the story of a self-conscious wrongdoer who deliberately hatched a scheme of misconduct. Were Gellene simply an amoral actor indifferent to ethical demands, the tale might be more graphic but less instructive. The ambitions and anxieties that motivated Gellene's decision, however, likely mirror those of many lawyers in major law firms. Furthermore, the influences that lent support to his rationalizations are pervasive in the world that these lawyers inhabit. Finally, lawyers are especially adept at constructing rationalizations in support of certain preestablished positions. Indeed, this is a highly valuable trait for someone engaged in representing clients.

The way in which these forces came together in John Gellene's life is of course unique. No other lawyer will ever come to the same end in quite the same way. It would have been impossible to foretell all the influences that ultimately resulted in his conviction. At the same time, it's too comforting to attribute his fall simply to defective character or a corrupt law firm. Far better instead to see it as a cautionary tale about the ethical landscape that highly accomplished lawyers in powerful law firms must navigate at the dawn of the twentieth-first century.

EPILOGUE

IN THE FALL of 1999, John Gellene was released from confinement at Fort Dix Correctional Facility in New Jersey. According to the terms of his sentence, he was on supervised release for two more years, required periodically to report to a probation officer. Unable to practice law, he reportedly is now working at an investment company. The main prosecutor in his case, Steven Biskupic, was named in 2002 as the U.S. attorney for the Eastern District of Wisconsin, in which Milwaukee is located. The assistant U.S. trustee in the Bucyrus bankruptcy, John Byrnes, has moved to the U.S. Trustee's Office in Roanoke, Virginia. Jeff Werbalowsky is still with Houlihan, Lokey in Minneapolis, heading up that firm's financial restructuring services. In the course of his work, on at least one occasion he has come in contact with John Gellene. John Stark has left Jackson National Life. In March 2001, he followed the path of Mikael Salovaara and founded his own vulture capital fund, Water Tower Capital in Chicago.

Larry Lederman remains a partner at Milbank Tweed, head of the international corporate practice. Milbank itself is now one of the most profitable law firms in the country. In 2002, it had $381 million in gross revenues. Its $1.785 million in profits per partner put it in seventh place in the *American Lawyer* rankings.[1] With the conviction of Gellene and the departure of seven of its ten bankruptcy partners around the same time, the firm's bankruptcy practice "seemed a goner" in late 1998. The arrival of lateral bankruptcy partner Luc Despins shortly afterward, however, has helped revive the practice. Milbank's bankruptcy group now has become a major presence in some of the largest corporate bankruptcies in recent years.

THE STORY of John Gellene involves a tale of intertwined strands of character and circumstance. These channeled him toward a destination he would not have chosen had he seen it from the start. His character is of course unique, but also is similar to many persons who hold positions of high responsibility. Gellene drew much of his sense of worth from professional success in arduous competitions. He was self-disciplined and willing to put in grueling hours on whatever task he undertook. He often seemed spread a bit too thin, loading up his plate with new challenges on top of already demanding ones. He tended to ignore what he considered minor technical duties in the face of consuming work responsibilities.

The circumstances he faced were distinctive, but also mirror broader historical trends. Gellene brought his personal attributes to a setting in which large law firms face the most intense competition for clients in their history. He arrived just as his own firm began taking steps to avoid being left behind in this newly volatile market. Milbank brought in Larry Lederman to help transform the firm by training a cadre of lawyers in cutting-edge transactional practice. It was Lederman who tapped Gellene to represent two of his clients simultaneously: Bucyrus on the one hand and Salovaara and South Street on the other. It was, of course, Gellene's failure to disclose this arrangement that led to his downfall.

Gellene also found himself at Milbank just as a surge in bankruptcy practice was starting. Several companies were beginning to break under the strain of large debt loads acquired in the 1980s. In many cases, this debt had been incurred in the course of leveraged buyouts. These and other novel transactions were the brainchild of investment banking firms who, similar to law firms, faced fierce competition because of the decline of long-term ties with their clients. Large corporate bankruptcies promised extremely lucrative fees for lawyers who represented debtors. Wall Street law firms, however, risked being shut out of this business because of potential conflicts of interest. Their efforts to persuade courts to adopt what they regarded as a realistic interpretation of bankruptcy conflict rules started to bear fruit in New

York and Delaware. It also, however, began to create a divide in legal culture between bankruptcy courts in those and other states.

In addition, the Bucyrus bankruptcy occurred at a time when tensions in bankruptcy were high between creditors holding the junk bonds of the 1980s, and vulture investors who had bought some of that debt for pennies on the dollar when the companies that issued it began to falter. Most bondholders exchanged their debt for shares in a reorganized company, which gave them some incentive to look to its long-term viability. Vulture investors, however, are essentially speculators. They bank on an increase in the value of a reorganized company as an opportunity to cash in their chips and move on. The two major creditors of Bucyrus were a holder of junk bonds and a vulture investor. The bitterness between them permeated the bankruptcy and may have influenced Gellene not to disclose Milbank's ties to Salovaara and South Street.

Furthermore, the Bucyrus bankruptcy in some ways was the paradigm of a traditional model of Chapter 11 that has lost its dominance in the decade since.[2] The effort to gain agreement on a prepackaged plan did make the Bucyrus reorganization a harbinger of the increasing tendency to use Chapter 11 to confirm deals created before the petition is filed. Otherwise, however, the bankruptcy represented the fading of the old order. Bucyrus was an "old economy" manufacturing company with hard assets whose value lay in their specific combination in the form of particular production facilities. For such a company, a reorganization that preserved the essential structure of the firm could well generate more value than the sale of its separate assets.

Negotiations thus focused on the relative priority of different claimants in the reorganized company, rather than on the possibility of liquidating the company or auctioning it off. Bucyrus management, and Gellene in particular, played a key role in, and exerted considerable influence over, those negotiations. With its major secured creditor holding a relatively modest $35 million in secured debt, Bucyrus had enough unencumbered assets that it didn't need to obtain debtor-in-possession (DIP) financing to operate during bankruptcy. This enabled it to avoid loan provisions that could have significantly limited its freedom of action during the negotiations.

Finally, as Gellene suspected, the Bucyrus reorganization occurred near the end of a boom in bankruptcy business. By 1994 the work of restructuring companies with onerous debt loads incurred in the previous decade was almost complete. Thus, even as they enjoyed the fruits of a growth spurt in bankruptcy work, perceptive lawyers already were looking over their shoulders for the lean years that would likely soon arrive.

HISTORICAL DYNAMICS already are creating new challenges for corporate bankruptcy practice. Noncompliance with Rule 2014 may be less of a current concern in bankruptcy cases than it was at the time of the Bucyrus bankruptcy. Gellene's conviction, along with severe sanctions on other firms for disclosure violations around the same time, seems to have led to more serious attention to disclosure obligations. In addition, large firms now may meet informally with a trustee before filing a Chapter 11 petition, as Milbank did in the Enron bankruptcy, to see if its ties to interested parties will prevent it from being appointed to represent the debtor or the creditors committee. Given increasing competition among courts for large corporate bankruptcies,[3] many trustees may be amenable to working around potential conflicts in order to attract cases to their districts. Large-firm lawyers thus may regard disclosure as less risky than it was a few years ago. As a result, different ethical concerns may become more salient. Debtor's counsel may have an incentive to offer advice that avoids a dispute that would trigger use of a special counsel, for instance, or lawyers within the firm may face temptations to breach the firm's firewall to obtain confidential information.

Another development since the Bucyrus bankruptcy has been a significant change in Chapter 11 bargaining dynamics. Unlike Bucyrus, many firms contemplating bankruptcy today rely heavily on human capital and other intangible assets whose profitability is not tied to their deployment in a specific form or location. In many cases, using Chapter 11 as a vehicle for preserving the company as a going concern may be less efficient than using it to sell off assets or radically transform its operations.⁴ Because it is less essential to the future of the company, the debtor's management has less bargaining power vis-à-vis major creditors than it did a decade ago. This shift has been reinforced by the greater use of DIP financing to dictate the terms of the reorganization to companies whose debt loads make them dependent on this source of capital.⁵

We can only begin to speculate what distinctive ethical issues will arise in this new landscape. Debtor's counsel may be inclined, for instance, to look out for the interest of its other clients when advising the company on which lender to use for DIP financing or to which bidders various assets of the company should be sold.⁶ While we can't be certain what forms they will take, we can be sure that new situations will continue to arise that will test the ethical mettle of bankruptcy lawyers in numerous ways.

More generally, dynamics peculiar to numerous other practice areas will produce their own evolving challenges for the lawyers who work in those settings. Each field contains its own distinctive set of pressures, incentives, challenges, and temptations. Appreciating the ways in which these forces interact in daily practice is crucial in any effort to understand the ethical challenges that lawyers will face in the years to come.

My primary purpose in this book has been to use John Gellene's story to explore in some depth the factors that shape modern large-firm lawyers' encounters with ethical issues. To that end, I have offered a multilayered account of the events that led to Gellene's downfall. This account does not lead inexorably to a comprehensive list of recommendations for the reform of legal ethics regulation. Nonetheless, it is natural to ask what Gellene's experience suggests about how we might better promote ethical behavior by practicing lawyers. It is worth sketching at least the outlines of an answer in order to provoke a discussion that grapples more realistically with the realities of modern practice.

One especially important lesson is that ethical law practice does not depend simply on the moral probity of individual lawyers. Personal character is of course relevant. Lawyers, however, work within law firms and practice groups that themselves operate within the broader context of the market for legal services. How these practice organizations respond to the demands of this market shapes the ethical environment in which their lawyers work. This occurs through both official policies and more subtle, informal signals. Appreciating that modern organizations "create an internal moral and intellectual world"7 that serves as a frame of reference for those who work within them underscores that any effort to enhance the likelihood of ethical conduct by lawyers needs to draw on the insights of organizational theory.

We should focus in particular on what we have learned about the behavior of business organizations. For better or worse, modern law firms are business enterprises that are subject to powerful market forces. They operate increasingly as self-conscious economic entities that must attend to profits, market share, and the efficient provision of service. Acknowledging this unavoidable reality is more productive than proclaiming that law practice has declined from being a profession to a business. We need to find ways to harness or constrain market forces to promote ethical ideals—to identify measures that more effectively regulate law firms as market actors. This is precisely what law attempts to do in its regulation of corporations. That effort offers a rich fund of experience from which we can draw insights.

One such insight is the importance of an "ethical infrastructure" within an organization: formal policies and procedures, as well as cultural norms, that promote compliance with ethical obligations in the face of competitive pressures.8 In the law firm context, formal elements of this infrastructure may include a variety of measures: a new business committee to review possible conflicts of interest from new clients or new matters; a full-time in-house ethics adviser; requiring that a conflicts check be conducted for a new matter before an attorney can obtain a billing code; mandating that all legal opinions issued on behalf of the firm be reviewed by a second partner; requiring partner approval of letters prepared in response to requests for information by client auditors; designating a liaison with the firm's malpractice insurer; peer review procedures; and ethics training for both lawyers and staff.

Such formal measures by themselves, however, are not enough. Experience with corporate legal compliance programs makes this clear. The organization must foster an ethos or culture that emphasizes the importance of ethical behavior.[9] Enron, for example, had what has been called "a good model of key provisions for the sort of audit committee charter that corporate governance advocates have promoted in recent years."[10] It also had a company code of conduct organized around the concepts of respect, integrity, communication, and excellence.[11] Yet critics have charged that the culture at Enron diverged radically from such formal policies and was a crucial element in the downfall of the company.[12] Rules and procedures thus can contribute to an ethical ethos, but won't ensure it if other features of the organization undermine them.

Research on corporate legal compliance suggests that several characteristics of an organization provide clues to its ethos. We can look for analogies to these features in large law firms. First is the organizational hierarchy.[13] Does the board of directors or one of its committees monitor legal compliance? If so, does it have the resources and access to information necessary to do so effectively? Does the organization make the budgets of internal auditors independent of the groups that they audit? Do auditors report to the heads of the divisions that they audit, or to an auditing director who reports to the board of directors? Are there inadequately supervised positions within the company where illegal behavior could easily occur? If so, is this an oversight or an attempt to shield management from incriminating knowledge?

A second concern is organizational goals.[14] Are they so unrealistic that they effectively encourage illegal behavior in order to meet them? For instance, basing rewards and penalties on overly ambitious revenue targets may have far more influence on conduct than establishing a company code of ethics.[15] A third concern is educating employees about legal requirements.[16] Are the appropriate employees informed of regulatory provisions that affect their duties? Are they informed of changes in these requirements? Are there regular meetings to discuss compliance issues? To what extent do training programs include material on ethics and legal compliance?

A fourth consideration is the organization's efforts to monitor compliance with legal requirements.[17] Does the corporation conduct internal audits? Are communication channels open throughout the hierarchy? Must employees periodically certify that they are familiar with relevant regulations and that the programs under their supervision satisfy them? Is there someone designated to receive reports of unethical conduct? To what extent is this person insulated from management pressure? How much is employee compensation tied to compliance performance? Finally, how has the organization dealt in the past with those who have engaged in unlawful or unethical behavior?[18]

Law firms thus will need both to establish an ethical infrastructure and to reinforce it with an organizational ethos that clearly places value on meeting ethical responsibilities. What can be done to encourage them to do this? The analogy to corporate compliance programs provides a clue. Corporations are subject to regulation by government bodies that have specialized expertise. Such regulation, of course, encompasses a wide variety of topics, such as securities, tax, employment discrimination, worker safety, environmental quality, pensions and employee benefits, antitrust, and others. Different specialized agencies establish and enforce regulations designed to implement these directives, and can refer cases to the Department of Justice for criminal prosecution. Corporations can be civilly or criminally liable for the actions of their employees in many cases.

There are, however, specific incentives for companies to establish compliance programs. They may avoid prosecution or receive lenient treatment if they take the initiative to monitor compliance with the law, investigate possible violations, and disclose the results of their investigation to appropriate government authorities. Furthermore, the Organizational Sentencing Guidelines specifically provide that an organization may be subject to a lesser penalty than otherwise would apply if it has implemented an "effective program to prevent and detect violations of law" at the time of the offense. The guidelines describe the general elements of such a program.[19]

These provisions have not, to say the least, eliminated corporate illegality. They are credited, however, with increasing attention to ethics and regulatory compliance in many corporations.[20] Compliance programs are tailored to the particular activities that are subject to specific legal requirements. Employees working in different areas of corporate operations receive training and supervision appropriate to the tasks that they perform and the legal provisions to which they are subject. The creation of corporate ethics officer positions has resulted in the emergence of a distinct profession that provides a reference group outside the company that can reduce unreflective deference to bottom-line demands.[21] A large literature has emerged that is devoted to discussing and evaluating corporate compliance programs.[22]

The ideal result is a company-wide commitment to compliance that is implemented in a manner suitable for both the industry in which the company operates and for each group of employees within the corporation. Effective programs don't simply acquaint employees with a company's general code of conduct. They also integrate an understanding of ethical requirements into everyday activities, so that it becomes part of the way that employees carry out their responsibilities.

This experience suggests that lawyers should be subject to regulation by agencies that have familiarity with the matters on which different lawyers work. To an increasing extent, this appears to be exactly what is happening. In the law firm context, specialized practice groups are analogous to different corporate departments. As lawyers concentrate on particular fields of practice, they often become subject to specific rules of practice that regulate their conduct. These rules are established by legislatures, administrative agencies, and courts with expertise in specialized fields.

The Sarbanes-Oxley legislation,[23] for instance, both set forth certain standards of conduct for securities lawyers and authorized the Securities and Exchange Commission (SEC) to promulgate rules governing lawyers who practice or appear before the commission.[24] Such lawyers are required to report evidence of a material violation of "securities law or breach of fiduciary duty or similar violation" to superiors, and are authorized to make disclosure outside the company in certain circumstances. The rules expressly provide that they supersede any state ethics rules that impose a lesser obligation on attorneys.[25] The rationale for such regulations is that securities lawyers may have unique opportunities to prevent corporate misconduct that could injure shareholders, employees, and the larger public.

Similarly, the Internal Revenue Service (IRS) has issued regulations governing the conduct of lawyers involved in providing tax advice and preparing tax returns,[26] as well as lawyers who prepare opinion letters in connection with tax shelters.[27] The rules establish a standard for presenting a position in favor of the taxpayer that is more stringent than state ethics rules impose on a lawyer presenting a client's case.[28] In addition, the IRS has decreed that a lawyer evaluating the likelihood that a tax position will prevail may not take into account the likelihood that the client will be audited.[29] The rationale for the IRS regulations is that the viability of the tax system depends primarily on voluntary compliance by taxpayers and public confidence in such compliance.

Banking practice also involves distinctive questions about lawyers' ethical obligations. Courts have upheld claims by federal banking regulators against law firms based on the notion that, as one observer puts it, "the lawyer has a de facto duty of care that runs to the depositors" of federally insured banks.[30] In addition, the Office of Thrift Supervision (OTS) has asserted that lawyers owe substantial fiduciary duties to the federal insurance funds that provide protection for their financial institution clients.[31] Furthermore, Federal Home Loan Bank Board regulations prohibit "unethical or improper professional conduct" before the board[32] and willfully aiding and abetting violations of federal banking laws and regulations.[33]

A similar rationale underlies the Patent and Trademark Office's (PTO) rules of practice. The PTO requires that attorneys representing a client applying for a patent must disclose any "prior art" that may be the basis for denial of the application.[34] Patent and trademark law's carefully calibrated balance between recognition of proprietary rights and desire to stimulate creativity requires accurate information about the current state of innovation. The lawyer and client often are in the best position to possess such information and therefore have an obligation to bring it to the attention of the agency. By contrast, under state ethics rules a lawyer generally is under no obligation to disclose any weakness in a client's case in the course of either negotiations or litigation.

Federal Rule of Civil Procedure 11 also represents a grant of authority beyond state bar rules to regulate and punish the behavior of attorneys.[35] Rule 11 authorizes federal judges to sanction attorneys for filing misleading papers and permits the court to impose a sanction on the attorney's firm as well. State ethics rules make no provision for sanctioning law firms for the transgressions of their lawyers, absent an egregiously defective ethical compliance program. Preserving the integrity of the judicial process nonetheless is regarded as sufficient to warrant authorizing federal judges to hold the entire firm responsible for violations of Rule 11.

With respect to John Gellene's specialty of bankruptcy, Nancy Rapoport has argued that it is time to adopt a code of ethics specifically for bankruptcy practitioners.[36] All bankruptcy lawyers practice with respect to a single federal Bankruptcy Code. Corporate bankruptcy practitioners in particular comprise a group of attorneys who encounter one another with regularity and thus have the ability to identify and the incentive to comply with common understandings about the range of acceptable conduct. Furthermore, state ethics provisions map poorly onto bankruptcy practice, creating considerable uncertainty about how to harmonize them with bankruptcy rules. In addition, some critics argue that even the specialized law dealing with bankruptcy conflicts is an anachronism carried over from a prior bankruptcy regime with very different features.

Finally, Congress, which enacts bankruptcy law, and bankruptcy courts, which apply it, are in a position to establish ethical standards. These standards could provide more guidance on issues such as how to characterize the DIP's obligations and those of its lawyer; whether and under what conditions parties may waive conflicts of interest; situations that represent actual rather than potential conflicts of interest; whether the appearance of impropriety can be a basis for disqualification; and whether and under what circumstances arrangements such as the appointment of special counsel and the use of firewalls can avoid disqualification.

The trend toward regulation of attorney conduct by specialized bodies appears to be increasing, and it should. It offers an opportunity to clarify what constitutes acceptable conduct for lawyers whose work has distinctive features and consequences. The argument that such entities should not establish or enforce rules of practice because they lack expertise in professional responsibility is unpersuasive. Ethical rules take on meaning in particular practice settings. Assessing lawyers' conduct requires awareness of the specific contexts in which lawyers work and appreciation of the competing values at stake in determining the obligations of lawyers who practice in those settings. Bar disciplinary officials who enforce general rules designed to govern all lawyers usually are in a poorer position to do this than are specialized agencies who deal on a regular basis with lawyers and their clients. Regulation of conduct by such agencies should give lawyers more finely tailored guidance about how to respond to the particular kinds of ethical issues that tend to arise in their practices.

As John Gellene's story suggests, compliance with ethical rules will depend to some extent on whether practitioners regard such rules as fair and realistic. The creation of rules by an entity familiar with a given area of practice should provide some reassurance on this score. In addition, what Ted Schneyer calls "bar corporatism" may contribute to the perceived legitimacy of specialized ethical rules.[37] Practitioners will be involved in dialogue with rule-makers about appropriate rules of practice, much as other regulated entities have opportunities to express their views and exert some influence in the regulatory process.

Schneyer suggests that this process already occurs to some degree in certain areas of practice. The IRS, for instance, has incorporated many of the American Bar Association's (ABA) Section of Taxation guidelines for the issuance of tax shelter opinions and has made them enforceable in IRS disciplinary hearings.[38] OTS consent agreements with law firms accused of misconduct in representing savings and loan associations accept the due diligence standards for preparing third-party legal opinions that have been drafted by the ABA Business Law Section. In addition, OTS has worked with a committee of that section to craft a standard letter that thrift institutions will be required to send to counsel as part of the regulatory examination process.[39]

In corporate law practice, the ABA formed the task force on Corporate Responsibility to explore possible responses to the alleged misconduct of officials in Enron and other major companies that came to light around the same time. The task force has proposed changes in the Model Rules of Professional Conduct that would clarify the options available to attorneys confronted with misconduct by their corporate clients.[40] It also was in contact with the SEC about the commission's proposed rules on attorney conduct. These examples suggest that bar corporatism may provide a way for the bar to continue to play a role in establishing ethical obligations and practice standards—even as it relinquishes any claim of exclusive authority to regulate lawyers.

There is, of course, the danger that institutions will become captives of the bar, just as critics charge that some agencies have been captured by the constituencies that they regulate. Designating a public entity as a key participant in the regulation of lawyers who practice in a particular field, however, will give greater voice to social concerns than under the bar disciplinary system. In addition, the political accountability of these institutions should impose some constraint on willingness simply to accede to the wishes of practicing lawyers. In any event, such a system is already in place in some areas of practice. Acknowledging its legitimacy would direct greater attention to it and provide opportunities explicitly to consider the competing values that should be balanced in determining the obligations of lawyers in different areas of practice.

Just as corporations must establish compliance programs that deal with specific regulatory mandates, so law firms would need to develop systems to address the ethical issues distinctive to specialized areas of practice. This reflects the fact that law firms have come to resemble organizations with various groups of employees who must comply with regulations specific to the departments in which they work. The firm would need a general system with features such as a database of clients for conflicts checks, a new business committee, and standardized billing guidelines. It also, however, should have compliance measures specific to particular practice areas, with compliance responsibility vested in practitioners who are specialists. The firm could, for instance, designate an ethics partner for each practice group. He or she would be available for consultation and would encourage attention to the particular ethics issues that lawyers in that group tend to confront.

Ethical guidance therefore would be provided not simply by a firm-wide ethics committee, but by lawyers who are in a position to help resolve the issues that arise in the course of daily practice. In doing so, these lawyers would draw on specialized ethical rules, suggested best practices, and familiarity with how state ethical rules have been construed to apply to the practice specialty in question. Courts or agencies would then take into account the adequacy of the particular compliance system in determining how the firm should be treated in the event of ethical violations by its lawyers—just as authorities do in deciding how to deal with corporations whose employees have engaged in illegal behavior.

As law firms become more significant economic enterprises, we need to look more to regulation of corporate behavior as a model for promoting ethical conduct by lawyers. Such regulation has been sensitive to the crucial influence of organizational culture and to the pressures generated by competitive markets—factors increasingly important in the lives of lawyers. In short, recognizing that much of modern law practice is big business can be the first step in developing standards that offer a realistic possibility of preserving the distinctive values of the legal profession.

DAVID GOELZER WAS the general counsel of Bucyrus during its bankruptcy. He grew up in the Midwest and, except for his college years studying engineering at Cornell, has lived and worked there all his life. He came to Milwaukee to join Bucyrus in 1972. He stayed until September 1995, when the reorganized company's new board of directors asked him and other long-time officials to leave. He is now in solo practice in Milwaukee.

EPILOGUE

Goelzer's appearance and demeanor are measured, prudent, conscientious, and precise—the embodiment of the traditional careful lawyer. Nothing about him is flamboyant. Around sixty, he is short and wiry, with thinning reddish-blond hair and glasses, attired in conservative suit and tie. Those who worked with Goelzer on the bankruptcy were impressed by his low-key but thorough style. His extensive knowledge of the events surrounding the reorganization, and his detailed contemporaneous notes recounting them, made him invaluable to lawyers in both the civil and criminal proceedings that were launched in response to Gellene's disclosure violation. Prosecutors joked that his notes were virtually a verbatim transcript, while another person who dealt with him described him as "the person in law school you want to sit next to in class."

Goelzer was, of course, the first witness the prosecution called in Gellene's criminal trial. Prosecutors regarded him as best suited to lay out the background of the events involving Gellene. More important, they wanted his testimony to establish that Gellene had never told Goelzer about his ties to Salovaara and South Street, and that such information would have been important to him. As Biskupic put it, Goelzer was credible because "he had absolutely no axe to grind against John Gellene; in fact he thought very highly of him." The prosecution "had tremendous confidence in him as a witness because he wasn't going to say anything too outlandish; it's not in his personality . . . His personality was precision."

Goelzer probably worked more intimately with Gellene during the Bucyrus bankruptcy than did anyone else. He spoke with him virtually every day, often several times, under the intense pressure of an extremely bitter reorganization process. He had great admiration for the work that Gellene did under extremely stressful conditions. The bankruptcy and Gellene's prosecution remain the most vivid events of Goelzer's professional life. He still struggles to make sense of those events, to incorporate them somehow into his understanding of both John Gellene and the practice of law. "To this day," he says, "I view the central issue here as being just unbelievable. The idea that a lawyer would—particularly Milbank Tweed—you know it's historically a very conservative law firm, and we had dealings with them in the 1980s." He observes, "I had good relationships with a number of the corporate lawyers there and they were the kind of people you would just trust completely."

"We had a big antitrust case in the middle 1980s," Goelzer recalls. The Milbank lawyer representing Bucyrus "was William Jackson, who is the son of a Supreme Court justice and chief prosecutor at Nuremberg—a very impressive man, just the pillar of rectitude." Indeed, Jackson had assisted his father in the Nuremberg prosecutions. Goelzer leans forward and continues, "You just couldn't imagine this guy . . . the idea that he would consider representing someone opposed to his client or would be shading things with his own client—you just couldn't imagine it . . ." His voice trails off, and he is lost for a moment in his own thoughts.

"Maybe I'm just naive," he says softly.

NOTES

PROLOGUE

1. *See generally* MARC GALANTER & THOMAS PALAY, TOURNAMENT OF LAWYERS: THE TRANSFORMATION OF THE BIG LAW FIRM (1991).

CHAPTER 1

1. WAYNE K. HOBSON, THE AMERICAN LEGAL PROFESSION AND THE ORGANIZATIONAL SOCIETY, 1890–1930 146 (1986).

2. *Id.* at 143.

3. Thomas Paul Pinansky, *The Emergence of Law Firms in the American Legal Profession*, 9 U. ARK. LITTLE ROCK L. REV. 593, 601–2 (1986–87).

4. MARC GALANTER & THOMAS PALAY, TOURNAMENT OF LAWYERS: THE TRANSFORMATION OF THE BIG LAW FIRM 14 (1991).

5. On the contrast between engineers and lawyers, see HOBSON, *supra* note 1, at 94–101.

6. *Id.* at 101.

7. *Id.* at 101–3; 2 ROBERT T. SWAINE, THE CRAVATH FIRM AND ITS PREDECESSORS, 1819–1948 1 (1948).

8. SWAINE, *supra* note 7, at 1.

9. *Id.* at 3.

10. ERWIN SMIGEL, THE WALL STREET LAWYER: PROFESSIONAL ORGANIZATION MAN? 37 (1964).

11. *Id.* at 39.

12. *Id.* at 9.

13. *Id.* at 116.

14. *Id.* at 7.

15. *See* GALANTER & PALAY, *supra* note 1, at 77–120.

16. David B. Wilkins & G. Mitu Gulati, *Reconceiving the Tournament of Lawyers: Tracking, Seeding, and Information Control in the Internal Labor Markets of Elite Law Firms*, 84 VA. L. REV. 1581 (1998).

17. George Rutherglen & Kevin A. Kordana, *A Farewell to Tournaments? The Need for an Alternative Explanation of Law Firm Structure and Growth*, 84 VA. L. REV. 1695 (1998).

18. Swaine, *supra* note 7, at 10.

19. *Id.* at 9.

20. PAUL HOFFMAN, LIONS IN THE STREET 8 (1973).

21. *Id.* at 2.

22. GALANTER & PALAY, *supra* note 4, at 34.

23. *Id.*
24. Hoffman, *supra* note 20, at 59.
25. *Id.* at 76.
26. *See* Ronald Gilson & Robert Mnookin, *Sharing among the Human Capitalists: An Economic Inquiry into the Corporate Law Firm and How Partners Split Profits*, 37 Stan. L. Rev. 313 (1985).
27. Hoffman, *supra* note 20, at 60.
28. Smigel, *supra* note 10, at 209.
29. *Id.* at 334.
30. Hoffman, *supra* note 20, at 2.
31. Mark Stevens, Power of Attorney 8–9 (1987).
32. Hoffman, *supra* note 20, at 5.
33. *Id.* at 50.
34. *Id.* at 60.
35. Smigel, *supra* note 10, at 59.
36. Hoffman, *supra* note 20, at 2.
37. Smigel, *supra* note 10, at 12.
38. *Id.* at 270.
39. Galanter & Palay, *supra* note 4, at 16.
40. Ellen Joan Pollock, Turks and Brahmins 96–97, 99 (1990).
41. *Id.* at 99.
42. Hoffman, *supra* note 20, at 100–101.
43. Pollock, *supra* note 40, at 34. Much of the account of the firm's history that follows is drawn from Pollock's book.
44. Hoffman, *supra* note 20, at 77.
45. Pollock, *supra* note 40, at 36.
46. *Id.* at 43.
47. Hoffman, *supra* note 20, at 76.
48. *Id.*
49. *Id.* at 51.
50. Galanter & Palay, *supra* note 4, at 115.
51. *Id.* at 43.
52. Ward Bower, *The Changing Face of Partnership*, in The Altman Weil Pensa Archive on Strategic Planning and Management for Law Firms and Corporate Legal Departments 179, 182 (Susan D. Sjostrom ed., 1996).
53. *See* Michael Orey, *Two Law Firms Set to Announce Plan to Merge*, Wall St. J., July 17, 2001, at B2; *Law Firms Sidley Austin and Brown Wood Merge*, Wall St. J., Apr. 24, 2001, at A6.
54. *See, e.g.*, Susan Hansen, *The Young and the Restless*, Am. Law., Sept. 1995, 67.
55. Paul Braverman and Robert Lennon, *In Motion*, Am. Law., Feb. 2002, 88.
56. *See, e.g.*, Hansen, *supra* note 54, at 69 on Rogers & Wells.
57. Michael D. Wiley, *A Closer Look at Loyalty*, Legal Times, March 31, 2003, at 18.
58. *Id.*
59. *Id.*

60. MICHAEL TROTTER, PROFIT AND THE PRACTICE OF LAW 48 (1997); Bower, *supra* note 52, at 186.

61. Nathan Koppel, *Sidley's Big Gamble*, AM. LAW., July 2001, at 108.

62. *See, e.g.*, Jan Hoffman, *Oldest Law Firm Is Courtly, Loyal, and Defunct*, N.Y. TIMES, Oct. 2, 1994, at 33.

63. Koppel, *supra* note 61, at 110.

64. *See, e.g.*, Brenda Sandburg, *The Last Days of Brobeck, Phleger & Harrison*, LEGAL TIMES, Apr. 21, 2003, at 20.

65. D. M. Osborne, *Rude Awakening*, AM. LAW., Mar. 1998, at 70.

66. One survey by a law firm consulting organization indicates that in 75 percent of the large firms studied, almost three-fourths grant "origination credit" to partners for as long as the client generates work for the firm. ALT-MAN, WEIL, INC., COMPENSATION SYSTEMS IN PRIVATE LAW FIRMS: 2003 SURVEY REPORT 28 (2003).

67. *Talking Shop*, AM. LAW., June 2003, at 86, 88.

68. Randall S. Thomas, Stewart J. Schwab, & Robert G. Hansen, *Megafirms*, 80 N.C. L. REV. 115, 127 (2001).

69. *See* RICHARD SENNETT, THE CORROSION OF CHARACTER: THE PERSONAL CONSEQUENCES OF WORK IN THE NEW CAPITALISM (1998).

70. IRVING JANIS, GROUPTHINK (1982); Jack Eaton, *Management Communication: The Threat of Groupthink*, 6 CORP. COMM. 183 (2001); Annette R. Flippen, *Understanding Groupthink from a Self-Regulatory Perspective*, 30 SMALL GROUP RES. 139 (1999). For discussion of a similar group phenomenon, see Paul F. Levy, *The Nut Island Effect: When Good Teams Go Wrong*, HARV. BUS. REV., March 2001, at 51.

71. *See generally* POLLOCK, *supra* note 40.

72. *Id.* at 224.

73. *Id.* at 264.

CHAPTER 2

1. ELLEN JOAN POLLOCK, TURKS AND BRAHMINS 46 (1990).

2. *Id.*

3. *Id.* at 25.

4. Edward A. Adams, *Bar Groups to Curb Unlicensed Lawyers*, N.Y.L.J., December 21, 1989, 1.

5. *Id.*

6. *See* LINCOLN CAPLAN, SKADDEN: POWER, MONEY, AND THE RISE OF A LEGAL EMPIRE (1993).

7. LAWRENCE LEDERMAN, TOMBSTONES: A LAWYER'S TALES FROM THE TAKEOVER DECADES 118 (1992).

8. *Id.*

CHAPTER 3

1. Stephanie Strom, *An Investment Vulture in a Tangle on Wall Street*, N.Y. TIMES, Sept. 25, 1996, at C1.

2. *Id.* at C16.

3. *Id.* at C1.

CHAPTER 4

1. Draft Complaint, *Jackson National Life Insurance Co. v. Goldman, Sachs, et al.*, Exhibit 6, p. 15, *United States v. Gellene*, Criminal No. 97-CR-221, E.D. Wis.

2. *Id.* at 24.

3. *See* Bruce A. Markell, *The Folly of Representing Insolvent Corporations: Examining Lawyer Liability and Ethical Issues in Extending Fiduciary Duties to Creditors*, 6 J. BANKR. LAW & PRACT. 403 (1997).

4. Goelzer testimony, Dec. 4, 1995, 717–18, *United States v. Gellene*, Criminal No. 97-CR-221, E.D. Wis.

5. Section 364 of the Bankruptcy Code, for instance, authorizes the court to treat repayment of a DIP loan as an administrative expense, thereby placing the DIP creditor ahead of all unsecured creditors. 11 U.S.C. Sec. 364.

CHAPTER 5

1. *See* Arthur J. Gonzalez, *Conflicts of Interest and Other Ethical Issues Facing Bankruptcy Lawyers: Is Disinterestedness Necessary to Preserve the Integrity of the Bankruptcy System?* 28 HOFSTRA L. REV. 67, 72 (1999–2000). Under one theory, the DIP has a duty to shareholders only until it is insolvent, at which point its obligation runs only to shareholders. *See* Commodity Futures Trading Commission v. Weintraub, 471 U.S. 343, 355 (1985). For an overview of the different theories about the duties of the DIP, see C. R. Bowles Jr. and Nancy B. Rapoport, *Has the DIP's Attorney Become the Ultimate Creditors' Lawyer in Bankruptcy Reorganization Cases?* 5 AM. BANKR. LAW INST. L. REV. 47 (1997).

2. In the Enron bankruptcy, for instance, the trustee appointed a second creditors' committee to represent former employees with interests in severance payments and retirement accounts.

3. One federal appeals court has stated that if the debtor's management seeks to pursue any course of action that the attorney believes is not in the interest of the estate, counsel must seek to dissuade management or resign from the representation. In re Perez, 30 F.3d 1209 (9th Cir. 1994). The same court went on to reach the controversial conclusion that counsel for the DIP also may have a duty to a specific creditor. For a criticism of the latter holding, see Bowles and Rapoport, *supra* note 1, at 83–85.

4. Dickinson Indus. Site v. Cowan, 309 U.S. 382, 388 (1940).

5. Todd J. Zywicki, *Mend It, Don't End It: The Case for Retaining the Disinterestedness Requirement for Debtor in Possession's Professionals*, 18 MISS. COLL. L. REV. 291, 302 (1998).

6. *See* DAVID SKEEL, DEBT'S DOMINION: A HISTORY OF BANKRUPTCY LAW IN AMERICA 110–12 (2001).

7. By its terms, Section 327(a) applies only to professionals employed by the trustee. Because, however, the DIP is given all the rights and powers of a trustee, and is subject to the same limitations, this section has been deemed applicable to professionals employed by the DIP as well.

8. In re Roberts 46 B.R. 815 (Bankr. D. Utah 1985).

CHAPTER 7

1. Barbara Benson, *Lawyers Seek Last Chapter: Bankruptcy Lawyers Seeking a New Chapter*, CRAIN'S N.Y. BUS., Jan. 30, 1995, 1.
2. *Id.*
3. Frankel Alison, *It's Back to Normal in Bankruptcy Practice, Now That the Last of the Mega-Cases Have Sputtered to a Close*, AM. LAW., April 1995, 70.
4. *A Behind the Scenes Look at Milbank Tweed's $1.86 Million Settlement*, 31 BANKR. COURT DEC., *News & Comment*, Jan. 20, 1998, at A1.
5. Barrett Paul, *How Ex-Milbank Partner Gellene Ended Up on Trial over a Conflict*, WALL ST. J., Feb. 23, 1998, at B6.
6. *Id.*
7. *Id.*
8. *Id.*
9. *Id.*
10. *Id.*

CHAPTER 8

1. *Why John Gellene Received the Sentence He Did*, 33 BANKR. COURT DEC., Sept. 29, 1998, at A1.
2. Karen Donovan, *John Gellene Sentenced to 15 Months*, NAT'L. L.J., Aug. 10, 1998, at A6
3. *Why John Gellene Received the Sentence He Did*, *supra* note 1, at A1.
4. *Is John Gellene's Appeal Persuasive?* 33 BANKR. COURT DEC., October 20, 1998, at A3.
5. United States v. Key, 859 F.2d 1257 (7th Cir. 1988).
6. United States v. McIntosh, 124 F.3d 1330 (10th Cir. 1997); United States v. Cherek, 734 F.2d 1248 (7th Cir. 1984).
7. United States v. Jackson, 836 F.2d 324 (7th Cir. 1987).
8. United States v. Phillips, 606 F.2d 884 (9th Cir. 1979); United States v. O'Donnell, 539 F.2d 1233 (9th Cir. 1976); United States v. Yagow, 953 F.2d 427 (8th Cir. 1992); United States v. Ellis, 50 F.3d 419 (7th Cir. 1995); United States v. Lindholm, 24 F.3d 1078 (9th Cir. 1994).
9. Steven M. Biskupic, *A Criminal Prosecution for Violating Bankruptcy Rule 2014: A Strong Standard or Simply Strong Proof?* 9 J. BANKR. L. & PRACT. 301, 319 (2000).
10. Indeed, just two months before Gellene went on trial, the U.S. Court of Appeals for the Seventh Circuit, whose rulings govern federal courts in Wisconsin and other nearby states, rejected the claim by John Byrnes that the Bankruptcy Code requires that a court automatically deny all compensation to any lawyer who withholds information under Rule 2014 that would have disqualified him from appointment. In re Crivello, 134 F.3d 831 (7th Cir. 1998).
11. BISKUPIC, *supra* note 9, at 316.
12. *Id.* at 319.
13. Wayne D. Holly, *United States v. Gellene: Bankruptcy Crime Prosecu-*

tion Continues Justice Department's Aggressive Enforcement Trend, 6 N.Y. ST. B.A. 71, 76 (1998).

14. *Introduction: Bankruptcy Fraud: A Roundtable Discussion*, 6 AM. BANKR. INST. L. REV. 275, 278 (1998).

15. *Attorney General Unveils Nationwide Crackdown on Bankruptcy Fraud*, Dept. of Justice News Release, Feb. 29, 1996.

16. Sandra Taliani Rasnak & Joe Brown, *Our First Line of Defense in Bankruptcy Fraud: The U.S. Trustees*, BUS. CREDIT, April 1998, at 2.

17. 6 AM. BANKR. INST. L. REV., at 276.

18. *See, e.g., Jones Day Settles Conflicts Charges*, 33 BANKR. COURT DEC., Sept. 29, 1998, at A1.

19. Matthew Goldstein, *Lawyers Go Over Limit: Bankruptcy Attorneys Learn Lessons in Disclosure*, CRAIN'S N.Y. BUS., June 1, 1998, at 3.

20. Karen Donovan, *Pleas for Ex-Partner*, NAT'L. L.J., July 20, 1998, at A4.

CHAPTER 9

1. See the comments of John Stark and Andrew Rahl, *The Issue Is Failure to Disclose: Should Milbank Tweed Be Required to Disgorge $1.8 Million Fee?* 31 BANKR. COURT DEC., Sept. 16, 1997, at A1, A10.

2. *See* Susan Daicoff, *Lawyer, Know Thyself: A Review of Empirical Research on Attorney Attributes Bearing on Professionalism*, 46 AM. U. L. REV. 1337, 1349–52 (1997).

3. *Id.* at 1392.

4. *Id.* at 1373–78.

5. *Id.* at 1420.

6. Edward A. Adams, *Bar Groups to Curb Unlicensed Lawyers*, N.Y.L. J., Dec. 21, 1989, 1.

7. *See, e.g.*, ROBERT JACKALL, MORAL MAZES: THE WORLD OF CORPORATE MANAGERS (1988): Samuel Bowles, et al., *The Determinants of Earnings: A Behavioral Approach*, 39 J. ECON. LIT . 1137, 1161–62 (2001); Myron Gable and Frank Dangello, *Locus of Control, Machiavellianism, and Managerial Job Performance*, 128 J. PSYCH. 599 (1994).

8. Donald Langevoort, *The Organizational Psychology of Hypercompetition: Corporate Irresponsibility and the Lessons of Enron*, 70 GEO. WASH. L. REV. 968, 970 (2002).

9. *Id.* at 971.

10. *See, e.g.*, SOCIAL INFLUENCES ON ETHICAL BEHAVIOR IN ORGANIZATIONS (John M. Darley et al. eds., 2001); CODES OF CONDUCT: BEHAVIORAL RESEARCH INTO BUSINESS ETHICS (David M. Messick and Ann E. Tenbrunsel eds., 1996); ROBERT JACKALL, MORAL MAZES: THE WORLD OF CORPORATE MANAGERS (1988); Harvey S. James Jr., *Reinforcing Ethical Decision Making through Organizational Structure*, 28 J. BUS. ETHICS 43 (2000).

11. Stephanie Strom, *Investment "Vulture" Leaves Blackstone*, N.Y. TIMES, October 8, 1996, at D2.

12. State bar rules are relevant to corporate firm lawyers not so much because of the possibility that state bar counsel may bring a disciplinary action against them for violating the rules. Bar counsel rarely have the resources or inclination to pursue prosecutions of lawyers in large law firms. Rather, the rules matter because they can be used as evidence in litigation by corporate clients against lawyers and law firms for malpractice and breach of fiduciary duty.

13. American Bar Association, Model Rules of Professional Conduct, Rule 1.7(a)(1) and Comment.

14. *Id.*, Rule 1.7(a)(2) and Comment.

15. *Id.*, Rule 1.7, Comment 26.

16. SUSAN SHAPIRO, TANGLED LOYALTIES: CONFLICT OF INTEREST IN LEGAL PRACTICE 10 (2002).

17. Richard Painter, *Advance Waiver of Conflicts*, 13 GEO. J. LEGAL ETHICS 289, 293 (2000).

18. On the evolution of investment banking during this period, see LISA ENDLICH, GOLDMAN SACHS: THE CULTURE OF SUCCESS 70–224 (2000); NILS LINDSKOOG, LONG-TERM GREEDY: THE TRIUMPH OF GOLDMAN SACHS 26–142 (1999); DAVID P. McCAFFREY & DAVID W. HART, WALL STREET POLICES ITSELF: HOW SECURITIES FIRMS MANAGE THE LEGAL HAZARDS OF COMPETITIVE PRESSURES (1998); ROBERT G. ECCLES & DWIGHT B. CRANE, DOING DEALS: INVESTMENT BANKERS AT WORK 9 (1988).

19. Brandt v. Hicks Muse & Co., 213 B.R. 784, 789 (D. Mass. 1997).

20. LAWRENCE LEDERMAN, TOMBSTONES: A LAWYER'S TALES FROM THE TAKEOVER DECADES 119 (1992).

21. John M. Darley, *How Organizations Socialize Individuals into Evildoing*, in MESSICK & TENBRUNSEL, *supra* note 10, at 25.

CHAPTER 10

1. *See, e.g.,* RICCARDO ORIZIO, TALK OF THE DEVIL: ENCOUNTERS WITH SEVEN DICTATORS (2003).

2. Gerald K. Smith, *Standards for the Employment of Professionals in Bankruptcy Cases: A Response to Professor Smith's "Case for Retaining the Disinterestedness Requirement for Debtor in Possession's Professionals,"* 18 MISS. COLL. L. REV. 327, 885 (1998) (describing position of Judge Carolyn Dineen King).

3. *Id.* at 866 n. 325 (noting position of Donald Bernstein of Davis Polk & Wardwell).

4. Nancy B. Rapoport, *Turning and Turning in the Widening Gyre: The Problem of Potential Conflicts of Interest in Bankruptcy*, 26 CONN. L. REV. 913, 924 (1994).

5. Roger J. Au & Son, Inc. v. Aetna Ins. Co., 64 B.R. 600 (N.D. Ohio 1986); In re Butterfield Ltd. Partn., 131 B.R. 67 (Bankr. E.D. Mich. 1990).

6. In re Martin, 817 F.2d 175 (1st Cir. 1987).

7. In re Marvel Entertainment, 140 F.3d 463, 476 (3d. Cir. 1998).

8. *See, e.g.,* In re Global Marine, Inc., 108 B.R. 998 (S.D. Tex. 1987); In

re Waterfall Village of Atlanta, Ltd., 103 B.R. 340 (N.D. Ga. 1989); In re Stamford Color Photo, Inc., 98 B.R. 135 (D. Conn. 1989); Freeman v. Chicago Musical Instrument Co., 689 F.2d 715, 720–22 (7th Cir. 1982).

9. In re Leslie Fay Companies, 175 B.R. 525, 532–33 (Bankr. S.D.N.Y. 1994).

10. In re Tinley Plaza Associates, 142 B.R. 272 (Bankr. N.D. Ill. 1992).

11. Teresa A. Sullivan et al., *The Persistence of Local Legal Culture: Twenty Years of Experience from the Federal Bankruptcy Courts*, 17 HARV. J.L. & PUB. POL'Y. 801, 804 (1994).

12. *See* Lynn M. LoPucki and Sara D. Kalin, *The Failure of Public Company Bankruptcies in Delaware and New York: Empirical Evidence of a "Race to the Bottom,"* 54 VAND. L. REV. 231 (2001).

13. Todd J. Zywicki, *Mend It, Don't End It: The Case for Retaining the Disinterestedness Requirement for Debtor in Possession's Professionals*, 18 MISS. COLL. L. REV. 291, 296 (1998).

14. *Id.* at 297.

15. Stephanie Strom, *Law Firm's Role Questioned in Macy Case*, N.Y. TIMES, Apr. 7, 1994, at D1.

16. *Id.*

17. Mr. Gonzalez later was appointed a bankruptcy judge, and presided over the bankruptcy of Enron Corporation.

18. In re Leslie Fay Companies,175 B.R., at 526.

19. *Id.* at 534.

20. *Id.* at 535.

21. *Id.* at 536.

22. *Id.* at 537.

23. *Id.* at 537.

24. *Id.* at 538.

25. *Id.* at 538–39.

26. On this "commitment effect," see Donald Langevoort, *Where Were the Lawyers? A Behavioral Inquiry into Lawyers' Responsibility for Clients' Fraud*, 46 VAND. L. REV. 75, 103–4 (1993).

27. Brenda Sapino, *Weil, Gotshal's Mcorp Take Cut $4.4M*, TEX. LAW., Oct. 9, 1995, at 7.

EPILOGUE

1. *The Am Law100: America's Highest Grossing Law Firms in 2002*, AM. LAW., July 2003, 127, 147.

2. Nathan Kopel et al., *Up Go the Walls: In Big Chapter 11 Cases, Papering Over Client Conflicts Is Part of the Game*, AM. LAW., Feb. 2002, 21.

3. Amy Merrick, *Chicago Court Adeptly Attracts Chapter 11 Cases*, WALL ST. J., Dec. 10, 2002, at A1.

4. Douglas G. Baird & Robert K. Rasmussen, *The End of Bankruptcy*, 55 STAN. L. REV. 751 (2002).

5. *See* David A. Skeel Jr., *Creditors' Ball: The "New" New Corporate Governance in Chapter 11*, 152 U. PA. L. REV. 917 (2003).

6. The allegation was made unsuccessfully against Milbank Tweed in the

Enron bankruptcy that the firm arranged for only its clients to bid on the sale of Enron's profitable trading unit. Milbank served in that case as counsel to the unsecured creditors' committee. Exco Corp., et al. v. Milbank, Tweed, Hadley, & McCloy, 2003 WL 2233455 (S.D.N.Y., Feb. 3, 2003).

7. DIANE VAUGAN, CONTROLLING UNLAWFUL ORGANIZATIONAL BEHAVIOR 70 (1983).

8. Elizabeth Chambliss and David B. Wilkins, *Promoting Effective Infrastructure in a Large Law Firm Practice: A Call for Research and Reporting*, 30 HOFSTRA L. REV. 691 (2002); Ted Schneyer, *A Tale of Four Systems: Reflections on How Law Influences the "Ethical Infrastructure" of Law Firms*, 39 S. TEX. L. REV. 245 (1998).

9. *See* Pamela H. Bucy, *Corporate Ethos: A Standard for Imposing Corporate Criminal Liability*, 75 MINN. L. REV. 1095 (1991).

10. Jonathan L. Freedman and Bart R. Schwartz, *Audit Committees of the Boards of Directors: How Much Responsibility Do They Have? How Much Responsibility Should They Have?* 20 ACCA DOCKET 48 (2002).

11. *See* BRIAN CRUVER, ANATOMY OF GREED (2002).

12. *See* BETHANY MCLEAN & PETER ELKIND, THE SMARTEST GUYS IN THE ROOM: THE AMAZING RISE AND SCANDALOUS FALL OF ENRON (2003); Loren Fox, ENRON: THE RISE AND FALL (2002).

13. Bucy, *supra* note 9, at 1129–33.

14. *Id.* at 1133–34.

15. PATRICIA WERHANE, MORAL IMAGINATION AND MANAGEMENT DECISION MAKING 34–35 (1999).

16. Bucy, *supra* note 9, at 1134–35.

17. *Id.*

18. *Id.* at 1138–39.

19. FEDERAL SENTENCING GUIDELINES MANUAL, chap. 8 (2002).

20. Diane E. Murphy, *The Federal Sentencing Guidelines for Organizations: A Decade of Promoting Compliance and Ethics*, 87 IOWA L. REV. 697 (2002); Dan K. Webb and Steven F. Molo, *Some Practical Considerations in Developing Effective Compliance Programs: A Framework for Meeting the Requirements of the Sentencing Guidelines*, 71 WASH. U. L.Q. 375 (1993).

21. Corporate ethics officers, for instance, are responsible for the publication of the periodical ETHIKOS, which focuses on ethics and compliance issues.

22. *See, e.g.*, GABI EBBERS, A COMPARATIVE ANALYSIS OF REGULATORY STRATEGIES IN ACCOUNTING AND THEIR IMPACT ON CORPORATE COMPLIANCE (2001); Kelly Walsh and Roxann Bulman, *Creating a Corporate Compliance Program From Scratch: A Bank of Hawaii Case Study*, 24 ABA BANK COMPLIANCE 20 (2003); H. Lowell Brown, *The Corporate Director's Compliance Oversight Responsibility in the Post-Caremark Era*, 26 DEL. J. CORP. L. 1 (2001); Elizabeth Ryan, *Building an Effective Corporate Compliance Plan*, 51 HEALTHCARE FINANCIAL MGT. 60 (1997).

23. Pub. L. No. 107–204, 116 Stat. 745 (2002) (codified as amended in 15 U.S.C. Sections 7201-7266 and scattered sections of 18 U.S.C.).

24. 15 U.S.C. Section 7245 (Matthew Bender 2004).

25. 17 C.F.R. Part 205 (Lexis 2004).

26. 31 C.F.R. Part 10 (Lexis 2004).

27. 31 C.F.R. Section 10.33 (Lexis 2004).

28. A tax preparer is subject to penalty if any part of an understatement of liability on a return or claim for refund is due to a position "for which there was not a realistic possibility of success." 26 U.S.C. Section 6694(a)(1) (Lexis 2004). That possibility is defined in I.R.S. regulations as "approximately a one in three, or greater, likelihood." 26 C.F.R. 1-6694-2(b). By contrast, the Model Rules of Professional Conduct provide that a lawyer may present a position before a tribunal as long as it is "not frivolous." MODEL RULE 3.1.

29. 26 C.F.R. 1-6694-2(b) (Lexis 2004).

30. George H. Brown, *Financial Institution Lawyers as Quasi-Public Enforcers*, 7 GEO. J. LEGAL ETHICS 637 (1994); *See, e.g.*, FDIC v. Mmhat, 907 F.2d 546 (5th Cir. 1990); FDIC v. Clark, 978 F.2d 1541 (10th Cir. 1992).

31. Notice of Charges, *In re* Fishbein, Katzman, Fisher & Kaye, Scholer, Fierman, Hays & Handler, OTS AP No. 92-19 at 26, P54 (Mar. 1, 1992). *See also*, Order to Cease and Desist, *In re* Fishbein, Katzman, Fisher & Kaye, Scholer, Fierman, Hays & Handler, OTS Ap. No. 92-24, P16(ii) (Mar. 11, 1992). *See also*, Remarks by Harris Weinstein, Chief Counsel, Office of Thrift Supervision, at National Conference of Bar Presidents (August 8, 1992), *summarized in* BNA CORPORATE COUNSEL WEEKLY 4 (August 26, 1992); Speech by OTS Chief Counsel Weinstein on Duties of Depository Institution Fiduciaries, *in* 55 BNA BANKING REP. 508, 510 (1990).

32. 12 C.F.R. Section 513.4(a)(3) (Lexis 2004).

33. 12 C.F.R. Section 513.4(a)(4) (Lexis 2004).

34. 37 C.F.R. Section 1.56 (Lexis 2004).

35. FEDERAL RULE OF CIVIL PROCEDURE 11 (Matthew Bender 2004).

36. Nancy B. Rapoport, *The Intractable Problem of Bankruptcy Ethics: Square Peg, Round Hole*, 11 J. BANKR. LAW & PRACT. 391 (2002).

37. Ted Schneyer, *From Self-Regulation to Bar Corporatism: What the S&L Crisis Means for the Regulation of Lawyers*, 35 S. TEX. L. REV. 639 (1994).

38. *Id.* at 657–58.

39. *Id.* at 671–72.

40. Report of the ABA Task Force on Corporate Responsibility, March 31, 2003, http://www.abanet.org.

NOTES ON SOURCES

ABBREVIATIONS

CCM   Milbank Tweed compensation committee memorandum
GTT   Gellene trial transcript (*United States v. Gellene*, Criminal No. 97-CR-221, E.D. Wis.)
FTT   Fee trial transcript (In Re: B-E Holdings & Bucyrus-Erie Company, Case No. 84-20786 & 20787, U.S. Bankr. Ct., E.D. Wis.)
DSTT Disclosure statement trial transcript (In Re: B-E Holdings & Bucyrus-Erie Company, Case No. 84-20786 & 20787, U.S. Bankr. Ct., E.D. Wis.)
BPT   Bankruptcy proceedings transcript (In Re: B-E Holdings & Bucyrus-Erie Company, Case No. 84-20786 & 20787, U.S. Bankr. Ct., E.D. Wis.)

PROLOGUE

1   Events at arraignment and plea: Arraignment and Plea, GTT, Dec. 12, 1997.

CHAPTER 1

15   Lederman call to Gellene: Gellene testimony, GTT, 1131–32.
15   "800 pound gorilla": Cynthia Revesz testimony, GTT, 465.

CHAPTER 2

50   Gellene background: Gellene testimony, GTT, 1111–14.
51   "gifts of my intellect": Gellene testimony, GTT, 1218.
52   Milbank "extremely competitive": Gellene testimony, GTT, 1119.
52   Working hours: Gellene testimony, GTT, 1119–20.
52   Hours billed 1993: 1993 CCM, Exhibit 361, Gellene trial, B-E4989.
52   Hours billed 1994: 1994 CCM, Exhibit 362, Gellene trial, B-E4981.
53   "works tremendously hard": 1993 CCM, B-E4990.
53   "a very hard worker": 1994 CCM, B-E4982.
53   "tireless worker": 1993 CCM, B-E4990.
53   "overworked": 1994 CCM, B-E4982.
53   "fiendishly hard": 1994 CCM, B-E4978.
53   "share the burden": 1995 CCM, B-E4974.
53   "control freak and a loner": 1994 CCM, B-E4982.
53   "develop better working relationships": 1995 Feedback Message, in 1996 CCM, Exhibit 394, Gellene trial, B-E4959.

379

53 "if I needed help": Gellene testimony, GTT, 1203.

53 "doesn't follow administrative rules": 1993 CCM, B-E4990.

54 "comes into compliance": 1994 CCM, B-E4982.

54 Penalties for delinquent daynotes: 1995 CCM, B-E4971, B-E4972.

54 Summer associate program: 1992 CCM, Exhibit 393, Gellene trial, B-E4984.

54 Recruiting and interviewing: 1994 CCM, B-E4982.

55 Gellene's work with Jerome: Gellene testimony, GTT, 1226–27.

56 Worked "very closely and very intensely" with Jerome: Gellene testimony, GTT, 1126.

56 Jerome "taught me how to be a lawyer": Gellene testimony, GTT, 1127, 1123–27.

57 "a bit of an enigma": 1990 Comments, in 1991 CCM, Exhibit 392, Gellene trial, B-E5013.

57 "can get depressed": 1991 CCM, B-E5012.

57 "gets out on a limb": 1992 CCM, B-E4996.

57 "civilize himself more": 1993 CCM, B-E4990.

58 "engage in practice on the debtor side": 1991 CCM, B-E5009.

58 bankruptcy practice as commodity: 1992 CCM, B-E5006.

58 "too many lawyers": 1992 CCM, B-E5007.

58 "fee-based practice": 1993 CCM, B-E4986.

59 "less business and more competition": 1994 CCM, B-E4978.

59 "pipeline": 1994 CCM, B-E4978.

59 "business has shrunk": 1994 CCM, B-E4978.

59 "find adequate new work": 1993 CCM, B-E4986.

59 concerns about practice management: 1995 CCM, Exhibit 363, Gellene trial, B-E4974.

59 "critical mass of partners": 1991 CCM, B-E5009.

59 "crush of daily work": 1991 CCM, B-E5009.

59 "staffing and business development": 1991 CCM, B-E5009.

59 "what drove the process last year": 1991 CCM, B-E5010.

59 "higher principle": 1991 CCM, B-E5011.

59 "unfavorable market developments": 1993 CCM, B-E4987.

59 "under-performers": 1992 CCM, B-E5007.

60 "creates anxiety in 100 percent": 1992 CCM, B-E5007.

60 Bar membership problem: Gellene testimony, GTT, 1114–18, 1123–27; Edward A. Adams, *Bar Groups to Curb Unlicensed Lawyers*, N.Y.L.J., Dec. 21, 1989, at A1.

62 Reinstatement at Milbank: Gellene testimony, GTT, 1128–29.

62 1991 compensation committee memo: Exhibit 392, Gellene trial.

63 Lederman's background and career are set forth in LAWRENCE LEDERMAN, TOMBSTONES: A LAWYER'S TALES FROM THE TAKEOVER DECADES (1992).

65 Milbank's Executive Committee report on Lederman: Memorandum to Partners Re: Lawrence Lederman, Oct. 28, 1991 (Exhibit 360, Gellene trial).

66 Lederman departure from Wachtell: Paul M. Barrett, *Inside a White-Shoe Law Firm's Conflict Case*, WALL ST. J., Jan. 23, 1998, A1; Laurie P.

Cohen, *A Former Partner Throws the Book at His Law Firm*, WALL ST. J., June 7, 1991, at B4.

70 "no longer Jerome's boy": 1991 CCM, B-E5013.
70 "exiting my orbit": 1994 CCM, B-E4982.

CHAPTER 3

72 Background on Becor Western is contained in GEORGE B. ANDERSON, ONE HUNDRED BOOMING YEARS: A HISTORY OF BUCYRUS-ERIE COMPANY 1880–1980 (1980); Prospectus, B-E Holdings, Inc., and Proxy Statement, Becor Western, Inc., for the Leveraged Buy-Out of Becor Western (LBO Prospectus and Proxy Statement), Nov. 3, 1987, at 25; and Goelzer testimony, GTT, 99–102.

74 Background on the LBO is contained in the LBO Prospectus and Proxy Statement at 25–30.

74 The terms of the capital structure for the new enterprises created by the LBO are set forth in the LBO Prospectus and Proxy Statement at 71–82.

76 Salovaara's background is described in Strom, *Investment Vulture*; and HILLARY ROSENBERG, THE VULTURE INVESTORS 319–20 (2000).

77 Formation of Broad Street: Eckert testimony, GTT, 563; DAVID P. MCCAFFREY AND DAVID W. HART, WALL STREET POLICES ITSELF: HOW SECURITIES' FIRMS MANAGE THE CASE HAZARDS OF COMPETITIVE PRESSURES (1998).

78 Dependence on dividends: LBO Prospectus and Proxy Statement at 13.
78 Company Outlook after LBO: Goelzer testimony, GTT, 116–17.
78 On defaults on debt in the late 1980s and early 1990s, see ROSENBERG, THE VULTURE INVESTORS at 16–17.

80 Events surrounding Goldman purchase of 9 percent bonds: Salovaara, May 25, 1994, deposition read into record, DSTT, 586–91.

80 Exchange offer: Salovaara, May 25, 1994, deposition, DSTT, 582–91; Goelzer testimony, GTT, 117–19; Bucyrus-Erie Solicitation of Consents to Exchange offer, Dec. 13, 1988.

80 Goldman profits from exchange offer: *The Issue Is Failure to Disclose: Should Milbank Tweed Be Required to Disgorge $1.8 Million Fee?* 31 BANKR. COURT DEC. (Sept. 16, 1997), at A1, A9.

82 Sale of notes to JNL: Goelzer testimony, GTT, 122–24.

84 Background on vulture investment: *see generally* ROSENBERG, THE VULTURE INVESTORS.

86 Events involving Water Street: ROSENBERG, THE VULTURE INVESTORS at 320–27; LISA ENDLICH, GOLDMAN SACHS: THE CULTURE OF SUCCESS 126–27 (2000); Eckert testimony, GTT, 563–66.

86 "Chinese Wall in the middle of his brain": ROSENBERG, THE VULTURE INVESTORS at 323.

87 Formation of Greycliff and South Street: Eckert testimony, GTT, 565–71.

87 Cash flow problems: Goelzer testimony, GTT, 127–28; Interview with David Goelzer, Milwaukee, Wisconsin, November 14–15, 2001.

88 Bucyrus switch to Milbank: Goelzer testimony, GTT, 125–27; Declaration

of John G. Gellene to U.S. Bankruptcy Court, E.D. Wis., Dec. 3, 1997, exhibit containing Goelzer notes, BCF 249042, BCF 245306, BCF 249039–40, BCF 245294, BCF 249032, BCF 245282–83, BCF 245278–81; Goelzer interview.

88 Discussion of Bucyrus financial alternatives in 1991–92: Exhibit to Gellene declaration, Dec. 3, 1997, BCF 246864–65, BCF 246854–56, BCF 246843–44.

89 Deloitte and Touche statement: Goelzer testimony, GTT, 126–27, Goelzer interview.

89 "Credit card had been closed": Interview with David Goelzer, Milwaukee, Wisconsin, Nov. 14, 2001.

89 Discussions re: South Street financing: Exhibit to Gellene declaration, Dec. 3, 1997, BCF 246843–44, BCF 246947–53, BCF 246950–53.

90 South Street does not want to be insider: Goelzer June 26, 1992, notes, exhibit to Gellene declaration, Dec. 3, 1997, BCF 246956–59.

91 Terms of South Street financing: Goelzer testimony, GTT, 131–35; Disclosure Statement and Proxy Statement for Proposed Reorganization Plan, Jan. 12, 1994, 13–14.

92 Downturn in last quarter of 1992: Goelzer testimony, GTT, 548.

94 Bucyrus, Nov. 19, 1992, meeting with Houlihan, Lokey: Goelzer testimony, GTT, 136, 321–24; interview with David Goelzer, Milwaukee, Wisconsin, Nov. 14–15, 2001; interview with Jeff Werbalowsky, Minneapolis, Minnesota, Sept. 25, 2002.

94 Lederman needs to designate bankruptcy lawyer: Goelzer testimony, GTT, 324.

CHAPTER 4

97 February 20, 1993, meeting: Gellene testimony, GTT, 1133–37; Goelzer testimony, GTT, 139–42; interview with David Goelzer, Milwaukee, Wisconsin, Nov. 14–15, 2001.

97 Press release: Goelzer testimony, GTT, 142; Goelzer testimony, FTT, 549.

99 Hours billed by Gellene for BR case through plan confirmation: FTT, 630 (1119.7 hours).

100 Chapter 11 of the Bankruptcy Code is set forth at 11 U.S.C. 1101–74.

100 On the history of U.S. bankruptcy law, see DAVID A. SKEEL, DEBT'S DOMINION: A HISTORY OF BANKRUPTCY LAW IN AMERICA (2001).

103 More than two thousand creditors: Gellene testimony, GTT, 1155.

103 Unofficial bondholders committee: Victor testimony, DSTT, 144–48.

104 Gellene contact with Goelzer: Goelzer testimony, GTT, 233; Interview with David Goelzer, Milwaukee, Wisconsin, Nov. 14, 2001.

104 March 31 meeting: Goelzer testimony, GTT, 143–44; Interview with David Goelzer, Milwaukee, Wisconsin, Nov. 14, 2001.

105 Salovaara main negotiator for South Street: Goelzer testimony, GTT, 183; Interview with David Goelzer, Milwaukee, Wisconsin, Nov. 14, 2001; Interview with Jeff Werbalowsky, Minneapolis, Minnesota, Sept. 25, 2002.

105 Werbalowsky meeting with Bank One: Interview with Jeff Werbalowsky, Minneapolis, Minnesota, Sept. 25, 2002.

105 Werbalowsky report about difficulties: Goelzer testimony, GTT, 162.

105 Lederman providing information on Salovaara: Goelzer testimony, GTT, 179–80, 368–69.

105 Gellene contact with Salovaara: Goelzer testimony, GTT, 364–65.

106 June 1993 meeting with Salovaara: Goelzer testimony, GTT, 212–13.

107 July 16, 1993, Gellene report to Goelzer: Goelzer testimony, GTT, 179–80.

107 July 28, 1993, discussion: Goelzer testimony, GTT, 180–84.

108 Stark background: Rachel Brash, *Inside Moves: The Man Who Blew the Whistle on Milbank*, AM. LAW., May 1998, at 47; *Bloomberg Profile: PPM's John Stark Brings Activism to Bonds*, BLOOMBERG NEWS, Aug. 10, 1993, 1.

108 Marriott lawsuit and "bondholders were left howling": *Bloomberg Profile*, Aug. 10, 1993, at 1.

108 Stark 1990 visit to Bucyrus: Stark testimony, FTT, 905–8.

108 Bucyrus press release: Stark testimony, FTT, 920–21.

109 March 1993 Stark and Gellene meeting: Gellene testimony, GTT, 1145–48,1151.

109 Anderson, Kill request for documents: Gellene testimony, GTT, 1148–50.

110 JNL refusal to join creditors' committee: Stark testimony, FTT, 930–33; Victor testimony, DSTT, 151–52.

111 Gellene fax of complaint: Interview with David Goelzer, Milwaukee, Wisconsin, Nov. 14, 2001.

111 JNL draft fraudulent conveyance complaint: Goelzer testimony, GTT, 146–50; Interview with David Goelzer, Milwaukee, Wisconsin, Nov. 14, 2001; Draft Complaint and Demand for Trial by Jury, Jackson National Life Insurance Co. v. Goldman, Sachs & Co., Inc. et al., April 1993 (Exhibit 6, Gellene trial).

117 April 23 meetings: Goelzer testimony, GTT, 151–59.

118 "[Other] bondholders' interests must be extinguished": Outline of Gellene Testimony for Fee Trial, Nov. 25, 1995, Draft, B-E 5297 (Exhibit 422, Gellene trial).

118 Milbank responsibility for "good faith" letter: Goelzer testimony, GTT, 166–68.

122 May 1993 Bucyrus proposals: Stark testimony, FTT, 940–43.

122 May 1993 JNL counterproposal: Stark testimony, FTT, 943–46 (Exhibit 371, Gellene trial).

122 Possible JNL hostility to Houlihan: Werbalowsky testimony, DSTT, 608–9, 611–13.

122 Tolling agreement: Disclosure Statement and Proxy Statement for Proposed Reorganization Plan at 17.

123 South Street negotiations: Disclosure Statement and Proxy Statement for Proposed Reorganization Plan at 21.

124 Calculation of potential claims against Goldman: Gellene testimony, FTT, 329.

125 Intention not to send draft plan to JNL: Goelzer testimony, DSTT, 77–78.

125 Mistaken distribution of solicitation of material to JNL: Goelzer testimony, DSTT, 83–85; Stark testimony, FTT, 962–64.

126 Stark Sept. 21, 1993, letter to Mork: Exhibit 213, fee trial.

126 JNL termination of Milbank in Phar-Mor: Stark testimony, FTT, 971.

126 Nov. 4, 1993, meeting: Werbalowsky testimony, DSTT, 602–4; Stark testimony, FTT, 976–78.

127 Dec. 20, 1993, letter: Exhibit 213, fee trial.

127 Three options: Goelzer testimony, FTT, 587–90.

128 Danger of "piecemeal sale": Werbalowsky testimony, DSTT, 605.

128 Terms of Bucyrus reorganization plan: Exhibit 371, Gellene trial.

130 Werbalowsky-Gellene disagreement on Goldman release: Goelzer testimony, GTT, 192–95; Werbalowsky interview.

131 Gellene reasons for release: Goelzer testimony, GTT, 195.

132 Milbank issuance of "good faith" opinion: Exhibit 4, Gellene trial.

132 1993 compensation committee memo: Exhibit 361, Gellene trial.

134 "Circus": Interview with David Goelzer, Milwaukee, Wisconsin, Nov. 15, 2001.

134 Successful push to file petition: Gellene testimony, GTT, 1179–82.

CHAPTER 5

136 Prepetition meetings with Byrnes: Byrnes testimony, GTT, 896; interview with John Byrnes, Milwaukee, Wisconsin, Nov. 15, 2001.

137 First-day hearing transcript: BPT, Feb. 18, 1994, 3–148.

137 Colloquy between Gellene and Eisenberg: BPT, Feb. 18, 1994, 11–13.

137 Colloquy between Arnold and Eisenberg: BPT, Feb. 18, 1994, 15–16.

138 Gellene on "South Street funds": BPT, Feb. 18, 1994, 17–18.

138 Eisenberg, "gist of what I'm hearing": BPT, Feb. 18, 1994, 20–21.

138 Colloquy between Gellene and Eisenberg: BPT, Feb. 18, 1994, 21–22.

139 Colloquy between Arnold and Eisenberg: BPT, Feb. 18, 1994, 30–33.

139 Eisenberg block quote: BPT, Feb. 25, 1994, 141–42.

140 Colloquy between Eisenberg and Gellene: BPT, Feb. 25, 1994, 142–46.

140 Rahl comments: BPT, Feb. 25, 1994, 145–46.

144 Social and professional relationship among Lederman, Salovaara, and Eckert: Eckert testimony, GTT, 578.

144 Social relationship between Lederman and Salovaara: Paul M. Barrett, *Inside a White-Shoe Law Firm's Conflicts Case*, WALL ST. J., Jan. 23, 1998, at B1, B5.

144 Salovaara and Eckert dispute: Eckert testimony, GTT, 577–81.

144 Milbank involvement on behalf of Salovaara: Lichstein testimony, GTT, 688–89.

145 New case memo regarding work on Salovaara-Eckert dispute: Exhibit 381, Gellene trial.

145 Conflict search for Eckert and Primerica: Exhibit 382, Gellene trial.

145 New case memo regarding work on Eckert estate planning: Exhibit 383, Gellene trial.

145 Lederman said no problem: Lichstein testimony, GTT, 754.

145 "Mikael ha[s] a deal for us": Gellene testimony, GTT, 1165.

145 Details of Busse matter: Gellene testimony, GTT, 1165–70.

146 Lederman asked Gellene to join discussion: Gellene testimony, GTT, 1171.

146 Salovaara on speaker phone: Gellene testimony GTT, 1174.

146 Time billed on Dec. 9 and Dec. 19: Exhibit 14, B-E 003785, Gellene trial.

146 Gellene conversation with Salovaara: Gellene testimony, GTT, 1175–76; Lichstein testimony, GTT, 696–97.

146 Discussion of possible conflict: Gellene testimony, GTT, 1177–78; Lichstein testimony, GTT, 693–96.

147 Gellene billed 1.7 hrs.: Exhibit 20, B-E 003827, Gellene trial.

147 New case memo and conflicts check regarding work on Busse: Exhibit 353, Gellene trial.

147 Lichstein work on Salovaara-Eckert dispute: Exhibit 20, Gellene trial.

147 Lichstein conversation about Salovaara's deposition: Lichstein testimony, GTT, 699.

147 Busse purchase agreement: Exhibit 16, Gellene trial.

148 Gellene conversation with Lederman: Gellene testimony, GTT, 1181–84.

148 Time billed on Busse: Exhibit 14, Gellene trial.

149 Time billed on Salovaara-Eckert dispute: Exhibit 20, Gellene trial.

149 Bucyrus request to retain Milbank: Exhibit 7, Gellene trial.

149 Milbank drafted Bucyrus request: Goelzer testimony, GTT, 205–6.

149 Gellene affidavit: Exhibit 22, Gellene trial.

149 "Equity security holders" and "institutional creditors": Gellene testimony, GTT, 1186–87.

150 Goelzer comments on Milbank representation of Goldman: Goelzer testimony, GTT, 207–9.

150 Milbank removal would be "cataclysmic": Goelzer testimony, GTT, 402.

150 JNL opposition to Milbank retention: Exhibit 419, Gellene trial.

152 Eisenberg remarks at Feb. 24, 1994, hearing: Read into the record during testimony of Byrnes, GTT, 979–86.

152 Byrnes objection to Milbank retention: Exhibit 24, Gellene trial.

153 Eisenberg remarks at March 17, 1994, hearing: Read into the record during testimony of Byrnes, GTT, 1002–9.

153 Eisenberg remarks at March 23, 1994, hearing: Read into the record during testimony of Byrnes, GTT, 1009–22.

153 "New York is different from Milwaukee": Read into the record during Byrnes testimony, GTT, 916.

153 "Just clean up our papers": Gellene testimony, GTT, 1188.

154 Gellene's sense that Eisenberg would be reluctant to disqualify Milbank: Gellene testimony, GTT, 1189.

154 Supplemental affidavit: Exhibit 27, Gellene trial.

155 Lichstein involvement in bankruptcy case discovery: Lichstein testimony, GTT, 699–700.

155 Lichstein work on Salovaara-Eckert dispute: Exhibit 20, Gellene trial.

155 Lichstein attendance at South Street investors meeting: Lichstein testimony: GTT, 700–703.

156 Lichstein conversation with Gellene about potential conflict: Lichstein testimony, GTT, 703–4.

156 Lichstein belated discovery of firewall: Lichstein testimony, GTT, 704–5.

156 Lichstein discussions with Lederman about potential conflict: Lichstein testimony, GTT, 705–6.

156 Milbank billing on Salovaara-Eckert dispute: Exhibit 20, Gellene trial.

156 Dec. 23, 1994, memorandum: Exhibit 49, Gellene trial.

157 Colorado court notice of claim transfer: Exhibit 52, Gellene trial.

157 Gellene billing on Busse: Exhibit 14, Gellene trial.

157 Nov. 8, 1994, memorandum: Exhibit 48, Gellene trial.

157 Milbank billing records on Busse: Exhibit 14, Gellene trial.

159 JNL request to file alternative plan: Stark testimony, Dec. 6, 1995, 1009–12.

159 "Sweeps under the prepack rug": Arnold opening statement, DSTT, 11.

159 JNL's objections to the disclosure statement and proposed amendments to it are set forth in Jackson National Life Company's Specific Proposed Changes to the Prepetition Disclosure Statement, filed June 13, 1994.

159 JNL claim that plan would never have been approved: DSTT, May 26, 1994, 52.

160 Bucyrus refusal to amend disclosure statement: Gellene testimony, FTT, Nov. 30, 1995, 390–92.

161 Eisenberg block quote: DSTT, May 26, 1994, 41.

161 Rahl statements: DSTT, May 26, 1994, 49–50.

161 Colloquy between Rahl and Eisenberg: DSTT, May 26, 1994, 51–53.

163 Lederman prepetition "relationship partner": Gellene testimony, FTT, 321–22.

163 Lederman Bucyrus bankruptcy billings: Milbank, Tweed, Hadley, McCloy, Attorney Summary, Bucyrus-Erie Chapter 11, MT008635.

163 Gellene "just totally running the show": Interview with David Goelzer, Milwaukee, Wisconsin, Nov. 15, 2001.

163 Revesz transfer: Interview with David Goelzer, Milwaukee, Wisconsin, Nov. 15, 2001.

163 "Always rushed": Interview with David Goelzer, Milwaukee, Wisconsin, Nov. 15, 2001.

163 JNL document request: Gellene testimony, FTT, Nov. 29, 1995, 168–71; JNL Request for Production of Documents, In the Matters of B-E Holdings, Inc. and Bucyrus-Erie Co., March 4, 1994.

163 Bucyrus response to JNL document request: Gellene testimony, FTT, Nov. 29, 1995, 171–74, 179–81, Response of Debtors to Jackson National's Request for Production of Documents, In re: B-E Holdings, Inc. and Bucyrus-Erie Co., Mar. 22, 1994.

164 Goldman refusal to produce documents: Gellene testimony, FTT, Dec. 1, 1995, 451–52.

164 JNL motion: Gellene testimony, FTT, Nov. 30, 1995, 198.

164 Creditors' committee support of JNL motion: Rochelle, Nov. 22, 1995, deposition read into the record FTT, Dec. 5, 1995, 843–44.

164 Rochelle's conversation with Gellene: Memorandum from William J. Rochelle III, to official Committee of Unsecured Creditors of Bucyrus-Erie Company, Apr. 18, 1994 (Exhibit 204, fee trial).

164 Decision to produce Bucyrus documents: Gellene testimony, FTT, Nov. 30, 1995, 210–11, 225–28.

164 Document production activity: Gellene testimony, FTT, Nov. 30, 242–45; Interview with David Goelzer, Milwaukee, Wisconsin, Nov. 15, 2001.

165 Depositions: List of Depositions on file.

165 Conflict over six-hour rule: Arnold question during Gellene testimony, FTT, Nov. 30, 1995, 261–62.

165 1,288 objections to form: Colloquy between Eisenberg and Arnold, FTT, 12.

166 Gellene declined to meet with creditors' committee: Gellene testimony, FTT, Nov. 30, 1995, 239–42.

166 April 27 memorandum: Memorandum from William J. Rochelle III and David A. Rosenzweig to Official Committee of Unsecured Creditors of Bucyrus-Erie Co., Apr. 27, 1994 (Exhibit 206, Fee Trial).

167 April 18 memo: Memorandum from Rochelle to Creditors Committee, Apr. 18, 1994. The emphasis is Rochelle's.

168 April 27 Rochelle conclusion about confirmation: Memorandum from Fulbright & Jaworski to Official Committee of Unsecured Creditors Re: Minutes of May 17, 1994, Committee Meeting, June 30, 1994, 2 (Exhibit 208, Fee Trial).

168 May 17 conference call: *Id.*

168 May 23 conference call: Memorandum from Fulbright & Jaworski to official Committee of Unsecured Creditors Re: minutes of May 23, 1994, Committee meeting, June 30, 1994 (Exhibit 209, Fee Trial).

169 Committee vote to support disclosure statement: Stark testimony, FTT, Dec. 6, 1995, 1107–8.

169 Examiner's Report: Report of the Examiner, June 13, 1994, In the Matter of B-E Holdings, Inc. and Bucyrus-Erie Company.

170 JNL disclosure statement amendment: Jackson National Life Insurance Company's Specific Environmental Changes to the Pre-petition Disclosure Statement, filed June 13, 1994.

172 Byrnes motion for sanctions: Gellene testimony, FTT, Dec. 1, 1995, 461–62.

CHAPTER 6

174 Gellene opening argument: DSTT, June 16, 1994, 4–10.

175 Arnold opening statement: DSTT, June 16, 1994, 10–19.

175 Goelzer testimony: DSTT, June 16, 1994, 41–90.

176 Werbalowsky testimony: DSTT, June 16, 1994, 91–139.

177 Colloquy between Rahl and Werbalowsky: DSTT, June 16, 1994, 137–39.

177 Victor testimony: DSTT, June 1994, 142–207.

178 Radecki testimony: DSTT, June 16, 1994, 209–89; Feb 17, 1994, 296–442.

179 Discussion among Radecki, Stark, and Rahl during break: DSTT, June 17, 1994, 350–53.

180 Radecki looking to audience while testifying: DSTT, June 17, 1994, 379–81.

181 Radecki estimate of equity to which JNL entitled: DSTT, June 17, 1994, 419.

181 Eisenberg irritation at Radecki: DSTT, June 17, 1994, 420–21.

181 Verville testimony: DSTT, June 17, 1994, 456–99.

182 Stark testimony: DSTT, June 17, 1994, 514–71.

182 Stark list of problems with disclosure statement: DSTT, June 17, 1994, 515–21.

183 Salovaara deposition read into record: DSTT, June 17, 1994, 578–91.

184 Eisenberg on research following two separate tracks: DSTT, June 17, 1994, 619.

184 Gellene closing argument: DSTT, June 20, 1994, 625–53, 728–35.

185 Arnold closing argument: DSTT, June 20, 1994, 674–719.

185 Byrnes closing argument: DSTT, June 20, 1994, 719–28.

186 Eisenberg decision: DSTT, June 20, 1994, 742–813.

189 Werbalowsky conversation with Stark: Interview with Jeff Werbalowsky, Minneapolis, Minnesota, Sept. 25, 2002.

189 Stark negotiations with Bucyrus after Eisenberg decision: Stark testimony, FTT, Dec. 6, 1995, 1129–75.

189 August 12 conversation between Rahl and Werbalowsky: Rahl testimony, FTT, Jan. 19, 1996, 321.

190 August 15 meetings: Rahl testimony, FTT, Jan. 19, 1996, 322–24.

190 Discussions between Rahl and Preston on intercompany claim: Rahl testimony FTT, Jan. 19, 1996, 324–26.

191 Eventual reduction of holding company value to 8.5 percent: Rahl testimony, FTT, Jan. 19, 1996, 341.

191 Final negotiations: Outline of Gellene Testimony for Fee Trial, Nov. 28, 1995, Draft, B-E 5325 (Exhibit 423, Gellene trial).

191 Terms of final plan: Second Amendment Joint Plan of Reorganization of B-E Holdings, Inc. and Bucyrus-Erie Company under Chapter 11 of the Bankruptcy Code as Modified Dec. 1, 1994, Conformed Copy Dec. 8, 1994; Supplement to Disclosure Statement and Proxy Statement—Prospectus for the Solicitation of Votes for the Second Amended Joint Plan of Reorganization.

192 Goldman objection and settlement: Outline of Gellene Testimony for Fee Trial, B-E 5326.

192 1994 compensation committee memo: Exhibit 362, Gellene trial.

194 Milbank fee request: Gellene statement, FTT, Apr. 18, 1996, 721–25, 891–93.

194 JNL fee request: Arnold closing argument, FTT, April 18, 1996, 787.

195 JNL willingness to accept stock: Arnold statement, FTT, Nov. 29, 1995, at 6.

195 Bucyrus opposition to JNL fee request: Gellene testimony, GTT, 1198.

195　Trustee's opposition to JNL fee request: Byrnes's testimony, GTT, 932–33.

195　JNL objection to Milbank fee request: Princi statement, FTT, Dec. 5, 1995, 867; Jackson National Life Insurance Company's objection to the Final Application of Milbank, Tweed, Hadley & McCloy for Allowance of Compensation and Reimbursement of Expenses, March 31, 1995 (Exhibit 340, Gellene trial).

195　"Sacrifice value for speed": JNL objection to Milbank compensation request, 18.

195　Gelfand involvement in fee trial: Gelfand testimony, GTT, 790–95, 825–52.

196　Gellene testimony: FTT, Nov. 29, 1995, 41–193; Nov. 30, 1995, 197–403; Dec. 1, 1995, 408–527.

196　Reference to affidavits in Gellene testimony: Gellene testimony, FTT, Nov. 29, 1995, 90–93.

196　Milbank representation of Goldman: Gellene testimony, FTT, Nov. 30, 1995, 316–17.

198　18.5 hours: Gellene testimony, FTT, Dec. 1, 1995, 465–66.

198　Father's Day: Gellene testimony, FTT, Dec. 1, 1995, 525.

198　Lotus Cab colloquy: FTT, Dec. 4, 1995, 534–37.

199　"Spread a bit too thin": Goelzer testimony, FTT, 611–12.

199　Lotus Cab colloquy on additional information: FTT, Jan. 29, 1996, 548–55.

200　Byrnes closing argument: FTT, Apr. 18, 1996, 857–90.

201　Eisenberg fee decision: FTT, May 31, 1996, 955–1132.

201　Eisenberg comments on Milbank representation of Goldman: FTT, May 31, 1996, 999–1001.

202　"Most litigious, angry, and bitter cases": FTT, May 31, 1996, 1066.

CHAPTER 7

205　Conversation between Lichstein and Edelman: Lichstein testimony, GTT, 707–8.

205　Gellene transfer to M&A practice: Gellene testimony, GTT, 1200–1203.

206　Gellene billable hours through Nov. 1995: Exhibit 363.

207　Events in Busse matter: Jessop testimony, GTT, 605–19.

208　Hindes discussion with Gellene about documents in late July: Hindes testimony, GTT, 635–37.

209　Stark discovery of Milbank tie to Salovaara: Rachel Brash, *Inside Moves: The Man Who Blew the Whistle on Milbank*, AM. LAW., May 1998, at 47.

209　Dec. 12, 1996, JNL motion: Memorandum of Law in Support of JNL's Rule 9024 Motion (Exhibit 42, Gellene trial).

210　Block quote from JNL memorandum of law: Exhibit 42, 17.

211　Gellene receipt of motion: Gellene testimony, GTT, 1204–7.

211　Lichstein attempts to get documents connected with JNL motion: Lichstein testimony, GTT, 707–11.

211　JNL memo of law had no date: Exhibit 43, Gellene trial.

212 Milbank partners' meeting: Lichstein testimony, GTT, 711–14.
212 Lichstein's continued efforts to obtain documents: Lichstein testimony, GTT, 714–15, 716.
212 Lichstein noticed affidavit was dated Dec. 12, 1996: Lichstein testimony, GTT, 715–16.
213 Gellene meeting with Lichstein and Gelfand: Lichstein testimony, GTT, 716–18, 764–65, Gelfand testimony, GTT, 802–4.
213 Gellene's last day at Milbank: Gellene testimony, GTT, 1214.
213 Gellene on medical leave: Kurt Eichenwald, *Milbank, Tweed Is Accused of a Conflict*, N.Y. TIMES, Feb. 28, 1997, at D2.
214 "Very seriously" and "thoroughly and completely respond": *Id.*
214 Blauner on continuation of JNL effort to reduce Milbank fees: Paul M. Barrett, *Law Firm Milbank Faces Accusation of Conflict of Interest in Bucyrus Case*, WALL ST. J., Feb. 28, 1997, at A9.
214 "Conflict is incredible": *Id.*
214 Gelfand conducted preliminary investigation: Matthew Goldstein, *Milbank Partners Hire Counsel in Fee Suit*, N.Y.L.J., Oct. 1, 1997, 1.
214 Gelfand affidavit regarding motions: Eichenwald, *Milbank, Tweed Is Accused of a Conflict*, D2.
214 Extension until March 21: Cary Spivak, *Bucyrus Accuses Law Firm of Conflict*, MILWAUKEE JOURNAL-SENTINEL ONLINE, Mar. 4, 1997.
214 Gellene assistance in Milbank investigation: Gellene testimony, GTT, 1214.
214 Gellene March affidavit to bankruptcy court: Declaration of John Gellene, In The Matter of B-E Holdings and Bucyrus-Erie Company, Mar. 12, 1997.
214 Milbank April 30 response: Cary Spivak, *Lawyer Admits Conflicts*, MILWAUKEE JOURNAL-SENTINEL, May 2, 1997, at B1; Paul M. Barrett, *Milbank Admits It Didn't Disclose Conflict*, WALL ST. J., May 2, 1997, at B18.
215 Bucyrus brief in response: Cary Spivak, *Bucyrus Demands Fine for Law Firm*, MILWAUKEE JOURNAL-SENTINEL, May 16, 1997, at B1.
215 Byrnes comment: Karen Donovan, *"No Conflict Existed," Milbank Says, Sorry, But . . .* NAT'L. L.J., June 9, 1997, at A4.
215 Broader scheme to benefit Salovaara: *The Issue Is Disclosure: Should Milbank Tweed Be Required to Disgorge $1.8 Million Fee?* 31 BANKRUPTCY COURT DEC., Sept. 16, 1997, 3, at A1, A10.
216 "Absolute rubbish": Roger Lowenstein, *Why Milbank Tweed Has Deep Regret*, WALL ST. J., May 22, 1997, at C1.
216 "[I]f an apology after the fact . . .": *Id.*
216 Eisenberg ruling on Rule 2014 violation: Cary Spivak, *Trial to Decide Whether Bucyrus to Get Fees*, MILWAUKEE JOURNAL-SENTINEL, June 7, 1997, at B1.
216 Byrnes motion: *Briefly . . .* , NAT'L. L.J., Aug. 11, 1997, at A5.
216 Goelzer work with Lammiman: Interview with David Goelzer, Milwaukee, Wisconsin, Nov. 15, 2001.
217 Byrnes notification of Biskupic: Interview with Steven Biskupic, Milwaukee, Wisconsin, Nov. 15, 2001.
217 Byrnes "laid out the paper trail": Paul M. Barrett, *How Ex-Milbank*

Partner Gellene Ended Up on Trial over a Conflict, WALL ST. J., Feb. 23, 1998, at B6.

217 "Venerable local company": *Id.*

218 Grand jury began to subpoena documents: Matthew Goldstein, *Grand Jury Subpoenas Issued in Inquiry on Milbank Conflict*, N.Y.L.J., June 11, 1997, at 1.

218 Biskupic background: Interview with Steven Biskupic, Milwaukee, Wisconsin, Nov. 15, 2001.

218 Bankruptcy fraud cases in Milwaukee U.S. Attorney's Office: Biskupic interview.

218 Biskupic approach to and conduct of investigation: Biskupic interview.

220 Gellene application for admission to practice in federal court in Milwaukee: Exhibit 39, Gellene trial.

221 Rotert background: Interview with Mark Rotert, Chicago, Illinois, Nov. 14, 2001.

221 Rotert involvement in and investigation of Gellene case: Interview with Mark Rotert, Chicago, Illinois, Nov. 14, 2001.

222 American Industrial Partners acquisition of Bucyrus: Tony Anderson, *Investment Firm to Buy Bucyrus*, DAILY REPORTER, July 31, 1977, at 1; Kathleen Gallagher, *Investment Firm Buying Bucyrus*, MILWAUKEE JOURNAL-SENTINEL, Aug. 1, 1997, at B1; Alby Gallon, *Investors Agonize over Bucyrus International Acquisition*, BUS. J., Aug. 8, 1977, at 6.

223 Denial of Milbank motion for protective order: Matthew Goldstein, *Milbank Partners Face Deposition in Forfeiture Suit*, N.Y.L.J., Aug. 25, 1997, at 1.

223 Biskupic meeting with Gellene: Interview with Mark Rotert, Chicago, Illinois, Nov. 14, 2001; Interview with Steven Biskupic, Milwaukee, Wisconsin, Nov. 15, 2001.

224 Withdrawal of misdemeanor plea agreement: Interview with Mark Rotert, Chicago, Illinois, Nov. 14, 2001; Interview with Steven Biskupic, Milwaukee, Wisconsin, Nov. 15, 2001.

225 "wasn't a close call": Interview with Steven Biskupic, Milwaukee, Wisconsin, Nov. 15, 2001.

226 Bucyrus suit against Milbank: Cary Spivak, *Bucyrus Sues Law Firm over Conflict Allegation*, MILWAUKEE JOURNAL-SENTINEL, Sept. 26, 1997, at 1; *Milbank Tweed Sued by a Former Client in Bankruptcy Case*, WALL ST. J., Sept. 26, 1997; Tony Anderson, DAILY REP., Sept. 26, 1997, at 1.

227 Milbank motion to seal documents and depositions: Cary Spivak, *Judge opens Bucyrus Documents*, MILWAUKEE JOURNAL-SENTINEL, Oct. 2, 1997, at 2D.

227 Gellene deposition testimony: *Milbank Client Instructed Firm to Conceal Conflict*, WALL ST. J., Oct. 15, 1997, at 1.

227 Salovaara deposition testimony: *Salovaara Denies He Asked Milbank to Keep Tie Secret*, WALL ST. J., Oct. 29, 1997, at 1.

227 Gellene: Lederman on Salovaara request to keep representation confidential: Paul Barrett, *Inside a White-Shoe Law Firm's Conflicts Case*, WALL ST. J., Jan. 23, 1998, at A1.

227 Lederman and Lichstein testimony: Goldstein, *Milbank Partners Hire Counsel*, at 1.

228 $600,000 claim: Matthew Goldstein, *Milbank Agrees to Refund Fee of $1.9 Million in Settlement*, N.Y.L.J., Dec. 18, 1997, at 1.

228 Stark comments: 31 BANKR. COURT DEC., *The Issue Is Disclosure: Should Milbank Tweed Be Required to Disgorge $1.8 Million Fee?* Sept. 16, 1997, A12.

228 "No way to turn back the clocks": *Id.* at A9.

228 Westbrook comment: *Id.* at A11.

229 "Blatant scheme" or "conflict on the surface": *Id.* at A9.

229 November 1: Declaration of John G. Gellene, to U.S. Bankruptcy Court, E.D. Wis. Dec. 3, 1997.

229 Nov. 18 memo: *Update*, N.Y. LAW J., Nov. 21, 1997, at 1; *Milbank Fires Partner Allegedly Involved in Conflict of Interest*, WALL ST. J., Nov. 21, 1997, at B8A.

229 Speculation about expulsion: Paul M. Barrett, *Milbank Tweed Ex-Partner Convicted*, WALL ST. J., Mar. 4, 1998, at B13.

229 Dec. 3 Gellene affidavit: Gellene declaration, Dec. 3, 1997.

229 Goelzer's notes: Attachment to Gellene declaration, Dec. 3, 1997.

230 Gellene indictment: United States v. John G. Gellene, Indictment, Dec. 9, 1997.

231 Maximum sentence: Cary Spivak, *Lawyer Indicted in Bucyrus Case*, MILWAUKEE JOURNAL-SENTINEL, Dec. 10, 1997, at D1, 8.

231 "Just a mistake": Spivak, *Lawyer Indicted in Bucyrus Case*, at D8.

231 Milbank statement after Gellene indictment: Spivak, *Lawyer Indicted in Bucyrus Case*, at D8.

231 Settlement of disgorgement suit: Paul M. Barrett, *Milbank Agrees to Repay Ex-Client $1.9 Million in Fees to End Litigation*, WALL ST. J., Dec. 18, 1997, at B10; Goldstein, *Milbank Agrees to Refund Fee*, at 1.

232 Gibbons involvement: Anna Snider, *Bucyrus Role Continues to Haunt Milbank*, N.Y.L.J., Apr. 15, 1998, at 1, 5.

232 $50 Million: Lisa Brennan, *Milbank Settles Conflict Case; Millions Paid*, NAT'L. L.J., Mar. 8, 1999, at A4.

232 $27 Million: Matthew Goldstein, *Bankruptcy Practice Restricts Itself*, N.Y.L.J., Apr. 19, 1999, at 1.

232 Dec. 18 Hearing: *A Behind the Scenes Look at Milbank Tweed's $1.86 Million Settlement*, Bankruptcy Court, Dec., Jan. 20, 1998.

232 Stark e-mail controversy: *Stark Ethics*, CORPORATE COUNSEL MAGAZINE, Aug. 1998, at 23.

233 Minnesota Office of Lawyer's Professional Responsibility: Karen Donovan, *Bucyrus Drags On*, NAT'L. L.J., Oct. 5, 1998.

CHAPTER 8

235 Jury selection: GTT, Transcript of Jury Voir Dire, Feb. 23, 1998.

235 Dispute over introduction of New York bar membership evidence: GTT, Feb. 23, 1998, 20–34.

236 Biskupic opening argument: GTT, Feb. 23, 1998, 37–57.

NOTES ON SOURCES

237 Rotert opening argument: GTT, Feb. 23, 1998, 57–92.

239 Goelzer testimony: Direct examination: GTT, Feb. 23, 1998, 94–168, Feb. 24, 1998, 176–234; cross-examination: 235–310, 315–434.

244 Revesz testimony: Direct examination: GTT, Feb. 24, 1998, 435–60; cross-examination: 461–84; redirect: 485.

245 Reder testimony: Direct examination: GTT, Feb. 25, 1998, 492–505; cross-examination: 506–47, redirect: 548–49; recross: 550–53.

246 Eckert testimony: Direct examination: GTT, Feb. 25, 1997, 559–81; cross-examination: 581–600.

247 Jessop testimony: Direct examination: GTT, Feb. 25, 1997, 601–19; cross-examination: 619–23.

247 Hindes testimony: Direct examination: GTT, Feb. 25, 1997, 632–37; cross-examination: 637–42.

248 Jerome testimony: Direct examination: GTT, Feb. 25, 1997, 643–53. cross-examination: 654–80.

249 Stipulation: GTT, Feb. 25, 1997, 682–83.

250 Lichstein testimony: Direct examination: GTT, Feb. 25, 1997, 683–719; cross-examination: 719–66; redirect: 766–76; recross: 776.

254 Gelfand testimony: Direct examination: GTT, Feb. 26, 1997, 785–811; cross-examination: 811–83; redirect: 868–77, recross, 878–83; second redirect: 883.

257 Byrnes testimony: Direct examination: GTT, Feb. 26, 1997, 887–942; cross-examination: 943–1026; Feb. 27, 1997, 1032–93; redirect: 1093–98.

259 Directed verdict motion: GTT, Feb. 26, 1997, 1099–1110.

259 Gellene testimony: Direct examination: GTT, Feb. 27, 1997, 1111–41, 1145–1221; cross-examination: 1221–56.

266 Discussion of jury instructions: GTT, Mar. 2, 1997, 1264–98.

267 Closing arguments: Wall: GTT, Mar. 2, 1997, 1299–1349; Rotert: 1353–1435; Biskupic: 1436–61.

272 Jury verdict: GTT, Mar. 3, 1997, 1471–73.

273 Conlon comment: Barrett, Mar. 4, 1998.

284 Sentencing hearing: Transcript of Sentencing Hearing, *United States v. Gellene*, Criminal No. 97-CR-221, E.D. Wis., July 24, 1998.

CHAPTER 9

293 Write-off of prebankruptcy fees and expenses: Exhibit 50, Gellene trial.

318 Oral Goldman waiver: Gellene testimony, FTT, Nov. 30, 1995, 332.

319 For overviews of the changes in investment banking over the past few decades, see LISA ENDLICH, GOLDMAN SACHS: THE CULTURE OF SUCCESS 70–274 (2000); NILS LINDSKOOG, LONG-TERM GREEDY: THE TRIUMPH OF GOLDMAN SACHS 26–142 (2d ed. 1999); DAVID W. HART ET AL., DOING DEALS: INVESTMENT BANKS AT WORK (1988).

CHAPTER 10

339 *Leslie Fay* decision: 175 B.R. 525 (Bankr. S.D. N.Y. 1994).

339 Trustee's motion: Memorandum of Law of the United States Trustee in Support of His Motion to Disqualify Weil, Gotshal & Manges As

Debtor's Counsel and to Impose An Economic Sanction Against Weil, Gotshal & Manges, Oct. 19, 1994.

340 Weil, Gotshal opposition: Memorandum of Law by Weil, Gotshal & Marges in Opposition to Motion by United States Trustee to Disqualify Weil, Gotshal & Manges as Debtors' Counsel and Impose an Economic Sanction, Nov. 3, 1994.

341 Final penalty $1 million: *Leslie Fay Lawyers Fined $1 Million by Court*, WOMEN's WEAR DAILY, Jan. 10, 1995, at 2.

343 Elizabeth Warren comment: *Judge Assails Lawyers for Leslie Fay*, N.Y. TIMES, Dec. 16, 1994, at D1.

EPILOGUE

353 Gellene's release from prison: Federal Bureau of Prisons, Inmate Locator, Inmate Register Number 05140-089.

366 Goelzer background and comments: Interview with David Goelzer, Milwaukee, Wisconsin, Nov. 14, 2001.

INDEX

INDEX

INDEX

INDEX

INDEX

INDEX